RENAISSANCE
AND
REFORMATION

RENAISSANCE
AND
REFORMATION

Editor

JAMES A. PATRICK
Chancellor, College of Saint Thomas More

Advisers

CHRISTOPHER FLETCHER
Queen Mary, University of London
Department of History

NATALIA NOWAKOWSKA
Oxford University
History Faculty

NORMAN TANNER, SJ
Pontificia Università Gregoriana
Faculty of Theology

RENAISSANCE
— AND —
REFORMATION

Editor

James A. Patrick

Chancellor, College of Saint Thomas More

2

Descartes, René – Households

Marshall Cavendish
Reference

New York

Marshall Cavendish
99 White Plains Road
Tarrytown, New York 10591-9001

www.marshallcavendish.us

MARSHALL CAVENDISH
EDITOR: Thomas McCarthy
EDITORIAL DIRECTOR: Paul Bernabeo
PRODUCTION MANAGER: Michael Esposito

WHITE-THOMSON PUBLISHING
EDITORS: Steven Maddocks and Cath Senker
DESIGN: Derek Lee and Ross George
CARTOGRAPHER: Peter Bull Design
PICTURE RESEARCH: Amy Sparks
INDEXER: Cynthia Crippen, AEIOU, Inc.

Library of Congress Cataloging-in-Publication Data
Renaissance and Reformation / editor, James A. Patrick.
    p. cm.
  Includes bibliographical references.
  Contents: 1. Agincourt, Battle of–Dams and drainage -- 2. Descartes, Rene-
Households -- 3. Humanism and learning–Medicis, the -- 4. Michelangelo-
Portugal -- 5. Preaching–Wren, Christopher -- 6. Index.
  ISBN-13: 978-0-7614-7650-4 (set: alk. paper)
  ISBN-10: 0-7614-7650-4 (set: alk. paper)
   1. Renaissance--Encyclopedias. 2. Reformation--Encyclopedias. I. Patrick,
James, 1933-

  CB359.R455 2007
  940.2'1--dc22

                                       2006042600

ISBN-13: 978-0-7614-7650-4   (set)
ISBN-10: 0-7614-7650-4   (set)
ISBN-13: 978-0-7614-7652-8-   (vol. 2)
ISBN-10: 0-7614-7652-0   (vol. 2)

Printed in Malaysia

10 09 08 07 06 5 4 3 2 1

ILLUSTRATION CREDITS
See page 576.

COVER: Leonardo da Vinci, *Madonna of the Rocks,* 1483 (Art Archive/Musée du
  Louvre, Paris/Dagli Orti).
TITLE PAGE: Flagellants praying, Italian, early fifteenth century (Art Archive/Musée
  du Petit Palais, Avignon/Dagli Orti).

Contents

Descartes, René

WIDELY REGARDED AS THE FOUNDER OF THE MODERN PHILOSOPHICAL TRADITION, THE FRENCHMAN RENÉ DESCARTES (1596–1650) ALSO MADE SIGNIFICANT CONTRIBUTIONS TO MATHEMATICS, PHYSICS, AND OTHER FIELDS OF KNOWLEDGE.

▼ *A portrait of René Descartes as he appeared around the time he left the renowned Jesuit school at La Flèche. Descartes would later be a major catalyst in the widespread rejection of the classically based Scholastic educational system the school excelled at providing.*

René Descartes was born in La Haye, a village in Touraine, in central France. His mother died while he was still an infant, and he was raised by his maternal grandmother. A brilliant and talented child, Descartes left home at the age of ten to study at La Flèche, a college in Anjou run by the Jesuits (a Roman Catholic order). Descartes remained at La Flèche, where students were taught in Latin, for nine years. Although he greatly admired his teachers, he disliked the emphasis the medieval Scholastic curriculum placed on the works of classical philosophers. Descartes's rejection of the education he received at La Flèche would serve as the basis for his own radically new system of reasoning.

A New Approach

Descartes would later write that he learned little of value at La Flèche, with the exception of precise mathematical work. Even so, he was an excellent student, and by the time he left the college, he was firmly grounded in the classical system of thought that he would later repudiate.

Descartes was troubled by what he perceived as the lack of certainty in the science of the time. Indeed, he believed that the Latin word *scientia*, which literally means "things known," should be applied only to knowledge that was beyond question.

Descartes's long and circuitous route toward the fulfillment of his early promise was directly influenced by acquaintance with two of his contemporaries: the Dutch mathematician and physicist Isaac Beeckman and Father Marin Mersenne, a fellow graduate of La Flèche who was around eight years Descartes's senior.

Through his friendship with Beeckman, Descartes gained the insight that mathematics could serve as the basis for an irrefutable system of thought. Such certainty would answer the claims of epistemological relativism—that each system of thought offers a version of truth and that none is inherently better—as well as the more general objections of skepticism to any claim to indisputable knowledge. Mersenne provided Descartes with the basis for the mechanistic conception of nature that would later serve as a pillar of Cartesian (that is, Descartes's) thought.

Descartes was also greatly influenced by his adventures as a young man. He sought out experiences that would help him fulfill his commitment "to seek no knowledge other than that which could be found either in myself or in the great book of the world." In 1618 the young scholar joined the army of Maurice of Nassau and traveled to Holland and Germany. In 1619,

◆ Marin Mersenne, the subject of this engraving, graduated from La Flèche a number of years before Descartes. Mersenne, who became a Roman Catholic priest, was an active contributor to the intellectual life of the seventeenth century; he is widely credited with inspiring Descartes's mechanistic view of nature.

CHRONOLOGY

1596
René Descartes is born in La Haye (the town was later renamed Descartes).

1616
Earns a law degree at Poitiers.

1618
Sets out on several years of travel, largely in Holland and Germany.

1622
Returns to France but continues to travel.

1628
Moves to Holland.

1634
Suppresses publication of a recently completed work, *The World*.

1637
Discourse on the Method is published.

1641
First edition of *Meditations on First Philosophy* is published.

1642
Second edition of *Meditations on First Philosophy*, along with his *Objections and Replies*, is published.

1644
The Principles of Philosophy is published.

1650
Descartes dies of pneumonia in Stockholm on February 11.

Isaac Beeckman 1588–1637

Descartes's friendship with the Dutch physicist and mathematician Isaac Beeckman had a significant effect on the subsequent development of Descartes's philosophical thought. Under Beeckman's influence, Descartes gained a new appreciation for the potential of mathematics to serve as a pillar of a new scientific method. Beeckman, a strong advocate of the integration of mathematics and science, was also a leading thinker in his own right. His contributions in the field of physics included work on the conception of free fall and inertia, as well as research into the behavior of flowing water under controlled conditions.

the year after his enlistment, Descartes found himself in Ulm, Germany, on November 10. During a fitful night of sleep, Descartes had a succession of dreams. The dreams had the effect of persuading him that he was to originate a new philosophical system that would radically restructure the approach to scientific knowledge.

A Slow Start

Despite the apparent intellectual mandate provided by his dreams, Descartes did not immediately set out to develop a new philosophical system; he chose instead to continue traveling and gathering insights from the great book of the world. His first attempt at a systematic work, *Regulae ad Directionem Ingenii (Rules for the Direction of the Mind)*, which he began around 1628, ended in an intellectual impasse. Descartes found himself unable to finish the work, which was published posthumously in 1701.

Though never completed, *Regulae* combines a mathematician's zeal for exactness and certitude with a philosopher's interest in the very nature of rational inquiry. In *Regulae*, Descartes attempted to universalize an essentially mathematical way of thinking, one that would apply to literally all fields of inquiry. This vision would continue to inspire Descartes as he worked toward the creation of his best-known and most influential works, *Discourse on the Method* (1637) and *Meditations on First Philosophy* (1641).

In the interim Descartes was becoming known as an eloquent proponent of the need for absolute certainty in the sciences. While in Paris in November 1628, he engaged in a disputation with one Monsieur Chandoux, an alchemist who believed that no science could be founded on absolute certainty. Chandoux argued in favor of probability rather than certainty as the appropriate starting point for scientific inquiry.

Descartes's powerful and well-received rebuke of Chandoux brought him to the attention of Cardinal Bérulle, the former chaplain to the late King Henry IV of France and a leading figure in the Counter-Reformation effort to convert Protestants to Catholicism. Bérulle encouraged Descartes to develop his system further. Around the same time, Descartes moved to the Netherlands. Except for occasional travels abroad, he remained in his adopted land until 1649.

Developing the System

Descartes completed the first systematic exposition of his views in *Le monde (The World)*, which was finished by 1634. *Le monde* was noteworthy for its advocacy of the Copernican system of astronomy (named for the sixteenth-century Polish astronomer Nicolaus Copernicus), which proposed a sun-centered universe. The long-held Ptolemaic theory of an earth-centered universe (named for the second-century Greek astronomer Ptolemy) was supported by the Roman Catholic Church. In light of the church's condemnation of the Italian astronomer Galileo Galilei in 1633 for asserting as fact views similar to those expressed in *Le monde,* Descartes decided not to publish his own work and instead began writing a treatise covering themes of mathematics and natural science, which was published in 1637. The work was organized under three main headings: "Geometry," "Dioptrics," and "Meteors." Although none of these studies is of much more than historical interest, the preface to the entire volume was to be of lasting significance.

This preface, the *Discours de la méthode (Discourse on the Method),* was remarkable for its concise, clear, and systematic exposition of the Cartesian method of avoiding error in the pursuit of absolute truth. Uncharacteristically, Descartes wrote in French—rather than Latin—with the effect that the *Discourse on the Method* bypassed the intellectual and religious elite and aimed directly at ordinary educated Frenchmen, whom Descartes hoped to sway to his point of view.

It is also in *Discourse on the Method* that Descartes's signature phrase, "I think, therefore I am" (in Latin, *Cogito, ergo sum*), appears for the first time. This famous phrase summarizes the key insight of Descartes's early thought—namely, that no matter how much I may doubt the reality of the appearances that surround me, I cannot doubt the simple fact that I exist. Indeed, the very act of doubting necessarily implies that I, the doubter, must in fact exist. This principle, which

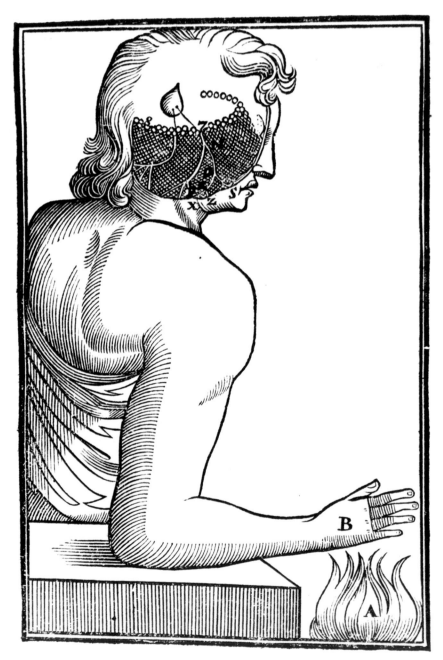

▼ *Among Descartes's many areas of specialized knowledge was medicine. He attempted, with limited success, to apply his mechanistic worldview to the human body and soul. This engraving is taken from* The Passions of the Soul *(1649), in which Descartes attempts to formulate explanations for human behavior in terms of responses to external stimuli.*

would be fundamental to the later work *Meditations on First Philosophy* (1641), is described by some commentators as Descartes's Archimedean Point, a hypothetical vantage point named in reference to the claim made by the ancient Greek philosopher Archimedes that he could lift the earth if he had a place to stand and a lever long enough.

Meditations on First Philosophy

In 1642 an updated version of Descartes's method appeared in the second edition of his *Meditations on First Philosophy in Which Are Demonstrated the Existence of God and the Distinction between the Human Soul and Body.* Less practical in both style and content than the *Discourse,* the *Meditations* as a whole is divided into six separate meditations, supposed to have taken place over six successive days (although this structure is merely a literary conceit). Descartes claims to have set aside these days for the express purpose of devoting himself "sincerely and without reservation to the general demolition of [his] own opinions."

Descartes's purpose is of course not primarily destructive. In fact, he hopes to rid himself of any opinion or belief that admits even the slightest possibility of doubt precisely in order to find at least one thing that can in no way be doubted. In a brilliant rhetorical and methodological turn, Descartes aims to use doubt in order to overcome doubt and thereby find one absolutely certain truth upon which to build his entire system.

In the first meditation, "What Can Be Called into Doubt," Descartes notes that he has often been mistaken about matters that he had assumed to be true. He observes that everything he knows has come to him either from his senses or through his senses and notes that the senses

DISCOVRS

DE LA METHODE

Pour bien conduire fa raifon, & chercher la verité dans les fciences.

Si ce difcours femble trop long pour eftre tout leu en vnefois, on le pourra diftinguer en fix parties. Et en la premiere on trouuera diuerfes confiderations touchant les fciences. En la feconde, les principales regles de la Methode que l'Autheur a cherchée. En la 3, quelques vnes de celles de la Morale qu'il a tirée de cette Methode. En la 4, les raifons par lefquelles il prouue l'exiftence de Dieu, & de l'ame humaine, qui font les fondemens de fa Metaphyfique. En la 5, l'ordre des queftions de Phyfique qu'il a cherchées, & particulierement l'explication du mouuement du cœur, & de quelques autres difficultez qui appartiennent a la Medecine, puis auffy la difference qui eft entre noftre ame & celle des beftes. Et en la derniere, quelles chofes il croit eftre requifes pour aller plus auant en la recherche de la Nature qu'il n'a efté, & quelles raifons l'ont fait efcrire.

E bon fens eft la chofe du monde la mieux partagée : car chafcun penfe en eftre fi bien pourueû, que ceux mefme qui font les plus difficiles a contenter en toute autre chofe, n'ont point couftume d'en defirer plus qu'ils en ont. En quoy il n'eft pas vray femblable que tous fe trôpent : Mais pluftoft cela tefmoigne que la puiffance de bien iuger, & diftinguer le vray d'auec le faux, qui eft proprement ce qu'on nomme le bon fens, ou la raifon, eft naturellement efgale en tous les hommes ; Et ainfi que la diuerfité de nos opinions ne vient pas de ce que les vns font plus raifonnables que les autres,

PREMIERE PARTIE.

4 2.

often err. Accordingly, he concludes that even the most theoretical understanding he possesses—including his knowledge of mathematics and geometry—is subject to doubt. In addition, he recognizes that he has sometimes found it difficult to distinguish his waking and sleeping states and comments on how the most clearly insane people remain convinced of their sanity.

▲ *The frontispiece to an early edition of the* Discourse. *Ostensibly written as a preface to another, largely forgotten, work, the* Discourse *became a magnum opus in its own right and a pillar of modern philosophical thought.*

Toward the end of the first meditation, Descartes goes so far as to theorize that everything he thinks he knows could have been implanted in him by a *malin génie* ("evil deceiver" or "malicious demon"). He concludes that he has no basis whatsoever for accepting the truth of any proposition.

In the second meditation Descartes considers the doubts that now plague him as a result of the previous day's reflections. He struggles to devise some way to address these ever-deepening doubts. Indeed, he begins to wonder even at his own nature. Does he have a body? Is the world he perceives around him in fact real? He finds that he can no longer answer these or many other equally perplexing questions. He acknowledges that his previous conception of himself as a man will no longer do, since not even his perception of himself can survive the doubts raised by his earlier "evil deceiver" argument.

▶ *An engraving of a telescopic instrument from Descartes's "Dioptrics" (1637), a work that examines the refraction of light and the properties of lenses. Like many other thinkers of his time, Descartes was a man of diverse interests. His work in physics, however, suffered from fundamental flaws and is no longer studied.*

THE ROLE OF GOD IN THE *MEDITATIONS*

In his third meditation Descartes discovers that among the ideas in his mind, there is one that stands out: his idea of God. Descartes claims that this idea is of "a supreme God, eternal, infinite, omniscient [all knowing], omnipotent [all powerful], and the creator of all things that exist apart from him." Descartes also claims that a lesser being (such as Descartes himself) could not have created the idea of a greater being (such as God). Accordingly, Descartes concludes that the idea of God can only have been implanted in him by God himself. Therefore, God exists.

Though often criticized, this proof of God's existence in effect justifies Descartes's confidence in his perceptions. In the fourth meditation Descartes notes that God, by nature good, would not deceive, since "in every case of trickery or deception some imperfection is to be found; and although the ability to deceive appears to be an indication of cleverness or power, the will to deceive is undoubtedly evidence of malice or weakness, and so cannot apply to God." God cannot deceive, not because he is not clever enough (he is), but because it would be contrary to his omnibenevolent (all-good) nature. God's role in Descartes's *Meditations* is thus not foundational but instrumental. That is, the fact that God would neither deceive Descartes nor allow him to be deceived about any clear and distinct perception guarantees the truth of Descartes's perceptions, even though God is not their source. Man is the center of Descartes's philosophical universe; God's existence simply assures Descartes that he can trust the evidence of his senses and the ideas in his mind.

This revelation serves as the basis for the rest of his system. In the self Descartes has found his one unalterable truth. However, a serious problem remains. What can Descartes do with this newfound knowledge when he cannot even be sure that the world to which he would apply it exists? Descartes's proof of God's existence in his third meditation resolves this problem by demonstrating that at least one being—God—must exist in addition to Descartes himself.

Applying the Method and Avoiding Error

When Descartes further proves, in the fourth meditation, that God would not deceive him, he is only a short distance from his goal. Since God would not deceive him, he need only identify the source of error and learn to avoid it. He finds the source of error in the disparity between will and intellect. Descartes claims that human will is equal to the will of God. By this statement he does not mean that the human will has the same efficacy as that of God but merely that a person can wish for or desire anything, just as God can. In both cases will is infinite.

The difference between God and man thus lies in their respective intellects. God's intellect is infinitely superior to that of man. God does not err, precisely because both his will and his intellect are infinite. He has infinite knowledge of all things; so every judgment he makes is both clear and distinct, as it is based on a thoroughgoing understanding of the matter at hand. People, on the other hand, err when they claim to know more than they in fact do, when their will to make a judgment or come to a conclusion about a particular matter exceeds their knowledge of the matter.

If people restrict their will to what they do in fact know, they may be absolutely certain in their judgment. Descartes claims that there can be no doubt of the truth of any sense experience or proposition of the mind that he perceives both clearly and distinctly. This claim resolves the problems that Descartes noted earlier. He need no longer doubt, for example, that he has a body, since he perceives his body clearly, and his body is distinct from other objects. God's proven existence and goodness are essential to his certainty of the truth of such judgments. The fact that

Despite the uncertainties into which these lines of thought plunge him, Descartes cannot doubt one thing: that he thinks. He writes, "the statement 'I am, I exist' is necessarily true whenever I utter it or conceive it in my mind." In other words, no matter what else he doubts, Descartes cannot doubt that he exists. He may not know what physical form he has (if any) or whether or not anything that he perceives is real, but he does at least know one thing: he exists.

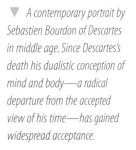

▼ *A contemporary portrait by Sebastien Bourdon of Descartes in middle age. Since Descartes's death his dualistic conception of mind and body—a radical departure from the accepted view of his time—has gained widespread acceptance.*

God is no deceiver allows Descartes to be sure that he is not being fooled by an external source into believing something false. In short, although it is the self, rather than God, that serves as the foundational Archimedean Point in Descartes's *Meditations,* God underlies the Cartesian system in that he guarantees the legitimacy of Descartes's perceptions. Without God acting as guarantor, Descartes would remain trapped in a universe of one, unable to make any definitively true statement about anything other than the simple fact of his own existence.

Implications of the *Meditations*

The remaining meditations (the fifth includes a second proof of God's existence) are of principally historical interest. The implications of the first four meditations, however, are profound. First and perhaps foremost, according to the Cartesian system people have a moral duty to avoid error. Sin, in Descartes's view, is a kind of error, and since the avoidance of sin is a moral imperative, so too is the avoidance of error. To neglect the conscientious application of Descartes's method is more than a simple mistake—to do so is to countenance wickedness and depravity.

Second, there is the problem of solipsism, that is, the belief that the self may be the only entity that actually exists. Although Descartes addresses this problem by debunking the "evil deceiver" argument and spends a great deal of effort in the fifth and sixth meditations addressing the question of the existence of the external world, he never quite manages to put to rest the lingering doubts regarding the actual nature of other minds.

Thus, the third implication of the meditations is that, while the existence of the world and of other people is assured, the precise nature of the "world" of other minds remains no more than an inference based on the individual's sense experience. That is, I perceive other people who resemble me doing things that resemble things that I do, and thus I conclude that the thought processes that I experience resemble those of other people. While not entirely unsatisfactory, since this conclusion is merely an inference rather than a direct observation, it is at best secondhand information. Since Descartes claims that the truths perceived directly by the mind (for example, those of arithmetic and geometry) are known with greater certainty than the evidence of the senses, this aspect of his work remains an unresolved and methodologically troublesome element of Cartesian philosophy.

Descartes's Influence and Last Days

Descartes's clear division of the human being into a body and a soul put into philosophical terms what had hitherto been essentially a theological abstraction. Cartesianism remains a major influence in contemporary philosophy. In addition to his well-known contributions to philosophy and the foundations of modern science, Descartes's innovations in mathematics were of great value at the time, and many remain in use to this day.

Following the publication in 1649 of his last major work, *The Passions of the Soul,* Descartes accepted an invitation to join the court of Queen Christina of Sweden, who was assembling a group of prominent thinkers to instruct her in philosophy. The following year, while still in Stockholm, Descartes succumbed to a fatal bout of pneumonia, brought on by a combination of bad weather and a demanding schedule. He left

▲ A detail of an eighteenth-century French painting depicting the court of Queen Christina of Sweden (reigned 1632–1654). Descartes's career ended at Christina's court when he died of pneumonia in 1650. Hired to instruct Christina in philosophy during chilly early morning sessions, Descartes suffered serious health problems that were brought on by the very cold weather.

behind a tremendous and impressive body of work—in fields as diverse as medicine, physics, optics, and philosophy—the relevance of which remains undimmed more than three and a half centuries after his death.

FURTHER READING
Cottingham, John. *The Cambridge Companion to Descartes.* Cambridge, 1992.
Descartes, René. *The Philosophical Writings of Descartes.* (3 vols.). Translated by J. Cottingham. Cambridge, 1993.

Daniel Horace Fernald

SEE ALSO
• Galilei, Galileo • Paris • Philosophy • Sweden

Disease

THE NATURE AND PATTERNS OF DISEASE IN THE FOUR-CENTURY PERIOD FROM 1300 TO 1700 ARE DIRECTLY RELATED TO THE APPEARANCE OF RADICALLY NEW PATTERNS OF LIVING.

People develop immunity to disease by remaining over a long period of time in a controlled and static environment. Moving from a home environment into a foreign environment exposes the traveler to new pathogens (bacteria and viruses that cause disease) and exposes the new environment to the pathogens carried by the traveler. Historians have deduced that the most significant rises in occurrences of disease follow seemingly unrelated developments. Such developments include the evolution of new trade networks and advances in transportation technology; both of these developments are major causes of new movements of people over large distances to unfamiliar places. During the Renaissance the movement of people between one geographical region and another made every trading post and seaport an incubator for disease.

By the second century BCE, caravans regularly traveled across Asia along a number of routes that Europeans referred to collectively as the Silk Road. During this period merchant ships also sailed from the coasts of Arabia, Mesopotamia, and Persia (areas that lay within a short distance overland of the eastern Mediterranean) across the Indian Ocean to India and China. As a result of this contact between Asia and Europe, severe disease outbreaks hit both the Chinese Han

► In the sixteenth century scholars began to investigate the human body in detail. Andreas Vesalius (1514–1564), the leading exponent of the science of anatomy and the subject of this seventeenth-century portrait, gathered much of his knowledge by dissecting cadavers.

Andreas Vesalius, chair of surgery and anatomy at the University of Padua, published the results of his dissections of human subjects, as well as dogs, pigs, cats, and the occasional monkey, in 1543. The public, however, was not ready for a radical new understanding of human anatomy.

Those physicians you know of had made to the emperor and to the nobles a most unfavorable report of my books and of all that is published nowadays for the promotion of study; I therefore burnt all these works that I have mentioned, thinking at the same time that it would be an easy matter to abstain from writing for the future. I must show that I have since repented more than once of my impatience and regretted that I did not take the advice of the friends who were then with me.

Andreas Vesalius, *De humani corporis fabrica*

Empire and the Roman Empire in Europe during the first centuries CE. The result—serious depopulation—eventually made such intercontinental trade less profitable.

Immunity and Medicine

As people within a community become immune, a disease moves from an active stage, described as epidemic, to a dormant state, described as endemic, in which the pathogens remain present in the community. Infections that pass directly from person to person change from being epidemic to endemic over the course of four to five human generations. When other carriers, such as animals or insects, are involved, the pattern differs and remains unpredictable.

The course of diseases can be altered by applying medical knowledge to protect people from infection. Owing to the work of Andreas Vesalius (1514–1564) and other scientists, people began to take a more proactive approach to disease control after 1500. Whether learning about human anatomy or the treatment of illness, physicians made huge advances during this era. Nevertheless, it was not until the nineteenth century that sufficient medical knowledge was available to begin to control epidemics.

The Black Death

The first large-scale global experience with disease was the devastating fourteenth-century outbreak of bubonic plague that became known as the Black Death. For historians the Black Death, which arrived in Europe in the 1340s, marks a dividing line between the central and the late Middle Ages. The period of the later Middle Ages is usually characterized as an era of crisis and trouble. The historical record reveals that the dark cloud of disease that hung over Europe in this period contributed considerably to its overall bleak image. While the Black Death did not cause all of the cultural crises of the period, the extent and ferocity of the disease certainly exacerbated existing problems and added new ones. Clearly, societies were forced to change considerably in the latter half of the fourteenth century to contend with the fearsome impact of the plague.

The Black Death is believed to have originated in the Gobi Desert, in present-day Mongolia, in the late 1320s. However, historians believe the plague bacillus (the disease-producing bacterium) was alive and active long before that date. Indeed, scholars believe that Europe had suffered a plague epidemic in the sixth century and that the disease had become dormant in the succeeding centuries. Some scholars attribute this period of dormancy to climatic changes. According to this theory the cooling of the earth's climate in the fourteenth century (during the so-called Little Ice Age) helped to stir the disease back to life.

The bubonic plague was carried great distances across Europe via the infected animals that traders, whether intentionally or not, took with them on their journeys. The plague was most often spread by rats and other rodents that carried the fleas that carried the disease. When the fleas migrated from their animal hosts to humans, they took the bacillus with them. The fleas passed on the bacillus either directly, by biting their new host and infecting the blood, or indirectly, by leaving deposits of excrement that entered the bloodstream through contact with scratches or lesions on the skin. In the majority of cases, the host, whether rodent or human, would die soon after contracting the bubonic plague.

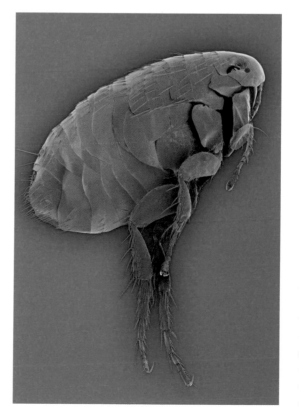

◄ A modern microscopic photograph of the oriental rat flea that carried the bubonic plague. The rats that hosted the fleas were frequently carried on ships to all parts of the world. During the voyage the rats fed on grain, and when they reached their destination, they infected the local rat population, which in turn infected people.

One of the reasons for the fearful reaction to the plague was its awful impact on those who contracted it. An infected person's early symptoms included a high fever, aching limbs, and the vomiting of blood. The most characteristic symptom was a swelling of the lymph nodes, glands found in the neck, armpits, and groin. The swellings protruded and turned blackish (hence, the name Black Death). The swellings continued to expand until they eventually burst, an occurrence that normally indicated impending death. The whole process, from first symptoms of fever and aches to death, lasted only three or four days. The swiftness of the disease, the terrible pain, and the grotesque appearance of the victims all served to make the plague especially terrifying.

The mortality rate generally ranged between 60 and 80 percent of those who became infected with the plague. If the victim was already at risk, through malnutrition or other illness, the plague was more easily contracted. The fact that during the 1300s many people in famine-stricken Europe fell into this category may explain the extraordinarily high mortality rate of the 1348 outbreak. Some scholars believe more than one disease is responsible for the devastation across Europe; even so, the bubonic plague is certain to have been at least the primary culprit.

Spread of the Bubonic Plague

In general, the plague traveled by ship as readily as by land and spread rapidly to both the eastern and western Mediterranean lands. In 1347 the plague hit Sicily and Cyprus; fleets subsequently carried it to Italy. By 1348, the worst year of the plague, the disease was recorded in France and England. Next the plague moved along the Rhine

▲ As countless families and communities watched their loved ones fall ill and die, suffering overwhelmed European society. The term Black Death, which originally described the skin discoloration caused by the bubonic plague, gained dark emotional overtones. In this anonymous fifteenth-century French fresco, a doctor attempts to treat a patient who has fallen victim to the disease.

This account of the Black Death was written around 1357:

Soon the corpses were lying forsaken in the houses. No ecclesiastic, no son, no father, and no relation dared to enter, but they hired servants with high wages to bury the dead. The houses of the deceased remained open with all their valuables, gold and jewels.... When the catastrophe had reached its climax the Messinians [citizens of the Italian city of Messina] resolved to emigrate. One portion of them settled in the vineyards and fields, but a larger portion sought refuge in the town of Catania. The disease clung to the fugitives and accompanied them everywhere they turned in search of help. Many of the fleeing fell down by the roadside and dragged themselves into the fields and bushes to expire. Those who reached Catania breathed their last in the hospitals there. The terrified citizens would not permit the burying of fugitives from Messina within the town, and so they were all thrown into deep trenches outside the walls. Thus the people of Messina dispersed over the whole island of Sicily and with them the disease, so that innumerable people died.

Michael Platiensis, quoted in Johannes Nohl, *The Black Death*

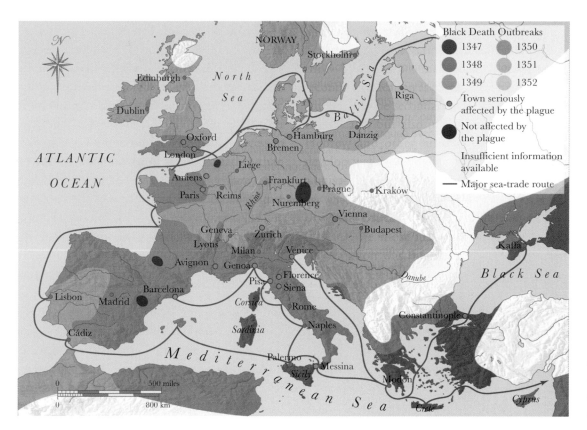

◀ *This map illustrates the spread of the plague in fourteenth-century Europe. The disease followed the path of new trade links.*

River trade routes and reached Germany. It reached Norway in 1349, eastern European countries in 1350, and Russia in 1351. Overall, because the disease tended to follow trade routes and to concentrate in cities, its route was nearly circuitous: traveling from the Near East to the western Mediterranean, then into northern Europe, and finally into Russia. The progress of the plague very neatly parallels the expanding geography of medieval trade.

The impact of the plague was felt across the trading world of the 1300s. Asian nations suffered significantly; China, for instance, suffered a drop in population from around 125 million to around 90 million over the course of the fourteenth century. In Europe the density of the population exacerbated the impact of the plague. The most conservative estimate is that 20 percent of Europe's population died. Other estimates, however, range as high as 40 percent. Writers of the time claimed that one-third of the continent, an estimated 20 million people, died during only a few plague years. In England, for instance, the Black Death killed 1.5 million people out of an estimated population of 4 million between 1348 and 1350. Both the Italian state of Pisa and Vienna, in modern-day Austria, lost 500 people

per day; the Italian states of Florence and Venice and the German states of Hamburg and Bremen lost a minimum of 60 percent of their population. At the peak of the epidemic, Paris, France, lost 800 people per day; in total, one-half of its population of 100,000 died. The city of Florence had 114,000 inhabitants in 1338 and between 45,000 and 50,000 in 1351.

The partial recovery that followed in most localities was halted by the return of the plague, with the result that the population of the northern German cities was at least 20 percent lower at the end of the fifteenth century than it had been at the beginning of the fourteenth. Zurich, in modern-day Switzerland, had 12,375 inhabitants in 1350 but only 4,713 in 1468.

Reactions across Europe

The spread of the plague was accelerated by a total absence of sanitary procedures and a lack of general knowledge about health and hygiene. For instance, the dead were heaped in piles, whereupon rats and dogs fed on the corpses, and the cycle of the disease was extended. Many homes had straw roofs and walls and mud floors; animals were kept inside alongside human dwellers. Streets were covered with mud, garbage, and excrement.

The plague brought immediate social changes throughout Europe as communities attempted to arrest the spread of the disease. First, people found a way to contend with the massive numbers of infected corpses. At Avignon, France, the pope consecrated the river so that the bodies of plague victims could be thrown into it. Outside some ports, ships with dead crews drifted helplessly, forbidden to come into land. The Italian states imposed a forty-day quarantine on newly arrived ships. For many people the plague made normal working life impossible. Throughout Europe fields were left untilled and untended animals wandered freely.

Efforts to protect the uninfected ranged from the prescient to the bizarre. Preventive measures included fumigating infected areas by burning juniper. Physicians often wore overalls, gloves, and a nose bag soaked with cinnamon and herbs. Although anything that prevented the spread of germs—even if unintentional—was helpful, none of these measures worked. In their attempts to treat the disease, people rang church bells and fired cannons, dipped handkerchiefs in aromatic oils, bathed in human urine, wore talismans (lucky charms), removed a quantity of blood—either by using leeches or by bloodletting—and placed "stinks" (dead animals) in their dwellings.

None of these methods were in the least effective. However, in Europe some practical measures did help to combat the spread of the plague. In addition to the quarantining of ships, many nations set aside infected houses. In some regions entire cities in which the plague had broken out were quarantined. In Milan and many other Italian cities, houses in which inhabitants were found to have the plague were immediately walled up; with this measure the healthy were often isolated inside their home along with the sick. Venice adopted sophisticated and stringent quarantine and health measures, including the isolation of all incoming ships on a separate island. In general terms people improved their personal cleanliness and their housing.

These changes, combined with an increased immunity to the plague, brought the disease under control in Europe by 1718. (In parts of Asia where changes were not made, however, the disease continued to ravage the population.) The Black Death had a catastrophic impact wherever it struck. It changed everyday life all over Europe permanently and irrevocably.

Colonialism and Disease

Since the meeting of two peoples who have had no previous contact can stimulate an outbreak of disease, it is unsurprising that the era of global travel and exploration sparked epidemics. From the fifteenth century on, European explorers who ventured abroad into new environments took their germs with them. Most of these new environments, notably the Americas, had existed within biological vacuums, and their inhabitants had interacted primarily with their own pathogens.

The Age of Exploration began with the voyages of Christopher Columbus in the 1490s. In succeeding voyages Columbus explored the Caribbean Sea and reached the mainland coast of South America. His success inspired explorers from a few nations, particularly from Spain. By 1522 large parts of present-day Mexico and Peru were under Spanish control. The biological impact—what the historian Alfred Crosby referred to as the "ecological imperialism"—of European explorations began to wreak havoc on the New World.

▶ The costume depicted in this 1720 watercolor and others like it were worn by doctors in an attempt to protect themselves from infection when treating patients suffering from the plague. The mask was made from leather and had glass eyes, and the beak was filled with herbs and spices that were believed to ward off the plague.

▼ *This detail from an early-fifteenth-century Italian painting, The Virgin of the Misericordia, by Pietro di Domenico di Montepulciano, portrays flagellants kneeling in worship. Flagellants also sang hymns and proclaimed flagellation to be the route to salvation.*

The disease that had the most devastating impact on the native peoples of the Caribbean and the Americas was smallpox (named *viruelas* in Spanish), which was first recorded in Santo Domingo, on the island of Hispaniola, in December 1518 and soon spread to Yucatán (Mexico) and eventually to Peru. After a twelve-day incubation period, the symptoms include a rash, fever, and vomiting. The outbreak of smallpox was soon followed by measles, typhus, and later by yellow fever. The disease exterminated the native population of Hispaniola, and there was a massive death toll in the rest of Mesoamerica. Estimates vary from 50 to 90 percent mortality rates throughout the Americas; certainly more than 20 million people died. The drop in population, as well as the native people's ongoing struggle with disease, made the Spanish conquest much easier.

When the Spanish soldier Hernán Cortés arrived in Tenochtitlán, in present-day Mexico, in 1519, the Aztec Empire of Montezuma contained between 11 and 25 million inhabitants. The Aztecs had never been exposed to such European children's diseases as chicken pox, smallpox, measles, mumps, and whooping cough. In Europe almost every baby caught at least one of these diseases during its first year of life. Although large numbers of children died from these diseases, natural immunities inherited from parents helped many others to recover. In the areas of the New World that became infected, the diseases became epidemic: since no one had inherited immunities, young and old alike succumbed. Tenochtitlán fell to Cortés in 1521 at least partly because of the impact of smallpox and other diseases. Although the spreading of disease was not a conscious tactic on the part of the Spanish conquistadores, the massive death toll decimated their enemy's numbers and weakened and disorganized survivors. By 1650 the population of what was once the Aztec Empire is estimated to have fallen to 1.5 million.

The following account of the impact of Spanish explorers on the Aztec people, recorded from the point of view of the Aztecs, was gathered by a Spanish Franciscan friar.

There was then no sickness; they had no aching bones; they had then no high fever; they had then no smallpox; they had then no abdominal pain; they had then no consumption; they had then no headaches. At that time the course of humanity was orderly. The foreigners made it otherwise when they arrived here.

It was the month of Tepeilhuitl when it [smallpox] began and it spread over the people as great destruction. Some [victims] it quite covered with pustules on all parts—their faces, their heads, their breasts, etc. There was great havoc. Very many died of it. They could not walk; they only lay in their resting places and beds. They could not move; they could not stir; they could not change positions, nor lie in one side; nor face down, nor on their backs. And if they stirred, much did they cry out. Great was its destruction. Covered, mantled with pustules, many people died of them.

Fray Bernardino de Sahagun, *Florentine Codex*

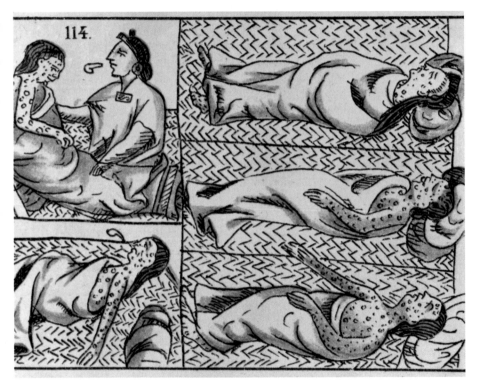

▲ *This Aztec image, from a late-sixteenth-century manuscript, illustrates the effects of the smallpox epidemic that swept through the Americas after the arrival of Spanish conquistadores.*

With the arrival of Europeans, native populations throughout the Americas plummeted. This numerical decline made it far easier for Spanish conquistadores in South and Central America and British settlers in North America to take over lands. In *Changes in the Land* (1985), the American historian William Cronon explains that the myth of North America as a "virgin land" is misleading. It is more realistic, he writes, to see North America as a "widowed land," whose occupants were largely gone within a few years of the Europeans' arrival. Native Americans suffered enormous loss of life because they lacked any established immunities to the standard European ailments, including influenza, measles, whooping cough, and smallpox.

Syphilis

The contact between the Old World and the New was also injurious to the health of peoples of the Old World. Among the New World diseases transmitted to Europe, the most significant is believed to be syphilis, a sexually transmitted disease that could cause deadly infection. While there is no certainty about whether or not syphilis existed previously in Europe, it is known that large numbers of visitors to the New World returned home infected with it.

Medical historians continue to debate the origins of syphilis. The primary hypothesis assumes a New World origin and holds that sailors who accompanied Columbus and other explorers brought the disease back to Europe. Another explanation is that syphilis was always present in the Old World but that before around 1500 it had not been identified as a separate disease from leprosy. Whatever its origin, syphilis was certainly waiting for Columbus and his crew in the 1490s. (Archaeologists continue to examine skeletal collections from the Bahamas in search of evidence of syphilis nearer to Columbus's first landfall. This evidence usually takes the form of scarring seen on the bones.) Contact with the New World, then, had at least one negative impact on the health of the Europeans who arrived there around 1500.

The fact that syphilis is transmitted through sexual intercourse, a subject that many people of the time were unprepared to discuss, made it one of the least understood diseases of the era.

The Impact of Modern Medicine

Disease had a marked but temporary impact on trade expansion and overall living patterns during the Renaissance. Interaction and trade among the world's peoples increased in the following centuries, and continued contact helped people build immunities to illness.

The birth of modern medicine can be dated to the late sixteenth century, when physicians began to gain a deeper understanding of the interaction of disease and the human anatomy. At the time of the Black Death, there was little that medical theory or practice could do to prevent its spread. However, between 1650 and 1850, deaths from epidemic disease were significantly reduced. This era undoubtedly benefited

from the development of new medicines and methods of treatment and from the fact that many epidemics had become endemic by this point. Perhaps the most important factor in combating disease was a realization of the importance of sharing knowledge among nations and peoples. In the case of the bubonic plague, the various reactions of different European communities was reflected in a considerable regional variance in the impact of the disease. From the seventeenth century, physicians were able to improve the common lot of all people thanks to the sharing of medical knowledge.

From the sixteenth century onward philosophers and physicians began to make outstanding advances in knowledge about bodily health and the workings of disease. Pupils of the Italian astronomer Galileo Galilei (1564–1642), for instance, used the microscope to build up a picture of the human body through what was known as artificial anatomy: by studying

▲ *In this 1570 engraving by Philip Galle (1537–1612), preparations are being made to treat a patient with guayaco, a resin from a Central American tree that was commonly used in the treatment of syphilis. Although this remedy had modest success, it was not a cure for the disease.*

Girolamo Fracastoro ▮ c. 1478–1553

The first syphilis epidemic broke out during the 1496 siege of Naples, in southern Italy, by the forces of King Charles VIII of France. Whatever the origins of the disease, it was understood from the beginning that syphilis was spread by sexual contact. In fact, it was commonly said during the Renaissance that the disease had developed from the union of a prostitute and a leper.

The Veronese medical anatomist Girolamo Fracastoro coined the word *syphilis* in a poem dedicated to the priest and poet Pietro Bembo (1470–1547). In an attempt to heal the afflicted, he and other physicians prescribed a number of different therapies and treatments in a trial-and-error method. Many prescribed mercury, which, as it was toxic to the sweat-producing and salivary glands, caused a very potent secretion from those glands. During the late fifteenth century Fracastoro and others treated syphilitic sweating and drooling by placing an incandescent (hot) iron bar on the patient's head (it was believed that saliva and sweat came from the brain). Although the efficacy of this and other treatments was unproven, many appeared successful, for an estimated 30 percent of patients recovered naturally.

Fracastoro believed that plague was spread by invisible living organisms. Fracastoro's putative organisms, which he called *seminaria* ("seeds") are somewhat akin to what are now known as bacteria or viruses. Fracastoro believed that *seminaria* could be transmitted from one person to another not only through direct contact but also indirectly through clothes, sheets, and other objects.

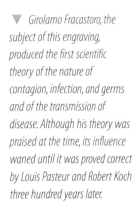

▼ Girolamo Fracastoro, the subject of this engraving, produced the first scientific theory of the nature of contagion, infection, and germs and of the transmission of disease. Although his theory was praised at the time, its influence waned until it was proved correct by Louis Pasteur and Robert Koch three hundred years later.

Crethæi docui arcanas Amythaonis artes,
Barbiton Aoniis & resonare modis.

portions of the anatomy of animals and insects, these physicians drew valuable conclusions about human anatomy. Although many of their assumptions were incorrect, their efforts resulted in the first published attempts to catalog the entire body of knowledge of human anatomy.

The plague outbreaks of the 1300s and 1400s stimulated the search for new medical cures. Even though new trading and living patterns resulted in more widespread infection, the new understanding that physicians accumulated by sharing theories and experimental results soon began to make the world safer from disease.

FURTHER READING

Arrizabalaga, Jon, John Henderson, and Roger French. *The Great Pox.* New Haven, CT, 1997.

Cantor, Norman F. *In the Wake of the Plague.* New York, 2002.

Crosby, Alfred W. *The Columbian Exchange: Biological and Cultural Consequences of 1492.* Westport, CT, 1972.

Dyson, J. *Columbus—for Gold, God, and Glory.* Toronto, 1991.

McNeill, W. H. *Plagues and Peoples.* New York, 1976.

Brian Black

SEE ALSO:
- Astrology • Columbus, Christopher
- Galilei, Galileo • Households • Magic • Medicine
- Trade

Dürer, Albrecht

GENERALLY REGARDED AS THE LEADING
GERMAN ARTIST OF THE RENAISSANCE,
ALBRECHT DÜRER (1471–1528) IS
BEST KNOWN FOR HIS WOODCUTS AND
ENGRAVINGS, WORKS THAT COMBINE
THE PRINCIPLES OF ITALIAN
RENAISSANCE ART WITH THE CON-
CERNS OF NORTHERN EUROPEAN
PROTESTANT HUMANISM.

Born the son of a Hungarian goldsmith in
Nuremberg, in the southern German state of
Franconia, Albrecht Dürer was apprenticed to his
father at age thirteen. This early exposure to the
meticulous demands of metalworking would
prove invaluable when Dürer later began to
produce the woodcuts and engravings for which

he is so famed. The first of Dürer's numerous self-
portraits, which dates from this time, was executed in the technically demanding medium of
silverpoint, in which a design is drawn on paper
with a small sharpened rod of silver. An inscription
states that Dürer drew his likeness from a mirror.

Eclectic Early Influences
Following his training as a goldsmith, Dürer was
accepted as a student by Michael Wolgemut, a
Nuremberg painter and graphic artist of some
renown. Presumably during his time with
Wolgemut, Dürer received further training in
draftsmanship (drawing) and oil-painting techniques, as well as in the skills required to produce
woodcuts and engravings.

Around 1489 or 1490, after five years of
apprenticeship, Dürer set off on what was known
as *Wanderjahre* ("years of wandering"), a period
of travel and study generally undertaken prior to
the submission of the masterpieces that would
win an artist full membership in the local craft
guild. Dürer left Nuremberg, apparently to travel
to a number of major art centers in northern
Europe. Although Dürer's travels to Italy would
have the greatest impact on his career, these early
northern trips added much to the artist's visual
experience and afforded him a broad base from
which to develop his own style.

Dürer headed to the Alsatian city of Colmar
to study with Martin Schongauer. An accomplished painter, Schongauer was also a master of
the newly perfected technique of engraving.
Given Dürer's apprenticeship, engraving held
particular appeal for him. However, upon arriv-
ing in Colmar in 1492, Dürer discovered that
Schongauer had died the previous year. After
befriending the Schongauer family, Dürer jour-
neyed to Basel, Switzerland, to meet up with
Martin's brother Georg, also an engraver.

◀ *Dürer's earliest surviving self-portrait, this silverpoint drawing bears
the distinctive facial features that are easily recognizable in the artist's
self-portraits during later life. Dürer's expert draftsmanship is already
apparent at the age of thirteen; the choice of silverpoint for this drawing
indicates the young Dürer's confidence, as it is extremely difficult to hide
mistakes when working in this medium.*

PERSPECTIVE IN NORTHERN PAINTING

Perspective is the attempt by an artist to create the illusion of three-dimensional space on the essentially flat surface of a panel or canvas. The accurate rendering of perspective became a major principle of Italian Renaissance painting from the fourteenth century; the mathematical rules of perspective were first discovered by the great architect FilippoBrunelleschi (1377–1466). By 1500 in Italy, illusory perspective had developed into a topic worthy of numerous theoretical tomes. In northern Europe perspective was generally dealt with much more casually and less scientifically than in the south. A sense of depth within a pictorial composition was created largely by guesswork on the part of the northern European artist, with the result that different parts of the composition typically recede into space at different rates. In 1525 Albrecht Dürer, convinced that northern artists should be schooled in the innovations of the Italians, published a treatise on geometry, *Underweysung der Messung mit dem Zirckel und Richtscheyt (Instruction for Measurement with the Compass and Ruler),* which he envisioned as a practical guide for art students. In this work Dürer outlines the ways in which geometric shapes and patterns can be usefully applied to architectural projects and painted compositions. The final section of the treatise, which comprises a description and analysis of single-point perspective, is the first notable contribution on this subject by a non-Italian artist.

▲ *This print by Dürer shows an artist using a grid system to transfer accurately the image before him onto paper. The eyepiece ensures that his viewpoint remains fixed; a single, ideal vantage point for the viewer is typically found in Italian paintings of the period.*

Basel was among the most important centers of humanism in northern Europe, and the young Dürer was no doubt influenced by the intellectual circles active there. During his time in Basel, Dürer executed his earliest known woodcuts, including *Saint Jerome and the Lion* (1492), as well as his first painted self-portrait. This work may be the earliest Western example of a self-portrait executed as an independent painting; earlier self-portraits survive but only as drawings or as likenesses within larger compositions, such as fresco cycles. After several years of travel around northern Europe, Dürer set out for Italy to familiarize himself with the work of the Italian Renaissance masters.

Dürer's Debt to the Italian Masters

Although Dürer continued to travel throughout his working life, his first two trips to the Italian city-states were undoubtedly the most important of his career. On the first, in 1495, he traveled throughout the northern states and encountered firsthand the Venetian school of painting, including the work of Giovanni Bellini (1430–1516) and Bellini's Paduan brother-in-law, Andrea Mantegna (c. 1431–1506). The newly developed concerns of the Italian artists of the period—including illusory perspective, a keen interest in the anatomical formation of human bodies, and the desire to match the great achievements of classical art—struck a chord with Dürer. Upon his return to Nuremberg, Dürer set out to incorporate the ideals of Italian Renaissance art into his own works. Though executed fundamentally in the late Gothic style characteristic of his northern European forebears, Dürer's paintings and graphic works of the years between 1495 and his second trip to Italy, late in

▲ *Commissioned and painted while Dürer was living in Venice,* The Feast of the Rose Garlands (1506) *epitomizes the rich colors and sumptuous effects often associated with the Venetian school. The main figures of the composition form a pyramid, a compositional device that Dürer may have helped to popularize. That Dürer himself was aware of the importance of this work is demonstrated by the rich clothes and bold gaze of his self-portrait in the upper right-hand corner.*

1505, demonstrate the artist's struggle to amalgamate his native German style with contemporary Italian innovations. Such works of this period as his woodcut of *The Four Horsemen of the Apocalypse* (1498) and his *Self-Portrait at 26* (1498) display compositions of Italian classical and contemporary inspiration as well as an emotional tension and love of symbolism that derive from late Gothic sensibilities. Dürer's second Italian trip once again centered mainly on Venice.

During his sojourn in the city, Dürer completed a number of paintings, among them *The Feast of the Rose Garlands* (1506), an altarpiece that displays Dürer's fully realized Renaissance style. This particular work, which was executed for the colony of German merchants living in Venice, was widely respected by Venetian artists and patrons alike, and Dürer's place as an honorary master of Italian Renaissance painting was secured.

Albrecht Dürer's greatest contribution to Western art is generally agreed to be within the graphic arts. His training as a goldsmith combined with his innate talent as a draftsman made him an expert in the skills required for engravings and woodcuts. His familiarity with the techniques of other noted graphic artists, including Martin Schongauer and Andrea Mantegna, provided an already fertile creativity with further inspiration. Throughout his career Dürer published various series of prints, some with added explanatory texts, as well as numerous images on single sheets. Easily affordable by even relatively modest patrons of the arts, these prints allowed Dürer to attain an impressive reputation and financial security early in his career and provided him with an important forum in which to develop his mature artistic style and express his strongly held personal beliefs.

Dürer's Apocalypse Cycle consists of fourteen large sheets, each with an image from the Revelation of Saint John (the last book of the New Testament) on one side and accompanying text on the reverse. The compositions are filled with movement, tension, and often with harrowing emotion. Dürer's technical skill is brilliantly showcased, and his interest in the innovations of the Italian artists of the period, whose work he encountered on his first trip to the Italian city-states (1495), is often apparent in his overt use of foreshortening and his obvious concern with anatomical rendering. However, the drama and detail of many of the scenes, as well as numerous stylistic details, derive directly from the northern tradition.

That Dürer intended to promote himself as well as the ideals of the Italian Renaissance through his Apocalypse series cannot be denied, but it is also possible that he sought to express his political and religious views through these scenes. Some scholars have detected German nationalist sentiments within the complex symbolism used in the prints. Dürer, already questioning the authority of Rome, may also have included hints in support of the anti-Catholic movement that was gaining momentum in parts of Germany at this time.

Artistic Maturity and International Celebrity

From an early age Albrecht Dürer possessed the ability to portray the emotional life and personality of his subjects, and his frequent return to his own figure throughout his career indicates that the pluck and self-knowledge present in adolescence remained with him into maturity. His self-portrait among the crowd in the background of *The Feast of the Rose Garlands* suggests not only that Dürer was conscious (and proud) of his new status but also that he, at least in some measure, understood the significance of his work within the history of Western art.

Upon his return to Nuremberg in the spring of 1507, Dürer continued to explore classical models and simple, monumental compositional groupings. Between 1507 and 1513 he worked on a series of woodcuts titled *The Passion of Christ*. Within the sixteen images in this cycle can be detected several attempts by Dürer to combine the serenity and timelessness of his classical ideals with a depiction of the harrowing emotions embodied in his subject matter. In 1514 Dürer completed his three masterpieces of graphic design: *The Knight, Death, and the Devil*;

◄ *The* Four Horsemen of the Apocalypse, *part of the Apocalypse Cycle, betrays Dürer's interest in Italian artistic concerns (including the use of foreshortening to indicate compositional depth), yet the overall mood of the series, with its focus on drama and complex symbolism, is northern.*

One of Dürer's three so-called master prints, this engraving, Melancholia I, captures the artist's philosophical dilemma as he tries to marry his native training in naturalism and complex iconography with the theoretical background generated by his study of Italian art. The melancholic temperament, best exemplified by the Italian Renaissance artist Michelangelo (1475–1564), often vacillated between the depths of despair and the sublime heights of artistic inspiration.

Saint Jerome in His Study; and *Melancholia I.* In these three copper engravings Dürer harnesses his opposing stylistic tendencies to create a set of works that transcend academic discussion of influence and inspiration; the works stand alone as compositions that express new depths of emotion and psychological insight.

In the final fifteen years of his life, Dürer enjoyed international renown and encountered many of his most influential contemporaries. The Holy Roman emperor Maximilian I was an important patron between 1512 and 1519. Dürer may have met the Protestant theologian Martin Luther in Augsburg in 1518; the artist's

DÜRER'S *FOUR APOSTLES*: A PROTESTANT INTERPRETATION

*T*he Four Apostles (1526), Dürer's last major painting, consists of two wooden panels, each depicting two saints; Saint John and Saint Peter appear on the left, and on the right Saint Paul stands in front of Saint Mark. There has always been some dispute over the work's title, which sometimes appears as *The Four Evangelists*, since only Saint John and Saint Peter were among the Twelve Apostles designated by Christ. However, Saint Paul, who was miraculously converted and who preached to the Gentiles, is also often numbered among the apostles. Saint Mark was one of the Four Evangelists (those who wrote the New Testament Gospels). Dürer presented the work to the leading men of Nuremberg to be hung in the city hall. In 1525 the city had officially adopted the tenets of Lutheranism, and Dürer's gift no doubt reflected his own devotion to the Protestant cause. The texts that appear on the frames come from the biblical writings of each of the four figures as they appear in Martin Luther's German translation of the New Testament (1522). Dürer's support for the new church is also apparent from the composition, notably from the positioning of Saint John and Saint Paul, both highly respected by Luther, in front; Saint Peter, typically awarded a central position in deference to his position as head of the Catholic Church, is relegated to the rear. Dürer's choice of texts warns viewers to take care and to avoid false teachings, perhaps a warning to the city leaders to adhere to Luther's principles and not to fall under the sway of the numerous more radical sectarians preaching throughout Germany.

The *Four Apostles* can also be viewed as the summation of Dürer's endeavors to unite Italian Renaissance ideals with northern humanism and the artistic heritage of the Gothic tradition. The figures' highly individualized, naturalistic faces are similar to those painted by the great early northern Renaissance artists, including Jan van Eyck (c. 1390–1441) and Rogier van der Weyden (1399–1464). The monumental figures, the simplicity of the composition, the pure colors, and the lack of fussy detail are obviously Italian in inspiration. Dürer's affinity with the humanists, who emphasised the value of the individual and sought to investigate the human condition, is reflected in the four faces, which can be seen to represent the Four Ages of Man or the four humors.

▼ *Dürer's most important late painting, The Four Apostles (1526), encapsulates both his artistic achievements and his religious views.*

deeply held Protestant beliefs would later be set out in the *The Four Apostles* (1526). During a trip through the Netherlands in 1520, Dürer met and sketched the Dutch humanist Desiderius Erasmus. He exchanged works with numerous important artists, including Raphael (1483–1520) and Matthias Grünewald (1480–1528). Dürer also wrote works that explained his own theories and expounded those championed by his Italian contemporaries; the most important of these are his *Vier Bücher von menschlicher Proportion (Four Books of Human Proportion)*, published in full after his death.

FURTHER READING

Eichler, Anja-Franziska. *Albrecht Dürer.* London, 1999.
Hutchison, Jane Campbell. *Albrecht Dürer: A Biography.* Princeton, NJ, 1990.
Panofsky, Erwin. *The Life and Art of Albrecht Dürer.* Princeton, NJ, 1955.

Caroline S. Hull

SEE ALSO

• Erasmus, Desiderius • Eyck, Jan van • Lutheranism
• Painting and Sculpture • Venice

Education

THE EXTENSIVE EDUCATIONAL REFORMS AND INNOVATIONS PUT IN PLACE DURING THE RENAISSANCE AND THE REFORMATION CONTINUE TO SERVE AS THE BASIS FOR MODERN SCHOOL SYSTEMS AND SCHOLARSHIP.

At the beginning of the Renaissance, educational opportunities were available only to the nobility and the clergy. Education was significantly influenced by the Catholic Church, and scholarship that was perceived to run counter to church doctrine was constrained. The Renaissance ushered in a period of remarkable discovery as scholars in science, art, and literature embraced classical themes found in rediscovered Latin and Greek works. Scholars began to dispute the prevailing medieval beliefs about the nature of man and the universe. In addition, new and innovative methods of teaching and scholarly inquiry were developed. The Renaissance period also saw the rise of the modern university system. During the Reformation educational systems underwent further changes; in particular, there were continued efforts to broaden education to the expanding middle class, and schools became increasingly independent of the church.

Educational Styles in the Renaissance

One significant change during the Renaissance was the refocusing of the philosophy of education away from instruction in specific skills toward the development of students' capability for critical thinking and reasoning. Higher education in the Middle Ages was directed by the church, and access was confined mainly to the social elite. Instruction was highly structured and based on memorization. During the Renaissance teachers increasingly tried to develop well-rounded students by teaching them *how* to think rather than *what* to think. Students were guided through the classical texts and then taught how to analyze the works so that they would be able to apply the philosophical and scientific principles contained within them to situations outside the classroom. In another break with the past, teachers often worked to develop the individual tastes and specialties of their students instead of trying to encourage everyone to excel in all areas. One motivation for this trend was the fact that teachers and tutors could charge more for individual tutoring of advanced students; therefore, they sought to find specific areas in which their students would perform well. In addition, since university classes tended to be large and included students of many ages, individual tutoring became even more important.

The spread of humanism during the Renaissance had a major impact on education. According to humanists the primary role of the educator was to help the student become a highly virtuous person and to provide the student with the skills necessary for a leadership

▼ A 1674 Persian painting of a teacher and his pupil. For many youths education began with individual tutoring rather than attendance at school.

role in society. The humanist education was founded on a study of ancient Greek and Roman literature, believed to be a source of "pure" knowledge that was uncluttered by years of medieval "superstition." Humanist schools and tutors also added physical exercise and the study of history to the traditional curriculum and promoted a greater awareness of the natural world.

   Although the availability of education spread dramatically during the Renaissance—hundreds of new schools and dozens of new universities were established during the period—it remained expensive, and the overwhelming majority of students were from the privileged classes. Only very rarely would a rich patron subsidize the education of a promising student from the lower classes. Nonetheless, the school system that was common during the Renaissance laid the basis for modern education.

Renaissance Schools

The educational system during the Renaissance functioned on three basic levels. The first level consisted of the primary, or elementary, schools. These schools were usually informal tutoring systems for the children of aristocrats, who would

▼ *Renaissance classrooms, small by modern standards, were often located in the teacher's own home or in an old barn, as depicted in this 1516 painting by Ambrosius Holbein.*

be taught at the palace or estate until they were able to begin secondary education. In some large cities children of the wealthy attended formally organized schools that were managed by church parishes. Students often began their primary education at age five or six. Pupils were predominantly male, although it was not uncommon for aristocratic and wealthy girls to be tutored or to attend private schools organized by royal courts. The aim of primary education was to teach languages, vocabulary, and philosophy and to provide an introduction to the fine arts, including music, sculpture, and painting. Reading and writing were taught as two distinct subjects. Generally, the language of instruction would be the local vernacular, and hence elementary schools were often known as vernacular schools.

The next level comprised the secondary schools, often known as grammar, or Latin, schools (since Latin was usually the language of instruction). The starting age varied greatly, but most students began grammar school between the ages of ten and twelve. The secondary school curriculum was based on the study of Greek and Roman literature and philosophy; students also participated in exercise regimens and games. As the Renaissance progressed, students were also increasingly exposed to the sciences, including arithmetic, astronomy, and geometry. Some

additional specialized secondary schools were designed for students expected to pursue a career in business or trade. Because the education program at such schools focused on mathematics, they were generally known as abacus schools (the abacus was used to make calculations during commercial transactions). Students at abacus schools were taught in their native language.

The third and highest level was the university. At the beginning of the Renaissance, most universities did not train students for a general education but instead prepared them for a specific career—in law, medicine, or the church, for example. However, as humanism became more widespread, universities began to offer more general curricula.

The primary mode of instruction at all levels of education was the lecture. Teachers presented material to the class in the form of long and intricate oral presentations. In other, separate classes it was permissible for students to ask questions and engage in discussion, but students were discouraged from interrupting the teacher. Students were usually given a single series of exams at the end of a particular course to determine whether they could advance to the next level. Any who failed would repeat the course. Corporal punishment was widely used to punish bad behavior or the failure to memorize lessons.

▲ *Students were primarily male during the Renaissance—as this sixteenth-century woodcut of a schoolmaster and his pupils demonstrates. Classrooms were usually bare and lacked amenities.*

THE GREEK REVIVAL

One of the most important aspects of Renaissance education was the revival of ancient Greek studies. Before this period Greek culture had had little direct impact on western Europe. The Greek language was not widely studied, and Roman authors tended to dominate the educational system. The fall of Constantinople in 1453 and the subsequent influx into Italy of Greek refugees helped spark the revival, and input from individual scholars, including the Italian Petrarch, also assisted the renewal of Greek studies. By 1500 Venice's printing presses began to reproduce Greek classics, and the city became the focal point of the Greek Renaissance. The newfound popularity of Greek studies spread, and Florence and other cities began to establish Platonic academies devoted to the study of ancient Greek culture and philosophy.

The reemergence of Greek studies formed one of the main currents of Renaissance scholarship. As scholars began to rediscover the literature of the ancient Greeks, they gradually introduced these works into the curricula of secondary schools and universities (this trend accelerated during the Reformation). As important as the rediscovery of Greek texts, the reemergence of Greek philosophy and Greek critical perspectives on art played a major role in the rise of humanism. The Greek revival in turn led to the rise of Neoplatonism in the northern Italian states, where scholars and theologians tried to reconcile Platonic philosophy with Christianity. At the core of this effort was the attempt to develop a cosmology (study of the universe) that could integrate advances in the natural sciences with existing religious doctrine. (Such scholarly work helped form the intellectual basis for the Counter-Reformation.) The Greek revival also influenced the thinking of the Protestant educational reformer Philipp Melanchthon, who is credited as the first Aristotelian Protestant philosopher—he even translated his name from the German name Schwarzerd (literally, "black earth") to its Greek version, Melanchthon.

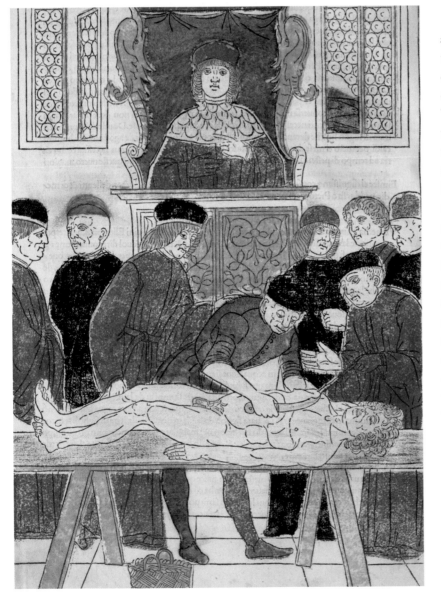

Initially, Renaissance teachers were divided along the lines of the educational system. Some teachers and tutors specialized in elementary education, others taught at the secondary level, and elite scholars were employed by universities. Teachers at the elementary and secondary levels were expected to be generalists who could teach a variety of subjects. However, as humanism spread, teachers increasingly began to specialize in specific fields, such as grammar, literature, and science. For instance, Latin teachers were expected to be masters of grammar and language, while other teachers specialized in philosophy or mathematics. At the university level there was an even greater trend toward specialization: professors began to concentrate on the work of a single author, such as Cato or Cicero, or in some cases, a specific style of writing. By the late fifteenth century, there were even marked differences in salaries and titles between the generalists at a university who taught grammar and specialists who were masters of narrower fields. The division of teaching into area specialties would continue through the Reformation. The newer models of teaching and of school organization originated in the northern Italian states and slowly spread across the European continent.

◄ *During the Renaissance scholars increasingly studied the natural world, of which human anatomy was a part. In this illustration from a medical work of 1491, students dissect a body.*

Educational Innovations of the Reformation

In their effort to win converts from Roman Catholicism, the first Protestant Reformers placed a strong emphasis on education. Through their efforts the notion of universal education came to be widely accepted. Both Martin Luther and John Calvin sought to give people access to the Bible in their native language rather than Latin, a language with which many were unfamiliar. They also recognized the need to increase literacy among the general population. Luther, Calvin, and other prominent Reformers also sought to spread their version of religion through schools. Protestant schools, even those operated by secular governments, continued to be heavily influenced by religion, and the clergy often played a major role in the establishment of the curriculum and the writing of textbooks. Many schools required children to attend church or catechism sessions. There were also daily prayers and mandatory religion courses.

Tensions over education often emerged between the growing Protestant churches and civil governments. The churches attempted to use the schools to teach children Protestant doctrine, while civil authorities wanted the schools to prepare the next generation of leaders. A major area of tension was the selection of suitable teachers; the churches often sought to have potential teachers tested to determine whether or not their beliefs conformed to orthodoxy. Towns and cities often used financial pressure, mainly the threat to revoke or limit funding, to ensure they maintained some control over education.

Protestant authorities continued to utilize the basic school structure of the late Middle Ages and the Renaissance. There were elementary and vernacular schools, secondary and grammar schools, and universities. However, some key differences emerged between Renaissance and Reformation schools. First, the Protestants emphasized the need to use local languages. While the vernacular schools of the Renaissance merely prepared students for the study of Latin, under the Protestant system elementary education was designed to prepare students to become fully literate in their native language. With the demise of Latin as a core subject, the curriculum broadened at the elementary and secondary levels; for example, the natural sciences gained a more prominent place in schools. Furthermore, the Protestants increasingly envisioned secondary education as preparation for university education. The secondary schools continued to teach Latin but also incorporated Greek and Hebrew and other subjects that would help develop well-rounded individuals prepared for a university education.

Universal Education and the Reformation

One of the most important impacts of the Reformation was the expansion of education. Protestant reformers wanted to wrest education away from the church and transfer responsibility to the secular governments. In a 1524 work entitled *To the Councilors of All German Cities That They Establish and Maintain Christian Schools,*

▼ *In this 1503 illustration the central position of arithmetic among the seven liberal arts reflects the view held by many that a thorough schooling in mathematics was the most fundamental aspect of education.*

▶ As time progressed, education became increasingly formal and began to resemble the system familiar today. In this seventeenth-century Spanish painting, a monk lectures to a group of university students.

Luther argued that towns or rulers should use confiscated church property to build and fund public schools for all citizens, rich and poor alike. This course of action was pursued in England and many of the German principalities in order to secure funding for public education.

Schools were the responsibility of local and regional governments, which offered varying levels of support. Governments paid the salaries of teachers, erected and maintained buildings, and provided other financial resources. Some cities (Zurich, Switzerland, for example) even provided scholarships for gifted rural children to attend secondary schools. Educational establishments varied in quality; wealthier cities were usually able to afford better teachers and facilities.

Public education during the period was usually limited to the elementary level and designed mainly to teach students to read and write and to provide a basic understanding of religion, history, and culture. Elementary education was free in many areas, and some cities and regions also provided free secondary education. Most secondary schools did charge fees, however, and even those with free tuition often charged boarding fees. Although scholarships were available, they were often provided by a wealthy benefactor; they were not part of a regular system designed to improve access for disadvantaged groups. A number of private schools throughout Europe served the wealthy and the powerful, including royal families.

Many Protestants, and even the Catholic Erasmus, echoed Luther's call that girls as well as boys should be educated. Although more girls began to attend elementary school, the sexes were separated and taught different curricula. Only girls from wealthy families were able to continue their education beyond elementary level, with a tutor or at a private girls' school.

EDUCATIONAL IMPACT OF THE PRINTING PRESS

Before the invention of the mechanical printing press in the 1450s, the availability of scholarly texts and books was limited. Schools typically had only one copy of any given text, a scarcity that reinforced the need for lessons to be based on memorization. After the printing press dramatically increased the availability of books, teaching styles changed in turn. For instance, with the large-scale production of grammar manuals, it became less important for students to memorize all of a language's rules, since they could look up any facts of which they were unsure. By 1500 at least a thousand active printing presses in Europe had produced some 30,000 titles.

Printing presses aided the expansion of education in a number of other ways. During the late Renaissance there appeared a consensus on what were the most important works for scholars to study. Schools increasingly abandoned the curricula of the Middle Ages, with their emphasis on memorization, and instead turned to the study of works by classical authors. Only with the rise of the printing press could schools accommodate the renewed interest in classical writers. Schools were now able to acquire these works more easily, and students could read such Greek and Roman authors as Plato, Aristotle, and Cicero for themselves. The general availability of texts and manuals also ensured that students received more uniform instruction.

By increasing literacy in general, the spread of books also generated a more widespread interest in education. During the Renaissance the number of students attending formal schools had not substantially increased. Only with the Reformation was there a dramatic expansion of educational opportunities. The printing presses helped fuel the spread of Reformation thought and new educational theories through the publication of works that expressed the new ideas and values that emerged during the period. Central to this dissemination of ideas was the increase in production of books in local languages and dialects as opposed to Latin. As a result, not only did more children attend school, but they increasingly came to be taught in their native language. In addition, printing presses made it easier for Protestant educators to publish their catechisms (instructive summaries of doctrine in question-and-answer form) and provide them to schools.

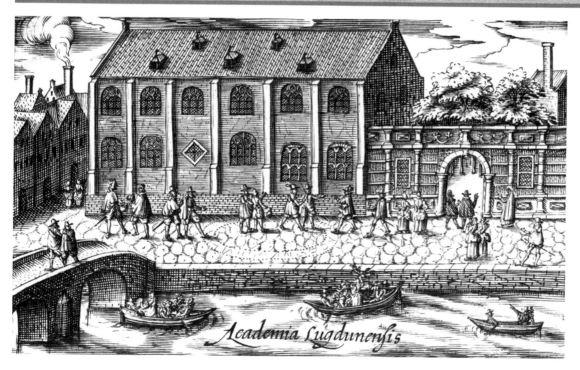

◀ *This 1625 engraving depicts the University of Leiden, which was founded in that Dutch city in 1575. Universities of the period usually had several hundred to a few thousand students.*

The Growth of Public Schools and Universities

In the Protestant states one result of the Reformation was the establishment of numerous new schools and the spread of free, universal public education. In England, for instance, some five hundred new schools had been founded by the seventeenth century. In Scotland in 1641, the crown established free education for all children at the elementary level. The spread of public education and the rise of the printing press led to a dramatic increase in literacy. By 1600 most states had literacy rates of around 30 percent. Some nations fared considerably better as public education spread. In Sweden 90 percent of the population was literate by 1700.

There was a corresponding growth in the number of universities. In 1500 there were 79 universities throughout Europe, and the number continued to rise: by 1700, 120 new universities had been established.

Philipp Melanchthon | 1497–1560

Many of the most influential educational reforms of the Reformation resulted from the work of Philipp Melanchthon, from Bretten, Germany. After a period of tutoring during his early youth, Melanchthon went to a Latin school in 1507. At thirteen he entered Heidelberg University, where he studied Greek philosophy and astronomy. When he applied for his degree, he was told by the university officials that he was too young; therefore he went to the University of Tübingen, where he finally received his masters degree in 1516. Melanchthon became a follower of Luther and later a professor at Wittenberg University. He wrote in both Greek and Latin and produced a number of scholarly works on Greek studies and theology; a strong ally of Luther, he also penned a range of works that helped define Protestant theology. However, his greatest impact was on education.

Melanchthon helped develop the school system for the German state of Saxony. This system later became the model for the majority of Protestant school systems throughout Germany and most of northern Europe. Melanchthon's main contributions were to introduce classes divided by age and to establish state control of education. Under Melanchthon's system state authorities issued licenses and fixed standards for teachers. He also wrote a number of textbooks that became widely used in schools throughout Europe. The heads of several universities asked the scholar to oversee reorganizations of their curriculum in order to inject Protestant theology into their teachings. Finally, Melanchthon developed and popularized the pedagogy (teaching methods) by which teachers were trained.

Melanchthon even influenced the training of the clergy. He insisted that future pastors should have a humanist education and be exposed to classical thought in addition to theology. He also wrote a phrase book, *Loci Communes,* which became the first widely used theological textbook for Protestants during the Reformation. Melanchthon continued to lecture at universities until the end of his life. At age sixty-three he collapsed while giving a lecture at Wittenberg University and died ten days later. In recognition of his accomplishments, Melanchthon became known as the "teacher of Germany."

▼ *Philipp Melanchthon, the subject of this portrait by Lucas Cranach the Elder (1472–1553), is regarded as the father of education in Germany. He helped found the universities of Königsberg, Jena, and Marburg and reformed eight other German universities.*

Many of these new universities were Protestant, and they often became centers of religious activism as scholars debated and examined theology free from the constraints of Catholic dogma.

In response, the Jesuits and other Catholic orders began to create new schools and universities and to expand opportunities at existing institutions. For example, in 1554 there were 23 Jesuit universities with 2,500 students; two years later, there were 26 colleges, and the number of students had grown to 5,700. The Jesuits also began to reform their pedagogy and incorporate some of the humanist themes of the Protestant school system.

John Calvin made his own contribution to higher education with the establishment in 1559, in the Swiss city of Geneva, of an academy to train pastors. Although the school was designed for religious training, it also incorporated the outlook and the ideals of humanism and aimed to provide a well-rounded education for the clergy. Student pastors studied ancient Greek and Roman philosophy and engaged in physical exercise. Calvin's academy was highly successful and came to be replicated throughout Protestant

◀ *Among the new universities established during the Reformation was Harvard University, which was founded in the British North American colony of Massachusetts in 1636. John Harvard, whose statue is depicted here, helped establish the university by bequeathing money and books to its founders—who named the college in his honor.*

Europe. The Jesuits even adopted Calvin's design and used his academy as a model for their own schools.

Lasting Influence

During the Renaissance and Reformation, most of the characteristics of modern education were established. The division of education into elementary, secondary, and higher education became widely accepted, and the importance of a well-rounded curriculum was recognized as school systems incorporated humanism and broadened the scope of studies. The principle of free, universal public education also became commonly accepted by those governments of Europe that adopted policies of financial support for public schools and efforts to promote literacy. Numerous other important components of modern education, including a common curriculum, common texts, and the use of local languages for instruction, all became widespread. Finally, the impact of educational development is demonstrated by the emergence during this period of thinkers and scholars who laid the groundwork for the subsequent age of scientific and philosophical discovery.

FURTHER READING

Black, Robert. *Humanism and Education in Medieval and Renaissance Italy: Tradition and Innovation in Latin Schools from the Twelfth to the Fifteenth Century.* New York, 2001.

Boyd, William, and Edmund J. King. *The History of Western Education.* 12th ed. Lanham, MD, 1995.

Eby, Frederick. *Early Protestant Educators: The Educational Writings of Martin Luther, John Calvin, and Other Leaders of Protestant Thought.* New York, 1971.

Strauss, Gerald. *Luther's House of Learning.* Baltimore, 1978.

Woodward, William Harrison. *Studies in Education during the Age of the Renaissance, 1400–1600.* 2nd ed. New York, 1965.

Tom Lansford

SEE ALSO
- Astrology • Calvinism • Erasmus, Desiderius
- Florence • Humanism and Learning • Literature
- Lutheranism • Mathematics • Medicine
- Petrarch • Platonism • Printing • Reformation
- Renaissance • Science and Technology • Sweden
- Universities

Elizabeth I

DURING THE REIGN OF ELIZABETH I (1533–1603), QUEEN OF ENGLAND AND IRELAND FROM 1558 TO 1603, PROTESTANTISM WAS ESTABLISHED AS THE PERMANENT NATIONAL RELIGION, AND ENGLAND REPUDIATED HOSTILE ATTACKS FROM CATHOLIC SPAIN.

Elizabeth Tudor was the daughter of Henry VIII, king of England and Ireland, and his second wife, Anne Boleyn. In order to marry Anne, Henry had broken with the Roman Catholic Church (the pope had refused to annul his first marriage to Catherine of Aragon) and, in 1534, declared himself supreme head of the English church. Many Roman Catholics did not accept that the annulment of Henry's first marriage was valid, and so in the eyes of many, his daughter Elizabeth was illegitimate. Henry, who already had another daughter, Lady Mary, desperately wanted a son to succeed him. In 1536 he was convinced by Anne Boleyn's enemies that the queen had been unfaithful to him. Anne was accused of having committed adultery with five men and executed.

The following day Henry married Jane Seymour, who gave birth to Henry's long desired son, the future King Edward VI. Henry declared his marriage to Anne null and void, and Elizabeth was formally declared illegitimate.

On the death of Henry VIII, Edward was crowned king. Henry's will made Mary and Elizabeth heirs after Edward, although both remained illegitimate in the eyes of the law. The young king and the leading politicians of the new regime, avowed Protestants, moved the Church of England in a radical direction. However, Edward became dangerously ill in 1553. He and his councillors tried to alter the succession in favor of Edward's Protestant cousin Lady Jane Grey and to disinherit Mary and Elizabeth, but upon Edward's death a popular rising placed Mary on the throne.

Mary was determined to restore Catholicism to its former position as the national religion, and many fearful Protestants fled into exile on the continent. Elizabeth's suspected Protestantism and her status as Mary's heir placed her in a dangerous position. Sir Thomas Wyatt the Younger (c. 1521–1554), a gentleman who objected to

▶ *Propaganda for the Reformed church: the dying Henry VIII passes on the legacy of the supremacy of the English church to his young son. The image shows the destruction of papal authority and the expulsion of monasticism—and through the window, the destruction of images.*

Elizabeth's superb education, steeped in Renaissance humanism, was centered around classical languages, history, rhetoric, and moral philosophy. Her tutors were the Cambridge scholar William Grindal and Roger Ascham, the greatest English educationalist of the Tudor period. In 1570 Ascham wrote that Elizabeth's abilities equaled those of any man.

I speak to you all, young gentlemen of England—that one maid should go beyond you, in all excellency of learning and knowledge of divers tongues.... Yea, I believe that beside her perfect readiness in Latin, Italian, French, and Spanish, she readeth here now at Windsor more Greek every day than some prebendary [canon] of this church doth read Latin in a whole week ... she hath obtained that excellency of learning, to understand, speak, and write, both wittily and fair with hand, as scarce one or two rare wits in both the universities have in many years reached unto.

Roger Ascham, *The Scholemaster*

CHRONOLOGY

1533
Elizabeth is born at Greenwich Palace.

1547
Henry VIII dies, and Edward VI becomes king.

1554
Elizabeth is temporarily imprisoned.

1558
Succeeds Mary as queen.

1559
Parliament passes the Acts of Supremacy and Uniformity; Mary, Queen of Scots, becomes queen of France.

1561
Returns from France to Scotland.

1570–1571
Henry, duke of Anjou, negotiates to marry Elizabeth.

1572–1579
Francis, duke of Anjou negotiates to marry Elizabeth.

1585
Elizabeth signs the Treaty of Nonsuch with the French.

1587
Mary, Queen of Scots, is executed.

1594
Rebellion breaks out in Ireland.

1598
William Cecil (Lord Burghley) dies.

1603
Elizabeth dies on March 24.

◄ *One of the best-known portraits of Queen Mary is this 1553 painting by Antonio Moro. Mary, pictured holding the Tudor rose, the symbol of her dynasty, was middle-aged when she came to the throne. Her appearance here may flatter her looks, and it has none of the majestic, iconic quality of the later images of Elizabeth.*

Mary's plan to marry the Catholic King Philip of Spain, led an armed uprising against Mary's rule and made contact with Elizabeth.

Although it is unlikely that Elizabeth herself was directly involved in the uprising, she was nevertheless imprisoned in the Tower of London and interrogated. Elizabeth defended herself with courage and wisdom, but the experience was a traumatic lesson in the dangerous game of high politics. Mary's desire to restore Catholicism permanently to England was hindered by the short duration of her rule and her failure to produce an heir. As her health deteriorated, she was forced to declare Elizabeth her successor.

A significant feature of the Elizabethan period was the development of a particularly fervent kind of Protestantism known as Puritanism. The word *Puritan* was originally an abusive insult—Puritans more commonly identified themselves as "the Godly." Puritans placed particular emphasis on the doctrine of predestination, that is, the belief that God had ordained some men to be saved in the afterlife and others to be damned. They were also united in their belief that further reform of the church was necessary and objected to customs and rituals prescribed by the 1559 Act of Uniformity, which Elizabeth passed on becoming head of the Church of England. The emphasis Puritans placed on the importance of preaching caused tension with the queen, who was suspicious of overzealous preachers and tried to limit their activities.

The easiest way to identify Puritans is to consider their social identity; they believed it was important to live an overtly godly way of life and devoted much energy to Bible reading, prayer, and attendance at sermons. In addition, Puritans were associated with strict social morality and hostility to certain forms of popular culture, including the public theater. The hostility between Elizabeth and the Puritans had not been resolved by the end of the queen's reign, and during the reign of her successor, James I, many Puritans chose to emigrate to America. The unresolved tensions in the Elizabethan church also played a central role in the events that led to civil war in the seventeenth century.

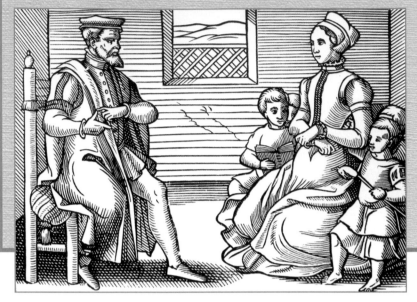

▲ *This image of a Puritan family comes from a 1563 woodcut; the family sits in a plain room with no decoration.*

The Elizabethan Religious Settlement

On November 17, 1558, Elizabeth was informed of the death of her sister. She immediately surrounded herself with supporters; the most important was William Cecil, who became Elizabeth's secretary of state. Cecil (made Lord Burghley in 1571) would remain Elizabeth's chief minister for the rest of his life. He and Elizabeth did not always agree on policy, but their relationship consistently remained one of mutual respect and admiration.

Cecil headed a new regime that was committed to the reestablishment of Protestantism in a country wary of yet more religious change. Elizabeth's accession depended on the political support of Protestants, the most zealous of whom returned from exile in continental Europe to celebrate the dawn of a new and hopeful era. Elizabeth's own religious attitudes, however, are difficult to assess. Although she openly rejected the Catholic Mass, she was devoted to aspects of worship that many of her Protestant subjects found worryingly unreformed: she venerated the cross, enjoyed church music, and maintained a strong dislike of clerical marriage. These practices

and views were seen by more fervent Protestants as hallmarks of Catholic belief.

Elizabeth was crowned on January 15, 1559. In her procession through London, she charmed the crowds that had flocked to cheer her with appealing speeches and gestures. Parliament met at Westminster in the same month to debate the new form of religion in England and declared Elizabeth the supreme governor of the Church of England. The Act of Uniformity returned English ritual and theology largely to that of the final years of Edward's reign.

Few people, however, were satisfied with this settlement. Catholics obviously rejected it; they were forced throughout Elizabeth's reign to pay increasingly large penalties for nonattendance at Protestant services, and as the reign progressed, Catholicism became a persecuted, minority religion in England. Many Protestants were also dissatisfied; those who had been in exile during Mary's reign were more radical in their vision of the new English church than the queen; they had expected that the 1559 settlement would merely be an initial step toward further reform. Protestants of this mentality are sometimes referred to as the "hotter sort of Protestants," or Puritans. Elizabeth clashed with her clergy and a wider body of Protestants, including members of her own council, over matters of church reform. She vetoed all petitions and bills in Parliament that aimed to persuade her to change the nature of church ritual and practices. She saw attempts to make her alter the settlement as an affront to her authority as queen and supreme governor of the English church.

Marriage and the Succession

Not only did Elizabeth clash with her subjects over religious policies, but she also experienced great pressure to marry and produce an heir to safeguard the future of Protestant England. Elizabeth is remembered as the Virgin Queen who decided not to marry for the good of the nation; portraits and poems that celebrated the queen's virginity date from the latter part of her reign, when it finally became accepted that Elizabeth would not marry. Earlier in her reign Elizabeth responded to pressure to marry with vague promises that she would attempt to find a husband, but she loathed the idea and prohibited open discussion of marriage and a potential successor. To her the matter was private.

It was virtually impossible for Elizabeth to find a suitable partner. Her ideal husband would be a man of sufficient status to be a worthy consort, preferably a Protestant or, at the very least, a man willing for his children to be brought up in the Protestant religion. Marriage was also a crucial diplomatic matter, and the offer of Elizabeth's hand was a key feature of foreign policy for the first twenty years of her reign. Many foreign princes approached her, but the proposals that Elizabeth appeared to take most seriously were those of the French princes, Henry and Francis, successive dukes of Anjou.

France was, however, a long-standing enemy, and the princes' Catholicism was widely disliked in England. In 1579 there was such open opposition to the proposal made by Francis, duke of Anjou, that Elizabeth was forced to abandon even the pretense of courtship. Later celebrations of Elizabeth as the Virgin Queen were a tacit acknowledgment that she would never marry.

The alternative to an unpopular foreign match would have been to marry within the realm. Elizabeth genuinely considered this option

in one case alone, that of Robert Dudley, earl of Leicester (from 1564), whom Elizabeth appeared to have truly loved. However, Dudley was already married, and gossip about his relationship with the queen developed into a scandal in 1560, when his wife, Amy Robsart, died in suspicious circumstances. Although historians now believe that neither Elizabeth nor Dudley had any hand in Amy Robsart's death, the scandal ended any question of the match (Leicester remained an important political and military figure, however). Elizabeth had many other favorite male courtiers, whose looks and charm contributed to their rise to power. Her courtiers made romantic protestations of their love to the queen, but these were artful games played out at court for the queen's attention and patronage: Elizabeth never again considered marrying one of her subjects.

▲ The new queen holds the orb and the scepter in a 1559 portrait that recalls the majestic images of her father. Elizabeth's hair is loose, as was the custom at the coronation of queens, although some believe that her loose hair symbolizes her virginity. She has the striking combination of her father's red hair and her mother's dark eyes.

Mary, Queen of Scots ❘ c. 1588–1637

Mary lived in France from the age of five and married the heir to the throne, the dauphin, in 1558. She became queen of France briefly in 1559 but was widowed in 1560 and returned the following year to her native Scotland a relative stranger. Mary was considered a great beauty who charmed most people that she met: Elizabeth was fiercely jealous of Mary's reputed beauty and talents and often boasted of her own, superior physical appearance and accomplishments. Mary's marriages proved to be her downfall. Her second husband, Henry, Lord Darnley, was murdered in 1567, and it appears that Mary was coerced into marriage with the man considered responsible, James Hepburn, the earl of Bothwell. Historians disagree about the evidence that implicates Mary in the murder, but her guilt was savagely asserted by hostile contemporaries. Mary was actively involved in plots against Elizabeth's life, but her correspondence with Anthony Babington, the young Catholic who sought to depose Elizabeth in Mary's favor, was contrived and manipulated by Francis Walsingham, who represented the fervent desire of Elizabeth's advisers and influential Protestant subjects to destroy the Catholic woman who might inherit the throne of England.

▼ *This unattributed portrait of Mary, Queen of Scots, dates from the time of Mary's wedding to the dauphin François in 1558. At this time Mary's future seemed assured, yet a decade later she would become a prisoner in England.*

Mary, Queen of Scots, and Catholicism

The problem of Elizabeth's marriage was particularly acute because her nearest heir was a Catholic—Mary, Queen of Scots. Mary had married Elizabeth's cousin, Henry, Lord Darnley, and had given birth to an heir, the future king James VI of Scotland and later James I of England, Scotland, and Ireland. Yet events in Scotland forced Mary off the throne, and she arrived in England in May 1568 in the hope that her cousin Elizabeth would protect her: instead Mary was imprisoned while Elizabeth and her council debated what to do with her. Mary attracted much sympathy among Catholics, and a small but significant number plotted to depose Elizabeth in the hope that Mary would inherit the throne and restore Catholicism. Mary's presence in England was, therefore, a severe challenge to the Protestant regime and to Elizabeth's safety.

Mary remained in captivity in England for the next eighteen years. In 1569 the Catholic duke of Norfolk hatched a plan to marry Mary and have her declared Elizabeth's successor. He was imprisoned in the Tower of London, but the Catholic nobility in the north of England rose in protest and attempted to raise the region in revolt. The rebellion was put down relatively easily by the queen's forces, but Pope Pius V excommunicated Elizabeth in 1570 and declared that her Catholic subjects were freed from their bonds of allegiance to the queen. The pope's action increased the likelihood of assassination plots against Elizabeth and drove a permanent wedge between the queen and her Catholic subjects; it also did much to cultivate anti-Catholic feeling in England. In 1570 and 1571 the Italian banker Roberto Ridolfi plotted another conspiracy that involved Spain, the papacy, and the duke of Norfolk, with the intention of deposing Elizabeth in favor of Mary. Following the discovery of the plot, Elizabeth reluctantly agreed to Norfolk's execution but refused to condemn Mary, despite tremendous pressure to do so from Parliament.

Further plots and intrigues came to a head with the Babington Conspiracy of 1586, when Elizabeth's principal secretary, Francis Walsingham, provided decisive evidence of Mary's involvement in another Catholic plot to depose Elizabeth. Mary was tried and found guilty, and Elizabeth reluctantly signed the death warrant. Elizabeth's council dispatched the warrant immediately, lest she change her mind, and Mary was executed at Fotheringhay Castle. When Elizabeth was told the news, she was openly devastated and so furious that she sent Lord Burghley from court, the only significant rift in their long political relationship.

The War with Spain

The year after Mary's execution, Elizabeth experienced another significant crisis. England had been unofficially involved in hostilities against Spain since the 1570s. In 1567 the Protestants in the Low Countries had rebelled against the rule of King Philip II of Spain (the Low Countries were part of Philip's Catholic Hapsburg Empire). English and Dutch Protestants called upon Elizabeth to help her co-religionists. However, the queen was unwilling to enter into open conflict; preferring instead to support private maritime operations, she licensed Francis Drake and other pirates—known more heroically as privateers—to attack and plunder Spanish ships.

In 1584 the assassination of William of Orange, the leader of the Dutch resistance to Spain, forced Elizabeth to make a formal military commitment. The earl of Leicester, Robert Dudley, went with an expeditionary force to the Netherlands in 1585, but his campaign had little success. In 1588 Philip finalized preparations to send the armada, a naval escort for the transport of an army that was to invade England. Elizabeth rallied her soldiers at Tilbury, in south-

▲ Robert Dudley, the subject of this unattributed portrait, possessed the masculine glamour that appealed to Elizabeth. More than a favorite, Dudley, the earl of Leicester, became a key adviser and military leader.

ern England; she inspected the troops on horseback in armor and made a stirring speech. On August 7 a combination of English ships and the prevailing weather conditions harried the Spanish and drove their fleet around the north of Scotland; many Spanish ships were wrecked on the Irish coast. The English offered prayers of thanksgiving and proclaimed their success to be God's vindication of their religion. The experience of war with Catholic Spain helped develop a strong sense of Protestant national identity in England.

Robert Devereux, 2nd Earl of Essex | 1565–1601

Educated and handsome, the earl of Essex possessed a paranoid ambition. He attracted Elizabeth's attention and favor as a courtier, but his desire for military glory was at odds with the queen's cautious martial policy. As a woman Elizabeth felt her authority was challenged in times of war, and she was proved right when Essex repeatedly ignored her instructions on campaign. Essex grew increasingly resentful that he could not dominate the queen as he wished, and his behavior toward his mistress grew increasingly belligerent and hostile. After the failure of his Irish campaign and his subsequent disgrace, expressions of public support for the earl greatly worried the authorities and gave Essex unrealistic expectations of his ability to command loyalty in London. His crazed attempt to raise the city failed miserably, and Essex died a convicted traitor after making a contrite confession of his sins on the scaffold.

The Final Years

The final years of Elizabeth's reign were marked by a sense of frustration, stagnation, and decline. People were eager for the new reign but still unsure of who would succeed, as the queen continued to refuse to name an heir. It was, however, widely hoped that the Protestant king James VI of Scotland, the son of Mary, Queen of Scots, would succeed. The defeat of the armada did not signal the end of the threat from Spain: Spanish ships were sighted in the English Channel at various times in the 1590s, although they did little harm to the English coastline. England

remained committed to the assistance of the Dutch with troops until the end of Elizabeth's reign, and from 1590 until 1594, Elizabeth sent military assistance to the Huguenots (French Protestants) in northern France. These alliances were born of a shared hostility to the mutual enemy, Philip II of Spain.

Robert Devereux, the young earl of Essex and Elizabeth's last great favorite, was determined that England continue the war against Spain, despite Elizabeth's reluctant attitude. In 1596 Essex led a successful attack in which he sacked the Spanish port of Cádiz and thus gained glory and renown

▶ *Through the windows in the background of this iconic 1588 image, the so-called Armada Portrait, can be seen the approach of the armada and then its destruction off the coast of Scotland. Elizabeth's hand rests on a globe, a representation of her new international might.*

In this 1601 painting Queen Elizabeth I is carried under a canopy, supported by her courtiers. Although she appears as majestic as ever, reports of her physical appearance in the last decade of her reign paint a very different image: an aging, toothless queen caked in makeup yet still dressed in sumptuous gowns and adorned with jewels and her famous red wig.

in Europe. However, in 1599 a rebellion in Ireland forced the redirection of English money and manpower. Although the Tudors claimed sovereignty over Ireland, their power was limited; attempts to force the Irish to adopt Protestantism had been generally unsuccessful, and the great majority of the Irish population was settled into a defiant Catholicism. Essex, England's leading military commander, was sent to put down the rebellion, but he failed spectacularly. After making an unauthorized truce with the rebels, he returned to London, where he was imprisoned for misconduct and stripped of his offices. His replacement, Lord Mountjoy, was sent to Ireland, and after a bitter campaign, he put down the rebellion in the final months of Elizabeth's reign.

The earl of Essex had became convinced that enemies at court, in particular Robert Cecil (Lord Burghley's son and political heir), had blocked his path to power and turned the queen against him. In 1601 he tried to raise London in a disastrous attempt to overpower the court and banish his enemies. Tried and found guilty of treason, Essex was executed in the Tower of London; his gloomy story dominated the end of Elizabeth's reign. In February 1603, an ill and depressed Elizabeth died, and her cousin, James VI of Scotland, succeeded peacefully to the English throne as King James I.

The Judgment of Posterity

In the following reign dissatisfaction with Elizabeth was forgotten. Disillusionment with the policies of King James prompted nostalgic representations of the myth of the "golden age of Elizabeth," a potent legend that has survived into modern times. Elizabeth demonstrated extraordinary skill as a ruler. Forced to learn the art of survival during the testing days of her youth, she remained on the throne for forty-four years, despite crises at home and abroad. She achieved all that she did as an exceptional figure—a female ruler in a man's world.

FURTHER READING

Doran, S. *Monarchy and Matrimony: The Courtships of Elizabeth.* London, 1996.

Guy, J. *The Reign of Elizabeth I: Court and Culture in the Last Decade.* Cambridge, 1995.

Haigh, C. *Elizabeth I.* 2nd ed. London, 1998.

Marcus, L., J. Mueller, and M. B. Rose. *Elizabeth I: Collected Works.* Chicago, 2000.

Starkey, D. *Elizabeth.* London, 2001.

Alexandra Gajda

SEE ALSO
• Armada, Spanish • Church of England • England
• Henry VIII • Philip II • Scotland

England

THE RENAISSANCE IN ENGLAND, WHICH LASTED FROM THE LATE 1400S TO AROUND 1700, SAW AN EXPLOSION IN ARTISTIC, CULTURAL, AND INTELLECTUAL ENDEAVOR. THE REFORMATION BEGAN IN THE 1530S; ENGLAND BROKE WITH ROME AND GRADUALLY ADOPTED PROTESTANTISM.

Although the Renaissance began in Italy in the mid-fourteenth century, it did not fully emerge in England until the last decade of the fifteenth. The major source of inspiration was not Italy but France and Burgundy, areas the English nobility often visited. However, the English Renaissance was influenced as much by domestic affairs as by French or Italian practice, and the transformation of English culture was slow, patchy, and inconsistent. Nevertheless, the English Renaissance marked the transition from medieval to early modern society.

Architecture

One hallmark of the Renaissance in England was the transformation of architecture; a Renaissance architectural style first appeared in England around 1540. King Henry VIII's cardinal, Thomas Wolsey, was ahead of his countrymen; he planned Hampton Court Palace, perhaps the first English building to imitate classical models. Completed in 1515, the palace featured many busts of Roman emperors. Classical themes developed with the construction of Gonville Hall in Cambridge in 1559, a building that featured a Gate of Humility, a Gate of Virtue, and a Gate of Honor—named for human qualities that featured prominently in Greek and Roman writing.

Renaissance architecture was intended to express a general belief in divine harmony and particularly the ancient Greek philosopher Pythagoras's idea that the universe is mathematically constructed. Renaissance architects created precise and symmetrical designs in which function and beauty were perfectly integrated.

The new passion for continental architecture was most ardent among the nobility, who sought to create houses that would impress the king during royal visits. Therefore, the main focus of Renaissance architecture in England was on the creation of stately country homes. However, while there were some Italian craftsmen working in England, a widespread hostility to foreign workmen, especially Catholics, ensured that the spread of ideas in this area was both slow and inconsistent. Nevertheless, since this prejudice was directed more against the Italians' religion than their nationality, the hostility to Italian influences did not extend to the ideas that were being disseminated from Flanders and other Protestant areas. In the early seventeenth century a huge book trade developed in Antwerp (in present-day Belgium). Numerous writings on Renaissance architecture were shipped to England, where they found a large audience.

Renaissance Literature

The greatest influence of the Renaissance on English culture was in the realm of literature. Initially, because of the Renaissance emphasis on imitating the great classical writers, advances in English literature were restricted to writers from the upper level of society (those who could write

▼ Built on the instruction of Cardinal Wolsey in honor of Henry VIII, Hampton Court Palace, southwest of London, was one of the first English buildings to show the influence of Renaissance architectural ideals.

Edmund Spenser's *Faerie Queene* (1591) is perhaps the greatest epic poem of its age. A tribute to Elizabeth I, *The Faerie Queene* is full of allusions to great works of classical literature and mythology. This remarkable and complex work is important in two respects. First, it confirmed the status of English as a language of sublime artistic expression. Spenser drew a great deal of inspiration from Petrarch (1304–1374), whose poems had done much the same for the Italian language. In this respect, then, *The Faerie Queene* represents the adoption of the Italian Renaissance (albeit in an altered form) in England. Second, its rich and vivid imagery represents an important trend in the English Renaissance. Visual art was widely distrusted and associated with Catholicism. The written word, associated with the Protestant emphasis on Bible reading, was the main force in English culture. Through language Spenser was able to create a visual feast that would not displease his Protestant patron.

Latin). Thomas More's *Utopia* (1516) was one of the greatest works of Latin scholarship and classical rhetoric of its time. However, as the sixteenth century progressed, other trends of Renaissance thought encouraged the development of more popular forms of writing in vernacular languages. The emergence of drama during the reigns of Elizabeth I and James I has given this era its reputation as a golden age of English literature. Although William Shakespeare (1564–1616) later became the most celebrated writer of his age, he was not the most acclaimed at the time. The playwrights Christopher Marlowe (1564–1593) and Ben Jonson (1572–1637) and the poet Edmund Spenser (c. 1553–1599) all earned great praise from their contemporaries.

Much of the literature that emerged in England embodies the paradoxical view of humankind that was typical of the Renaissance. On the one hand, the view that humans are the greatest of God's creations, capable of glorious achievement, tended to inspire an optimism about human potential. Yet the great tragic dramas of the age portray people whose sinfulness, malevolence, or foolishness brings about their ruin.

Much dramatic writing of the time was organized around the concept of the Great Chain of Being—the belief that all things occupy a fixed position in a hierarchical scheme topped by God. The principle of order was both challenged and reinforced by contemporary drama. Typically, the opening scene is one of harmony. One or more characters then violates that harmony through malevolent or misguided actions. Finally harmony is reestablished, and the perpetrator is punished for his transgression. For instance, a man sides with the devil in Marlowe's *Doctor Faustus* and is brought to destruction for his evil

▲ *The Red Cross Knight, the Christian hero of book 1 of* The Faerie Queene, *fights a dragon in this image from the 1590 first edition of one of the great works of English literature.*

choice. In Shakespeare's *Othello*, the eponymous hero is brought down by sexual jealousy, awakened in him by the evil insinuations of Iago. The play ends with Othello and his wife dead, Iago punished, and some sort of normality restored. This basic narrative pattern—a righting of wrongs that, though it may cost many lives, ends redemptively—provided the backbone of English tragedy, a genre that differs from its classical and medieval antecedents in its focus on the plight of the individual: on the drama of being human.

Humanism

The earliest English humanists, exponents of the particular way of thinking that underpinned the Renaissance, tended to be not practitioners but patrons: that is, they used their wealth and influence to foster young academics, to promote centers of learning, and to collect and preserve books and manuscripts they considered worthy of study. Perhaps the most important of these humanists was Humphrey, duke of Gloucester (1391–1447). Humphrey translated the works of such ancient authors as Plato, Aristotle, and Plutarch and accumulated a huge collection of books by newer humanist authors, such as the Italians Petrarch (1304–1374), Poggio Bracciolini (1380–1459), and Leonardo Bruni (c. 1370–1444). Humphrey also persuaded Oxford University to add Ovid, Cicero, and Virgil to a new rhetoric curriculum, and between 1439 and 1444 he donated 280 volumes to the university's library.

Another influential humanist patron was William Grey, bishop of Ely (d. 1478), who, unusually, had lived in Rome and had Italian humanist friends, many of whom were persuaded to lecture in England. He translated many of their works into English and donated 200 manuscripts to university libraries. Owing to Grey, Humphrey, and other such humanist patrons, by 1499 there were 114 specialist humanist schools, an increase of 85 from 1450. These centers of humanism were vital to the spread of the "new learning," as it soon became known. Although humanism remained the preserve of the educated elite, such schools ensured that generations of new scholars were bought up with an increased understanding of humanist principles.

Humanism was not a political, religious, or ethical ideology as such. Rather, it established a set of ideas that aided critical analysis and supported self-expression (a humanist was taught how to think, not what to think). For example, one of the major goals of humanism was the rediscovery of classical Greek and Latin texts. A deeper understanding of the two languages and a concern with the principles of translation resulted in a more rigorous approach to grammatical and

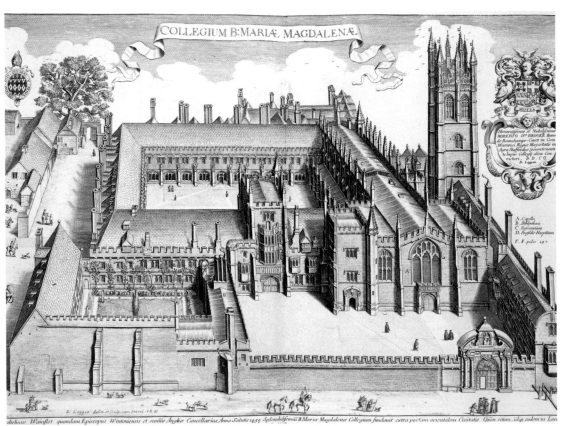

▶ A 1675 engraving of Magdalen College, Oxford. Founded in 1448, Magdalen became a center for the development of humanist learning.

No single belief system with a clearly stated body of doctrines underpinned humanist thought. The simple fact that humanists believed at once in the value of reasoned argument and the importance of studying classical texts led to frequent disagreements among humanists about the meaning of a given author's writing or how a "humane" person should respond in a given situation. Some humanist scholars preferred Latin texts, whereas others preferred Greek ones, and humanists argued over which tongue gave truer expression to individual thought. Similarly, while some scholars sought to attain a greater understanding of the Bible by reading the scriptures in their ancient languages, others were content to accept the authority of the church's approved translation, the Latin Vulgate. They exploited the capacity of reason in other areas.

Many humanists also disagreed with one another over whether their brand of learning was an escape from the murky world of politics or a way to improve it. For instance, while the great Dutch humanist Desiderius Erasmus said of John Colet, "when I hear him speak I might be listening to Plato!" he fiercely disagreed with Colet's decision to become an adviser to King Henry VIII. Erasmus believed that individuals should have "peace of mind," critical insight, and a skeptical eye concerning the machinations of princes and politics. Because of his antipolitical inclinations, some characterized Erasmus as a dreamer, whereas Colet, at the risk of compromising his conscience, decided to trust in his king and attempt to make a difference in the "sinful world." Such disputes among humanists stemmed in part from the types of sources that they stressed. Those who read about Greek ideas of virtue and civic democracy often tended toward political participation, while those who chose to withdraw often cited stories of corrupt Roman emperors—or indeed Niccolò Machiavelli's contemporary book *The Prince* (1513), which portrayed self-serving rulers motivated not by virtue but by the desire to retain power.

▼ *This eighteenth-century engraving of the English scholar John Colet was copied from a portrait by Hans Holbein the Younger. Colet was a leading humanist; his mockery of religious superstition and monastic corruption struck a chord in a period in which old values were being questioned.*

linguistic precision. From this approach sprang a new stress on the concept of historical context, that is, how the original author interacted with his social environment: how far his circumstances dictated what he wrote and how he wrote. For instance, John Colet (c. 1467–1519) broke new ground in 1497 and 1498 with a series of university lectures on the New Testament Epistles of Saint Paul. Colet's lectures treated Paul as an individual personality (rather than an anonymous exemplar of a tradition) and described the historical circumstances in which Paul was writing.

Another important humanist idea was the exaltation of reason. Considered and informed judgment was regarded as an essential prerequisite for a person to become "humane." For the first time, many traditional assumptions were questioned and reassessed. This rationalist development was accompanied by a yearning for new modes of artistic expression. Although the great works of visual art that sprang from the Renaissance were largely restricted to mainland Europe, the importance of the written word was heavily emphasized in England. The writing of "learned letters," beautiful poetry, and (in the sixteenth century) plays was seen as a supreme act of self-expression that enlivened the spirit.

Henry VIII and the Reformation

The Reformation in England can be defined as England's break with Rome and adoption of Protestantism as its national religion. However, the process was both complex and protracted. Henry VIII, who reigned from 1509 to 1547, oversaw the beginnings of this great shift toward a new national church. Unlike the campaigns for religious reform on the continent (for instance, the one led by Martin Luther in Germany from around 1520), the origins of the Reformation in England owed less to a widespread desire for religious change than it did to Henry's personal and political ambitions. Indeed, Henry was not a Protestant but, at one stage at least, a loyal and conventional Catholic—the pope went as far as to dub him Defender of the Faith in 1521 after Henry penned a critique of Luther.

In the late 1520s, however, Henry's relations with the papacy became increasingly strained. Henry was determined to divorce his wife, Catherine of Aragon, and marry Anne Boleyn. However, Catholicism did not permit divorce, and so it was necessary for Henry to prove that the marriage to Catherine had been invalid in the first place in order for an annulment to be granted by the pope. Henry's major concern was that his marriage had not produced a male heir. In this period of relative dynastic insecurity, a male heir was the surest way of achieving an undisputed succession to the throne. Henry argued that the pope had no right to refuse an annulment. Despite the best efforts of Thomas Wolsey, Henry's cardinal, to have the case heard in England by favorable judges, the case was finally revoked to Rome in 1529, an almost certain indication that Henry's appeal would fail. Wolsey was dismissed as a consequence.

When it became clear that Henry would not get his way through papal assent, he opted to assert that this matter was for England alone. There was no single moment when England definitively broke with Rome but rather a series of events and pieces of legislation that whittled away the pope's authority in England and replaced it with the king's. In 1531 Henry was declared the supreme head of the English church, and the Protestant Thomas Cranmer was appointed archbishop of Canterbury in 1533. The year 1534 saw the passing of the Act of Supremacy, a sweeping measure that banned all appeals to Rome, confirmed Henry's leadership of the church, and banned the pope from creating new bishops in England.

Although Henry was not a Protestant, his key advisers increasingly were. Cranmer had the king's confidence, as at one time did Anne Boleyn, who had Lutheran sympathies. Perhaps the most important of the figures who helped to popularize Henry's reforms was his secretary Thomas Cromwell (c. 1485–1540). Cromwell, who became Henry's most powerful adviser and government official, was central to the propaganda machine; he ensured that a vast literature of antipapal polemic and Lutheran theology was disseminated as widely as possible. He was also a leading figure in the campaign to have the Bible translated into English and ensured that "popish" relics and symbols were removed from English churches.

▼ This cartoon, taken from a contemporary broadsheet, shows Henry VIII humiliating the pope. England's conflict with Rome generated a great deal of comment, from lengthy academic tomes to lurid popular accounts. Thanks to the printing press, large numbers of people were kept abreast of developments.

The relationship between the humanist movement and the Reformation is difficult to establish; certainly humanism was not strictly a cause of the Reformation. Indeed, some of the Reformers' most vocal critics, including Thomas More, were humanist scholars. On the other hand, the development of humanism did influence the expression of Reformed ideas. For instance, the humanist stress on the written word was seized on by many Protestants, who wrote far more propaganda than Catholics did. Similarly, the humanist interest in history and historical context led many writers to pen histories of England that often stressed a national consciousness—a patriotism of sorts—that could be used to slur Rome and its attempts at intervention.

Because of this new consciousness, Henry's claim that religion was a matter for him, not the pope, gained a new credibility. There was also a new emphasis on the workings and correct interpretation of national law. This peculiarly English Renaissance trend resulted in a new class of highly trained lawyers who aimed to clarify the precedents that are the basis of English common law. Thus, many humanist lawyers came to contrast common law with papal law and found inconsistencies between the two. It was sometimes argued that papal law was inferior, a conclusion that Henry found extremely useful when justifying his break with Rome.

However, humanism and Protestantism were in many senses inimical. Whereas humanists stressed the importance of reason, Protestantism was a reaction against exactly that tendency in Catholicism. By stressing original sin and the unique power of God to dispense salvation, Protestants tended to shun exactly the potential for human development that humanists argued for. Martin Luther and Erasmus were famously hostile to each other; Luther saw Erasmus's endeavors as a misguided waste of time.

Although it would therefore be incorrect to assume that humanist thought was a cause or even a consistent ally of the Reformation, humanism did help to shape the Reformation. One example of this ambiguous relationship was the campaign to have the Bible translated into English. In 1539, largely as a result of Thomas Cromwell's efforts, the Great Bible was published and placed in all churches, and literate parishioners were encouraged to read it. Public access to the Bible and to religious literature in general aided the spread of Protestantism. Yet the project to translate the Bible into English was not an exclusively Protestant concern; Thomas More, the noted Catholic humanist, for example,

▲ *The frontispiece of the first official Bible to be published in English, the Great Bible (1539), depicts Henry VIII surrounded by his advisers and by the English people. That Henry allowed his image to be so strongly associated with the publication is an indication of his initial enthusiasm for the project.*

In the world of high politics, Thomas More and Bishop John Fisher were executed in 1535 for refusing to swear to the Act of Supremacy. Both had also strongly opposed Henry's divorce from Catherine. On the popular level there was a serious rebellion, known as the Pilgrimage of Grace, in 1536. Led by Robert Aske, this rising began in the north and made significant gains before being outmaneuvered; the ringleaders were executed. The rebels' motives were mixed, but opposition to Henry's religious reforms was certainly a strong factor.

▲ Queen Elizabeth I, the subject of this unattributed contemporary portrait, reigned for over forty years and brought stability to a previously fraught political and religious situation. The many depictions of Elizabeth, more than any other Tudor monarch, came to symbolize a new and more confident England.

was a supporter. Humanists could thus support religious reform without necessarily being associated with Protestantism.

Despite the religious changes in the country, it is unlikely that many ordinary Englishmen would have felt that the country was becoming significantly more Protestant; the positive reforms were few in number and were rarely sustained with great governmental vigor. Yet many people would probably have agreed that the country was becoming far less Catholic. The dissolution of the monasteries between 1536 and 1539 removed a large chunk of the Catholic

social and religious infrastructure from local communities. However, the reasons for this reform were more economic than religious: Henry coveted the vast income from these lands to wage foreign wars and to reward those people who had assisted his reforms.

Queen Elizabeth I

Henry died on January 28, 1547; two reigns followed that were too short to make a serious impact. First, Henry's son came to the throne aged just nine. Edward VI had two protectors, Northumberland and Somerset, who governed while he was a minor; both, like Edward, were Protestants. The religious reforms during this period were more sustained and more clearly Protestant than during Henry's reign. However, Edward VI, a sickly child, died of tuberculosis in 1553 and was succeeded by his older half sister, Mary. A devout Catholic, Mary sought to bring England back under papal authority. In some respects she proceeded cautiously—testament to how much public opinion had swung against papal rule over the previous twenty years—but her reign was also characterized by the persecutions that have led to her being dubbed Bloody Mary. During the last three years of her reign alone, about three hundred Protestants were burned at the stake. Mary died childless in 1558 and was succeeded by her Protestant half sister, Elizabeth, the daughter of Anne Boleyn. Queen Elizabeth I, who reigned for forty-four years, is one of the most important monarchs in English history. She inherited a religiously divided nation, and yet by her death in 1603, England was undeniably a Protestant country.

One of the most pressing objectives at the start of Elizabeth's reign was to establish a new religious settlement that would reverse Mary's Catholic alterations and yet be acceptable to as many of her subjects as possible. Elizabeth sought stability and consensus rather than a doctrinal purity that might prove divisive. The so-called Elizabethan settlement of 1559 rejected papal authority and confirmed Elizabeth as supreme governor of the English church. A revised prayer book, published in 1559, was broadly Protestant in outlook, and rigorous provisions were made for uniformity of church services. England's confession of faith, the Thirty-Nine Articles (1563) espoused a clear, if moderate, Protestant position. Salvation by faith alone (rather than by good works) was affirmed, transubstantiation (the doctrine that the body and blood of Christ are literally present in the Eucharistic bread and wine) was rejected, and the controversial doctrine of predestination (the belief that God elected some and reprobated others by a decree before the beginning of time) was cautiously affirmed.

Elizabeth's concern was to balance the competing demands of powerful Catholic families and zealous Puritans. Although she knew that she could never satisfy both, she hoped to minimize instability by, wherever possible, not alienating either. However, events sometimes intervened to make this compromise impossible. For instance, Elizabeth was excommunicated by the pope in 1570 after she had suppressed a Catholic rising in the north. This event placed English Catholics in a dilemma: they were forced to choose between loyalty to the papacy and to their queen. Insofar as Elizabeth ever persecuted Catholics, her actions were guided by an understanding of Catholicism as a political threat rather than as a heresy.

Elizabeth was equally determined in her treatment of Puritanism. While she supported some Puritan campaigns—the attempts to educate the clergy and to establish more ministries, for example—she was also very suspicious of where their loyalties lay. Her Puritan archbishop Edmund Grindal wrote to her shortly before his dismissal, "Although ye are a mighty prince, yet remember that he which dwelleth in heaven is mightier." He added, "I choose rather to offend your earthly majesty, than to offend the heavenly majesty of God." This attitude was typical of many Puritans during this period. Once again, Elizabeth was faced with powerful subjects who had divided loyalties.

Reverendissimus in Christo Pater D.D. EDMUNDUS GRINDALLUS Archiepiscopus Cantuariensis

Elizabeth faced many challenges during her long reign. Her survival in power for such a long time gave a degree of stability and moderation to English society that had previously been lacking. By 1603 England was a Protestant nation that had achieved relative security against foreign invasion. Elizabeth's successor was to inherit a healthier nation than she had in 1558.

▲ This eighteenth-century engraving depicts Edmund Grindal, the archbishop of Canterbury whose Puritan sympathies brought him into conflict with Elizabeth I.

Many Protestant ministers had fled England while Elizabeth's predecesssor, Queen Mary, was on the throne. They tended to locate themselves in hotbeds of Protestant activity, such as John Calvin's Geneva (in present-day Switzerland). They returned determined to reform the English church more thoroughly than Elizabeth and other moderates would countenance. Puritans were Calvinists who believed in predestination, godly living, and the suppression of "popish" ceremony and pagan village festivities (such as maypole dancing). Many also supported a Presbyterian system of church government that bypassed bishops and gave increased power to local congregations. Such campaigns ran counter to Elizabeth's desire for uniformity of religion and led to many legal conflicts. A great number of Puritan priests who refused to wear surplices were deprived of their living as a consequence.

▲ A 1557 portrait of Lady Ingram, a Puritan, and her two sons. In common with most Puritans, the Ingram family wore simple dark clothes and prided themselves on their zeal and piety.

James I

Elizabeth died on March 24, 1603. The accession of James VI of Scotland as James I of England, Ireland, and Scotland was greeted with a wave of optimism. For the first time since the reign of Henry VIII, England was to be ruled by an adult male who was an avowed Protestant. Moreover, James was a very experienced ruler—he had been crowned king of Scotland in 1567 at just thirteen months of age. Indeed, James sometimes referred to himself as "the cradle king." James's accession to the English throne also united the kingdoms of England, Ireland, and Scotland for the first time. Many therefore had high hopes of a successful reign.

While it may be possible to propose an approximate starting point of the Reformation (during the period when Henry broke with Rome), it is much more difficult to identify a clear end point. The identity of the English church remained hotly disputed throughout James's reign and beyond. With the benefit of hindsight, it is clear that England was less vulnerable to invasion by foreign Catholic powers in the seventeenth century than it was in the sixteenth, but this point of view was by no means prevalent at the time. If anything, there was more paranoia about "popish plots" during this period than during Elizabeth's reign.

Fears of Catholic plots were by no means groundless. In 1605 Guy Fawkes, a Catholic insurgent, attempted to blow up Parliament while it was in session. The Gunpowder Plot, as it has become known, was easily foiled, and Fawkes was executed, but this outcome did nothing to allay Protestant suspicions. Even James I was not immune from suspicion. In 1604, after James ended the war with Spain (which had become financially crippling), rumors circulated that he was considering converting to Catholicism. Why else, it was reasoned, would he refuse to fight for the Reformed cause?

Ridiculous though this charge was, James did not always help himself in such matters; he was not as careful of his friends as some would have wished. Particularly damaging was his relationship with George Villiers, the first duke of Buckingham. Buckingham became a tremendously influential and corrupt adviser to James. Some of his advice—for instance, that James's son Charles should marry a Spanish princess—

was taken as proof of his Catholicism. Buckingham was murdered by an embittered soldier, John Felton, in 1628. Felton was cheered through the streets en route to his execution.

James, despite his weaknesses—financial profligacy, laziness, and arrogance—was an intelligent man who ruled with moderation. In matters of religion and particularly foreign policy, however, many of his subjects were rather less sensible than he was. In 1618 the Thirty Years War broke out in Europe. The territorial feuds that had dogged Europe for centuries had now become a matter of religion, too. Unlike most of his subjects, James chose not to see the conflict as a battle between God and the devil. Indeed, James desired peace, and he sought to marry his son Charles to a Catholic princess in order to create a moderate alliance. James had long nurtured an ambition to end Europe's religious divide, but as he found over time, his parliaments wanted not to heal the wound but to win the war.

However, James's reign was by no means characterized by such conflict. To some extent, the disappointments of many Protestants were a result of high expectations borne of James's success as a monarch. His domestic religious policy, highly pro-Protestant, brought greater doctrinal consistency than Elizabeth's had done. James, not only a Protestant but a Calvinist, led an English church that espoused the central Reformed doctrines of predestination, salvation by faith alone, and a metaphorical interpretation of the Lord's Supper. James instinctively sought consensus and moderation, and like Elizabeth, he rejected the extremist demands of Puritans on the one hand and Catholics on the other. Though moderate, his church can be described as largely Calvinist in character.

James died in March 1625, having presided successfully over a period of religious peace in his three kingdoms of England, Scotland, and Ireland.

▼ This contemporary engraving by Johann Theodore de Bry shows the January 1606 execution of the Catholic dissenter Guy Fawkes and several other conspirators after their failed attempt in the preceding November to blow up the Houses of Parliament while the members were sitting and the king and his court were in attendance. Although easily foiled in the end, the Gunpowder Plot rekindled Protestant fears of a Catholic threat.

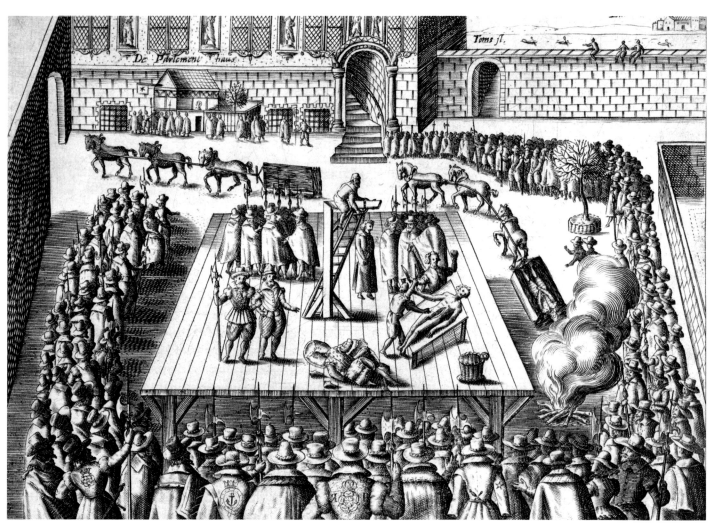

Controversy came to a head in 1637. Three Puritan pamphleteers, William Prynne, Henry Burton, and John Bastwick, who had criticized the Arminian and arbitrary nature of Charles's rule, were arrested and sentenced to have their ears cut off. Although the action was intended to make examples of them, they in fact became heroes to the Puritan cause. In the same year Laud insensitively attempted to introduce his reforms into Scotland, a more clearly Calvinist country, and was rebuffed. Riots resulted, and a Scottish army gathered at the English border in an attempt to stave off what was perceived to be an imposition directed from London. The problems that had largely simmered under the surface during Charles's rule without Parliament now reached a head, for he was forced to recall the House of Commons. Nine years later, following a protracted civil war, Charles was executed.

The Ministers and people solemnly take the Protestation in all Churches over the Kingdome,

Mr Burton, Dr Bastwick, & Mr Prinne, triumphantly from perpetuall captivity, those 3 famous witnesses of Truth, return home to London, attended with thousands of horse and foot,

▶ *Suspicions that William Laud's reforms were a smokescreen for "popery" were most famously voiced by William Prynne, Henry Burton, and John Bastwick in 1637. Brutally punished, the three men became heroes to their fellow Puritans and, as this piece of contemporary propaganda shows, were cheered through the streets of London upon their eventual release in November 1640.*

Legacy of the Reformation

While it would be foolish to suggest that the execution in 1649 of a monarch widely perceived to be a Catholic had any direct connection to Henry VIII's break from Rome over a century earlier, both these dramatic events can certainly be seen as important aspects of the prolonged English Reformation. Although Charles was a blinkered monarch—unlike his predecessors, he proved incapable of adapting to circumstances— the religious and political tensions that he so mishandled were the product of a century-long process. Indeed, so entrenched were these instabilities that it was not until the Glorious Revolution (the bloodless coup of 1688 in which King James II, a Catholic, was supplanted by the moderate Protestants William of Orange and Mary) and the 1689 Bill of Rights that the tensions were resolved. The final settlement ended the religious dispute by prohibiting a Catholic from sitting on the English throne and thereby irrevocably cementing Protestantism as the national religion. It also enshrined the right of Parliament to act as a fully legislative body and thus ended the political dispute in favor of parliamentary monarchy over absolutism.

FURTHER READING
Guy, John. *Tudor England.* Oxford, 1990.
Russell, Conrad. *The Crisis of Parliaments: English History 1509–1660.* Oxford, 1971.
Williams, Penry. *The Later Tudors.* Oxford, 1998.

Leif Dixon

SEE ALSO
• Architecture • Elizabeth I • Erasmus, Desiderius
• Henry VIII • Humanism and Learning
• Literature • Lutheranism • Marlowe, Christopher
• Reformation • Spenser, Edmund

English Civil Wars

THE ENGLISH CIVIL WARS WERE THE CONFLICTS BETWEEN KING CHARLES I AND PARLIAMENT THAT BEGAN IN 1642 AND ENDED IN 1649 WITH THE EXECUTION OF THE KING AND THE ESTABLISHMENT OF A REPUBLIC.

King Charles I clashed with Parliament from the very beginning of his reign in 1625. The House of Commons (the lower of the two houses of Parliament) had particularly strong grievances concerning the king's financial exactions, his favoring of the extremely unpopular duke of Buckingham, his conduct of the wars against Spain and France, and his religious policy, which many felt was turning the Church of England back toward Catholicism. Charles believed that, as king by divine right, he could conduct matters as he saw fit and perceived Parliament's expressions of grievance as an encroachment on his royal prerogative.

▼ In common with many other paintings of Charles I, this equestrian portrait, painted by the Flemish artist Anthony van Dyck in the 1630s, projects a powerful image of kingship.

Charles was frustrated and angered by the stubbornness of his parliaments' insistence on their right to counsel him and to have their concerns addressed before they granted him taxation. Unlike his father, James I, after arguments with Parliament, Charles was incapable of conciliation. In 1626, rather than make any concessions to Parliament, which was calling for the impeachment of Buckingham, Charles decided to dissolve Parliament. As a result, he had to forgo tax revenue. However, he needed to finance his wars, and so he imposed a forced loan on the nation without parliamentary consent. Fears grew that Charles was attempting to extend the royal prerogative and limit the role of Parliament in government. Despite the reasonable sum of money brought in by the loan, owing to Buckingham's disastrous military campaign in France, Parliament had to be called again in March 1628 to provide further taxes. This Parliament presented Charles with the Petition of Right, a statement of its grievances and an assertion of parliamentary privileges.

This Parliament was prorogued (suspended). However, one major grievance was removed on August 23, 1628, when Buckingham was assassinated. The ill-concealed pleasure of many of his subjects at this turn of events simply added to Charles's resentment. In 1629 matters came to a head. The recalled Parliament demonstrated its determination to assert its right, and the House of Commons forcefully passed a Protestation against changes in the religious settlement and against Charles's illegal collection of tonnage and poundage (customs dues that, contrary to precedent, Parliament had not granted to Charles for life). On March 10 a furious Charles once again dissolved Parliament.

The Personal Rule

The eleven-year period of Charles's reign when he governed England without any parliament is known as the Personal Rule. Superficially, the regime was effective. Charles made peace with France and Spain and thus needed less money. His financial measures were largely successful and produced little outright resistance. The most

According to early modern political thought, a king was the representative of God on earth and thus had a divine right to rule. This aspect of kingship was increasingly stressed in the seventeenth century, when theories of monarchical absolutism developed. However, it was also thought that monarchy was limited by institutions of state (such as parliaments), by the law, by good counsel, and by the reasonable behavior of the king himself. The divine right did not constitute freedom to rule arbitrarily, and alongside the veneration of kings ran a fear of tyranny. Charles I placed particular emphasis on his divine right and on his prerogative powers and justified many of his more provocative actions (especially during the Personal Rule) in these terms.

The image of the king that was promoted during Charles's reign also served to emphasize the sacred nature of kingship. Charles's court was organized to maintain distance between him and his subjects, and court ceremony heightened the reverence with which he was treated. While at the time there seemed many advantages in the promotion of such an elevated image of the king and the insistence on his prerogative power, Charles's rule was later interpreted as arbitrary or tyrannical. Charles's exercise of his divine right seemed arrogant to many and was often exceptionally maladroit.

The Arch-Prelate of St Andrewes in Scotland reading the new Service-booke in his pontificalibus assaulted by men & women, with Cricketts stooles Stickes and Stones.

The rising of Prentises and Sea-men on Southwark side to assault the Arch-bishops of Canterburys House at Lambeth.

▲ *This engraving depicts the riots in Edinburgh in 1637 over the revisions made to the prayer book (above) and protests directed at Archbishop Laud in 1640 outside his palace in Lambeth, London (below).*

notorious of these measures was the imposition from 1634 of "ship money." Originally, the Royal Navy had levied a contribution of ships from the coastal counties during times of war. During the Personal Rule the contribution was converted into a payment of money and extended to all counties at a time of peace.

At the same time, the reforms of William Laud, archbishop of Canterbury from 1633, took effect, and the Puritan element (the more radical Protestants) within the Church of England was suppressed. Laud placed great emphasis on ceremony; many people who had been brought up in a Reformed tradition believed that such an emphasis hinted at an imminent return to Catholicism. The high-profile presence of Catholics at court, Queen Henrietta Maria among them, did nothing to dispel fears that the king was surrounded by popery.

While the Personal Rule appeared harmonious, with little explicit opposition to its policies, tensions perhaps existed under the surface. When Parliament was finally recalled in 1640, there was an explosion of grievances about the measures imposed in its absence.

The British Context

Charles inherited three kingdoms from his father: England, Scotland, and Ireland. Events in his other kingdoms were to provide the catalyst for the conflict in England and to produce civil conflicts of their own on an equal scale. The English civil wars cannot be understood without examining the wider British context.

Like his father, Charles was interested in bringing the Calvinist Kirk of Scotland (Scotland's national church, established in 1560) more closely in line with its less reformed counterpart, the Church of England. Yet unlike James, Charles did not govern his northern kingdom competently and attacked the situation with an astonishing lack of tact. With the English archbishop Laud in charge of the policy, a new prayer book similar to the English one was imposed on the Kirk in 1637. A series of coordinated riots broke out in Edinburgh at its introduction on July 23, and resistance spread throughout Scotland. In February 1638 the so-called National Covenant was drawn up; it sought to defend the "true religion, liberties, and laws of the kingdom." The vast majority of Scottish ministers, nobles, and lairds (landowners), as well as ordinary men, subscribed. Although the Scots' intention was to air their grievance in a traditional Scottish form and to negotiate with Charles, the king perceived the covenant as a direct challenge and raised an army to force the obedience of the Scots. In the consequent Bishops' Wars, Charles entered into military conflict with his own subjects.

The first campaign against the Covenanters in June 1639 was an abject failure; the English army sued for peace before any engagement had taken place. In order to make effective war on the Scots, a parliament had to be called. The summoning of the English Parliament in April 1640 finally marked the end of the Personal Rule. However, an uncooperative Parliament insisted on the hearing of grievances before the supply of taxes would be considered. Unwilling to make concessions to either the English Parliament or to the Scottish Covenanters, Charles dissolved the so-called Short Parliament on May 5. The Scottish Covenanters now took the initiative; in the Second Bishops' War, they swept into England in August and occupied the northeast. The Scots, now able to impose terms on Charles, insisted on a settlement ratified by the English Parliament. In November 1640 Charles was thus forced to call what was to become known as the Long Parliament.

With a broad consensus of the English and Scottish political nations ranged against him,

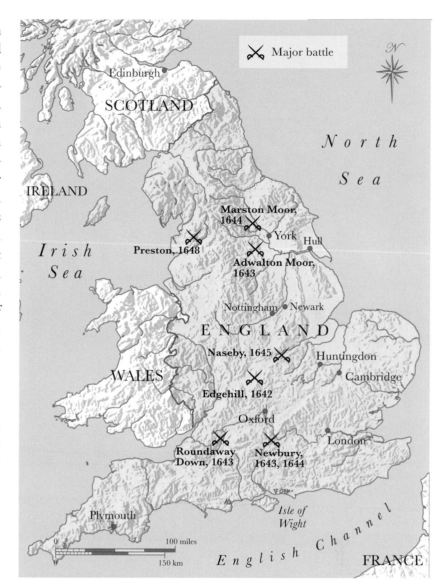

Charles had to make concessions. A settlement was reached with the Scots in summer 1641, by which time a number of substantial measures taken by the English Parliament included the Triennial Act—a guarantee of at least one parliament every three years. However, the question of church reform in England was much more problematic: divisions were already starkly apparent.

Some hoped to take the opportunity to push the church farther along the road of reform; others simply wanted a return to the moderate and inclusive settlement of the Elizabethan and Jacobean churches. As the debates on religion in the Long Parliament wore on in the autumn of 1641, Charles had reason to feel more optimistic: neither Parliament nor the Scots were the threat they had been, and he had won back the support of many of his subjects.

▲ *This map of England during the time of the English civil wars indicates the sites of the major battles.*

▲ News of conflict in Ireland was spread in England by printed reports and woodcut illustrations. This 1641 engraving portrays the killing of Irish Protestants by Catholics.

At the end of October, the situation changed radically. News arrived of a massive rebellion of Irish Catholics in Ulster and the massacre of thousands of Irish Protestants. All the old fears about a "popish plot" were resurrected, and the Irish rebels implicated Charles himself in their uprising. The events leading directly to the outbreak of war in England had begun.

Ireland had long presented a major problem of governance for the English crown. From 1632 Charles's rule in Ireland was conducted by Thomas Wentworth, later earl of Strafford, whose government was authoritarian and exacting. With his probing financial measures, disregard for property rights, and contempt for compromise, Wentworth managed to alienate all sections of Irish society. During the crisis of 1639, Charles recalled him to England, where he was regarded as an obdurate and innovating defender of royal power and tyranny. Parliament forced the execution of Wentworth on May 12, 1641.

The rebellion of the Irish Catholics, essentially defensive, was provoked by the anti-Catholic rhetoric emerging from the increasingly successful Scottish Covenanters and the English Parliament. Soon the resentments of the ill-treated Catholic population and the religious divisions in the country were stirred into a full-scale rebellion with its own momentum. Exaggerated reports of the atrocities committed against Protestants whipped up frantic anxiety in England, and Parliament turned immediately to raising an army. It was the question of who was to lead this army that resulted in war.

The Outbreak of War in England

Charles naturally claimed the right to raise and control the army of suppression. However, Parliament, perhaps mindful of the example of the Bishops' Wars, feared that the king was quite capable of turning military power against them. Parliament attempted to lay claim to the control of the army.

On November 8, 1641, John Pym, the leader of the parliamentary opposition to Charles, presented the House of Commons with an indictment of Charles's misgovernment that came to be known as the Grand Remonstrance. Opinion was fiercely divided over this indictment, and political divisions became sharper across the kingdom. Pym's blatant propagandism and his proposals for further religious reform helped to turn some people against Parliament. Charles, who believed that the solution lay in the elimination of the leaders of the opposition, tried to arrest Pym and four other members of the Commons on January 4, 1642. Charles's attempt to take members of the Commons by force was a great breach of parliamentary privilege. However, the so-called Five Members had already escaped. The incident further enhanced fears that Charles was prepared to use unconstitutional measures.

Hostility to Charles in London was now severe. When the king withdrew from the city on January 10, the center of government was left in the hands of Parliament. Over the subsequent months, both Parliament and the king attempted to lay claim to military authority. On March 5 Parliament passed the Militia Ordinance, which asserted the right to legislate without the assent of the king. In April, Charles attempted to gain control of the arsenal in Hull but was denied access to the town.

Oliver Cromwell   1599–1658

Oliver Cromwell was born in Huntingdon, Cambridgeshire, to a gentry family on April 25, 1599. After an unremarkable four decades, he became a member of Parliament for Cambridge in the Short and Long Parliaments of 1640. Although socially conservative, Cromwell had strong Puritan sensibilities and expressed himself forcefully in Parliament. He came to prominence as a parliamentary military leader in the First Civil War and was made General of the Horse in the newly formed New Model Army in 1645. His role at the Battle of Naseby was pivotal.

By this time Cromwell was a committed Independent (the Independents wanted to separate from the Church of England and form local churches). Although he seems to have been reluctant to engage in regicide (the killing of a monarch), during the trial of the king that followed the Second Civil War, Cromwell saw the necessity of that course. He was one of the fifty-nine men, the regicides, who signed the king's death warrant.

Cromwell took a leading role in the Commonwealth government established after the king's death. The failure of the Rump Parliament to agree on electoral reform and dissolve itself led Cromwell to expel this Parliament in April 1653. A new constitutional experiment followed in the form of a Nominated Assembly (known as Barebone's Parliament), which consisted of "godly" men selected by Cromwell. It, too, collapsed, and in December 1653, Cromwell was made head of state as Lord Protector of England, Scotland, and Ireland. He repeatedly tried and failed to cooperate with Parliament and resorted to increasingly extreme measures to govern. Although he accepted greater powers in 1657, he refused to accept the crown despite calls for him to become king.

Cromwell died on September 3, 1658. He was succeeded as protector by his son, Richard. Richard did not have his father's political capability, and his government collapsed. In May 1660 Charles II was made king, and both the Stuart line and the institution of monarchy were restored.

▲ This unfinished miniature of Oliver Cromwell was painted by Samuel Cooper (1609–1672).

On June 2 Parliament presented Charles with its demands in a document called the Nineteen Propositions. The king rejected the propositions as a "total subversion" of the laws and constitution of the kingdom. Both sides were now convinced that the other could not be trusted and that raising forces was necessary. On August 18 Parliament declared all those who supported the king traitors. On August 22, 1642, the king raised his standard at Nottingham and formally opened the hostilities against Parliament.

The First Civil War

The armies of Charles met those of the earl of Essex, Parliament's military leader, at Edgehill, in Warwickshire, in the first major engagement of the war. Neither side won a decisive victory. Over the following months, the military advantage lay with the Royalists. Parliament turned to the Scots for help, and on September 25, 1643, the Solemn League and Covenant was concluded.

However, this document alienated many Scots nobles, and the royalist cause in Scotland now became viable. The earl of Montrose, Charles's leader in the northern kingdom, rallied support against the Covenanters, and full-scale civil war began in Scotland in 1644. Meanwhile in England, Parliament had suffered a blow with the death of Pym in December 1643. The leadership of the Commons passed to more aggressive men—among them Oliver Cromwell. In March 1644 Laud, who had been in the Tower of London for three years, was impeached (charged with misconduct in office). He was executed the following January after a show trial.

During 1644 the war in England began to turn against the king. Cromwell's military brilliance was proved on July 2 at the Battle of Marston Moor in Yorkshire, where a parliamentary victory decided control of the north. In early 1645 the military resources of Parliament were greatly improved by the founding of the New

On June 14, 1645, the royalist commanders princes Rupert and Maurice met the parliamentarian forces led by Oliver Cromwell, Thomas Fairfax, and Henry Ireton. Although the parliamentarian forces significantly outnumbered those of the king, the battle was very close. Cromwell led the last parliamentary charge, and his success was the decisive factor; Cromwell's cavalry managed to break the royalist infantry. The enormous losses suffered by King Charles made a parliamentarian victory in the First Civil War almost inevitable. His private correspondence was captured; it revealed his plans to use Irish troops in England and indicated that he was considering extending toleration to Catholics and allying with foreign princes. These letters, published as *The King's Cabinet Opened*, did lasting damage to Charles's reputation.

▲ *The prominent role played by cavalry on the battlefield during the English civil wars is indicated in this print depicting the Battle of Naseby.*

cessions to the Irish Catholics in return for military aid. (Charles's private correspondence, captured at Naseby, had revealed the plan to use Irish troops in England; his enemy's worst fears were thus confirmed.) On May 5, 1646, Charles gave himself up to the Scots at Newark in the hope that he would gain better terms from them than from the English Parliament. On June 24 the remaining Royalists in Oxford surrendered. The First Civil War was over.

War in England

The conflict took place across the kingdom and involved all levels of society. Large numbers of people, able to base clear political judgments on the vast quantity of news and propaganda that was distributed throughout the country from 1641, became strongly committed to one side or the other. Nevertheless, the priorities of many lay with their family, their home, and their local community, not with national politics. Toward the end of the war, defensive organizations, known as Clubmen, were formed in some counties to protect local communities against the intrusion and devastation of war.

The war cost a great deal of money, and both sides resorted to extreme measures to fund their military effort. Over the course of the war, Parliament was better able than the king to impose taxes and exactions on the population, and so the New Model Army was much better paid than its royal counterpart by 1645. The fiscal burden was not the only consequence of the war. Up to one-quarter of the adult male population bore arms at some point during the civil wars; of the entire population about one person in thirty died in combat or from disease.

The Second Civil War

By 1646 Parliament had achieved many of the reforms that it had aimed for. The episcopacy (the hierarchical church government) had been abolished, and the Church of England extensively reformed. Parliament was now in a position to force the king to accept the constitutional measures its members thought necessary to curtail his tyranny and ensure Parliament's role in the government. At this stage nobody seriously envisaged a settlement without the king: republicanism was

Model Army. Unlike its predecessors, the New Model Army was a centralized national force. It was put to the test at the Battle of Naseby (June 14, 1645), where the brilliance of Cromwell and his cavalry was again demonstrated

More parliamentary victories followed Naseby. Charles's position was further damaged by the news in late 1645 that his envoy in Ireland, the earl of Glamorgan, had offered con-

far from the mainstream of political thought. Despite the apparent strengths of the king's opponents, however, they faced substantial difficulties in the search for a settlement.

There was extensive disagreement both within Parliament and between Parliament and its Scots allies. Furthermore, many of those who had supported the parliamentary cause had done so because they thought Charles had threatened the existing settlement; they simply wanted a return to the previous situation. Now Parliament looked like the dangerous innovator.

The principal line of division within Parliament was between the Presbyterians, who argued for a national church structure like that in Scotland, and the Independents, who opposed any form of national church. The Presbyterians dominated the houses of Parliament, while the Independents had allies in the army, where religious fervor, often radical, was a powerful force. In February 1647 the Scots delivered the king to Parliament and returned home. Parliament

attempted to disband the army, which responded on June 4 by seizing the king. The army was now a serious political entity. Charles took advantage of these divisions. He continually stalled during peace talks and tried to play the different elements within Parliament off against each other. He also pursued negotiations with the Scots.

Charles was alarmed by the emergence of radical sentiment in the army, and in November 1647 he fled to the Isle of Wight. In December his negotiations with the Scots bore fruit in an engagement that pledged Scottish support for Charles's conditional return to authority in England in return for his establishment of a Presbyterian church in Scotland. Charles also received assurance of aid from his Irish deputy James Butler, earl of Ormond. The king now felt able to reject Parliament's terms. The scene was set for a renewal of hostilities.

The provincial uprisings against Parliament that broke out in the spring and summer of 1648 were claimed by the Royalists for their side in the

Second Civil War. However, this military campaign was by no means coordinated, and the New Model Army suppressed the risings. The projected Irish assistance did not materialize, and

THE
Declaration and Standard

Of the *Levellers* of England ;

Delivered in a Speech to his Excellency the Lord Gen.*Fairfax*, on *Friday* laft at White-Hall, by Mr.*Everard*, a late Member of the Army, and his Prophefie in reference thereunto ; fhewing what will befall the Nobility and Gentry of this Nation, by their fubmitting to community ; With their invitation and promife unto the people, and their proceedings in *Windfor* Park, *Oatlands* Park, and feverall other places ; alfo, the Examination and confeffion of the faid Mr.*Everard* before his Excellency, the manner of his deportment with his Hat on, and his feverall fpeeches and expreffions, when he was commanded to put it off. Togsther with a Lift of the feverall Regiments of Horfe and Foot that have caft Lots to go for *Ireland*.

Imprinted at *London*, for G.*Laurenfon*, *Aprill* 23. 1649.

▲ *Radical literature, such as this document produced by the Levellers, flooded the presses during the civil wars and the Interregnum (the period when England was ruled without a monarch).*

the Scots Engagers (as they were called) were too few and too late. Charles was defeated once again. His decision to renew hostilities caused a fundamental shift in the army's position. Parliament's victory in the First Civil War was seen as a clear indication from God that right was on its side. Charles, in waging further war against Parliament, was seen as rejecting God's verdict. At a prayer meeting in April 1648, the officers of the army called Charles a "man of blood" who could be brought to account for making war on his people. Victory in the Second Civil War confirmed God's judgment. The army now wanted Charles brought to justice.

Parliament, however, reopened negotiations with the king in September 1648. The army presented a remonstrance to Parliament, and when this call was ignored, the army entered London. On December 6, Colonel Thomas Pride led troops to the entrance of the Commons. They arrested or secluded 231 members, and others withdrew. This incident, known as Pride's Purge, reduced the House of Commons to a rump that was willing to try the king.

The Execution of Charles I

On January 4, 1649, the House of Commons asserted its right to govern unilaterally, without the king or the House of Lords. A high court of justice was established, and on January 20 Charles's trial began. Accused of making war against his people, as represented by Parliament, Charles was impeached as a "tyrant, traitor, and murderer, and a public and implacable enemy to the Commonwealth of England." Charles refused to acknowledge the legitimacy of the court and was not prepared to plead guilty or otherwise. He denounced the procedure as arbitrary and claimed that the court itself threatened the liberty

THE LEVELLERS

Notable among the radical ideas developed in the army were those of the Levellers, who advocated religious toleration, universal male suffrage, drastic reforms to the legal and taxation systems, and the abolition of the monarchy and the House of Lords. The Levellers conducted sophisticated campaigns of petitioning and printing in order to influence public opinion. Many army generals, including Cromwell, considered these influences dangerous. On October 28, 1647, the Putney Debates opened between Leveller agitators and the army's general council. Though inconclusive, the debates exposed many of the tensions within the army and within Cromwell's own thinking. By early 1648, Leveller influence was reduced, and army unrest receded.

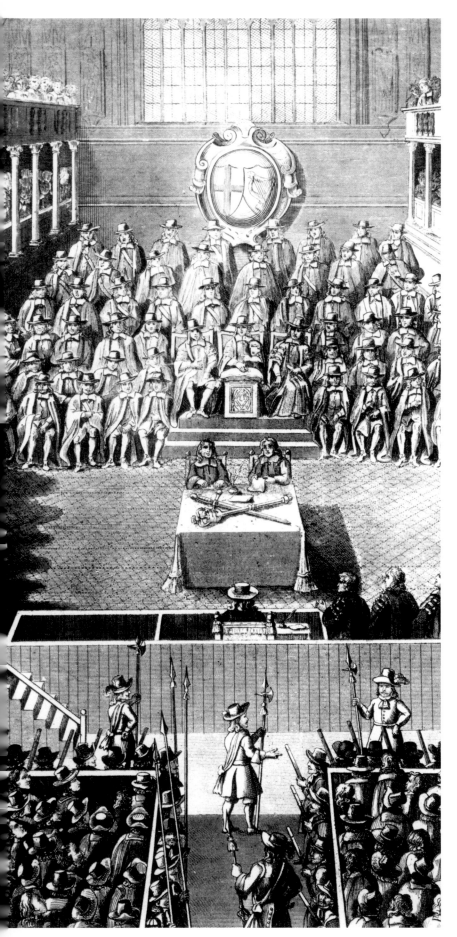

◄ *The conclusion of the trial of Charles I was probably foregone, but the propaganda victory went to the Royalists. This engraving depicts Charles I awaiting his sentence before the high court of justice at Whitehall, London, on January 27, 1649.*

of his subjects. The court, deprived of the opportunity to conduct a public exposure of Charles's crimes by the king's refusal to take part in the trial, sentenced him to death on January 27.

On January 30, 1649, Charles was beheaded on a scaffold erected outside the Banqueting House in Whitehall in front of a shocked crowd. Soon after, on March 17 and 19, the Rump Parliament passed acts that abolished the House of Lords and the monarchy. In their place the republican Commonwealth government was established.

In his death Charles achieved an enormous propaganda victory. Few if any outside the political elite of the army and Rump had considered republican government a possibility, and regicide was a step that horrified the vast majority of the population, who had always accepted monarchy as the natural state of the polity. Charles's criticisms of the court that had been set up to try him resonated with wider fears that the measures taken by Parliament and the army during the civil wars were unprecedented and arbitrary. The dignity of Charles at his execution also helped to strengthen the royalist cause in the long term; he became a martyr associated with the defense of liberty and freedom. The bitter religious and political conflicts that had raged between and within the forces that contested the civil wars were far from over.

FURTHER READING

Cust, Richard, and Anne Hughes, eds. *The English Civil War.* New York, 1997.

Scott, Jonathan. *England's Troubles.* Cambridge, 2000.

Smith, David L. *A History of the Modern British Isles, 1603–1707: The Double Crown.* Oxford, 1998.

Woolrych, A. *Britain in Revolution.* Oxford, 2002.

Anna Bayman

SEE ALSO

• Calvinism • Church of England • England
• Scotland • Stuarts, The • Thirty Years War

Erasmus, Desiderius

ONE OF THE FOREMOST SCHOLARS OF THE RENAISSANCE, DESIDERIUS ERASMUS (C. 1466–1536) WAS A CHRISTIAN HUMANIST FAMOUS FOR HIS DISPUTES WITH MARTIN LUTHER AND FOR THE SKILLFUL USE OF SATIRE IN HIS WRITINGS.

Desiderius Erasmus was born in the Netherlands around 1466, probably in the city of Rotterdam. The illegitimate son of a Catholic priest, Erasmus spent his early years in Gouda. In 1475 he took up studies with the devout and scholarly Brethren of the Common Life in Deventer, where he remained until 1483. After further studies at Hertogenbosch, Erasmus entered the monastery at Saint Gregory's, near Gouda, around 1486. He was ordained a priest in 1492 and—although he would soon leave Saint Gregory's—he remained faithful to his Roman Catholic roots. In later years he engaged the Protestant Reformer Martin Luther in vigorous theological debate.

Early Life

In 1494 Erasmus quit the monastic life in favor of a position as private secretary to a prominent cleric, the bishop of Cambrai. He did not,

► A contemporary Flemish portrait of Desiderius Erasmus at his desk. Best known for his humorous work The Praise of Folly, Erasmus was among the most widely read and influential scholars of his day. He expended a great deal of intellectual effort attempting to mend the growing schism between the Roman Catholic Church and the Reformed Protestant churches. Although his efforts ended in failure, Erasmus is remembered respectfully by many Protestants and Catholics alike for his desire to preserve the unity of Christendom.

however, leave the church or repudiate his calling as a priest. During this time he wrote his first work, *Adagia,* which was published several years later, in 1500. In keeping with Erasmus's overall focus on the ancient world, reintroduced to Europe through the rediscovery of classical texts during the Renaissance, the *Adagia* consisted of Erasmus's annotations on many Latin adages (proverbs). Erasmus also served as an adviser to the Holy Roman emperor Charles V. He would later dedicate his *Institutio principii Christiani,* published in 1516, to Charles.

Erasmus's pursuit of theological studies at the University of Paris from 1495 represented an attempt to find a place for himself within the church that would fit with his rather particular intellectual and personal tastes. Unfortunately he found little of value in the Scholastic philosophy that dominated his studies at Paris and disliked the life he was forced to lead as a student there. Soon after, he was introduced to Thomas More, with whom he was to strike up a long-lasting and productive friendship.

Torn between Two Worlds

Erasmus was an archetypal Renaissance humanist: he was committed to the ideals of *bonae literae,* the study of classical Greek and Latin texts with an eye to applying the insights and virtues of

▲ A fifteenth-century manuscript illumination of lectures given at the University of Paris. Erasmus himself gave lectures at the university—an institution that later condemned his views.

the ancient world to his own. In this respect Erasmus followed in the footsteps of such earlier humanists as the Italians Petrarch (1304–1374) and Leonardo Bruni (c. 1370–1444). On the other hand, Erasmus's dedication to the Roman Catholic Church was clear, unequivocal, and sincere. Unlike certain other Renaissance humanists, Erasmus was not a secular thinker forced to clothe his views in religious language in order to please those in ecclesiastical authority. Indeed, Erasmus's evident sympathy with the complaints of Protestant Reformers against the perceived opulence and decadence of the Catholic Church earned him as much enmity from his fellow Catholics as his refusal to side with the Reformers against the church did from Martin Luther and his supporters.

Erasmus had been profoundly influenced by the *Annotationes,* a commentary on the New Testament written by the Italian humanist Lorenzo Valla (1407–1457). In fact, Erasmus was so inspired by Valla's work that he went on to complete a new Latin translation of the New Testament as well as a commentary on Valla's work. He also wrote a number of commentaries and edited early works of theology by the church fathers. His motivation for this work, in addition to simple piety, was his desire to reawaken interest in the spiritual life of the early Christian church, whose ideals he believed had become somewhat fossilized in the church of his day. Erasmus also hoped to heal the growing rupture between church leaders and increasingly aggressive Reformers, most notably Martin Luther.

In his life and works Erasmus consistently tried to create and also to embody a central position between the most extreme Reformers (Luther, for example) and what many saw as the most reprehensible elements of the Catholic Church. However, Reformers subjected him to scathing attacks.

Erasmus's work was also condemned by the University of Paris, and many leading church figures regarded him as a heretic. Indeed, Erasmus so alienated some of his fellow Catholics that he was buried without having received the sacraments. Facing rebuke on every side, Erasmus, who had a sensitive temperament and was deeply affected by criticism, nevertheless continued to insist on what he called the "philosophy of Christ." His was a straightforward faith, embedded in practice rather than theory. He had little patience for the sorts of categorizing and pigeonholing typical of the theological disputes at the University of Paris and other leading schools.

Erasmus's philosophy of Christ stood in stark contrast with the theology of Thomas Aquinas (1225–1274) and other earlier religious thinkers, whose abstract theological musings had left such a profound mark on church teaching. Erasmus regarded such musings as symbolic of how rigid the church had become. In Erasmus's view, the church, like the synagogues before it, had fallen prey to the worship of its own rules and history rather than the adoration of the Bible, the only source of the true word of God. Pious, reflective

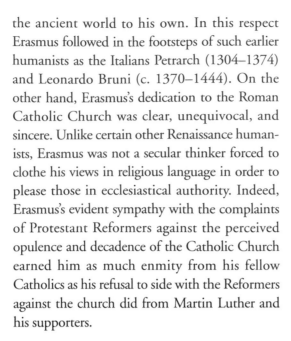

▼ *In this sixteenth-century illustration, the doctors of the University of Paris—whose Scholastic philosophy Erasmus repudiated—are pictured at an official meeting.*

Lorenzo Valla ▌ 1405–1457

Lorenzo Valla was born in Rome in 1405. Erasmus, deeply impressed with Valla's *Annotationes*, published a commentary on that work in 1505. A renowned humanist in his day, Valla held a chair in eloquence at the University of Pavia. In his writing Valla was intensely critical of Scholasticism and of the Aristotelian philosophy that lay at its base.

Valla, an innovator in the updating of medieval Latin for the Renaissance age, was himself the subject of powerful invective directed against him by Poggio Bracciolini (1380–1459) and other prominent Renaissance thinkers. Erasmus's writing style and playful, witty use of Latin may have been influenced by Valla, who had previously expanded the rather narrow boundaries of the stripped-down, dialectical (logically formulated) Latin of the Scholastics.

Defuncto Valla Musis plorantibus inquit Phoebus, hic antistes nostri Hiliconis erit

▲ *Erasmus owes much of his stylistic excellence and skillful Latin wordplay to Lorenzo Valla, the subject of this engraving. Valla, a Renaissance humanist, is remembered for his restoration of classical eloquence to the Latin language, which had been largely denuded of its sweeping rhetorical power by the Scholastics during the Middle Ages.*

study of God's word was the core of a philosophy centered on Christ. This emphasis on personal study, independent of church teaching, put him at odds with church authorities. Erasmus is reported to have said to Luther, "I will put up with this church until I find a better," a statement that, in the eyes of the Reformers, marked him out as lacking the resolve necessary to effect much-needed church reform. Erasmus's commitment to finding a middle ground left him very much isolated in a theologically polarized world.

Dispute with Luther

Erasmus was convinced of the weakness of the human will and the inability of people to face the temptations of the world and their own nature without the sort of pious reflection he advocated in his philosophy of Christ. This skeptical and even pessimistic view of human nature lay at the core of his refusal to enter into theological debates, his opinion being that such disputation was a waste of talent, time, and effort.

Erasmus's lack of confidence in the ability of people to govern their own affairs by means of unaided reason was also behind his reluctance to break with the Catholic Church, even though he acknowledged the central objections lodged against the church by the Reformers. Better, he reasoned, to work to correct the church's errors from the inside than to destroy an important though admittedly flawed institution. The Reformers were, in Erasmus's view, threatening the foundation of human society with their attacks on the church.

Even so, as the church on one side and the Reformers on the other each became more rigid in their insistence on their own position, Erasmus attempted to remain above the fray; he either refrained from contributing to the ongoing debate or sought to reconcile the opposing parties by encouraging each to see the merits of the other's position and the defects in its own. This approach earned Erasmus few friends on either side, as he resisted increasingly aggressive demands from both sides that he declare his allegiance. Finally, in 1524, Erasmus took a stand against the views of Martin Luther in *De libero arbitrio (On Free Will)*.

THEODICY

Central to the dispute between Luther and Erasmus was the issue of God's sovereignty, debated in the context of theodicy. A theodicy is any theological or philosophical system that attempts to provide support for God's goodness in light of the self-evident existence of evil. In other words, the fact that everyone sees evil in the world on a daily basis raises the obvious question, "What is the source of evil?"

To answer that God is the author, or source, of evil is entirely unacceptable from any Christian perspective (including both the Protestant and Roman Catholic standpoints), since this view denies God's omnibenevolence, the idea that God's character is entirely good and contains no evil whatsoever. Omnibenevolence is one of the three characteristics of God on which nearly all Roman Catholics and Reformers agreed; the other two are omniscience (the quality of being all-knowing) and omnipotence (the quality of being all-powerful). While other attributes of God—for instance, his omnipresence—are generally acknowledged by Christians, these three form a kind of core, since they are interdependent; the denial of one leads to a complete alteration in the meaning of the others.

If, for example, it is claimed that God is not omnibenevolent, his omniscience and omnipotence become sinister rather than benign qualities. Similarly, an omnibenevolent and omnipotent God who was not all-knowing would be something of a divine and well-intentioned bumbler, likely to do unwitting harm where he meant to do good. Finally, to deny God's omnipotence while granting him omniscience and omnipotence would make God a wise, well-meaning, but ineffectual deity who could see the good and wish to do it but who would lack the power to carry out his will.

Therefore, the insistence on all three of these attributes was central to the Reformers' efforts to create an acceptable theology that would justify their decision to break with the church of Rome. Although the church's position on this particular matter was in most ways markedly similar to that of the Reformers, a difference arose between the church and some of the Reformers regarding the role of free will.

▶ *Martin Luther, depicted preaching from a pulpit in this sixteenth-century Danish altarpiece, was both a leading Reformer and a passionate opponent of Erasmus. Luther sought certainty and precision in religion, while Erasmus more modestly held that man should humble himself before God and acknowledge that some questions—such as the precise nature of free will—were beyond the scope of mere human reason. Erasmus criticized Luther for what he saw as Luther's unjustified confidence in the ability of human reason, unaided by divine insight, to solve thorny theological problems.*

Further Disputes with Luther

On the one hand, it seemed necessary to affirm the existence of free will in order to be able to place the blame for sin squarely on human shoulders. If God withheld from people the ability to choose between good and evil, then sin could be blamed on God; yet to do so would be to deny God's omnibenevolence.

Conversely, in the view of Luther and others, to allow people free will was to deny God's omnipotence and hence his sovereignty. After all, they reasoned, to claim that human will is truly free is to claim that people are capable of doing what God wishes to prevent them from doing or of refusing to do what God wills them to do. A God whose will can be disobeyed by people is no sovereign God at all—hence Luther's insistence that only God's will is free and that people have no free will.

In *De libero arbitrio* (1524) Erasmus argued that Luther's denial of free will was dogmatic and unjustified. Erasmus pointed out that the Bible was far from clear on this matter and that consequently the matter should either be left to church authorities or, alternatively, not addressed at all. Erasmus also objected to Luther's excessive reliance on unaided reason in coming to his conclusions. Given Erasmus's longstanding suspicion of theology in general, this objection is far from surprising. In short, Erasmus accused Luther, however indirectly, of relying too much on his own questionable train of reasoning; Erasmus rather humbly confessed that the matter was beyond the reach of his or any other intellect.

Luther's reply, *De servo arbitrio* (1525), was vehement in its denunciation of Erasmus and his position. Against Erasmus's modest proposal that a Christian not attempt to navigate religious mazes without the benefit of clear biblical or ecclesiastical guidance, Luther's angry, almost wrathful reply insisted on the need for absolute precision and certainty in theological matters. To rest one's salvation on a belief system based on skeptical doubt was to Luther absurd, even indecent. In Luther's words, *"Spiritus sanctus non est scepticus"* (the Holy Spirit is not a skeptic). To settle for less than certainty was not merely improper in Luther's eyes but impious as well. A Christian who trusted in uncertainties was likely to find himself grossly disappointed on Judgment Day, when God came to gather his people.

Erasmus replied to *De servo arbitrio* with *Hyperaspistes* (1526), the broader dissemination of which led to his final alienation from most of the Reformers with whom he had stayed in contact until then. When Reformers gained effective control of the university at Basel where Erasmus was teaching, Erasmus moved on to Freiburg, in southern Germany. In spite of many disappointments (most notably his diminishing influence among Reformers and many church leaders), Erasmus continued to campaign for reconciliation and unity within Christendom (the community of all Christians). Although he earned the respect of some moderate members of both factions and was even considered as a candidate for cardinal by Pope Paul III, his noble efforts were largely wasted on increasingly strident Catholic and Protestant leaders.

BASILEA — Basell

M. D. I.

▲ Erasmus taught in Basel, Switzerland, pictured here in a contemporary German manuscript. Erasmus left Basel for Freiburg when Protestant Reformers gained control of the city's university and effectively denied the Catholic Erasmus any meaningful say in academic governance.

Erasmus was no more popular among his fellow Catholics than among the many Reformers who felt betrayed by what they saw as his lukewarm support for true church reform. Erasmus found himself denounced by some Catholics as a political operator who set both sides against each other for his own benefit in order to garner support for his own heretical, anti-Catholic religious beliefs. In the Iberian Peninsula, church authorities used the Spanish Inquisition quite effectively to suppress the activities of reform-minded Catholics and others who had been influenced by Erasmus's thought.

The Praise of Folly

As deeply as Erasmus was affected by the opposition to his religious views on two fronts, he continued to satirize what he saw as absurd elements in religious thought and practice. The best known of these efforts was his *Encomium moriae, id est Laus stultitiae (The Praise of Folly)*, published in 1511—more than a decade prior to his dispute with Luther. The inspiration for *The Praise of Folly* came to Erasmus during the summer of 1509, when he was traveling back from Italy to England. During his stay Erasmus had been greatly distressed at the lack of propriety in both the secular and ecclesiastical realms and had been simultaneously very much taken by his contact with Italian humanism. While traveling back to England, where he planned to stay with his good friend Thomas More, the English humanist, Erasmus was struck with the idea of writing a mock, or ironic, encomium (work of praise) to Folly, ostensibly written by Folly herself.

▲ This wood engraving from The Praise of Folly is intended in part to show the madness that can overcome the solitary scholar. Erasmus saw God as the ultimate source of wisdom. As a Christian humanist he took issue with those who denigrated reason as well as with those who deified it. Erasmus believed that reason was among God's greatest gifts to man but that it should be tempered by humility and reverence.

BONAE LITERAE, RES, AND VERBUM

Erasmus was committed to the notion of *bonae literae*. The precise meaning of this term is difficult to specify, but at its center is the idea that presentation (or what is often called "style") is a significant element of persuasive writing and argument. *Bonae literae* thus stands in sharp contrast to the Scholasticism that Erasmus found so distasteful as both a priest and student of theology.

Connected to *bonae literae* are the further elements of *res* and *verbum*. *Res*, Latin for "thing," has the additional meaning of "subject matter." The dialectical Scholasticism of the church of Erasmus's time focused on the bare subject matter, very often to the exclusion of *verbum*—the well-placed word or clever turn of phrase. Rather than approach the truth in a strictly logical or dialectical way, the practitioner of *bonae literae* makes use of the full range of linguistic expression in order to illuminate and illustrate the key points of an argument. The clearest example of this approach in Erasmus's work is to be found in his *Praise of Folly*, in which ridicule and satire are used to great effect in the criticism of abusive church practices and degraded public mores.

It is worth noting that the very beginning of the work's title, *Encomium moriae,* is itself a kind of joke, being a learned play on the similarity between the Latin word for "folly" and the name of Erasmus's friend More. The fact that Erasmus also dedicated the work to Thomas More gave a new, ironic meaning to the title of the book—which could in fact be rendered as "In Praise of More." Although *The Praise of Folly* can be read simply as learned entertainment, in it Erasmus also expounds on education, religion, and numerous other subjects. As such, *The Praise of Folly* is itself an example of the *bonae literae* for which Erasmus was such an outspoken advocate. In common with the ancient poetic texts that served as Erasmus's models, *The Praise of Folly* was designed to do more than simply amuse; it aimed also to present, in an agreeable form, substantive commentary and social criticism.

The Praise of Folly also gave practical voice to Erasmus's view, shared by More, that it was not enough simply to state the truth in straightforward terms. Simply to expound accurately on the bare subject matter, or what ancient rhetoricians called the *res nudas,* was to fall short; in addition to being true, a narrative should also be persuasive. Thus, the writer necessarily had to draw on the kind of rhetorical techniques that had been largely purged from medieval universities, along with the study of grammar, in favor of logic. While by no means hostile to logic, Erasmus was critical of the neglect of the actual means of communicating a philosophical message. He laid the blame for this unfortunate state of affairs at the feet of the churchmen who remained in charge of many of Europe's most influential and prestigious universities. Doing so earned him further enmity from many within the Roman Catholic Church.

Erasmus remained an active and productive scholar until his death in Basel on July 12, 1536.

FURTHER READING

Erasmus, Desiderius. *The Praise of Folly.* Translated by C. Miller. New Haven, CT, 1979.

Erasmus, Desiderius, and Martin Luther. *Discourse on Free Will.* Translated by Ernst F. Winter. New York, 1997.

Rummel, Erika, ed. *Erasmus on Women.* Toronto, 1996.

Daniel Horace Fernald

SEE ALSO

• Aristotle • Charles V • More, Thomas • Papacy • Philosophy • Platonism • Reformation • Renaissance • Rome • Venice

Established Churches

IN THE REFORMATION'S WAKE RULERS IN NORTHERN EUROPE ESTABLISHED NATIONAL CHURCHES TO PROVIDE THE RELIGIOUS UNITY ONCE SUPPLIED BY CATHOLICISM.

Before the Reformation in the 1520s, western Europe shared a single religion and a single political ideal. The religion was Catholicism, headed by the pope in Rome. The political ideal was Christian Europe. At the political heart of Europe was the Holy Roman Empire, ruled from 1519 by an emperor, Charles V (1500–1558), who was more effective than many of his predecessors had been. Other kingdoms surrounded the empire—England, France, and the Scandinavian countries, for instance. Historically all had shared the Latin language, which was still the language of scholarship, church liturgy, and government. Kingdoms were not compact national states but sovereignties; kings often ruled widely separated territories whose inhabitants by 1500 spoke different languages. There was no place in pre-Reformation Europe for the idea that a kingdom or empire could have more than one religion or that the choice of religion was a personal matter that had nothing to do with the state.

Reformation and National States

The political unity of the Holy Roman Empire would be dissolved by nationalism, the notion that Europe consisted not of a single civilization with one language but of many small kingdoms, each with its own language: Spanish, French, English, German, or any one of the dozen other vernacular languages that occupied the field as Latin broke down. Nationalism and the Reformation reinforced one another. The major reform movement led by the German Martin Luther from around 1520 benefited from the idea that Germans ought not to be subservient to distant Roman Catholic authorities, and Henry VIII likewise urged Englishmen not to give their loyalty to a foreign power. Between 1517 and 1545, Martin Luther and John Calvin (for religious reasons) and then Henry VIII (for political and personal reasons) denied that Rome was the necessary standard of faith and center of unity. Their reasons varied, but charges of theological error and corruption were always leveled against the Catholic Church by the Reformers. Nationalism thus had a religious face, and

◄ *A portrait of the Holy Roman emperor Charles V painted by Titian (c. 1490–1576). Though a loyal Catholic, Charles was unable to prevent the establishment of national churches in his German territories.*

Control of appointments to offices in the newly established churches was always the first concern of Renaissance monarchs, but this control was imperfect unless the monarch also controlled the wealth of the church. Around 1530 the monasteries, convents, cathedrals, and parishes of England owned about one-fourth of the best land in England. Between 1536 and 1540 Henry VIII closed the monasteries and confiscated their wealth, which he used partly to found new dioceses and partly for education but mostly to enrich the Tudor nobility. The patrons of parish churches had the right to appoint the priest subject to the approval of the bishop. During the reign of Elizabeth I, many parishes were given to lay persons. In 1605 the English bishops estimated that five-sixths of the parishes were controlled by laymen. Often these lay patrons were interested in gaining the highest possible income—an end they achieved by paying the minister who lived in the parish as little as possible. Some wealthy dioceses and local churches were presided over by bishops. After 1559 Queen Elizabeth seized the bishops' assets and gave them pensions in return.

conversely, religious reform, because it involved a separation of national churches from Rome, always encouraged nationalism. One idea that survived the breakup of medieval Catholicism was the idea that religion was a political matter—that every state, even the new national states, should have one religion.

The Peace of Augsburg

The decision that every kingdom should have its own religion was a provision of the 1555 Peace of Augsburg, which was promulgated by the Diet of the Holy Roman Empire. By then England and parts of present-day Germany and Switzerland no longer shared one common faith. Since political loyalty without a common religion was unimaginable in this era, kingdoms with more than one religion were thought to be unnatural and ungovernable. Those present at Augsburg decided to consider the official religion of every kingdom or principality either Lutheranism or Catholicism, depending upon the religion of its ruler. The principle was summed up in four Latin words: *cuius regio, eius religio* ("whose is the territory, his is the religion"). If the prince was Lutheran, his subjects were expected to be Lutherans. If the ruler was Catholic, his subjects were expected to practice Catholicism. Those who found this principle unacceptable were expected to leave their country. National churches would then be "established churches"— churches established by the king's law.

In the background of the movement to make churches answerable to the king rather than to the pope was the ancient European quarrel called the investiture controversy. Broadly, in the feudal system that characterized political life in the

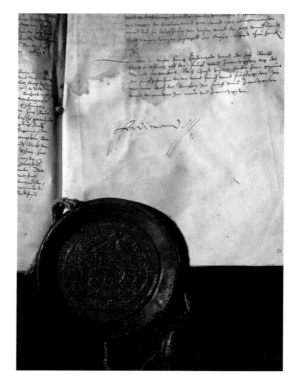

◀ *This document, the Peace of Augsburg, bears the signature and seal of Ferdinand I, brother of Charles V. By signing it in 1555, Ferdinand accepted the existence of Lutheranism in the German imperial territories—an act necessary to prevent perpetual warfare between Catholic and Protestant princes. Although wars of religion would trouble Europe throughout the 1600s, by conceding that Protestant principalities could exist, the Peace of Augsburg was the first step toward the toleration of Reformed religions.*

Middle Ages, officeholders were responsible to the person who gave them their office and who invested them with its symbols at the same time. The point of contention in the investiture controversy was the question of whether the local bishop should receive the symbols of his office, the shepherd's staff and ring, from the king or from the pope (or the pope's representative). If from the pope, the bishop owed loyalty to the pope; if from the king, the bishop was the king's man. The church had traditionally considered lay investiture—investiture to a church office by a layman—an impossibility; God had given all power in heaven and on earth to the church. The church then delegated temporal (secular) rule to the king at his coronation while continuing to exercise its own spiritual power directly.

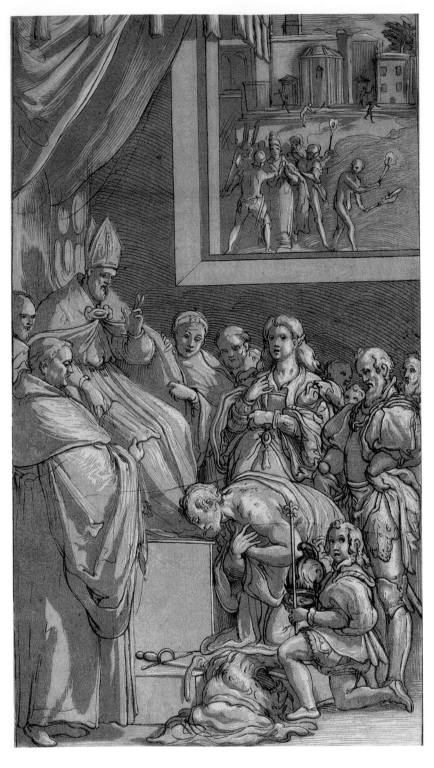

The best of Christian kings were from time to time unhappy with papal incursions on their authority and sought ways to limit papal power in their kingdom. The existence of a system of church courts, in which wills were settled and marriage law judged and in which clerics were charged and tried beyond the jurisdiction of the king, was at least an irritant. Bishops controlled not only spiritual matters but also extensive lands and great wealth. The tension between pope and king was often managed in a practical way. As long as his rights were maintained, the pope usually appointed to the highest offices men acceptable to the king, and when wars came, the bishops often helped raise money for the campaign. As tension mounted, the establishment of a church independent of Rome became for European kings and princes a tempting solution.

Royal Power versus the Pope

By 1550 a body of theory supported the proposition that the king ought to be head of the church in his realm. In the background was the example of the Byzantine emperor, who since the time of Constantine in the fourth century had exercised the right to call councils and, in extreme situations, to depose clerics in the Orthodox Church. This eastern theory, called caesaropapism, was disallowed in the West, where the pope insisted upon the exclusive right to appoint bishops and crown kings. In 1302 Boniface VIII had claimed in a letter that the pope had authority over every person, yet he did not specify whether this authority was moral or political. The response of the French king Philip IV was to take Boniface's successors to Avignon, a city surrounded by French territory, and to insist upon the election of French cardinals to important positions. These actions were an attempt to settle the investiture controversy on terms favorable to the king.

Later in the fourteenth century, the English Scholastic philosopher William of Ockham would defend the position that the emperor had a right to depose a heretical pope in his *Dialogue on the Dignity of the Pope and King*. The removal of the papacy to Avignon together with the political difficulty of returning the pope to Rome caused the Papal Schism (1378–1417), when there were two, and on one occasion three, popes.

▲ A drawing by Federico Zuccari (c. 1540–1609) of Pope Gregory VII blessing a repentant Emperor Henry IV in 1077. Excommunicated and unable to govern, Henry had to beg the pope's forgiveness but later defied his authority on several other occasions.

The church could make kings by crowning and anointing them and could also excommunicate rulers and thereby release subjects from obedience to their king. One significant moment in the investiture controversy was the excommunication of the Holy Roman emperor Henry IV by Pope Gregory VII in 1076 on the grounds that the emperor had appointed bishops without the consent of the pope.

This confusion tended to undermine the authority of the papacy and to popularize such arguments as those advanced by William of Ockham. In response to the difficulty of determining just where ultimate authority lay, there developed a body of thought that held the pope subject to a general council. This theory, called conciliarism, was advanced at the Council of Pisa in 1409. Although conciliarism did not directly propose the superiority of the king to the pope, it did establish the idea that papal authority was not absolute. The great defender of conciliarism was the Frenchman Jean Charlier (known as Jean de Gerson; 1363–1429), a brilliant theologian who proposed the superiority of general councils to the pope at a time when there seemed no other way out of the situation in which pope excommunicated pope. In the process Gerson defended several propositions that would later be adopted by the Gallicans in France. Among these propositions was the idea that the authority of the king was for all practical purposes as absolute in church affairs as it was in civil matters.

The work that most influenced the thinking of kings during the early sixteenth century was Marsilius of Padua's *Defensor pacis* (1342). While absolutist monarchs—Henry VIII of England and Louis XIV of France, for example—would not have liked Marsilius's emphatic claim that all power was vested in the people, who might therefore depose their ruler, they would have welcomed the idea that all authority rested in the state and that the church possessed no inherent power of its own. In the late sixteenth century this theory was restated by the Swiss theologian Thomas Erastus (1524–1583), who taught that the civil authority had complete jurisdiction over the church—including the power to excommunicate.

◀ Tobias Stimmer painted this portrait of Thomas Erastus in 1582. The significance of Erastus's Seventy-five Theses (1589) was reflected in the numerous translations of the title.

Thomas Erastus c. 1524–1583

The Swiss physician and theologian Thomas Erastus became famous because of his work the *Seventy-five Theses,* which took the position that there was no need for any power other than that of magistrates in matters of religious controversy. Erastus sought to illustrate that no such power existed within the church. In the last three of his theses, he argued that no ecclesiastical body had ever existed that had the power to excommunicate; that power belonged solely to the magistrate. In matters concerning church doctrine, pastors were to be consulted, but their authority was not final.

Erastus's arguments reinforced the opinion that the civil magistrate held ultimate authority. Erastus was widely cited in the controversies that led to the creation of established churches. Erastus's work was not published until 1589, but Richard Hooker knew of it when he wrote the first five books of *The Laws of Ecclesiastical Polity* (1593–1597). Two hundred years later Erastianism influenced the debates that resulted in the disestablishment of the Church of England in the United States after the American Revolution.

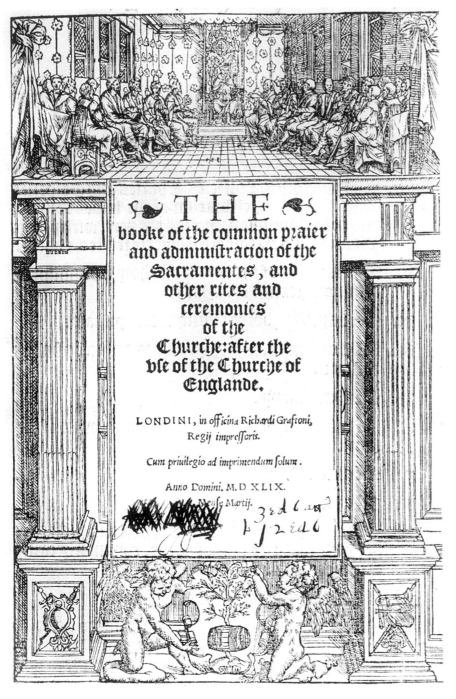

With the investiture controversy settled in their favor, rulers were free to drift toward a theory of kingship called absolutism. According to this system, the king ruled by divine right derived from God, the king's will was law, and disobedience could be sin. The millennium-long power of the church to check the ambition of rulers was broken in Protestant lands and increasingly ineffective in Catholic kingdoms.

England: The First Royal Establishment

In a series of acts passed between 1532 and 1534, English bishops were required to consider Henry VIII head of the church, never to call a convocation to revise church law without the king's permission, and never to appeal to the Roman courts. In 1536 the smaller monasteries were visited and condemned and their property confiscated. The church was thus in the hands of the English king. In the reign of Henry's son, Edward VI, the government authorized new ceremonies and issued the Book of Homilies (1547), a collection of government-approved sermons to be read in churches. During her brief reign (1553–1558), Queen Mary, a Catholic, returned the realm to Roman obedience. In May 1559 the new queen, Elizabeth I, persuaded Parliament to reinstate the acts of Henry VIII. The religion of the Elizabethan church was described in forty-two articles—later reduced to thirty-nine—that the queen herself approved and by the Book of Common Prayer, which was established by an act of Parliament in 1549. Bishops were now nominated to their office not by the pope but by the queen, who liked to remind her bishops that as she had made them, she could unmake them.

The established churches, the Church of England chief among them, were always shaped to some degree by political considerations. Elizabeth was anxious to create a constitution for the established church that would include as wide a range of English religious opinion as possible. There were to be no windows into men's souls so long as they conformed to the established church. Elizabeth's most vocal critics were not Catholics, who after the first decade of the reign were too timid to protest much, but Puritans. The great defender of the right of the Church of England to appeal to reason and tradition as well

The frontispiece of the first English Book of Common Prayer (1549) describes the book as representing the "use of the Churche of Englande." These words were revolutionary not only because they were written in the English language but also because the new liturgy was no longer that of international Catholicism.

The King as Head of the Church

Once religious loyalty to Rome was dissolved, the investiture controversy was settled in favor of local rulers, who became head of the church in their kingdom. The property of the church then became national property, and the support of the church became the business of the crown. Because it was hard to imagine that citizens who did not share the common religion could be politically reliable, the authority of the state was used to reinforce the authority of the king's church, now established by national law.

▼ *A nineteenth-century engraving of Richard Hooker, the scholar whose* Laws of Ecclesiastical Polity *answered the Puritans on behalf of the Elizabethan regime. The Puritans considered the Bible the only authority for church organization. Hooker appealed to the broad tradition that included Aristotle and Thomas Aquinas, in which reason and custom were also authorities.*

as to the Bible in the formation of its established religion was Richard Hooker, whose *Laws of Ecclesiastical Polity* (1594–1597) was written in part to convince the Puritans of the lawfulness of the Elizabethan establishment.

Presbyterianism in Scotland

In 1560 the Church of Scotland was established with the theology of the French Reformer John Calvin (1509–1564) and a collegiate form of government by presbyters (lay elders). In that year the Scottish Confession of Faith was adopted by the Scottish parliament. The Scottish church accepted the main Calvinist doctrines: justification by faith alone, election, and predestination. Apostolic succession—the doctrine that church authority was secured in a line of descent that passed from the apostles to bishops by the laying on of hands—was a doctrine dear to the leading divines of the Church of England in the seventeenth century. In Scotland it was considered a relic of Catholicism that gave the clergy too much power. The necessity of bishops was denied, and magistrates were empowered to protect and also correct the church when necessary. Whereas in England religion was established by royal authority, in Scotland, although the Scottish king was bound to protect Protestant interests, the church was ruled by laymen.

Lutheranism in Germany

From the beginning Lutheranism was a national movement, inspired in part by the longstanding hostility of the German emperor and the people

▲ *The Carthusians were the only religious order in England whose members resisted the claim of Henry VIII to be head of the church in England. This painting, by Domenico Gargiulio (1612–1679), dramatically depicts the Carthusians' grisly fate.*

of the Holy Roman Empire to the claims of the pope. In his *Appeal to the Christian Nobility of the German Nation* (1520), Luther urged the nobles to resist the impositions of Rome, a policy that many would have found pleasing.

When Martin Luther was threatened by Catholic authorities in 1518, he was protected by Elector Frederick III of Saxony. Thus began a long tradition that the Protestant German nobility would protect Protestant champions and interests. After the Peace of Augsburg established the principle that the religion of the king was the religion of the kingdom, the Lutheran rulers became the official protectors of the churches in their realm. In 1527 Elector John was instrumental in the imposition of Lutheranism in Saxony; he deprived Catholic priests of their benefices and expelled recalcitrant laymen. After its successes in Germany, Lutheranism was adopted in Denmark, Sweden, and Finland, with the king or king and parliament as head of the church.

A common feature of the governments of countries that had established Protestant churches was a marked hostility toward the Roman Catholicism they had rejected. In England after 1559, subjects were fined for failure to attend the services of the Church of England. After 1585, Jesuits and other Catholic missionaries found in the realm were subjected to the death penalty. In Denmark after 1624, Catholic priests found exercising their ministry were sentenced to death. In England the laws that prevented Catholics from practicing the professions were not removed until 1829 (on the other hand, the monarch was not permitted to profess the Roman Catholic faith). This hostility of the Protestant kingdoms to Catholics was reciprocated by the Catholic countries of Europe. Protestantism was illegal in France until 1787, and in Spain the last laws against the practice of a Protestant religion, although not rigidly enforced after 1900, were not removed until the constitution of 1978.

Royal Establishments in Catholic Kingdoms

The Protestant kingdoms of northern Europe were the only states that established their religion by law and made the king head of the church. In Catholic kingdoms, while the national church was not independent of Rome, rulers tended to behave as though the church in their dominion was a matter of local interest, its policies to be determined by the monarch. Philip II of Spain dominated the Catholic Church in Spain no less effectively than Elizabeth I dominated the Church of England. Although Philip was unquestionably orthodox, his relation to the papacy differed from Elizabeth's only in degree; Pope Clement VIII threatened him with excommunication, and Philip hinted at the desirability of a general council that might bring the pope to heel.

After the Peace of Augsburg established the *cuius regio* principle, Catholic kings often acted as though they were effectively the head of the Roman Catholic Church in their realm. These monarchs wanted to control the appointment of bishops no less than Henry VIII did in England; like Henry, they wanted to limit the authority of church courts and avoid paying money to Rome.

The creation of established churches, either by law in Protestant countries or by custom and royal policy in Catholic countries, introduced an intense period of religious conflict throughout Europe. The imposition of the Peace of Augsburg left Catholic German states with many Protestants, Lutheran states with many Catholics, Catholic France with many Calvinists, and Protestant England with a large Catholic minority. Queen Elizabeth was persuaded that many Catholics and all Catholic priests were agents of the pope and the Spanish king, while the Spanish, who ruled the Netherlands until 1573, considered Calvinism an anomaly to be removed with the sword. The Saint Bartholomew's Day Massacre of August 23 and 24, 1572, took the lives of between five and ten thousand Huguenots (French Calvinists) in Paris and other French cities.

The failure of the settlement envisioned by the Peace of Augsburg was an important cause of the Thirty Years War, which was provoked when the Protestant citizens of Prague threw two Catholic councillors from the window of the Hradschin Palace on May 23, 1618. During this long war the Catholic powers tended to prevail, and during the first half of the war, the issues were primarily religious. The French, unwilling to see the Holy Roman emperor Ferdinand triumphant, formed an alliance with Swedish Protestants, who were led by King Gustavus Adolphus. Between 1630 and 1648 the issues were increasingly political; the contest between the French king Louis XIII and the emperors Ferdinand II and Ferdinand III tended to overshadow religious concerns.

▼ *This contemporary engraving by Franz Hogenberg depicts the massacre of Huguenots (French Calvinists) in Paris on Saint Batholomew's Day, August 24, 1572. This event was the most dramatic expression of European princes' determination to maintain political control by requiring uniformity of religion through the violent suppression of dissent. Catholics in Elizabeth's England and in John Knox's Scotland suffered a similar fate, and in Germany, Protestants were often forced to flee from Catholic principalities, and Catholics from Protestant principalities.*

LOUIS XIV AND FRENCH NATIONAL CATHOLICISM

Louis XIV, who ruled France from 1661 until 1715, was always interested in religion; his reign was adorned by such great preachers as Jacques-Bénigne Bossuet and François Fenelon. Despite his acknowledged faithfulness to Catholic doctrine and the title Most Christian King, given to him by the pope, Louis strove to exert royal authority over the Catholic Church in France. A long dispute with Pope Innocent XI over Louis's right to appoint bishops led to the passing in 1682 of the Four Articles, a Gallican statement (that is, one arguing for administrative independence from papal control) that took France to the brink of schism with Rome because it upheld the king's right to appoint bishops and minimized the pope's authority over the French church. The Gallican articles were condemned by Pope Alexander VIII in 1690, and in 1693 Louis withdrew them, but the French church never abandoned the idea that as the church's eldest daughter, it deserved special freedom from Roman supervision. Following Henry VIII, Elizabeth I, and Louis XIV, the Austrian emperor Joseph II would assert his authority over the Catholic Church in the eighteenth century under a policy called Josephinism.

▲ This 1654 tapestry, made in the world-famous Gobelin factory, depicts the coronation of Louis XIV of France, a king who, in defense of Catholicism as the religion of his kingdom, in 1685 repealed the Edict of Nantes, which had allowed French Protestants some toleration. While staunchly defending Catholic orthodoxy, Louis resisted papal attempts to exercise authority over the appointment of bishops in France.

saw their church as a legitimate expression of their Christian faith. There was, however, especially in the British Isles, always some objection to the idea of the establishment of any religion, especially among the Scots, whose resistance to the plan of Charles I and Archbishop Laud to establish the Church of England in Scotland led to civil war in 1642. The phrase in the First Amendment to the Constitution of the United States that prevents the establishment of any religion is a reference to the sixteenth-century European practice of setting up established churches. The so-called establishment clause of the First Amendment to the Constitution prevented the establishment of a national church but left untouched the established Congregationalism of Massachusetts and Connecticut.

When the Thirty Years War ended in 1648, continental Europe was exhausted. Although minor territorial adjustments followed the war, the best that could be achieved was a return to the principles of the Peace of Augsburg. After such widespread slaughter and destruction, toleration seemed preferable to religious strife. Protestants still labored under restrictions in France, as did Catholics in England, Denmark, and Sweden, but the persecution of religious dissent faded. The last execution of a Catholic for his religion in England was in 1680.

The system of confessional churches, one religion for each kingdom, seems in retrospect to have been a failure, but the citizens of national states that had an established church generally

FURTHER READING

Cross, Claire. *Royal Supremacy in the Elizabethan Church*. New York, 1969.

Davies, E. T. *Episcopal and Royal Supremacy in the Church of England in the Sixteenth Century*. Oxford, 1950.

Ehler, Sidney Z., and J. B. Morall. *Church and State through the Centuries*. New York, 1967.

Hassal, Arthur. *Louis XIV and the Zenith of the French Monarchy*. Freeport, NY, 1972.

O'Brien, Louis. *Innocent XI and the Revocation of the Edict of Nantes*. Berkeley, CA, 1930.

James A. Patrick

SEE ALSO
• Calvinism • Church of England • France
• Lutheranism • Reformation • Thirty Years War

Exploration

DURING THE RENAISSANCE EXPLORERS SCOURED UNCHARTED AREAS TO FIND NEW TRADE ROUTES AND MARKETS, ASSERT POLITICAL POWER, CLAIM TERRITORY, ESTABLISH COLONIES, EXPAND GEOGRAPHICAL KNOWLEDGE, AND GAIN ACCESS TO EXOTIC GOODS.

The discovery of new lands by migrant peoples gave rise to legends of adventure that inspired later voyagers. In the ancient world accounts of adventurous journeys, both fictional and factual, were preserved in such writings as Homer's *Odyssey* and Ptolemy's *Geographia;* these texts influenced explorers when classical works became popular in the Renaissance. In the thirteenth century Marco Polo trekked across Asia and brought back silks, jewels, pearls, and spices. His account of Cathay (China) was another great source of inspiration to later European explorers.

During the Renaissance explorers were motivated variously by a sense of adventure, the possibility of acquiring personal wealth and fame, and the desire to win their country supremacy over its rivals. A primary goal of European explorers and the royal sponsors of their voyages was to find a direct route, by sea, to the Far East. The products of China and Southeast Asia—especially the spices that came from the Spice Islands (in present-day Indonesia)—were highly desired in Europe. However, between Christian Europe and the Far East lay a vast swath of Islamic territory. The lucrative trade in spices and silks was controlled by the Muslim merchants who oversaw the transportation of these goods overland from their source to the Mediterranean. By finding a maritime route to the Far East, Europeans would access the source and bypass the middlemen. Explorers hunted for a route to China by rounding Africa, searching for northern and southern passages, and traveling west across the Atlantic. Portugal and Spain vied to control trade routes and prices and used their military power to repel competitors. Much exploration was speculative; some trips benefited investors, while others failed. While searching for routes to China, explorers discovered many lands and thus opened up new markets and won territory for their sponsors.

In the fifteenth century China's Ming dynasty rulers sent Cheng Ho's treasure fleet on several voyages to India and East Africa. Cheng Ho's junks, like the Arabs' dhows, relied on seasonal ocean currents and monsoon winds to travel long distances. The nimble caravels of southern Europe, rigged with lateen (triangular) sails, were ideal for trading and exploring along coasts and shallow rivers. Christopher Columbus's ships were caravels, as were those despatched by Henry the Navigator from Portugal to Africa. The larger square-rigged *nao,* or carrack, endured long voyages and severe conditions on the open ocean, moved swiftly, and carried ample cargo. The first circumnavigation of the world (1519–1522), led by Ferdinand Magellan, was made in *naos.*

▼ An illustration from a sixteenth-century medical treatise of nutmeg, a highly precious commodity during the Renaissance. People used spices for health purposes and to make bland food palatable. The desire to control the importation of rare spices into Europe was a spur to world exploration.

Cartography

At the dawn of the Renaissance, cartographers were drawing heavily on classical sources, notably the descriptions in Ptolemy's *Geographia,* which was written in the second century and rediscovered around 1410. Maps of familiar European regions were reasonably accurate, but to Europeans the rest of the world remained a mystery. Cartographers illustrated unknown areas, particularly Africa, with pictures of the fantastical creatures and peoples they imagined lived there. By venturing into unknown regions, the first great explorers were overturning a picture of the world based on outdated knowledge and superstition.

One particularly curious misconception was the belief that land dominated the planet. Christopher Columbus stated, "the earth is small; six parts of it is dry land." The position of land-masses on maps was often incorrect, and their shape distorted. The equator was drawn far to the north of its actual location. The location and configuration of the islands of the Far East were uncertain. Some cartographers greatly underestimated the size of the Atlantic Ocean and were unsure of what lay on its western edge. Until Columbus's voyage, nobody in Europe suspected the existence of the Americas. On maps, to Europe's west lay a sea; beyond was Asia.

As explorers investigated the earth, Renaissance cartographers used their observations to correct and refine maps and achieve more accurate and proportionate depictions of land and water bodies. However, many explorers kept details of their journeys secret in order to avoid giving their political and commercial rivals any advantage.

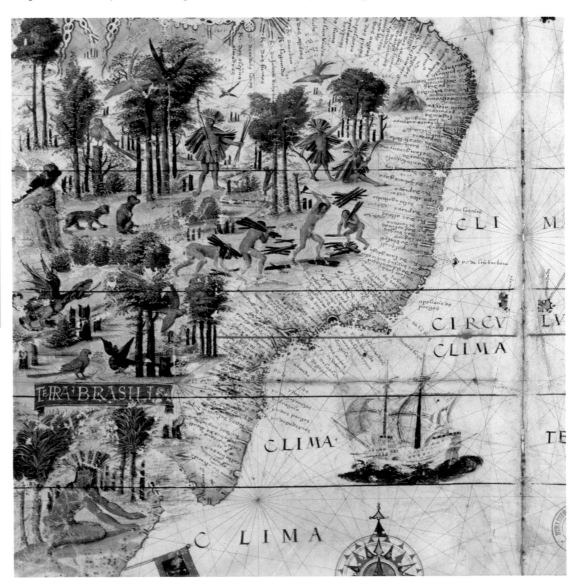

▶ *On this map of Brazil, published around 1519, the coastline, which had been visited and surveyed by Amerigo Vespucci (1454–1512) and other explorers, is drawn accurately, while the unexplored interior is filled with the animals, vegetation, and peoples of popular imagination.*

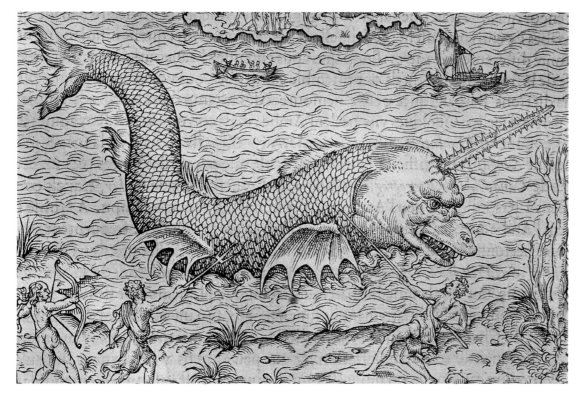

An illustration of a sea monster from a French book of 1575. Explorers' fears that fantastical creatures inhabited the mysterious depths of the ocean were in part borne out by the large and unfamiliar real ocean animals—whales and squid, for example—that could cause serious damage to ships.

Richard Hakluyt c. 1552–1616

The English scholar Richard Hakluyt had a significant influence on Renaissance exploration. He earned two degrees at Oxford University, where he probably received a comprehensive humanities education and specialized in geography. Having studied divinity, he became an ordained minister; he also learned cartography and gained navigational skills. Explorers respected Hakluyt and related to him their voyages to uncharted areas of the world. Hakluyt recorded these accounts and put them together with manuscripts he gathered, many of them "hidden in several hucksters' hands" or "long [having] lien miserably scattered in mustie corners" at risk of being "buried in perpetuall oblivion." In 1582 he published *Divers Voyages Touching the Discovery of America and the Islands Adjacent unto the Same.*

In 1583 England's ambassador to France, Edward Stafford, employed Hakluyt as a chaplain and secretary. While living in Paris, Hakluyt met explorers and their families and thus was able to collect, translate, and publish accounts of French and Spanish exploration in the New World. Captains and crews shared stories, some of them true and others fantastical tales of monsters. Hakluyt shaped these stories into his masterpiece *Principall Navigations, Voiages, Traffiques and Discoveries of the English Nation, Made by Sea or over Land to the Most Remote and Farthest Distant Quarters of the Earth at Any Time within the Compasse of These 1500 Yeeres*, which was issued initially in 1589 and then revised to form a three-volume set, with the revised subtitle *Within the Compasse of These 1600 Yeeres*, and published from 1598 to 1600. The East India Company, the English body charged with exploiting trading opportunities in Asia, hired Hakluyt as a consultant. Also a Virginia Company and Northwest Passage Company member, Hakluyt urged English people to colonize North America in the name of personal enrichment and English prosperity and pride. The tone of his promotional rhetoric was propagandist and anti-Spanish.

Since he expected to compile additional publications, Hakluyt continued to chronicle travelers' experiences; he interviewed explorers and preserved manuscripts for readers. After Hakluyt's death, Samuel Purchas, who had worked with him until they were estranged, acquired and prepared Hakluyt's narratives, in addition to other primary sources, for publication in 1625. The four volumes were collectively entitled *Hakluytus Posthumus, or Purchas His Pilgrimes; Contayning a History of the World in Sea Voyages and Land Travells by Englishmen and Others.* Although Purchas's editions did not match the quality of Hakluyt's work, they preserved the contents of manuscripts that have since vanished. The Hakluyt Society, established in 1846, continues Hakluyt's work by publishing books on subjects related to exploration and by translating obscure archival manuscripts. Reprints of Hakluyt's books, with their firsthand tales of Renaissance exploration, continue to amaze readers.

▲ *Lucas Janszoon Waghenaer's* Mariner's Mirror, *a navigational guide and atlas of the seas, was highly valued among mariners for centuries after its publication in 1584. This engraved frontispiece includes depictions of numerous navigational instruments, including quadrants, astrolabes, lead lines, cross-staffs, and magnetic compasses, as well as globes and a ship surrounded by sea creatures.*

Navigation

The realities of navigation were far removed from tales in books and the advice of experts who had never been to sea. Navigational theories were often incompatible with the realities of conditions at sea. Pilots were not usually well educated, and their success or failure often depended more on practical insight, courage, instinct, and experience than on theoretical knowledge of navigational procedures. Seamen had knowledge of seasonal climate changes; they were able to interpret the condition of the sky, wind, and water and knew important landmarks. Although most literate people accepted that the earth is round, not flat, mythology and superstition influenced the decisions made by captains and pilots. Most crew members believed the earth was flat and

that it was thus possible to sail over the world's edge. They were scared to travel beyond known landmarks and believed the equator would broil everyone who crossed it.

Navigational tools during the Renaissance were simple, and navigational techniques, with few exceptions and improvements, were essentially medieval. For centuries Chinese explorers had relied for directional guidance on the lodestone (known to scientists as magnetite), an iron oxide–rich mineral with magnetic properties that can be transferred to objects. Chinese sailors rubbed lodestones on wires to make "point-south needles" that indicated the direction north-south when hung from a thread or floated in a bowl of water. By the 1300s European navigators were placing the needle, stuck to a circular piece of card, on a pivot in a box. Navigators used these magnetic compasses in conjunction with portolan charts, special maps whose radiating rhumb lines (lines of constant compass bearing) helped the navigator plot a course from port to port.

During voyages across the ocean, where no landmarks were available, a navigator tracked the longitude (east-west position) of his ship by monitoring the distance sailed and the direction of travel (a procedure known as dead reckoning). To work out the distance traveled, some measure of the speed of the ship was necessary. A highly accomplished navigator could feel the speed of his ship. Others threw driftwood overboard and watched how quickly it receded behind the ship. From the sixteenth century navigators used the chip log, a rope knotted at regular intervals. The rope was let out for half a minute, timed with a sandglass. The number of knots paid out indicated the ship's speed. Changes in speed and direction were logged with pegs on a traverse board.

As ships neared shore, the navigator measured the depth of the water with a lead line, a device that was also used to collect water samples and sediment. For the benefit of future explorers, pilots described sea depths in books called rutters. They also recorded water characteristics, underwater vegetation, dangerous rocks and currents, star and sun readings, and birdlife. Captains used logbooks to record the course sailed, the local weather and sea conditions, and the location of notable places and things.

Voyagers on the open ocean faced many dangers, not least from violent weather. William Strachy gave an eyewitness account of a shipwreck near Bermuda on July 24, 1609.

... the cloudes gathering thicke upon us, and the windes singing, and whistling most unusually ... a dreadfull storme and hideous began to blow from out the North-east, which swelling, and roaring as it were by fits, some houres with more violence than others, at length did beate all light from heaven; which like an hell of darkenesse turned blacke upon us, so much the more fuller of horror.... For foure and twenty houres the storme in a restlesse tumult, had blowne so exceedingly, as we could not apprehend in our imaginations any possibility of greater violence, yet did wee still finde it, not onely more terrible, but more constant, fury added to fury, and one storme urging a second more outragious then the former.... Windes and Seas were as mad, as fury and rage could make them; for mine owne part, I had bin in some stormes before.... Yet all that I had ever suffered gathered together, might not hold comparison with this: there was not a moment in which the sodaine splitting, or instant over-setting of the Shippe was not expected.

Samuel Purchas, *Hakluytus Posthumus, or Purchas His Pilgrimes*

◄ *An unattributed fifteenth-century Flemish painting called* Shipwreck Caused by Demons. *Storms and sea calamities, which explorers sometimes personified as evil forces, often tore ships apart or forced them aground. Survivors prayed to express gratitude, mourn victims, and bolster spiritual strength before continuing with the voyage. Success often depended on a crew's resourcefulness and innovativeness; the men would utilize timber and objects found at their unexpected landing site to supplement recovered tools and supplies. They repaired crafts whenever possible or gathered supplies to build a new ship.*

In the early 1400s most navigators kept their vessels close to land. As navigators mastered the measuring of latitude (north-south position), chiefly through celestial observation, ships ranged farther out. Navigators used the cross-staff, quadrant, and astrolabe to work out their latitude from the configuration of the stars in the sky. In the north crews observed the angle and elevation of the sun or polestar above the horizon. In the Southern Hemisphere, where the polestar was not visible, sailors measured the height of the midday sun. Accuracy was affected when ship movement made devices unsteady, distracted crews forgot to turn sandglasses, or the ship was blown off course. Sailors used telescopes by the early seventeenth century to spy distant landmarks.

▲ *Explorers occasionally took on assignments other than exploratory voyages in order to strengthen ties with a patron or to earn a supplementary income. This illustration depicts the occasion when King Richard II of England (reigned 1377–1399) commissioned ships to transport cargoes of provisions for the English troops serving in Ireland.*

Planning a Voyage

Some explorers set off with one ship and a small crew and without state backing. Other expeditions consisted of several ships, each with a particular purpose—scout ships, messenger ships, and supply ships, for example. Until a given route was proven and merchants and bankers became willing to invest in voyages along that route, captains, officers, and shipbuilders might pay for the journey themselves. Monarchs arranged certain high-profile voyages and provided financial assistance. Scientists planned routes and told navigators where to sail and how to describe sites and collect details of local peoples and their customs and languages. Explorers sometimes transported a small pinnace (light sailing ship) for use in local reconnaissance, especially along shallow rivers and inlets.

Renaissance Crews

A typical crew consisted of a gentleman captain, a professional pilot, officers, occasionally an agent to deal with merchants, and seamen. Wages were low, and so money was seldom the sole motivation for pilots and officers. Many explored

to test geographical theories and to improve their skills. Captains sailed for fame and to serve their nation by beating rival foreign explorers to desirable lands and goods. Captains often had deep religious convictions and prayed to Saint Nicholas, the mariners' patron saint. Many crews included a priest, who would minister to those on board and perhaps undertake the evangelization of non-Christian native peoples (from the 1560s, the Catholic Church greatly increased missionary activity in newly discovered lands). The crew was often a ragtag bunch that included banished convicts and boys escaping from unpleasant homes.

Crews had to be self-reliant, versatile, and resourceful as they traveled to strange and remote places. Sailors had to be good leaders and willing risk takers. Though life on board a ship entailed challenging and dangerous work, at other times it could be tedious; sailors had to mend sails and clothes and repair broken equipment. To relieve boredom and loneliness, the crew played games and pranks and danced and performed music. (Music was not only a form of entertainment— certain melodies signaled routine activities or alerted the crew to danger.) Sailors participated in rituals when crossing the equator; they also gossiped and gambled (a forbidden activity). Punishments ranged from extra chores to whippings and even being cast away. Food and water were rarely fresh; men ate hardtack, salted meat, and rotting fruits and vegetables until ships could be restocked. The great English naval commander John Hawkins (1532–1595) summarized how to be a good explorer: "Serve God daily, love one another, preserve your victuals, beware of fire, and keep good company."

Explorers departed on voyages unsure of how long they would be gone and what conditions they would encounter. Leaders of expeditions involving multiple ships planned rendezvous sites in case the vessels became separated, and officers left messages for the crews of other ships in jars buried next to crosses. Navigators who naively relied on inaccurate maps risked the depletion of their supplies if the journey lasted longer than expected. A familiar route did not necessarily ensure security. Diseases decimated crews, hurricanes swept boats apart, and sometimes entire ships and crews were lost.

In his well-known book Samuel Purchas describes how Captain James Lancaster prevented his crew from succumbing to scurvy on a voyage to Asia in 1600 to establish trade for the English East India Company:

... the reason why the General's men stood better in health then [sic] the men of other ships, was this: he brought to Sea with him certaine Bottles of the Juice of Limons, which hee gave to each one, as long as it would last, three spoonfuls every morning fasting: not suffering them to eate any thing after it till noone. This Juice worketh much the better, if the partie keepe a short Dyet, and wholly refraine salt meate, which salt meate, and long being at the Sea is the only cause of the breeding of this Disease. By this meanes the Generall cured many of his men, and preserved the rest: so that in his ship (having the double of men that was in the rest of the ships) he had not so many sicke, nor lost so many men as they did, which was the mercie of God to us all.

Samuel Purchas, *Hakluytus Posthumus, or Purchas his Pilgrimes*

Portuguese Exploration

In the 1420s Portuguese explorers began to sail south to the North African coast and southwest into the Atlantic Ocean, where they located Madeira, the Azores, the Canary Islands, and the Cape Verde Islands. Financed by Prince Henry (called the Navigator by posterity), the explorers were looking for the source of the gold and ivory that Muslim traders were bringing north from beyond the Sahara Desert. In addition to accruing wealth, the Portuguese hoped to spread Christianity, claim global political superiority, and increase geographical knowledge. Their journeys initiated the Age of Exploration. They did much to improve on medieval maps, on which Africa's west coast was depicted only as far as the Gulf of Guinea. Africa was also speculatively joined to a mythical southern continent, and the Indian Ocean was landlocked. Many maps suggested that Africa contained monsters.

◄ *Music, an important source of entertainment on exploratory voyages, also had practical purposes. This gilded, embossed, and enameled brass depicts musicians and their instruments on the flagship of Holy Roman Emperor Charles V (reigned 1519–1556).*

Henry the Navigator ▮ c. 1394–1460

Prince Henry of Portugal, later called the Navigator, encouraged and funded a program of exploration that came to be the catalyst for European global expansion. His parents, King John I and Queen Philippa, provided the resources that allowed their third son to develop his interest in exploration. Henry, a devout Catholic, vowed to defeat Muslims and to convert to Christianity people he considered heathens—wherever they were to be found.

Associated with the military Order of Christ, Henry supported crusading campaigns to remove Muslims from North Africa and seize their land for Christian Portugal. He decided to wage war on Ceuta, a primarily Muslim North African port near the Strait of Gibraltar where pirates and slavers thrived. In 1415 Henry's invaders seized Ceuta and defeated the Muslim Moors there. Intrigued by Africa, Henry listened to prisoners' accounts and reviewed captured maps, which were more accurate and comprehensive than those available in Portugal. Certain that the interior of Africa was rich with gold, Henry began to conclude that further exploration of Africa might greatly benefit Portugal in economic, political, and religious terms.

Henry moved to the southwestern Portuguese port of Sagres, where he developed the natural resources of Cape Saint Vincent to build an observatory and an innovative navigational school. At the school Henry assembled experts in mathematics, astronomy, geography, and cartography. The school contributed to the improvement of navigational tools and influenced Portuguese shipbuilding. Research into the design and construction of ships led to the development of swift and nimble caravels, ships that were essential to many fifteenth- and sixteenth-century voyages. Henry sponsored numerous voyages of exploration along the coast of Africa and urged his students to promote Christianity wherever they traveled and to look for Christians to enlist in the struggle against the Muslims. He told his students to gather geographical data to improve maps and share with other Portuguese navigators.

The school's most important mission was to find a sea route via Africa to the spices and silks of Asia. Here Henry encountered difficulties: his crews were apprehensive about traveling by Cape Bojador (on the northwestern coast of the Sahara), which was associated with sea serpents and other perceived evil dangers. From 1424 through 1434, captains refused to complete the journey Henry had planned. He could not convince them that their fears were imaginary. Captain Gil Eannes agreed to try again and in 1434 maneuvered his ship sufficiently far west to prevent his crew from viewing the Cape as they passed it. Henry's explorers reached Cape Blanc by 1441. Five years later they sailed to the mouth of the Gambia River. After Henry's death his nephew, King John II, oversaw the Sagres institute and continued the exploration of Africa and, beyond, Asia.

Another motivation for early Portuguese exploration was the search for Prester John, a legendary Christian king whom Henry believed lived somewhere in Africa. Henry hoped that he and the mighty Prester John would form an alliance to drive the Muslims out of Africa. Another widespread belief held that Thomas the Apostle had set up a Christian colony in India.

Although his crews were reluctant to cross the equator, Henry's ships explored the coasts of West Africa as far south as present-day Sierra Leone. As they edged south, explorers stopped at ports and acquired gold, ivory, and slaves to bring to Portugal. By 1459 maps were indicating that ships could sail around Africa's southern extremity and from there east to China. Ten years later the papacy granted Portugal the exclusive right to trade in West Africa on the condition that explorers chart 350 coastal miles annually. By setting up *padrões* (stone crosses), the Portuguese laid claim to lands and established staging points for future voyages.

◄ *A detail from a painting by an unknown Portuguese artist: Prince Henry the Navigator, holding a map of his discoveries, is surrounded by cartographers and captains and by navigational instruments.*

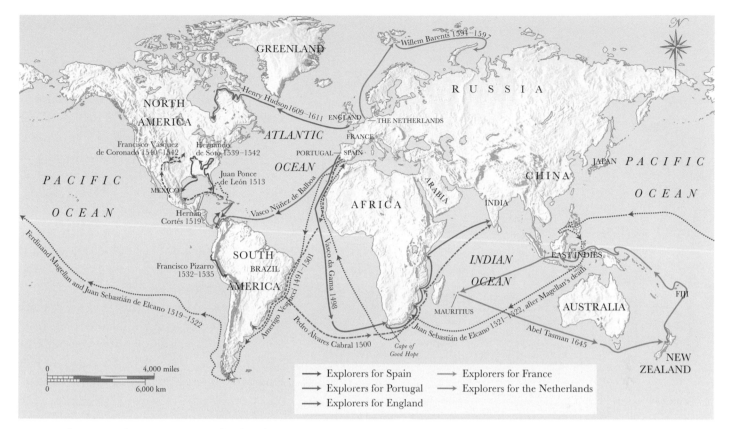

The map contains the following labels:

GREENLAND

Willem Barents 1594–1597

RUSSIA

NORTH AMERICA

Henry Hudson 1609–1611

ENGLAND

THE NETHERLANDS

FRANCE

ATLANTIC OCEAN

PORTUGAL — SPAIN

JAPAN

PACIFIC OCEAN

CHINA

Francisco Vásquez de Coronado 1540–1542

Hernando de Soto 1539–1542

Juan Ponce de León 1513

PACIFIC OCEAN

MEXICO

Hernán Cortés 1519

Vasco Núñez de Balboa

ARABIA

AFRICA

INDIA

SOUTH AMERICA

BRAZIL

Francisco Pizarro 1532–1535

Amerigo Vespucci 1491–1501

Vasco da Gama 1498

INDIAN OCEAN

EAST INDIES

...1522, after Magellan's death

AUSTRALIA

FIJI

Ferdinand Magellan and Juan Sebastián de Elcano 1519–1522

Pedro Álvares Cabral 1500

Cape of Good Hope

Juan Sebastián de Elcano 1521–1522, after Magellan's death

MAURITIUS

Abel Tasman 1645

NEW ZEALAND

0   4,000 miles
0   6,000 km

→ Explorers for Spain   → Explorers for France
→ Explorers for Portugal   → Explorers for the Netherlands
→ Explorers for England

▲ The routes of the most important European exploratory expeditions during the Renaissance.

In 1488 Bartolomeu Dias made the first European voyage around the Cape of Good Hope, at Africa's southern tip. Meanwhile Pero da Covilhã and Afonso de Paiva traveled by land to East Africa. Posing as merchants, they immersed themselves in the local culture and spoke in Arabic while examining the coastline for future exploration. Vasco da Gama reached the Cape of Good Hope in 1497 and then ventured up the East African coast. An Arabian who joined Gama's crew taught him how to use the monsoon winds to travel across the Indian Ocean to India, where he landed the following year. Portuguese rulers funded further journeys around the Cape of Good Hope to sustain trade in India and Asia. Control of these routes assured Portugal wealth and power both regionally and globally. By the late sixteenth century the Portuguese Empire extended across the Indian Ocean as far as China. Portugal's monetary success motivated other states to explore and cartographers to produce more maps to meet the demand.

Because of the rivalry between Portugal and Spain, both countries' explorers worked secretively; they did not share geographical and navigational information and drew deliberately vague maps and charts. Just as the Portuguese did not

want to share Asian spices, the Spanish did not want to share the silver and gold they were beginning to discover in the Americas. For each, control of these precious commodities was equated with political power. In 1493 Pope Alexander VI's *Inter caetera* granted Spain "all the islands and mainlands, found or to be found, discovered or to be discovered, westward or southward, by drawing and establishing a line running from the Arctic to the Antarctic Pole one hundred leagues west and south from any of the islands that are commonly called the Azores and Cape Verde." The 1494 Treaty of Tordesillas shifted the line to 46°37′ west. Spain had trading rights to all land west of the line, and Portugal to the east. The latter territory included Brazil, a country whose colonization began with Pedro Álvares Cabral's visit in 1500.

Spain and the New World

In an attempt to surpass Portugal, Spanish explorers searched for alternative western routes to China and the East Indies. In 1492 Christopher Columbus, attempting to reach Asia by sailing west across the Atlantic Ocean, happened upon the Americas, a continent previously unknown to Europeans (Columbus remained

▲ An engraving of Vasco Nuñez de Balboa (1475–1519), a Spanish explorer of Central America, and some of his soldiers, who appear surprised or excited as they look upon the treasures being placed before them. The engraver is illustrating the pragmatic nature of explorers' interactions with native peoples. Explorers brought gifts to emphasize their power and appease peoples whose land they sought to control. They traded European goods for food, shelter, and guides, whom they hoped would lead them to gold and other valuables.

native peoples and all but wiped out the Mayan and Incan civilizations (which were decimated by European diseases to which they had no immunity). A condition of the Treaty of Tordesillas was that Spain and Portugal spread Christianity to any newly discovered lands. The conquistadores were therefore accompanied by missionary priests, who worked with considerable (and in some cases excessive) zeal. Ships returned to Spain laden with silver, gold, and other treasures, much of it ransacked from temples.

Juan Ponce de León assumed Florida was an island when he reached it in 1513. A decade later, Giovanni da Verrazano headed north along America's eastern coast. "My intention in this navigation was to reach Cathay and the extreme east of Asia, not expecting to find such an obstacle of new land as I found," Verrazzano stated, "and if for some reason I expected to find it, I thought it not to be without some strait to penetrate to the Eastern Ocean. And this has been the opinion of all the ancients, believing certainly our Western Ocean to be one with the Eastern Ocean of India without interposition of land." He thought that Pamlico Sound, a body of water separated from the coast of present-day North Carolina by a ribbon of sandy islands, was the Eastern Ocean. Subsequent maps depicted a huge body of water in North America's center.

During the sixteenth century rumors circulated of cities of gold located somewhere in the Americas. While searching fruitlessly for such mythical locations, explorers greatly increased geographical knowledge. Hunting for gold from 1539, Hernando de Soto trekked through Florida and the southern states and crossed the Mississippi River. In 1540 Francisco Vásquez de Coronado explored western North America in search of the Seven Golden Cities of Cibola. He found no gold but saw the Grand Canyon.

Francis Drake led five ships on the first English circumnavigation of the globe (1577–1580). During the voyage Drake claimed land on North America's Pacific coast for England.

Northern Passages

Because Portugal and Spain controlled all southern routes from Europe to Asia, explorers from other nations decided to seek routes to the north.

convinced that the lands he discovered were continuous with Asia). A prime goal of his voyage was, in his words, "to make a new sailing chart. In it I will locate all of the sea and the lands of the Ocean Sea in their proper places." In 1499 and 1501 the Italian geographer Amerigo Vespucci sailed along the South American coast. Vespucci realized that the Americas was a New World and that Columbus had not therefore found a direct western sea route to China. On a world map of 1507, the German Martin Waldseemüller drew a single western continent and named it America in honor of Vespucci. He also included a new ocean between America and Asia.

In 1513 the Spaniard Vasco Nuñez Balboa crossed Panama and saw the Pacific Ocean. Realizing the ocean separated the New World from Asia, he claimed it for Spain. The first circumnavigation of the world, carried out between 1519 and 1522, was led by Ferdinand Magellan (who did not survive the journey). Also in 1519, the conquistador Hernán Cortés arrived in present-day Mexico. Thrilled when gold-bearing people greeted him, Cortés searched the interior for more riches. Within two years he had conquered the Aztec Empire with help from the Aztecs' rivals. Over the following decades Spanish conquistadores explored South and Central America. They won military victories over the

During the Renaissance many people were torn between suspicion that explorers' tales were too fantastical to be true and the desire to believe in the heroic deeds explorers recounted. Boasts about adventures in faraway places were difficult for people to disprove, and it was hard to distinguish exaggeration from fact. Time often distorted explorers' memories, and writers incorporated legendary events and inaccurate details in historical accounts. After the Renaissance people continued to embrace a nostalgic and romanticized view of explorers and exploration. Such sentimentality coupled with the desire to be personally associated with explorers made some people vulnerable to hoaxes. Vague narratives and the unfamiliarity of the places described abetted deceptions. Scam artists sold fraudulent exploration documents and appealing artifacts to unwary customers. Some pranksters produced false relics based on items described in expedition accounts to fool naive friends rather than for profit. Whether created for financial gain or fun, fakes often perpetuated historical misunderstandings.

Modern historians and scientists cooperated to resolve one of the twentieth century's most successful exploration-inspired hoaxes. In the 1930s a San Francisco group of book collectors and historians, formally called the Ancient and Honorable Order of E Clampus Vitus or ECV (known as the Clampers because they placed plaques at California historical sites), decided to play a joke on a member, Herbert Eugene Bolton, the director of the Bancroft Library at the University of California, Berkeley. Several Clampers created a brass plate resembling the one Francis Drake stated he had placed on a post near a California harbor in June 1579 to claim the surrounding land (which he named Nova Albion) for England. In 1936 Berlyle Shinn, a passerby, found the plate the Clampers had left on the Marin peninsula. Bolton and two metallurgists examined the plate; not seeing the initials ECV hidden on it, they declared it authentic. Representatives of the California Historical Society paid Shinn $3,500 for the plate, which the library exhibited.

Bolton was not swayed by suggestions the plate was a fake. The California Historical Society issued *Drake's Plate of Brasse: Evidence of His Visit to California in 1579*. Critics commented that the inscription and lettering were inconsistent with Renaissance language and the metal seemed newly etched. The Clampers wrote *Ye Preposterous Booke of Brasse* and urged Bolton to reconsider. He steadfastly refused. In 1976, the new library director James D. Hart asked the Massachusetts Institute of Technology metallurgist Cyril Stanley Smith to evaluate the plate microscopically. Smith reported he was "inclined to the opinion that the plate is a modern forgery." Investigators at Oxford University agreed. If it existed, Drake's original brass plate probably remains undiscovered somewhere near San Francisco.

Many explorers, cartographers, political rulers, and merchants believed in the Northwest Passage, an easily navigable waterway across the north of America that joined the Atlantic Ocean to the Pacific. Little did they know that between the east and west coast of the far north lay an ice-choked maze of unnavigable channels. Local fishermen, who well knew the perils, were ignored. Sir Humphey Gilbert's *Discourse of a Discoverie for a New Passage to Cataia* (1576) promoted voyages in the northwest. The merchant Robert Thorne stated that this northern route to Cathay "may so easily and with so little cost, labor, and danger be followed." Maps represented distances and topographical features inaccurately. Even when no viable routes were found, explorers persisted in the belief that such routes would be found if only they sought hard enough.

Explorers who attempted northwestern travel into the Canadian Arctic did not get far. Cold weather and gusty winds buffeted ships; ice capsized or trapped vessels; crews endured freezing temperatures, frostbite, and depleted supplies, and many perished. Icebergs and a mutiny stalled Sebastian Cabot's explorations of around 1509. Henry Hudson, representing the Dutch East India

▲ *This sixteenth-century illustration documents the role played by inhabitants of Tlaxcala, the capital of an anti-Aztec confederacy, in helping Hernán Cortés conquer the Aztecs in 1519.*

Company, was marooned in a boat and abandoned when his crew, stressed by extreme conditions, mutinied in 1611. Only three men from Jens Munk's Norwegian sixty-five-member crew survived being icebound in Button Bay in 1619.

The search for a northeast passage, across the top of Russia, was beset by similar disasters. In 1553 Hugh Willoughby's ship became icebound on the Russian coast, and all aboard perished. The magnetic pole may have affected compass readings and caused Willoughby to steer off course. In 1580 Richard Hakluyt and John Dee briefed Charles Jackman and Arthur Pet for a northeastern expedition. Telling the men how to interact with native peoples, they suggested Jackman and Pet perfume ships before landing to impress any they met. The frozen Kara Sea halted the men's progress, and crews suffered from exposure to the elements. Pet returned to England, while Jackman's ship floundered in Norway. Other explorers found conditions impossible. The Dutch explorer Willem Barents survived the winter of 1596/1597 in his ship when ice lifted it out of water, only to die during the trip home.

Many explorers died before they could share crucial details and advice about northern exploration. Those who survived stressed the need for sturdier ships, abundant supplies of medicine and food, and better methods of navigating icy water. Many admitted that the trade routes geographers, cartographers, and leaders envisioned did not exist.

Terra Australis

Terra Australis, the great southern continent, filled the earth's remotest and most mysterious regions in the popular imagination. A southern *Terra Incognita* ("unknown land") was included on the world map detailed by the second-century Greek geographer Ptolemy, whose works were rediscovered in the fifteenth century. Ptolemy accepted the theory put forward by Aristotle (384–322 BCE) that, since the earth was symmetrical, there must exist frozen lands in the south to balance those of the north. On a 1569 world map drawn by the great Flemish cartographer Gerardus Mercator, a huge *Terra Australis* (the Latin words literally mean "southern landmass") fills the world's southern extremity. Not until James Cook's circumnavigation of Antarctica in the late eighteenth century was the myth of *Terra Australis* finally exploded.

Perhaps the geographers of the Renaissance wanted to fill the unknown parts of the earth with land rather than ocean. Land was more enticing: it offered food, shelter, and people. Many explorers were convinced that *Terra Australis* contained the gold sources, particularly Solomon's Ophir, described in pre-Renaissance legends (after all, gold had not been found

▶ *Explorers seeking the Northeast Passage to China encountered harsh Arctic conditions and were slowed by icy waters. This illustration from the* Narrative of Barents's Last Voyage *(1598) depicts Barents's fleet at anchor while men spear and hunt bear. Icebound explorers either perished or survived by trapping wildlife. Although explorers failed to find a northeast passage until the nineteenth century, their descriptions of polar regions added to geographical knowledge.*

anywhere else). Francis Drake's route around South America in 1578 disproved Mercator's theory that South America was joined to a southern continent. Most explorers considered Australia (discovered by the Dutch in 1605 and known as New Holland) part of a large southern continent. Dirk Hartog explored Australia's west coast in 1616 and did not distinguish it from *Terra Australis*. In 1642 the Dutch explorer Abel Tasman sailed east of Australia and found the coast of New Zealand. Many speculated that Tasman had discovered the western edge of a land that stretched across the entire Pacific. As further exploration revealed nothing but ocean, the size of *Terra Australis* shrank on maps and in people's minds.

The endeavors of the Renaissance laid the ground for future exploration, which benefited from advances in communications, navigation, and transportation. Economic, scientific, and political ramifications aside, exploration influenced Renaissance culture, fueled the imagination, and inspired people to think beyond the local. The Portuguese epic poet and explorer Luis Vaz de Camões (c. 1524–1580) overheard a man summarize the personal benefits of exploration: "You are lured by the perils of the uncertain and the unknown, to the end that fame may exalt and flatter you." The same sense of adventure and desire for glory motivated countless future generations of explorers of the earth and beyond.

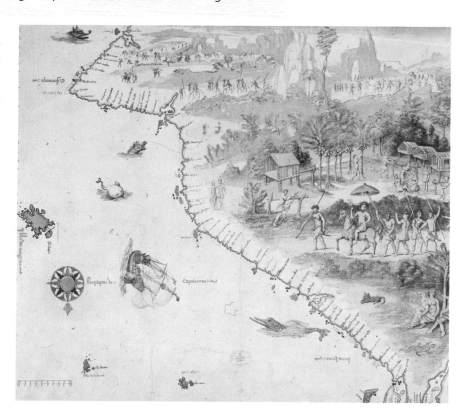

▲ This map, entitled The First Map of Australia, *appeared in a 1547 atlas. Prior to extensive exploration, imaginative mapmakers, influenced by legends, envisioned possible Australian human and animal coastal inhabitants, plants, and structures. As people explored that continent, maps incorporated their findings and became more realistic than this fantastical portrayal.*

FURTHER READING

Buisseret, David. *The Mapmakers' Quest: Depicting New Worlds in Renaissance Europe.* Oxford, 2003.

Hale, John R. *Renaissance Exploration.* New York, 1968.

Parry, John H. *The Establishment of the European Hegemony, 1415–1715: Trade and Exploration in the Age of the Renaissance.* New York, 1966.

Penrose, Boies. *Travel and Discovery in the Renaissance, 1420–1620.* New York, 1971.

Wright, Louis B. *Gold, Glory, and the Gospel: The Adventurous Lives and Times of the Renaissance Explorers.* New York, 1970.

Elizabeth D. Schafer

SEE ALSO
• Columbus, Christopher • Disease • Elizabeth I
• England • Magellan, Ferdinand • Mathematics
• Missionaries • Nationalism • Portugal
• Science and Technology • Spain • Trade • Warfare

Eyck, Jan van

JAN VAN EYCK (C. 1385/90–1441) IS
CELEBRATED FOR BRINGING AN ASTON-
ISHING NEW PICTORIAL REALISM TO
LATE MEDIEVAL ART. HIS WORK WAS
HIGHLY PRIZED THROUGHOUT EUROPE
AND SET THE STYLE FOR PANEL PAINT-
ING IN THE SUCCEEDING CENTURIES.

Jan van Eyck is the best-known painter of a family
of artists that probably originated from the town
of Maaseik in the diocese of Liège (in the eastern
part of modern-day Belgium). The surviving

work of the van Eycks consists of the large-scale
altarpiece *Adoration of the Mystic Lamb* (often
called the Ghent Altarpiece), nine signed and
dated works by Jan van Eyck, and a group of
anonymous paintings by their assistants and followers. Apart from Jan van Eyck's secular portraits, these paintings were used in a religious
context as altarpieces, memorial panels, or
objects for private devotion.

One of the greatest puzzles of Eyckian scholarship concerns the relative contributions of the
brothers Hubert and Jan van Eyck to the Ghent
Altarpiece, which was completed by Jan van Eyck
in the early 1430s after his brother's death in
September 1426. An inscription on its frame
reads, "The painter Hubert van Eyck, than
whom none was greater, began this work; Jan, his
brother, second in art, completed the heavy task
at the request of Joos Vijd. He [Vijd] invites you
by this verse on the sixth of May to look at what
has been done." The year 1432 appears as a
chronogram created by letters painted in red in
the inscription. Little is known of Hubert van
Eyck, who is recorded as living in Ghent in the
early 1420s. Although the style of the Ghent
Altarpiece is consistent with the style of Jan van
Eyck's signed works, it probably includes work by
Hubert, as well as by anonymous workshop assistants employed by both Hubert and Jan. In
reality, it is a collaborative production that has
been made to appear as stylistically unified as
possible.

A third brother, Lambert van Eyck, was probably also a painter, but his work is lost to history.
Finally, reports from the sixteenth century, not
necessarily reliable, indicate the existence of a
sister named Marguerite van Eyck reputed to
have been active as a painter in Ghent. Jan van
Eyck did not therefore achieve fame in isolation:
some of his clients would have known the work
of his siblings.

◀ *The fact that the subject looks directly at the viewer and that the
painter's motto appears on the upper frame may indicate that this work,
Man in a Red Turban, is a self-portrait. The date October 21, 1433, is
inscribed on the lower frame. Van Eyck uses a dark background to
amplify the volume of the head and picks out tiny details with light.*

THE PROGRAM OF THE GHENT ALTARPIECE

CHRONOLOGY

c. 1385–1390
Jan van Eyck is born.

1425–1428
Is based in Lille, Flanders.

1428–1429
On a ducal embassy to Portugal, paints the portrait of Isabella of Portugal.

1432
Buys a house in Bruges.

early 1430s
Marries.

1436
Is paid to travel abroad, perhaps on diplomatic missions.

1441
Dies.

Dedicated on May 6, 1432, in the Church of Saint John, Ghent (now Saint Bavo's Cathedral), the Ghent Altarpiece was commissioned by the wealthy patrician Joos Vijd and his wife Elizabeth Borluut. It decorated an altar in their private chapel at which mass was said daily "to the honor of God, His Blessed Mother, and all His saints," for the salvation of the souls of the founders and their ancestors. Commemorative portraits of the founders adorn the reverse of the altarpiece.

The iconography is based partly on the Catholic liturgy for All Saints' Day, which includes readings from the New Testament Book of Revelation, but the complex image does not rely on a single theological text. The work visualizes the redemptive mysteries of the Catholic faith. In the interior the remarkable nude figures of Adam and Eve, situated at the upper level, are present as the originators of sin in the world. The beginning of mankind's redemption (deliverance from evil) is represented by the incarnation of Christ at the moment of the Annunciation, painted on the exterior of the altarpiece. Inside, the muted colors and tones of the exterior wings give way to a glorious heavenly landscape. A multitude of holy figures travel on foot and on horseback to adore the mystic lamb of God that stands on the central altar. The lamb, whose blood flows into a chalice, symbolizes the Eucharistic sacrifice of Christ. Dominating the altarpiece is an imposing deesis (a representation of Christ between the Virgin Mary and John the Baptist). Mary and John are seated on either side of a figure who bears the attributes of Christ as king and priest. This arrangement is a symbolic indication that Mary and John will intercede on behalf of mankind at the Last Judgment.

▲ *The Rolin Virgin
(1437/1438) was installed in the
Chapel of Saint Sebastian in the
Church of Notre-Dame-du-Chastel
in Autun, Burgundy. It served as a
memorial painting for Chancellor
Nicholas Rolin, shown kneeling at
a prie-dieu (prayer bench) with a
devotional book in front of him.*

Jan van Eyck, Court Painter

In an age wherein the social status of the typical painter was relatively low, van Eyck gained
prestigious employment. He became court
painter first to Prince John of Bavaria, count of
Hainaut-Holland (c. 1422–1425), and then to
one of Europe's most powerful rulers, Philip the
Good, duke of Burgundy (1425–1441). The
van Eycks were probably from the gentry. Jan's

overt references to his own authorship, through
his signatures and self-portraits, underscore the
high status he achieved as a painter.

As court painter and valet de chambre to the
duke, van Eyck, besides painting, would have
conceived and executed the designs for court festivities and supplied the decorative programs for
the duke's palaces. His ability as a portraitist,
evident in *Man in a Red Turban* (see page 386),

In a work of 1456, the Italian humanist Bartolommeo Fazio described a lost work by van Eyck called the *Lomellini Triptych* (possibly painted around 1436). The triptych consisted of three scenes, the Annunciation, Saint Jerome in his study, and Saint John the Baptist, with portraits of the patrons on the exterior of the wings.

Jan of Gaul has been judged the leading painter of our time. He was not unlettered, particularly in geometry and such arts as contribute to the enrichment of painting, and he is thought for this reason to have discovered many things about the properties of colors recorded by the ancients and learned by him from reading Pliny and other authors. His is a remarkable picture in the private apartments of King Alfonso, in which there is a Virgin Mary notable for its grace and modesty, with an Angel Gabriel, of exceptional beauty and with hair surpassing reality, announcing that the Son of God will be born of her; and a John the Baptist that declares the wonderful sanctity and austerity of his life, and Jerome like a living being in a library done with rare art: for if you move away from it a little it seems it recedes inward and that it has complete books laid open in it, while if you go near it is evident that there is only a summary of these. On the outer side of the same picture is painted Battista Lomellini, whose picture it was—you would judge he lacked only a voice—and the woman whom he loved, of outstanding beauty; and she too is portrayed exactly as she was. Between them, as if through a chink in the wall, falls a ray of sun that you would take to be real sunlight.

Bartolommeo Fazio, *De viris illustribus*

◀ *The man in the* Arnolfini Portrait, *a double portrait of a married couple, may be Giovanni di Nicolao Arnolfini, a merchant from Lucca living in Bruges. His first wife, Costanza Trenta, whom he married in 1426, died before 1433. This portrait may show his second wife.*

was highly prized both at court and among wealthy urban clients. In contrast to Italian and French tradition, which favored the profile portrait, van Eyck painted his sitters in three-quarter view and thus emphasized the three-dimensional form of the sitter's head over abstract line. The almost scientific objectivity of his representations was not intended to capture the shifting moods of emotion or character but conveys a sense of the unchanging qualities of the individual.

Reality and Invention

Painters in the late Middle Ages in western Europe were admired for their ability to represent nature in a lifelike manner, for their powers of imagination, and for their technical skill. In all three areas Jan van Eyck displayed unsurpassed ability. His detailed and systematic scrutiny of the objects and phenomena of the natural world is evident from his unerring depictions of light effects and reflections, of botanically accurate plants and trees, and of the gleam of gold stitches in silk textiles. In short, Van Eyck's paintings appear to represent the world he observed. Yet his apparent realism is deceptive; he did not simply copy what he saw in front of him but also used his

The fountain in this painting, *The Virgin by a Fountain*, *symbolizes Mary's role as the source of life. On the frame is van Eyck's signature in Latin: "Johannes de eyck me fecit + complevit anno 1439" ("Jan van Eyck made and completed me in the year 1439").*

Arnolfini Portrait (1434), for example, van Eyck depicted in a convex mirror on the rear wall of the interior the reflection of two small figures entering the room through the doorway, one of them probably van Eyck himself. This optical device locates these small figures in the same spatial position as the viewer and thus extends the pictorial action into the world outside the painting. Inside the room the merchant Giovanni Arnolfini and his wife appear to greet their visitors. The mirror offers two viewpoints of this same event.

Van Eyck frequently attempts to extend the picture into the world of the spectator and to engage the spectator in the world of the picture. The foot of Adam in the Ghent Altarpiece projects over the ledge he stands on and is foreshortened as if seen from below. The figure is thus adjusted to the viewing point of the spectator and seems to project into real space. In the scene of the Annunciation, the wooden frames of the painting appear to cast diagonal shadows into the Virgin's chamber: by matching the direction of the shadows to that of the real light that shines in from the window in the Vijd Chapel, van Eyck suggests that light from the real world has traveled directly into the realm of the picture.

The Market for Devotional Works

There is good evidence that a number of small devotional works by van Eyck, such as his *Virgin by a Fountain* or his true portrait of Christ, were created in multiple versions. Van Eyck adapted the intimate pose of the Virgin and Child in his *Virgin by a Fountain* from well-known and deeply venerated Byzantine icons—for example, the Virgin Kykkotissa, versions of an image at Kykkos Monastery, on the Mediterranean island of Cyprus, traditionally attributed to Saint Luke. The fact that van Eyck's picture generated a series of copies and variations is evidence that it became a revered image in its own right. Van Eyck thus freely borrowed a recognizable motif from an ancient icon to invest his picture with comparable status.

Such devotional and iconic images for personal use had enormous appeal among a broad range of religious and lay patrons. In contrast to a commissioned painting such as the *Rolin Virgin*,

imagination. He was also aided in the creation of his works by a stock of workshop drawings that served as a storehouse of images and ideas. Van Eyck excelled in imagining things he had never seen, as is illustrated by the hybrid beasts carved in the stone capitals of his Romanesque architecture (seen in the *Rolin Virgin*), as well as in representing phenomena that he had observed only fleetingly in nature, such as shifting clouds or splashing water.

Van Eyck used his skill in mimicking nature and his inventive intellect to construct and guide the viewer's experience of his pictures. In the which contains a portrait of the patron, such small devotional images could be made speculatively and sold ready-made from the workshop. In such open market transactions, the price of the object depends not on a prior arrangement between the patron and the artist but on the market forces of supply and demand. By the later 1430s van Eyck's workshop assistants were evidently making copies and variations of popular devotional works for sale on the open market.

Van Eyck's clients included successful artisans, members of the wealthy middle classes and old patrician families of the Netherlands, foreign merchants, and rich noblemen and princes. The numerous foreign merchants resident in the major trading and commercial center of Bruges were important buyers. They not only commissioned paintings from van Eyck but probably also bought noncommissioned devotional works and exported all these paintings to Spain, Italy, Germany, or England along trade routes. Van Eyck's international reputation relied partly on the leading position of Bruges within a global trade network.

After van Eyck's death in 1441, his workshop continued in production. Some Eyckian panel paintings for private devotion date from that period, such as the *Saint Jerome in His Study* (now at the Detroit Institute of Arts) that is dated 1442. It is likely that Jan's widow, Margaret van Eyck, or perhaps his brother Lambert ran the workshop for a period in the early 1440s.

▲ *As a biblical scholar, Saint Jerome (d. 420) is shown in his study. In the Middle Ages the belief that he had been created a cardinal led him to be portrayed in the red robes and broad-brimmed hat of that office. In typical Eyckian fashion, the painting includes a number of everyday objects. Hanging from the shelf is a brass astrolabe, an instrument used for studying the heavens. This image was made in multiple versions in van Eyck's workshop.*

THE TRANSMISSION OF OIL PAINTING

By the sixteenth century Jan van Eyck was incorrectly credited with the "invention" of oil painting. The medium was in fact in use as early as the twelfth century in northern Europe, but Jan van Eyck perfected the technique.

In oil painting pigments are mixed with linseed or walnut oil to produce a paint medium that is slow to dry and highly flexible. Oil paint can produce many types of descriptive mark. These properties make it suitable for imitating the broad range of tones found in nature as well as for mimicking texture. The vibrant areas of red and green color in van Eyck's paintings were created by applying oil paint in thin, transparent layers called glazes. The extraordinary realism and visual brilliance of Eyckian painting was made possible in part by the medium of oil.

Early Netherlandish oil technique was admired as a novelty by Mediterranean painters trained to paint in the less versatile medium of egg tempera (in which the pigments are bound with egg yolk). The Neapolitan painter Niccolò Colantonio, for example, one of the first Italian artists to imitate Netherlandish realism, was working in an oil medium by about 1445. He had perhaps learned this technique around 1440 from the Netherlandish artist Bartélemy d'Eyck, possibly a relative of Jan van Eyck. By the early sixteenth century, oil had become the chief medium of European painting.

◄ *The Old Testament motifs van Eyck introduced into the* Rolin Virgin *(of which this is a detail) give a larger dimension to the picture's meaning.*

early decades of the sixteenth century. Well-known features of Eyckian art, such as the trademark depiction of a flight of geese flying in the sky in V-formation, were widely used by artists who intended to capitalize on van Eyck's success by associating themselves with him.

By the mid-sixteenth century, when humanists began to chart their lives and works, the van Eycks were regarded as the founders of the whole tradition of Netherlandish painting and as its most perfect exponents. The Ghent Altarpiece, described in 1495 as a summation of the whole art of painting, was held up as an exemplary painting that continued to offer a challenge to all later artists. The myth of van Eyck's invention of oil painting ensured his continued fame in literary works on the arts throughout the eighteenth and nineteenth centuries.

FURTHER READING

Dhanens, Elisabeth. *Hubert and Jan van Eyck.* New York, 1980.

———. *Van Eyck: The Ghent Altarpiece.* New York, 1973.

Foister, Susan, Susan Jones, and Delphine Cool, eds. *Investigating Jan van Eyck.* Turnhout, 2000.

Weale, W. H. J. *Hubert and John van Eyck.* London, 1908.

Susan Frances Jones

SEE ALSO:

• Burgundy • Painting and Sculpture • Renaissance
• Trade

Posthumous Reputation

Although few artists grasped the full range of optical and illusionistic devices van Eyck aimed at the spectator, his pictorial realism was copied everywhere. In Bruges and elsewhere, his innovations were imitated and exaggerated in panel painting and manuscript illumination into the

Ferdinand and Isabella

THE MARRIAGE OF KING FERDINAND OF ARAGON (1452–1516) AND QUEEN ISABELLA OF CASTILE (1451–1504) UNITED THEIR RESPECTIVE KINGDOMS TO FORM THE POWERFUL EARLY MODERN KINGDOM OF SPAIN.

Ferdinand and Isabella each ruled a kingdom of their own. Through their marriage they created the kingdom of Spain, conquered the Muslim kingdom of Granada, founded the Spanish Inquisition, expelled Jews and Muslims who refused conversion to Christianity, and underwrote the voyages of Christopher Columbus.

From Royal Childhood to Marriage

Isabella, the elder of the two monarchs, had a difficult childhood. Her father, King John II of Castile, died when Isabella was only three, and her mother was emotionally unstable. Isabella and her younger brother Alfonso were raised in large part by their grandmother while they lived far from the court and from their half brother, the new king Enrique (Henry) IV. Until Henry IV fathered a daughter, Alfonso and Isabella were next in line for the throne, and even after the birth of Henry's daughter, Joan la Beltraneja, instability continued. In 1464, when Isabella was thirteen, rebellious nobles who were tired of Henry's rule claimed Alfonso as their king and began a civil war. War in Castile would continue for over a decade. Alfonso's death in July 1468 did not bring hostilities to an immediate end. Instead, seventeen-year-old Isabella declared herself heir to the throne of Castile. Finally, in September both sides admitted to being exhausted by the conflict. The half siblings met at Los Toros de Guisando to declare their agreement: Henry IV would continue to rule, but Isabella would be his heir.

Ferdinand's stabler family was also touched by war. When Ferdinand was only five, his father, John II (a cousin of Isabella's father), was given the crown of Aragon, which was immediately plunged into civil war. Rebellious nobles from

▶ Ferdinand and Isabella's marriage in 1469 united a territory that extended across the Iberian Peninsula. This map shows the Spanish kingdoms during their reign

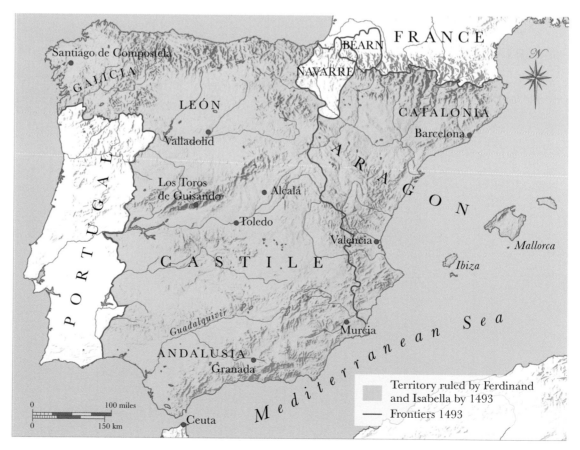

Catalonia, one of the kingdoms in Aragon, named Ferdinand's half brother its king. When the latter died in 1461, John II named nine-year-old Ferdinand his heir, to the nobility's dismay. Fighting continued, and the nobility looked to Henry IV, Isabella's half brother, for leadership. John II of Aragon also saw in Castile a counter to the pressures of the French and the rebellious Catalans. For him the solution was marriage between his intelligent, militarily gifted son and the heiress to the Castilian throne.

Henry IV, meanwhile, was hard pressed to control his half sister and erstwhile heir, Isabella. He had wanted to determine whom she would marry, but the independent-minded Isabella had her own ideas. After considering marriage to the king of Portugal, the heir to France, or a member of the English royal family, she determined to marry Ferdinand. She and Ferdinand were close in age; Ferdinand was by all accounts a dashing young man, and their alliance would be useful to Isabella. Ferdinand might have imagined that he would one day rule Castile as its king, but the agreement the couple signed before their wedding suggested otherwise. They would share all royal titles and sign all documents jointly, and Ferdinand would abide by Isabella's decisions in granting lordships or other honors. Negotiations were carried out in secret to avoid Henry IV's hostility. The marriage proved to be a political success; it was also, according to contemporaries, a genuine love affair.

Establishing Control

The young couple moved quickly to consolidate support for the marriage and the political alliance

▶ A fifteenth-century painting by an unknown artist of Queen Isabella as a young woman.

behind it. They needed that support because Henry named his daughter Joan as his heir the following year, in 1470. The Castilian nobility remained deeply divided, and Castile threatened to follow Aragon into civil war. John II was finally able to pacify Barcelona in 1472; Ferdinand's future kingdom was finally secure and ready to throw its support behind Isabella without distractions. That support was critical because when Henry IV died in 1474, Isabella was crowned queen of Castile, and her kingdom plunged back into civil war. Joan's supporters were not immediately pacified, and Isabella relied on Ferdinand's military ability to help her win the war against Joan and her supporters. The civil wars finally drew to a close in 1479, the same year that Ferdinand inherited the throne of Aragon. At the beginning of the year 1480, therefore, Ferdinand and Isabella were each secure on their respective thrones and well positioned to extend their authority over their subjects.

The years following 1479 were marked by a new aggressiveness in Isabella and Ferdinand's joint rule. Even beforehand, in 1476, they had established the *Santa Hermandad,* a centrally organized constabulary and judicial tribunal for

A sixteenth-century Spanish painting of King Ferdinand of Aragon. Though he was praised for his pragmatism by no less a figure than Machiavelli, it is unclear how Ferdinand himself would have greeted such praise.

In 1513 Ferdinand was cited by Niccolò Machiavelli as a prime example of a great prince:

Nothing makes a prince more esteemed than great undertakings and example of his unusual talents. In our own times we have Ferdinand of Aragon, the present King of Spain. This man can be called almost a new prince, since from being a weak ruler he became, through fame and glory, the first king of Christendom; and if you consider his accomplishments, you will find them all very grand and some even extraordinary. In the beginning of his reign he attacked Granada, and that enterprise was the basis of his state. First, he acted while things were peaceful and when he had no fear of opposition: he kept the minds of the barons of Castile busy with this, and they, concentrating on that war, did not consider changes at home. And he acquired, through that means, reputation and power over them without their noticing it; he was able to maintain armies with money from the church and the people, and with that long war he laid a basis for his own army, which has since brought him honor. Besides this, in order to be able to undertake greater enterprises, always using religion for his own purposes, he turned to a pious cruelty, hunting down and clearing out the Moors from his kingdom: no example could be more pathetic or more unusual than this. He attacked Africa, under the same cloak of religion; he undertook the invasion of Italy; he finally attacked France. And in such a manner, he has always done and planned great deeds which have always kept the minds of his subjects in suspense and amazed and occupied with their outcome. And one action of his would spring from another in such a way that between one and the other he would never give men enough time to be able to work calmly against him.

Niccolò Machiavelli, *The Prince*

THE HOLY OFFICE OF THE INQUISITION

When Isabella and Ferdinand authorized the Holy Office of the Inquisition, they did not create an entirely new institution; rather, they adapted existing institutions toward new ends. The Roman Catholic Church had run inquisitions during the Middle Ages, but most of them had ceased to function by the fifteenth century. Isabella's half brother, Enrique IV, had toyed with the idea of establishing a royal inquisition without success. When Isabella and Ferdinand wanted a means to investigate potential heresy among converted Jews, an inquisition (another name for an inquiry) was the logical solution. The monarchs successfully petitioned the pope to give them full authority over the Inquisition and thus made it a royal institution rather than a Catholic one. Furthermore, Isabella was worried that the accused might exact retribution against those who testified against them and insisted that prosecution testimony be anonymous. This ruling was a variation from the rules of Roman and canon (church) law that the Inquisition otherwise followed.

In many ways the Inquisition did not match the stereotypical image of it. It adhered to rules of evidence: for example, any charge required two witnesses to be proven, and hearsay by itself was not sufficient to convict. It had jurisdiction only over Christians, not Jews or Muslims (nor later, Native Americans in the New World). Most important, it was not an all-encompassing, terrifying institution that kept all of Spain cowed and in fear. In reality, it was little different from other secular or religious courts of the period.

Neither, however, was the Inquisition a benign influence. People were tortured and executed under its auspices, and even those found innocent sometimes had their goods seized by the court. In later years the Inquisition turned its attention to bigamy, Protestantism, and other crimes of nonconversos, or Old Christians. However, between 1480 and 1525 the Holy Office of the Inquisition tried a significant percentage of Spain's conversos (Jews who had converted to Christianity). Scholars vigorously debate whether these conversos were guilty of the Jewish practices ascribed to them. Certainly, some conversos did practice Judaism at some time for a variety of reasons, while others were genuinely devout Christians.

▼ *The Alhambra Palace, taken over by Ferdinand and Isabella in 1492, had been built mainly between 1238 and 1358 by the Muslim monarchs of Granada. Isabella and Ferdinand used this Muslim palace as their residence when they were in Granada.*

each town and village. Men from each community would band together to defend the community outside city bounds and administer justice to wrongdoers. Isabella and Ferdinand also sent *corregidores,* royal officials empowered to judge cases and supervise public order, into dozens of cities in Castile and Aragon. The monarchs established a uniform system of appellate (appeal) courts, the highest of which, located in Valladolid and Granada, were called *chancillerias.* They established the Holy Office of the Inquisition, the only institution to hold sway in all Spain, for the purpose of reforming and punishing heretics. In addition, they encouraged reform within the Roman Catholic Church.

Jews, Muslims, and Converts

One of Isabella's and Ferdinand's concerns was the number of unassimilated religious minorities in their combined kingdoms. There were large numbers of Muslims in Valencia and elsewhere in the crown of Aragon, smaller numbers of Muslims in Castile, and Jews in both kingdoms. In the minds of many people, this class of unassimilated religious minorities also included converted Jews and Muslims, known as conversos and Moriscos, respectively. Anxiety about this situation—and how the monarchs responded to it—would become one of the hallmarks of their reign.

Jews had suffered in Iberia since at least 1391, when anti-Jewish riots had swept across the peninsula. At that time numerous Jews were forced to convert to Christianity; others converted voluntarily in the months and years after the riots. Now Ferdinand and Isabella grew increasingly concerned about these conversos, who had begun to assimilate into Christian society. Apparently Isabella especially worried that at least some of these conversos continued to practice Judaism in secret. Isabella and Ferdinand considered such subterfuge dangerous for religious and political reasons. Their solution to this dilemma was to establish the Inquisition, a tribunal that would investigate and punish insincere Christians.

Unlike the predominantly urban Jews, Muslims lived largely in rural areas as agricultural laborers. In Ferdinand's Valencia, Muslims made up as much as 30 percent of the population and maintained their status without similar pressure to convert throughout Ferdinand's reign. In 1482, however, Ferdinand and Isabella began their war against Granada, and the status of Muslims in Castile soon changed. Ferdinand led the campaign personally and with success. In the years after that war, tolerance faded, and between 1499 and 1501, all of Granada was forcibly converted. One year later, on February 12, 1502, all of Castile's Muslims were forced to convert as well.

1492: The "Marvelous Year"

After a long period of civil and political unrest, in the 1480s Isabella and Ferdinand began to see the fruits of their pacification work. For the Catholic monarchs (their official style was "their Catholic majesties") the events of 1492 must have seemed a sign of divine favor. It was called in Latin the *annus mirabilis*, the "marvelous year."

The momentous events began on January 2, when the kingdom of Granada fell to the combined Spanish armies. Ferdinand's troops had besieged the city of Granada since the spring of 1491, and by fall it was clear that the city could not hold out much longer. Rulers on both sides signed formal documents of surrender on November 25, 1491, and set the formal surrender for January 2, 1492. Isabella and Ferdinand were present for the ceremony, in which Boabdil, ruler of Granada, handed the keys to the gates of the city to Ferdinand, who handed them to Isabella. Ferdinand and Isabella granted Boabdil and Granada's citizens relatively generous terms. The monarchs promised local residents that they could retain their land and remain in the city unharmed. The kingdom would become part of Castile (hence, technically under the dominion of Isabella rather than Ferdinand) and under the jurisdiction of a Castilian governor, but residents could continue to practice Islam and to operate under Muslim law. They could also continue Muslim systems of education and were exempt from taxation for a period of three years. Boabdil was even given territory in the nearby Alpujarras Mountains.

▼ *This 1485 painting by Pedro Berruguete is called Auto-da Fé, after the public ceremony at the conclusion of an inquisitorial trial when the sentences were read out and the condemned were subsequently punished or put to death by the secular authorities.*

Later stories claimed that Boabdil wept as he returned to his castle, the Alhambra. According to legend his mother berated him and said, "Do not weep like a woman for what you could not defend as a man." What is certain is that Christians in Castile and Aragon rejoiced to celebrate the end of nearly seven hundred years of Muslim rule on the Iberian peninsula.

Yet this event was only the beginning of the marvelous year. Only a few months later, at the end of March, Ferdinand and Isabella signed a royal decree to expel all Jews from their combined kingdoms by July 31. Scholars continue to debate the king and queen's intentions. Their stated reason—and it seems that they believed it—was that they were concerned that Jews were making it difficult for conversos to practice Christianity. Many scholars also suspect that Ferdinand and Isabella had assumed that most Jews would convert to Christianity rather than leave, as indeed some did. In addition, while it does not seem that profit was their primary motivation, the monarchs and others did profit from the expulsion. Whatever Ferdinand and Isabella had imagined, the consequences were grave for the Jews. Desperate Jewish families were impoverished as unscrupulous merchants bought their property for pennies; even if they had received a

▲ *In this anonymous sixteenth-century painting, called* The Virgin of the Catholic Monarchs, *Ferdinand and Isabella are depicted praying before Mary and the baby Jesus. The figure at the far left, behind Ferdinand, is Spain's inquisitor general, Tomás de Torquemada. The other figures on the left are Saint Thomas Aquinas and Ferdinand's son, John. Kneeling next to Isabella is her daughter, Isabel; the other figures on the right are Saint Dominic and the chronicler Pedro Mártir de Anglería. Religious devotion was an important part of Isabella and Ferdinand's justification of their rule.*

Although this legal document is dated March 31, it was actually published a month later and thus gave Jews a month less to prepare to leave. Many scholars believe that this delay was caused by influential advisers who were urging Ferdinand and Isabella not to expel the Jews:

You know well, or ought to know, that whereas we have been informed that in these our kingdoms there were some wicked Christians who Judaized and apostatized from our holy Catholic faith, the great cause of which was interaction between the Jews and these Christians. . . . Furthermore, we procured and gave orders that inquisition should be made in our aforementioned kingdoms and lordships. . . . we desired to content ourselves by commanding [the Jews] to leave all cities, towns, and villages of Andalusia where it appears that they have done the greatest injury, believing that that would be sufficient so that those of other cities, towns, and villages of our kingdoms and lordships would cease to do and commit the aforesaid acts. And since we are informed that neither that step nor the passing of sentence against the said Jews who have been most guilty of the said crimes and delicts against our holy Catholic faith have been sufficient as a complete remedy . . . therefore, we, with the counsel and advice of prelates, great noblemen of our kingdoms, and other persons of learning and wisdom of our council, having taken deliberation about this matter, resolve to order the said Jews and Jewesses of our kingdoms to depart and never to return or come back to them or to any of them.

Quoted in Edward Peters, trans., *Jewish History and Gentile Memory: The Expulsion of 1492*

fair price, Jews were forbidden from taking gold, silver, money, arms, or horses out of the country. Many of them left the country with few possessions. However, life away from Spain was hard, too. Many Jews who moved to North Africa suffered violent persecution there. Others relocated to Portugal, but all Portugal's Jews were forcibly converted in 1497. Navarre, another destination for fleeing Jews, expelled its Jewish population in 1499. Within a few years many emigrants chose to convert to Christianity and return to their homeland.

Most Jews had not yet left the country when Isabella and Ferdinand launched another project in Spain's miraculous year: their commission of Christopher Columbus. Columbus hoped to find a new route to the Spice Islands; what he found instead were the islands of the Caribbean. The full implications of this new venture were not at all clear in October 1492. The monarchs sensed, however, the potential boon of making landfall across the Atlantic.

Meanwhile a scholar at the University of Alcalá named Elio Antonio de Nebrija published a book in 1492. It was a new kind of book in Europe: a grammar not of a classical language such as Latin or Greek but of the everyday Castilian spoken in Isabella's kingdom. In justification of this original idea, Nebrija averred that language is the companion of empire. As such, Castilian, or Spanish, merited his scholarly attention. Indeed, by 1492 it was becoming increasingly clear that Castilian would be the language of a new empire that stretched across the Iberian Peninsula and beyond.

Spain after Isabella

When Isabella died in late 1504, it was not certain what would happen to the united kingdoms. Ferdinand and Isabella's only surviving child, Joan, was now queen of Castile, but she and her husband, Philip of Burgundy, remained elsewhere in Europe. While she was away, Ferdinand was administrator and later regent of Castile. Ferdinand remarried, and if his son by his new wife had survived, Castile and Aragon might well have been separated. However, Ferdinand's son died after only a few hours. Furthermore,

◀ This fourteenth-century drawing from Barcelona, Spain, portrays a Jewish service at a synagogue. The Spanish inquisitors believed that as long as there was an active Jewish community in Spain, all their attempts to deter and punish the practice of Judaism would fail.

According to the medieval code of courtly love, a man was to serve his beloved in much the same way as a vassal served a lord; indeed, many poets of the Middle Ages and the Renaissance borrowed heavily from the language of feudalism when describing amorous encounters:

...No cruelty, disdain, absence, despair,
No, nor her steadfast constancy, can deter
My vassal heart from ever hon'ring her.
Though these be powerful arguments to prove
I love in vain, yet I must ever love.
Say, if she frown, when you that word rehearse,
Service in prose is oft call'd love in verse ...
Thus has this cruel lady us'd a true
Servant and subject to herself and you;
Nor know I, great Love, if my life be lent
To show thy mercy or my punishment...."

Thomas Carew, "My Mistress Commanding Me to Return Her Letters"

► *This painting from a Bohemian cycle of months of around 1400 shows laborers making hay on their lord's land. Relations between lords and peasants are central to an economic understanding of feudalism.*

no powers over the people who worked the land; a man might declare himself to be the vassal of his beloved to signify his devotion to her; a man who was technically the vassal of a lord might feel himself under no obligation to serve and defend him. On the other hand, there was the fact that a territory technically a fief, though it might have had little or no consequence for centuries, could in certain circumstances become a significant possession and provide a legal underpinning to its lord's political claims.

Fiefs

The classic model of feudal society has been the so-called feudal pyramid. A ruler would grant land in fief to powerful men, who would be his tenants-in-chief in return for their loyalty and service, particularly military service. The tenant-in-chief would bring with him when summoned to accompany the ruler on campaign a specified number of soldiers, usually men trained in the specialized skills of fighting on horseback. In turn, the tenants-in-chief would subinfeudate their own men (that is, grant them lands), again in return for loyalty and service, in order to make up the contingent of troops they had to provide. Subinfeudation might proceed further; the tenants would have their own subtenants. The grant of a fief was not a grant of full ownership of the land but only of the possession of it for a period of years or even for life, but the fief would revert to the lord who had granted it at the end of that term.

Few historians now would argue that this description of how European society was organized in the Middle Ages was true. The only time at which it bore any relationship to reality was immediately after territory had been conquered, when the victorious commander and new ruler was able to reward those who had fought with him through the distribution of the lands that had been taken. England after the Norman Conquest of 1066, when Duke William of Normandy conquered the kingdom, took the crown, and gave great estates to the men who had come over with him from France, used to be seen as the prime example of how feudal society functioned. Yet it has long been recognized that many aspects of this system existed before the Norman Conquest under the Anglo-Saxon kings, that by no means all land was held in fief, and that the grants of fiefs soon deviated from the simple chain from king to tenant-in-chief to subtenant.

Clear and graphic as the concept of the feudal pyramid may be, it is wise to discard it. For most of western Europe, it would never have been an accurate picture. Much land was not held in fief, and in some areas there were very few fiefs at all. Not all fiefs were land: money fiefs—where a grant of revenue from a toll, for example, would be made in fief—are as old as grants of land. From the beginning it is evident that fiefs were inherited and that those who held fiefs would expect to pass the fief on to their heirs. Not to be allowed to inherit a fief would be a cause for grievance, even rebellion. Technically the grant might have to be renewed, but a lord would need good reason to refuse this renewal if he were not to be regarded as behaving unjustly.

Some lands held in fief were not originally granted to the man who held them or to his ancestors but had been lands held in full owner-

ship, which were surrendered to a lord, who then granted them back to the original owner in fief, as happened to some estates in the duchy of Milan in the fifteenth century, for example. In Portugal at the end of that century, the forceful king John II refused to take the customary oath made by Portuguese kings when they came to the throne to maintain the existing forms of land tenure; he insisted instead that all the powerful landholders hold their estates as fiefs from him. The conversion of lands into fiefs in this way would weaken the landholders' position and make them more dependent on the goodwill of the prince, as John plainly intended it should. He also wanted to make it easier for his own officials to have access to the great estates of the nobility. Until his reign the king's powers to raise troops or levy taxes or to exercise jurisdiction on privately owned estates had been very limited.

▲ *This statue of King John II of Portugal stands in the courtyard of the university he founded at Coimbra. John changed the pattern of relations with the great nobles of his kingdom by insisting that they hold their estates as fiefs.*

In other areas, to hold land in fief could give the landholder greater powers over its revenues and the people who lived and worked on it than the ownership of the land outright would do, because with the fief would come powers of jurisdiction and perhaps a share in the taxes that were levied on it. Often major fiefs were held with extensive powers of criminal jurisdiction, sometimes even including the right to execute those found guilty of serious crimes. Fief holders might be granted the right to collect public taxes and keep some or all of the proceeds, as some holders of major fiefs in France could do, as well as levy tolls or other dues for themselves. Some fief holders engaged in this practice even if they did not, in theory, have the right to do so. The association of fiefs with the exercise of public authority in this way gave fiefs a prestige that other forms of property did not have. The holding of an estate in fief, especially if it meant sharing in the powers of government, could confer greater prestige and revenues than outright ownership of the estate would do.

In France the prestige attached to fiefs became associated with noble status, even when fiefs could be bought and sold like other property—as lesser fiefs often could be. The acquisition of a fief was one way in which those who had made their fortune in trade, for example, could seek to be accepted as noblemen. However, some questioned whether a man who was not a noble could legitimately hold a fief at all.

There were disadvantages to holding lands in fief, other than the (usually remote) possibility that the grant might be withdrawn. Sometimes the lord could claim payments, for example, contributions if he had to pay a ransom following capture in battle. Most lucrative for the lord and most troublesome for the fief holders was the lord's claim to act as guardian of minor heirs until they reached the age of majority and to arrange the marriage of heiresses. These rights of wardship could be abused, sold, or granted to others, and the relatives of the children might buy out the rights of the lord so that they could take care of their offspring and their estates.

Problems could also arise if there was no direct male heir. Conventions about which relatives could inherit fiefs and whether women could inherit them or pass on rights to inherit them to their sons varied in different areas and at different times. To some extent, much depended

▼ *In this fifteenth-century manuscript illumination, King Henry VI of England invests John Talbot, earl of Shrewsbury, who kneels before him in homage, with the sword of office as great constable of France.*

The British historian Susan Reynolds has written an influential book, *Fiefs and Vassals,* in which she criticizes feudalism—both the word and the concept. She argues that, even though the words *fief* and *vassal* can be found in medieval sources, modern understanding of these terms has been shaped by definitions elaborated by lawyers and scholars in the sixteenth, seventeenth, and eighteenth centuries. The ultimate source of the definitions of the two words was a legal treatise on fiefs, written in Lombardy in the early twelfth century, that became known as the *Libri feudorum (The Books of Fiefs).* This treatise cannot, however, be read as an accurate picture of the nature of fiefs and the customs relating to them in twelfth-century Lombardy, let alone as an authoritative statement of laws applicable throughout western Europe over several centuries.

◀ *This seventeenth-century painting by Pieter Brueghel III (1589–1639) portrays peasants paying their dues. Often at least some dues would be paid in kind.*

on the circumstances of each case. If the estates were valuable and the rules uncertain, the lord might be ready to take the lands into his own possession or grant them to someone else, perhaps one of his relatives.

Vassals and Homage

According to the classic picture of feudal society, a man who received the grant of a fief would in return swear homage to the lord; he would promise loyal devotion and service to his lord, and the lord would promise to protect the man in return. The man who received the land would be considered to have become the vassal of the lord. In theory heirs who came into possession of a fief would renew their homage, just as the grant of the fief would be renewed. If a new lord took over lands in fief, all his vassals would come to pay homage to him.

It is once again true that different rules and conventions prevailed in different areas at different times. Not all men who held fiefs would be considered vassals; nor all men considered vassals would hold fiefs. Ceremonies of homage sometimes took place, particularly when the major barons came to swear homage to a new king or prince. Frequently, men would hold estates in fief from more than one lord, and conflicts of loyalty could arise. A powerful lord might demand that his vassals swear liege homage to him, whereby their vows of loyalty to him would take precedence over their vows of loyalty to any other lord. Rulers in particular would want obligations to them to override all other obligations.

It was a commonplace that society was divided into three groups, orders, or estates, but definitions of those three groups varied. Theologians favored the idea that they were defined by function: those who prayed, who were naturally the most important; those who fought and had the duty to defend those who prayed; and those who worked to support the other two groups. By the later Middle Ages, the prevailing definition was related to this view but with more emphasis on social status. At this time the orders were commonly seen as the clergy (those who prayed), the nobility (those who fought to defend society), and the commons, or third estate (those who worked in agriculture or as artisans or merchants). The tenure of fiefs and the status of vassals became particularly associated with the second order, the nobles.

▲ A portrait of Francesco Maria I della Rovere, duke of Urbino, who held his lands from the pope in fief but commanded the Venetian army.

man: who should swear homage to whom? Alternatively, a man might hold an estate of another man whom he would not acknowledge as his social superior and whom he would not want to recognize as his lord, let alone his liege lord. A man might be the vassal of two powerful lords, each of whom claimed liege homage. Dilemmas that arose out of such conflicts could persist for generations. John, duke of Brittany, owed his victory over a rival claimant to the duchy partly to the support of King Edward III of England, and he was reluctant to swear liege homage to the king of France. The terms of the oath of homage he swore to King Charles V of France in 1366 evaded the problem: he rendered homage to Charles as his predecessors had done, but it was not stipulated whether it was liege homage. This ambiguous solution continued to be employed for a century, until King Louis XI in 1461 told Duke Francis II of Brittany that he would not ask for liege homage. However, the king did not tell him that he wanted to regard the duke not as his vassal but as his subject, a greater degree of subordination.

The term *vassal* was not exclusively associated with the tenure of fiefs; it had the connotation of a personal association between lord and man. A ruler could claim that a man was his vassal not because that man held fiefs from him but because he wished to stress an element of personal obligation that should overcome other interests and loyalties. For example, the popes in the late fifteenth and early sixteenth centuries tried to lay a prior claim to the services of Roman barons who were sought after as military commanders by other powers by claiming that the barons were their vassals and could not serve others without the permission of the pope.

It was by no means clear, however, where the loyalties of many vassals should lie. Complex patterns of tenure of fiefs created complex networks of obligations. A man might hold an estate of a man who in turn held another estate of another

▲ Society's three orders, or estates, appear on this fifteenth-century manuscript page: clergy surround the pope at the top, nobles and soldiers surround the king in the center, and the commons are at the bottom.

Counsel and Consent

The obligations between lord and vassal were reciprocal. A lord could look for loyalty but not blind obedience. He would lose the loyalty of his vassals if he did not treat them well; if a vassal felt that he had been ill-treated or dishonored by his lord, he could renounce his homage, although if he did so, he had to give up any fiefs he held from him as well.

Among the duties and rights of a vassal were the duty to give counsel to his lord and the right to be consulted by him. As a rule, the major barons of a kingdom claimed the right to advise the king and to some degree represent the interests of the kingdom. If it was considered that a ruler governed too harshly, unjustly, or unwisely, the barons might claim the right to point out to him the error of his ways. The rights and duties of a ruler cannot be reduced to the attributes of a liege lord; his power and authority had other important foundations. Nevertheless, the idea that great landholders had a right to a voice in the conduct of the affairs of the kingdom was a significant political concept. If the king was a minor, landholders wanted at least some representation in the royal council so they could have some say in and bear some of the responsibility for the supervision of the kingdom. In general, barons were less interested in taking part in routine meetings or seeing to the daily business of administration.

The assumption that the major landed nobles were the natural counselors of the king contributed to the development of representative institutions such as Parliament in England and the States General in France. Large gatherings of the nobility, summoned to discuss important matters and to give their advice and perhaps their consent, were the forerunners of assemblies in which nobles were joined by representatives of the commons, or third estate, usually sent by towns and cities and sometimes by representatives of the clergy as well. In these larger assemblies nobles usually continued to meet separately. Historians have tended to pay more attention to the development of the assemblies of the commons—perhaps because these assemblies had the important role of giving consent to the levying of taxes; the power to do so gave the commoners considerable leverage when they made requests to the monarch in return for the money they had granted. This role was critical to the development of the House of Commons in England.

Barons could also claim to represent the community when they formed leagues against the monarch. Although it can be hard to disentangle

RICHARD
Earl of

▲ A detail from an unattributed seventeenth-century portrait of Richard Neville, earl of Warwick.

the personal motives—the grievances and feuds, resentments and jealousies—that usually drove the participants in the leagues to rebel, the rebellious barons were often concerned about wider issues as well. In times of peace or war, relations between the prince and the barons were still the core of political life in the sixteenth century in much of Europe.

Military Service

According to the classic model, the primary reason for the development of the system of fiefs was to enable lords to have men fully equipped and trained to fight on horseback whenever they were needed. Fiefs were granted to fighting men so that they had the support and resources they needed to acquire and maintain the expensive horses and arms that all mounted warriors required. In England, for example, fiefs were assessed for knight service, the *servitium debitum*, that is, the number of knights or fully equipped mounted soldiers they were bound to provide. Feudal levies—summons to the holders of fiefs to perform their military service in the feudal array—were last issued in England in the late fourteenth century, but Christian rulers in Spain issued feudal levies during the campaign to conquer Islamic Granada in the late fifteenth century, and feudal levies were still being issued in France in the late sixteenth century.

As a method of raising an effective army, however, feudal levies were problematic. One fundamental difficulty was that service was usually only for a limited period, such as forty days. This period might be enough for a warlord to gather his men for a raid on a neighbor but not for a full-scale military campaign, especially if the countdown began from when the contingent left home rather than from when it arrived at the mustering point. Many fiefs split up and were divided among heirs or had parts sold off to raise cash; the fact that an individual holding might entail only part of the service of a knight complicated the arrangements for the levy. Even when fiefs had not been divided up in this way, the expense of equipping a mounted warrior,

◀ *Military service by holders of fiefs was typically as armored horsemen—such as these mounted warriors from a painting of the Battle of San Romano (1432) by the Italian Paolo Uccello (1397–1475).*

especially a fully equipped knight, grew so much as weapons and armor for men and horses became more complex that more land was needed to support each man. Therefore, the number of men a given fief could be expected to supply was reduced. There might be limitations on how far away from home a vassal would be expected to fight. As a lord would expect to stay in command of the men he brought with him, it was difficult to establish an effective hierarchy of command and to use coordinated tactics on the battlefield. Additionally, there was the problem that the fief holder might be too young, too old,

too ill, or otherwise incapable of performing military service.

On the whole, it was easier to collect money from fief holders in lieu of military service and pay soldiers to fight. Paid soldiers had long been the core of medieval armies and increasingly became the dominant element. The English solution was the levy of a tax called scutage on those who owed military service, and the proceeds were used to raise paid troops. Even if they were being paid, barons might still bring more men than they were being paid for, partly out of pride or perhaps to attract the bounty of a grateful king.

Bastard feudalism has become a central focus of studies of late medieval England. Much emphasis has been put on the replacement of land by money as the foundation of the bond between lord and man and on the formal written contracts, called indentures, by which men promised service in peace and war in return for payment. The indentures made by John of Gaunt, son of Edward III, in the later fourteenth century have been analyzed closely and were long regarded as typical. Historians now recognize that not only was John of Gaunt's retinue exceptionally large but that he made more use of indentures than other lords tended to do. It is also recognized that grants of money rather than land were known long before the fourteenth century.

Much attention has also been paid to livery and maintenance, particularly to breaches of the peace by retinues of armed men wearing the badge or livery of their lord, who would be protected by him—by force if necessary—if they were brought before the courts. Legislation by the Tudor monarchs against retaining and restrictions on the grants of livery were held to have checked these abuses. Some historians argue that English noblemen up to the mid-seventeenth century could still maintain large retinues and show marked disrespect for the law in support of their men. It is clear that features identified as typical of bastard feudalism can be found long before and long after the period when it is supposed to have flourished.

▼ *Coats of arms and distinctive helmet crests helped identify a lord; badges (the symbols illustrated here by the shields) would be distributed to his retainers as jewel or cloth patches. These shields, crests, and badges belonged to lords in Yorkshire, in northern England.*

The solution of the French kings in the fifteenth century was to set up a professional core of troops, billeted throughout the kingdom and paid for from taxation; this army became established as a permanent institution. Feudal levies might be issued to provide extra men or as a justification for the exaction of payment in lieu of service. French nobles often joined the army and fought at their own expense, whether or not they held fiefs; such service was held to be one of the defining characteristics of the landed nobility, the "nobility of the sword."

Retainers and Fighting Men

Lords sought to have a force of fighting men at their disposal not just to fulfill any obligations they might have to provide troops but also to fight for the lords themselves. A great lord would be expected to appear with a substantial following, including men of rank as well as his tenants and household servants.

A monopoly of the legitimate use of force by the ruler has been seen as one of the defining characteristics of the modern state, in contrast to the private wars of feudal society. Many barons still had strong fortresses in the fifteenth and sixteenth centuries. Some castles were altered to make them comfortable residences, although they were built in such a way that they could be defended. Rulers might try to control the building of castles and fortifications by insisting that their permission was required. Private castles would often be garrisoned by paid soldiers, but

This knight in the retinue of King Ferdinand of Aragon and Queen Isabella of Castile wears the royal livery.

manning the defenses could also be one of the services expected of vassals and tenants. A lord's fortifications were expected to provide refuge and defense for his men and their families. Loyalty to a lord could be very strong, and his men did not necessarily need to be forced to fight for him, even against the prince. A lord could greatly value the fighting potential of his tenants and might consider it more important to maintain their goodwill than to extract the maximum revenue from them.

Lords and princes might also bind men to them by paying them; sometimes the parties entered into a formal written contract, made for a limited term or even for life. The support promised by these arrangements was mutual; the lord provided protection in return for support. A badge, a decorative symbol, was often given to retainers to display their allegiance; livery, for instance, a jacket with the lord's arms or in his colors, might also be handed out. Men might be retained by several lords at the same time. The more useful or influential the man, the more lords would want to establish links with him.

In itself, retaining was not considered an abuse; it was a kind of patronage that was a normal and accepted aspect of political society. It could be abused, however, and lead to corruption and injustice. Protection for a retainer might involve an attempt to prevent him from being tried for crimes he had committed, especially if they had been in the service of the lord. Bribery of judges, intimidation, and the use of force to halt trials could result. Some bands of retainers

The kingdom of Naples was a fief of the papacy from the mid-eleventh century, but in the mid-thirteenth century the pope invited the Angevin dynasty to take it over. The Angevins ruled the kingdom until 1435, when Alfonso of Aragon took the throne. Eventually he was invested with the kingdom as a fief, but throughout the fifteenth century the popes were inclined to interfere in the kingdom. The French heirs of the Angevin dynasty did not relinquish their claim, which passed to the French king Charles VIII. His invasion of the kingdom in 1494 was a watershed in the history of Italy, but his reign in Naples was short-lived. The throne of Naples was disputed between the French and Spanish kings, and the Spanish were eventually victorious.

The pope's power to confer title to the kingdom of Naples gave him a valuable diplomatic bargaining counter with aspirants to the throne, and he could threaten to depose the king if he were displeased with him. At times, however, when he did not want to anger either of two rival claimants, he faced an uncomfortable dilemma. Several popes were tempted by the idea of making one of their own relatives king of Naples, but since no one else favored such schemes, they were never realized. The pope wanted the king to make some payment as recognition of his overlordship, but from the reign of Alfonso, he had to settle for a symbolic annual tribute of a white horse.

▲ King Alfonso of Aragon insisted that he should be accompanied by the Neapolitan barons when he entered Naples in triumph in 1443. The scene is a detail from a fresco by Belisario Corenzio.

could behave like armed gangs and terrorize their neighborhood or rob travelers. Such disregard for the rule of law and the use of the bonds between lord and man to subvert public order have been regarded by some historians as characteristic of feudal society, which at the worst led to "feudal anarchy." To others, these tendencies represent a degeneration from feudalism as it should have functioned, or "bastard feudalism."

Fiefs and Vassals in International Relations

Whether or not a territory was a fief or a man was a vassal could become a question of importance in relations between states, especially if the man concerned was a prince. It was a question that sometimes found its answer in war. The king of France, for example, claimed that the king of England was his vassal for the duchy of Aquitaine in the southwest of France. A dispute over jurisdiction led the French king to seize the duchy in 1294, and although a settlement was reached in that dispute, the wars between the French and English kings that began in 1324 and 1337 both started with a declaration by the French king that Aquitaine had been confiscated owing to the disloyalty of his vassal, the English king.

The status of the duchy of Aquitaine was only one of the causes of the wars between England and France. Notions of vassalage and homage did have some force, and the fact that territory held by a prince might technically be a fief of another prince could provide a basis for legal arguments; it was a matter that could acquire greater significance in the right circumstances. In 1477 King Louis XI of France could justify his seizure of the duchy of Burgundy on the grounds that Duke Charles had left only a daughter, and women could not succeed to that fief. When the Holy Roman emperor was Charles V (reigned 1519–1556), the most powerful prince in Europe, it became much more important that much of Italy was technically part of the empire. In his capacity as emperor he could grant the duchy of Milan to his son Philip and thus make it a Spanish dominion. The republic of Siena was also granted to Philip in fief, who then granted it to Duke Cosimo de' Medici and thus brought the Sienese under the rule of their traditional rival, Florence. When the pope reclaimed Ferrara in 1598 from the d'Este family as a papal fief on the grounds that there was no legitimate male heir, the d'Este were able to keep their other major city, Modena, because it was an imperial rather than a papal fief.

Because of the differing conceptions of feudalism, some historians have proclaimed that it was dead by the sixteenth century, if not earlier, while others argue that it still flourished in the eighteenth century and even later. The concepts of fiefs and vassals were evidently still found useful in the sixteenth century and beyond and can help in understanding the political society of the time, but the survival of feudal elements does not render those societies truly feudal.

▼ King Louis XI of France (shown here in an unattributed court portrait) faced major rebellions by his barons, who justified their revolt by claiming they were acting in the public interest.

FURTHER READING

Bloch, Marc. *Feudal Society.* Translated by L. A. Manyon. Chicago, 1964.

Contamine, Philippe. *War in the Middle Ages.* Translated by Michael Jones. New York, 1984.

Fourquin, Guy. *Lordship and Feudalism in the Middle Ages.* London, 1976.

Hale, John R. *War and Society in Renaissance Europe, 1450–1620.* London, 1985.

Hicks, Michael. *Bastard Feudalism.* London, 1995.

Reynolds, Susan. *Fiefs and Vassals: The Medieval Evidence Reinterpreted.* New York, 1994.

Christine Shaw

SEE ALSO
• Burgundy • England • France
• Hundred Years War • Italian Wars • Lombardy
• Monarchy • Nobility and Rank • Peasants' Revolts
• Spain • Warfare

Florence

FOR MANY, FLORENCE EPITOMIZES THE
RENAISSANCE: THE ITALIAN CITY-STATE
WAS ONE OF EUROPE'S MOST IMPOR-
TANT PLACES IN TERMS OF ECONOMIC
AND POLITICAL POWER AND INFLUENCE,
INTELLECTUAL AND SPIRITUAL
ACCOMPLISHMENTS, AND SUBLIME
ARTISTIC ACHIEVEMENT.

In Italy, at the dawn of the fourteenth century, there began a gradual transition from the High Middle Ages to the age called the Renaissance. From their Italian beginnings, the forces behind this new age, spreading outward, prompted the development of a comparable process all across the European continent. Within Italy in particular, the transformation of economics, politics, security, philosophy, religion, and the arts that characterized the Renaissance had its genesis in Florence, a landlocked but prosperous and vibrant city situated in the Tuscan hills of north-central Italy. From the construction of a sophisticated banking system and the development of modern diplomacy to the conception and articulation of the philosophy of humanism and cultivation of innovative artistic and architectural styles, Florentines usually led the way.

Economics

The birth and subsequent progression of the High Middle Ages between the eleventh and thirteenth centuries was driven in large part by the establishment of a cluster of commercially powerful city-states situated between the Ligurian and Adriatic seas in northern Italy. Initially, coastal city-states such as Venice, Genoa, and Pisa proved the most economically prosperous and influential because they acted as hubs for the trade of raw materials and finished goods between Europe and the empires of the greater Middle East and Asia. Over the long term, however, two of their inland neighbors—Milan and Florence—were just as adept at generating

► A painting by Caspar Vanvitelli of Florence as it looked in the late seventeenth century. One of Europe's most economically powerful cities, Florence had vast cultural and political influence during the Renaissance.

The use of raw materials acquired from other regions of Europe and the world to produce finished goods for sale at home and abroad was one means through which Florence built one of the Italian city-states' strongest municipal economies. The growth of the city's economy in the fourteenth century in particular was driven primarily by the use of lower-class laborers, the most numerous of which were employed in the fabrication of woolen cloth acquired from England by way of the Flemish middlemen of northern Europe.

The Ciompi, whose ranks included wool weavers, beaters, and combers, were not well compensated and could be dismissed summarily by the wealthy merchants who reaped the greatest benefits from the laborers' efforts. The wool workers also were not permitted to form guilds and thus were denied the capacity for the collective representation necessary to turn to the Florentine government to lodge an effective protest against their employers. During the High Middle Ages and also in the early stages of the Renaissance in particular, guild membership was one of the principal means through which individuals and their families could play a direct role in the governance of Florence. The lack of such status was thus perceived correctly by the lower classes as an unambiguous form of political disenfranchisement.

Increasingly embittered over their lack of economic and political rights, the Ciompi took up arms and staged a violent revolt in July 1378, which drew support from a family destined to dominate Florence's economic and political systems over the ensuing three centuries—the Medicis. The revolt was broadly concurrent with and comparable to similar disputes in other powerful Italian city-states. The involvement of the Medici clan in the affair convinced government leaders to grant the Ciompi guild status. That concession, however, was only a transitory one. Within weeks the vast majority of the members of the city's manufacturing association, the Arte della Luna, successfully pressured the government to cancel the legislation passed during the crisis; the wool workers' representative rights were therefore eliminated, and the status quo restored. Over the longer term the Ciompi scare helped to push Florence toward an ever more oligarchic brand of governance under the auspices of the Medicis.

▼ *Florence's wool workers, the Ciompi, depicted in this 1572 painting of a wool factory by Mirabello Cavalori, played a central role in the city's thriving textile industry.*

wealth by capitalizing on their central location, which served as a geographic bridge that linked western Europe to both the east and the south.

One means by which Florence took advantage of its location in the twelfth and thirteenth centuries was by securing raw materials—especially English wool—at the annual trade fair sponsored by the Champagne region of France and other such gatherings. Craftsmen could then use the materials to produce considerably more valuable finished goods. Perhaps the best-known of these craftsmen were the Florentine wool workers, the Ciompi, whose skills helped the city's merchants generate the requisite capital to earn themselves positions among the elite of Italy—indeed, among the elite of Europe—by the turn of the fourteenth century.

Concurrent with Florence's growth as a trade power, the city bolstered its economic base by acquiring control over papal banking late in the thirteenth century. In particular, the city's mercantile families—most notably the Medicis—used their position as tax collectors for a series of popes to dominate European banking over the course of much of the Renaissance.

Aside from a brief period of economic instability that grew out of a 1344 decision by the English king Edward III (reigned 1327–1377) to repudiate his debts to several Florentine bankers, the economic structure of the city remained stable; its merchants and bankers funneled profits generated by insurance payments, investments, loans, and money exchanges into urban industries and architectural and artistic projects.

Ultimately, the Medicis proved to be the most sophisticated, financially prosperous, and politically influential of Florence's bankers. Established in 1397, the family's bank had branches in Avignon, Bruges, Geneva, London, Milan, Pisa, Rome, and Venice by the middle of the fifteenth century. The Medicis used that wealth to maintain near complete control over the culture and politics of the city down to the seventeenth century. The family's influence was manifested in pursuits that ranged from the construction of massive palaces and commissioning of paintings and sculptures to the cultivation of a relationship with the Catholic Church that yielded a variety of appointments to members of the clan in that institution's hierarchy over the centuries.

The Medici Dynasty

In the century prior to the rise of the Medicis as the wealthiest and most politically influential family in Florence, the city's system of governance underwent a gradual transition from mixed control by communal associations of free men on one hand and local feudal nobles on the other to a more broadly republican system and ultimately to the oligarchy most commonly associated with Renaissance Florence.

In theory the republican system of government that emerged in Florence over the latter half of the thirteenth century was designed to afford a much larger proportion of the city's population a

▶ Pages from the then secret journals of Florence's most prosperous Renaissance bank, the bank administered by the Medici family. Also pictured are golden florins used at the time.

Cosimo de' Medici c. 1389–1464

One of the most historically well known and politically gifted of the Medici family, Cosimo was the first member of the clan to seize and exercise near monopolistic control over Florentine internal affairs. Following an initial setback in the battle between the Medicis and Albizzis for influence in Florence's politics, which resulted in a yearlong exile (1433–1434), Cosimo returned home to the city, where he was the dominant figure until his death in 1464. Upon his arrival he repaid Rinaldo (1370–1442), a member of the Albizzi clan, by sending the latter's entire family into exile.

As was true of all the most successful Medici leaders, the principal base of Cosimo's power was economic. He inherited a substantial fortune from his father, Giovanni di Bicci (1360–1429), and used those resources to extend further the family's dominance of the European banking world. It was in part because Medici banking interests forced him to focus on international as well as municipal affairs that he proved so politically resourceful within the city as well.

Most significantly, the wealth generated from the family's holdings abroad helped Cosimo to secure more respect from Florence's politicians as well as the allegiance of current and prospective members and supporters of the city's military forces. One notable such ally was Francesco Sforza (1401–1466), a leading figure in the condottieri (essentially, mercenaries for hire) who later seized control of the duchy of Milan by force and became its duke.

Cosimo's personal and professional interests extended beyond but were contingent on his capacity to generate wealth and exercise political influence. Giovanni di Bicci had insisted on a high-quality education for his son, and Cosimo placed a similar emphasis on the cultivation of philosophy and the arts. He provided the necessary funds to lay the intellectual foundation for the work of the succeeding generation of humanist philosophers. He also subsidized extensive renovations at the Church of San Lorenzo and the monastery of San Marco, along with the construction of several elaborate personal palaces.

say in its political affairs. In practice, however, this victory of the *popolo*, or people, was a temporary one at best. Those members of the *popolo* who eventually acquired positions of influence in the municipal administration were unable to ensure civil order and in particular lacked assistance from the city's powerful merchant and banking families. By the turn of the fourteenth century, those families were themselves engaged in a struggle for economic and political predominance. In the aftermath of the Ciompi revolt, one such family—the Medicis—prevailed over its competitors.

The Medici family exercised power within a political system that featured a relatively broad-based popular assembly but one in which de facto power was vested in an executive body known as the Signoria. Membership in that body was typically limited to members of the wealthiest and thus most politically influential Florentine families. Consequently, it was rare that the Signoria did not include either one of the Medicis or someone loyal to the clan and willing to look after its interests.

Members of the Medici clan first began to arrive in Florence as migrants from the neighboring Mugello valley early in the thirteenth century. After prevailing in a battle for power against several rival families, including the Albizzi, Capponi, and Uzzano, the Medicis established a

virtual stranglehold on control over Florentine public and private affairs that extended beyond politics and economics to the cultural and religious arenas as well. Aside from three relatively brief periods of exile (1433–1434, 1494–1512, and 1527–1530), the family's authority faced few serious challenges from either internal or external actors for much of the fourteenth, fifteenth, sixteenth, and seventeenth centuries.

▲ *Cosimo de' Medici, depicted on this contemporary medal, presided over the Florentine political system from 1434 to 1464.*

► The facade of the Church of Santa Maria Novella, completed by the architect Leon Battista Alberti in 1470, is one of Florence's numerous architectural landmarks.

During their time atop the Florentine political system, the Medicis employed a range of means to exercise their authority. Most control was wielded from behind the scenes through the adroit maneuvering of such men as Cosimo (1389–1464), Lorenzo the Magnificent (1394–1444), and Cosimo I (1519–1574). So influential, for example, was Lorenzo that his son Giovanni (1475–1521) eventually became the first member of the family to be named pope. Giovanni presided over the church as Pope Leo X and reigned from 1513 to 1521. Two years after Giovanni's death, another Medici, Giulio (1478–1534), was elected pope and took the name Clement VII.

In addition to the generation of wealth and construction of a political dynasty, the Medicis used their power and influence to forge a place for Florence as a center of Renaissance intellectualism and artistic and architectural innovation. The family used its vast financial resources to fund the establishment and administration of the Florentine Platonic Academy and commission countless works from local architects, painters,

and sculptors. It is in the contexts of art and architecture in particular that the family's legacy is most evident in the present day, as the city the Medicis called home remains a center of European culture and one of the continent's leading tourist destinations.

Internal and External Security

One of the principal interests of any political actor, whether an individual, family, city, or state, is to ensure the security of the territory under its control. Concerns over threats to internal and external security were indeed prevalent in Florence during the Renaissance.

Put simply, Florentine rulers (most notably the Medicis but also their predecessors and successors) had two sets of related but distinct security interests to contend with between the fourteenth and seventeenth centuries: the maintenance of internal political stability on the one hand and, on the other, the defense of the city against threats posed by external powers to the Italian peninsula and also, at a broader level, to the European continent as a whole.

Niccolò Machiavelli (1469–1527), a prominent Florentine political theorist who represented the Medicis at royal courts across Europe, is credited by many historians as the creator of modern diplomacy. Machiavelli believed that human beings, naturally selfish, seek, as far as possible, to further their own interests at the expense of their competitors'.

You need to understand this: A ruler, and particularly a ruler who is new to power, cannot conform to all those rules that men who are thought good are expected to respect, for he is often obliged, in order to hold on to power, to break his word, to be uncharitable, inhumane, and irreligious. So he must be mentally prepared to act as circumstances and changes in fortune require. As I have said, he should do what is right if he can; but he must be prepared to do wrong if necessary.

The Prince

Internally, in general terms, two types of conflicts had the greatest tendency to foster both political and social instability in Renaissance Florence. The first type grew out of disputes between members of the city's wealthy mercantile and industrialist families and members of the lower classes, especially those workers who were denied the right to join guilds. The second type erupted as a result of disputes among the city's most powerful families over their economic and political interests and thus nearly always involved attempts by one clan or another to overthrow the Medicis.

The most significant and potentially destabilizing conflict of the first type was the Ciompi revolt, which gave Florence's wool workers transitory guild status and left the Medicis as the most influential family in the city. Conflicts of the second type resulted in the aforementioned three periods of Medici exile; however, in each case, the family ultimately returned to Florence and reasserted its economic and political predominance. Cosimo's exile, for example, lasted less than a year, and the democratization process that followed the expulsion of Piero de' Medici (1471–1503) was also relatively short-lived.

Externally, the Florentines generally and the Medicis specifically became embroiled in two sets of conflicts for control over territory on the Italian peninsula. Domestically, Italy's five most powerful city-states (Florence, the duchy of Milan, the kingdom of Naples, the Papal States, and Venice) engaged in an ongoing series of small-scale battles for territory and, to some extent, political authority over lesser city-states such as Ferrara, Mantua, Modena, and Siena.

These conflicts did prove enormously draining financially, especially in the fourteenth and early fifteenth centuries, a fact that led Italians to a greater reliance on diplomacy than war to settle intrapeninsular disputes in the succeeding centuries. Niccolò Machiavelli was especially proficient in the pursuit of Medici family interests through diplomatic means.

At the international level, Florence's principal competitors and occasionally battlefield foes during the Renaissance were France and Germany. The most damaging such encounters included invasions by the French kings Charles VIII (1470–1498) and Louis XII (1462–1515) in 1494 and 1508, respectively, and by the Holy Roman emperor Charles V (1500–1556) in 1527. Charles VIII's invasion in particular led Piero de' Medici (1471–1503) to seek peace terms with the French, a decision that contributed to his own exile in 1494.

▲ *The march of the French king Charles VIII on Florence, the subject of this painting by Francesco Granacci (1477–1543), led to Piero de' Medici's flight into exile at the behest of city leaders in 1494.*

EXILE AND RETURN

One means through which Medici leaders escaped conflict, remained alive, and thus retained the capacity to return to Florence and reassert their authority in the future was by accepting a period of exile elsewhere in Italy or perhaps farther afield. Three such episodes of varying length illustrate the family's perseverance under challenging circumstances. Cosimo was the first of the Medicis forced to endure a period of exile. After losing a vote in October 1434 for control of the Signoria (the city's upper ruling body), Cosimo avoided an extended conflict with the Albizzi family head, Rinaldo, by accepting banishment to Padua for a period of ten years. Yet within less than one year, the Medicis had regained control over the Signoria and the assembly below it. The family contacted Cosimo, who quickly returned to Florence, where he reigned supreme over the city's politics until his death in 1464.

The longest period of exile for the Medicis began in 1494. When the French invaded the northern Italian city-states and marched toward Florence, Lorenzo the Magnificent's son Piero responded by seeking out King Charles VIII in an effort to secure favorable terms of surrender for his family. The Florentine assembly deemed Piero's behavior to be traitorous to the city and banished the Medicis, who did not return until 1512 under the leadership of then Cardinal Giovanni de' Medici. Giovanni paved a path for the family's return to power by gaining the confidence of Pope Julius II (1443–1513) and arranging the marriage of his niece, Clarice, to the son of one of Florence's richest residents and power brokers, Filippo Strozzi (1428–1491). Another Medici, Giovanni's nephew Giulio, became Pope Clement VII in 1523.

A third and final exile followed the collapse of a deal Clement attempted to broker to secure an alliance under Medici auspices between the Florentine government and the Catholic Hapsburg Empire to the north. That absence from the city's political scene was short-lived. By 1531 Alessandro de' Medici (1511–1537) had been named duke of Florence. He and his successors remained ensconced atop the Florentine power structure throughout the remainder of the Renaissance, a period during which they would also exercise considerable influence across the region of Tuscany.

▲ The Treaty of Cateau-Cambrésis, which was negotiated by King Henry II of France and King Philip II of Spain in 1589, resulted in increased influence for the Hapsburg family in Florentine and broader Italian political affairs. This unattributed painting of the agreement between the two kings was made in Siena.

The incursions by both Charles VIII and Charles V were part of a broader series of conflicts known as the Wars of Italy, through which the French Valois and Austrian Hapsburg dynasties, respectively, grappled for control over the peninsula. Those wars began with Charles VIII's seizure of a large swath of the northern Italian city-states in 1494 and were ultimately settled by way of the negotiation of the Treaty of Cateau-Cambrésis of 1559, which left the Hapsburgs able to exercise direct or indirect control over much of the country, including Florence. Essentially, the treaty formalized the military gains Charles V had achieved during the previous two decades. In 1530, for example, Charles V's alignment of the Hapsburgs with the Medici family guaranteed the security of Florence so long as the city considered itself an imperial possession of the Holy Roman Empire.

The Medicis and the Papacy

Intellectual and religious developments in the context of the Florentine Renaissance were very much interrelated in the following general ways. First, connections between the Medici family and the papacy led to a perception, particularly among the lower social classes, that the latter institution was becoming increasingly corrupt. Second, Italian intellectuals responded by developing a new strain of philosophical thought that came to be known as humanism. Humanist thought promoted individualism and, along with it, a growing tendency to criticize the Catholic Church. Third, the Medicis themselves played a role that was, at least to some degree, contradictory. The family enjoyed close relations with Rome, so much so that two of the clan were elected as popes, but the Medicis also poured substantial resources into the development and refinement of humanist thought and the cultivation of the arts.

The development of mutually beneficial relations between Florence and the papacy dates to the papacy's granting control over the collection of its taxes to the city's leading families late in the thirteenth century. Those families had previously supported the papacy during the High Middle Ages. In Florence and other Italian city-states political parties known as Guelfs were aligned

▲ Giulio de' Medici, elected pope as Clement VII in 1523, is portrayed reading an edict in this illumination from a sixteenth-century manuscript.

with Rome and its interests against antipapal parties called Ghibellines.

The Medicis used the profits generated by their management of the papacy's banking business to bolster their economic power and political influence. Not surprisingly, the family remained loyal to the Italian branch of papacy when the Catholic Church split into competing branches during the Papal Schism of 1378–1417. The church repaid the favor via the election of two Medicis—Leo X and Clement VII—to the papacy. Born Giovanni de' Medici, Leo was named a cardinal at age thirteen and became pope at thirty-seven. He adopted an extravagant lifestyle while he served as pope from 1513 until his death in 1521 and attracted plenty of criticism through his use of profits generated from controversial practices, such as the sale of indulgences, to subsidize his private largesse and cultivation of the arts.

Marsilio Ficino c. 1433–1499

Every philosophical movement has a leading figure. For the Neoplatonists of the mid- to late fifteenth century in Florence, the man who filled that role was Marsilio Ficino, a scholar and priest who drew praise and support from both Cosimo and Lorenzo de' Medici prior to the family's temporary expulsion from the city in 1494.

After pursuing an education in medicine during his formative years, Ficino began to study Greek in the 1450s and engaged in the development and subsequent refinement of Neoplatonism in the ensuing decades. His relationship with the Medicis commenced when he was hired by Cosimo to translate the body of Plato's works into Latin, an undertaking that made all of the Greek philosopher's dialogues widely available in the West for the first time. It continued with Lorenzo the Magnificent's decision to facilitate Ficino's pursuit of a modest ecclesiastical career from 1473 to 1492. In addition to Plato's dialogues, Ficino translated the works of two other Greek philosophers, Plotinus and Proclus, of whom little was previously known in Renaissance Europe. He then used a series of commentaries on those translations to disseminate his own Neoplatonic views in an attempt to strike a balance between traditional Christian doctrine and the mysticism advocated by Girolamo Savonarola, the reformer who ruled Florence briefly during the Medicis' second exile.

In particular, Ficino suggested that rational thinking and the expression of individual will would help to free one's soul for an ascent to heaven. He also relished drawing parallels between Christianity and earlier Egyptian, Greek, and Hebrew religions and even dabbled in astrology. The latter pursuit led the papacy to investigate him for heresy in 1490, but in the end Rome declined to prosecute him.

Ficino's best-known contributions to the emerging humanist literature included his *Platonic Theology concerning the Immortality of the Soul* (1469–1474), *Concerning the Christian Religion* (1474), and *On the Threefold Life* (1489). In the latter two works he characterized the structure of the universe as hierarchical; human beings occupied the middle rung on an existential ladder of progression toward a union with God upon death.

The extravagance of prominent church officials, most significantly popes, cardinals, and bishops, was one factor that contributed to the conception and proliferation of the philosophy of humanism. Another was the willingness of the Medicis, especially Cosimo and Lorenzo the Magnificent, to provide the requisite funds for philosophers such as Marsilio Ficino (1433–1499) and Giovanni Pico della Mirandola (1463–1494) to spread their ideas.

Originally conceived by the Florentine rhetorician and historian Leonardo Bruni (1370–1444), humanism drew on the work of Greek scholars to develop a Neoplatonic philosophy that focused on human nature generally and the achievements, interests, and accomplishments of individuals specifically. However, it also placed an emphasis on Christian values, albeit not necessarily those propagated by the papacy.

In his *Oration on the Dignity of Man* (c. 1494), which was published and widely circulated only after his death, Pico della Mirandola stressed that individuals had an unlimited capacity for spiritual self-development. This argument

◄ *Marsilio Ficino, the subject of this unattributed portrait, was one of Florence's leading humanist philosophers during the Renaissance. After the expulsion of the Medicis in 1494, Ficino retired to the Tuscan countryside.*

brought him into direct conflict with the Catholic Church, as did his fascination with the controversial sermons of a Dominican monk named Girolama Savonarola (1452–1498). Savonarola, who moved to Florence after meeting Pico della Mirandola and was installed by Lorenzo the Magnificent at the monastery at San Marco, preached an apocalyptic message in an attempt to force reform in the behavior of the clergy. Savonarola claimed to have received a series of divine visions that forecast forthcoming doom for the citizens of Florence. In the end he succeeded only in isolating Florence from the papacy and eventually engendered such resentment among the general population that he was dragged away from the monastery by an angry mob and burned at the stake in 1498.

In addition to the intellectual and religious philosophical contributions put forward by Bruni, Ficino, and Pico della Mirandola, the Florentine humanist movement benefited from the work of Giovanni Boccaccio (1313–1375), who helped lay the foundation for subsequent critiques of the Catholic Church within and beyond Italy. Boccaccio's most famous book was *The Decameron* (c. 1350), through which he delivered a commentary on Florentine society in the context of a fictional tale that described the adventures of several city residents forced to flee the ravages of the Black Death in 1348.

Over the long term, the humanists of Florence proved to be the trendsetters for a movement that spread north to the heart of the Holy Roman Empire in the sixteenth century and helped to create an intellectual atmosphere that was conducive to the genesis and subsequent evolution of the Protestant Reformation in Germany. The development of movable type and subsequent growth of the European printing industry helped spread the ideas of Ficino, Pico della Mirandola, and others farther afield, where they were refined and built on by a continually increasing pool of reform-minded political and religious philosophers.

Two of the most notable members of that philosophical pool were a Dutch monk named Desiderius Erasmus (c. 1466–1536) and a German professor of religion named Martin Luther (1483–1546). Luther's vocal criticism of

▲ *This sixteenth-century Italian painting depicts the execution of the Dominican monk Girolamo Savonarola by an angry Florentine mob in 1498.*

the sale of indulgences—a practice that claimed to offer gullible or negligent Christians entrance to heaven in return for a payoff to corrupt priests, bishops, or even the pope—was part of the opening salvo of the Reformation, the sixteenth-century movement that began in northern Europe and eventually split Christianity into opposing camps.

Florentine Art and Architecture

Concurrent with the development of the humanist philosophy of Neoplatonism, Florentine society played host to a flowering of the arts as a result of the patronage of the Medici family. Like their philosophical counterparts, many of the city's architects, painters, and sculptors reproduced and refined forms of expression that originated in classical Greece.

▲ *Sandro Botticelli's Birth of Venus embodies a particularly fine illustration of Florentine artists' affinity for portraying women as creatures at once sensuous, serene, and self-possessed.*

Above all, architectural projects and works of art commissioned in Florence during the Renaissance were status symbols. Most were ordered by Medici clan members from a pool of artists as vast as in any city in Europe. Boasting of the scope of his family's largesse, Lorenzo the Magnificent declared in 1470 that the Medicis had spent the astonishing sum of 663,755 gold florins on architectural and artistic commissions over the previous thirty-five years.

Numerous architects, painters, and sculptors were the beneficiaries of the deep pockets and personal hubris (exaggerated self-confidence) of the Medicis, both financially and in terms of the prestige they could glean from the production of a work deemed a masterpiece by Florentine society. In general terms, most Florentine painters and sculptors attempted to mirror reality by producing portraits and busts of the city's powerful bankers, merchants, politicians, and clergymen. Human beings, for example, were typically portrayed in a more scientific and natural manner than had been the case during the Middle Ages, with the female figure represented as voluptuous and sensual and the male body as strong and heroic.

Those who achieved the highest status among this emerging artistic upper class included Donato di Niccolò di Betto Bardi (1386–1466; more commonly known as Donatello) along with Filippo Brunelleschi (1377–1446), Sandro Botticelli (1445–1510), Leonardo da Vinci (1452–1519), and Michelangelo Buonarroti (1475–1564). Donatello, a sculptor, spent a period of time in Rome studying the statues of Greek antiquity before moving to Florence, where he lived and worked. Among Donatello's most notable creations was his statue of David (c. 1446–1460), which was the first known life-size freestanding bronze nude made by a European artist since antiquity. Brunelleschi, who was a friend of Donatello's, studied with him in Rome and also drew inspiration from the many architectural remnants of the Roman Empire, which he incorporated into his work. In particular, Brunelleschi used classical columns in the interior of the Church of San Lorenzo in Florence.

Like the philosophers Ficino and Pico della Mirandola, the painter Sandro Botticelli (1445–1510) was a member of the court of Lorenzo the Magnificent. Born Alessandro di Moriano

PORTRAYAL OF WOMEN BY FLORENTINE RENAISSANCE ARTISTS

The growing tension in the relationship between the Catholic Church and humanist philosophers was reflected in a number of paintings and sculptures of women that were produced in Florence during the Renaissance. There were two general types of works—portraits of female members of influential families and religiously oriented paintings of the Virgin Mary, known as Madonnas.

Artists who sought to replicate themes prevalent in ancient Greece and Rome were eager to present the female body to Florentine society in its natural form. The resulting paintings frequently showed women as voluptuous, sensual beings and thus objects of desire. Examples include *Dance of the Nudes* (c. 1470s) and *Apollo and Daphne* (undated) by Antonio di Jacopo Benci Pollaiuolo (c. 1457–1498) and Botticelli's *Birth of Venus* (c. 1484–1486).

Unsurprisingly, the church had an aversion to the overt expression of such themes in artistic works. (It is worth noting that this aversion was at odds with popular and often accurate perceptions of the behavior of the upper ranks of the clergy, from the head of the church in Rome down to cardinals and local bishops.) Yet while opposed to sexually appealing paintings of Venus and other goddesses, members of the church hierarchy were supportive of spiritually oriented representations of the Virgin Mary. Examples include da Vinci's *Madonna of the Rocks* (1483) and *Madonna and Child with Saint Anne* (c. 1508–1513) and Michelangelo's *Madonna of the Stairs* (c. 1489–1492).

The contrasts in these two distinctive types of paintings mirrored the growing cleavage between, on the one hand, philosophers and religious reformers who stressed the merits of secularism and, on the other, church officials understandably reluctant to cede any authority whatsoever with respect to the traditional interpretation of Catholic doctrine. At their core such philosophical and artistic differences anticipated the gradual transition from Renaissance attitudes to those of the Reformation.

▼ *Leonardo da Vinci's* Madonna of the Rocks, *which he finished in 1483. The location of the Virgin Mary and Christ in a rocky cave, although spiritual in orientation, was quite controversial at the time.*

Filipepi, Botticelli drew broadly on Neoplatonic themes in his paintings. Among the best-known and most renowned of these works are *Primavera* (c. 1482) and the *Birth of Venus* (c. 1484–1486); both paintings are set in the garden of the goddess Venus.

Leonardo da Vinci, who divided his time between the cities of Florence and Milan, was both a scholar and painter. He studied constantly and even dissected human bodies in order to learn more about their structure. One of his best-known work is *The Last Supper* (c. 1495–1498), which he painted in Milan.

In addition to his painting and sculpting skills, Michelangelo was an accomplished and highly sought after architect. He spent much of his life living and working in both Florence and Rome, where he completed a range of artistic and architectural projects for the papacy and the Medici family. Michelangelo's first architectural works were commissioned by the Medicis. Those projects, however, proved to be among his least well known. After failing to complete renovations on the family's mausoleum in 1534, he left Florence for Rome, where he remained until his death in 1564. Nevertheless, while in Rome

▲ *Pope Leo X (center) with Cardinal Giulio de' Medici (right) and Luigi de Rossi (left) are depicted in this painting by Raphael (c. 1517). Leo remained pope until 1521.*

members' cultivation of close relationships with the hierarchy of the Catholic Church and somewhat contradictory willingness to subsidize the work of the leading philosophers and artists of the Renaissance. However, at least to some extent, Florence's support for these figures also helped lay the foundation for more widespread criticism of the papacy and in that sense contributed to the development of the Protestant Reformation in northern Europe in the sixteenth century. From there it quickly spread farther to the north and west. The spread of Protestantism contributed to a substantial decline in the influence of the Catholic Church, which had grown increasingly unpopular among lay officials during the Renaissance.

FURTHER READING

Brucker, Gene A. *Renaissance Florence.* New York, 1969.

Cronin, Vincent. *The Florentine Renaissance.* New York, 1967.

Goldthwaite, Richard A. *The Building of Renaissance Florence.* Baltimore, 1980.

Hale, J. R. *Florence and the Medici: The Pattern of Control.* London, 1977.

Robert J. Pauly Jr.

Michelangelo retained his ties to the Medicis through his professional relationship with Pope Clement VII.

From Renaissance to Reformation

Without question, Florence's most significant contributions to European history between the fourteenth and seventeenth centuries grew out of the Medici family's dominance of the city's economic and political systems, as well as its

Florence, Council of

THE COUNCIL OF FLORENCE, A SERIES
OF CHURCH MEETINGS IN FLORENCE
AND ROME BETWEEN 1439 AND 1443,
ENSURED THE POPE'S VICTORY OVER A
RIVAL COUNCIL AND ACHIEVED A BRIEF
REUNION OF THE CATHOLIC AND
ORTHODOX CHURCHES.

The Council of Florence arose out of a tense situation. There had been a long struggle between Pope Eugenius IV and a large council (meeting) of church leaders from all over Europe that had gathered in Basel, Switzerland in 1431. The quarrel centered on the fact that both the pope and the Council of Basel claimed to have final authority over the church. Pope Eugenius lost patience in 1437 and asked the council whether it was willing to transfer to Italy, where he hoped he would have more control over it. Two-thirds of the council fathers voted to remain in Basel, and one-third voted to accommodate the pope. Despite the majority vote to stay in Basel, Eugenius ordered the council to move, and it was eventually reestablished in the city-state of Florence. As a result, from 1439 onward, there were two rival councils in session, one of which consisted of the churchmen who moved to Florence and the other, of those who refused to move and remained at Basel. The Council of Florence, therefore, had its roots in the Council of Basel and was regarded by the pope and his supporters as the legitimate continuation of that council.

Relations between the Council of Florence and the continuing Council of Basel worsened. Each annulled the proceedings of the other and condemned its members. A key to the pope's victory was that a delegation of church leaders from the Orthodox Church, which was seeking reunion with the Catholic Church, decided to come to Florence rather than to Basel.

East-West Schism

The Orthodox and Catholic churches, which were sometimes known as the churches of the East and West, had been in schism since 1054. In that year a dispute caused a rift that was never healed, despite several attempts at a solution during the Middle Ages. Efforts to heal the schism were renewed in the 1430s. The Orthodox Church was under threat; much of its land had been conquered by the expanding Islamic Empire, and an army of Ottoman Turks had advanced to within a short distance of Constantinople, the capital city of the Orthodox world. The leaders of the Orthodox Church hoped that reunion with the Catholic Church might bring military and other aid from the West to save the city from defeat. The prospect of material aid was an important motive for reunion, but there were genuine religious motives as well.

The Decree of Reunion

When members of the councils of Basel and Florence realized that the political and religious

▼ A detail from the Carta della Catena, which shows the city of Florence shortly after the council. The large, domed church in the middle is the cathedral, where important sessions of the council took place and the decree of reunion, Laetentur Caeli, was read out.

FIORENZA

▶ This painting by Pinturicchio (c. 1454–1513) shows Pope Eugenius IV receiving the submission of Cardinal Enea Silvio Piccolomini—who later became Pope Pius II—after the cardinal had abandoned the rival Council of Basel.

Pope Eugenius IV ▌ c. 1383–1447

Pope Eugenius IV was born Gabriele Condulmaro to a wealthy family that lived in Venice, in northern Italy. The future pope became a monk, then bishop of Siena in 1407, and a cardinal a year later. He was appointed governor of part of the Papal States, and it was no surprise when he was elected pope in 1431, following the death of Pope Martin V. Threatened by many opponents, Pope Eugenius IV proved a forceful and able pontiff.

The Council of Basel had been called by his predecessor, Martin V, but when it first met, soon after his election, Eugenius tried to dissolve it. The council resisted, and he was obliged to back down. However, the tension that remained eventually led Eugenius to move the council to Florence. Eugenius had been forced by his enemies to leave Rome in 1434, and he spent most of the following nine years in Florence. After his successes at this council, he still had to deal with the continuing Council of Basel in its final stages and to win the support of the kings and other secular rulers of Europe for his actions.

The Council of Florence was the centerpiece and greatest achievement of Eugenius's long reign. He was also a patron of the Renaissance and employed such famous artists as Fra Angelico, Pisanello, Donatello, and Lorenzo Ghiberti.

leaders of the Orthodox Church were interested in discussing reunion with the Catholic Church, both councils issued invitations to the Eastern church to send representatives. In the end the Orthodox delegation preferred Florence to Basel. The choice was made, it seems, for several reasons: the Italian city was easier to reach from Constantinople; the delegation had doubts about the legitimacy of the Council of Basel; and the pope and the city of Florence were attentive and generous, at least at the beginning, regarding the details of payment for travel and the provision of decent accommodation.

The delegation from Constantinople was substantial. It was led by the heads of the state and church, Emperor John VIII Palaeologus and Patriarch Joseph II of Constantinople, and included a number of bishops and theologians of the Orthodox Church. There followed several months of discussion and debates between the Orthodox delegation and bishops and theologians of the Catholic Church, which were held in various churches and houses in the city. Eventually agreement was reached in the Decree of Reunion.

As well as obtaining the agreement of Pope Eugenius and the Catholic bishops at the council, the decree was approved by Emperor John and all the Orthodox bishops present except one, Mark of Ephesus. Patriarch Joseph, who backed the decree, died shortly before final agreement was reached. When the delegation returned to Constantinople, support for the reunion soon declined and eventually evaporated. There was hostility to the decree at the popular level; several bishops on the delegation who had signed the decree changed their mind, and the emperor did not press for its confirmation. The possibility of further discussion of the reunion effectively came to an end with the capture of Constantinople by the Turks in 1453 and the resulting loss of freedom for the Orthodox Church.

Results of the Council of Florence

Despite the fleeting nature of the reunion, the Council of Florence appeared at the time to be a notable victory for Pope Eugenius. As a result of this and other factors, the fortunes of the rival Council of Basel began to decline. This rival council deposed Pope Eugenius later in 1439 and elected in his place the Duke of Savoy, who took the name of Felix V. Thus, two men were recognized as pope: Felix V by the Council of Basel and Eugenius IV by the Council of Florence and by most Christians. Though a devout man, Felix V was, at the time of his election, a layman, not a bishop; he had been married and was a widower, the father of five children. Many people considered that his married and lay status made him unsuitable to the papacy. Moreover, few wanted a repetition of the Papal Schism, when first two and later three men claiming to be pope had divided and traumatized Europe between 1378 and 1417, a time that was still within living memory. Felix V never had much support outside the Council of Basel, and he finally resigned his claim to the papacy in 1449. Thus, what was generally seen as the Council of Basel's mistake in electing Felix V as a rival pope strengthened the position both of the Council of Florence and of Pope Eugenius IV.

The Council of Basel gradually withered away. After moving in 1447 to Lausanne, another city in Switzerland, it finally dissolved itself in 1449. In its later sessions the Council of Florence (which was moved by the pope to Rome in 1443 but continued to keep its old name) achieved reunions with several other Christian groups that had become separated from the Catholic Church: some Copts in Egypt and some Christian communities in Syria and Armenia. Though these groups were relatively small, the reunions produced further prestige for the council and for Pope Eugenius. The council finally came to an end in 1445.

Lasting Influences

The reunions between the Catholic Church and the Orthodox and other churches were either short lived or were limited to small groups within these churches. Nevertheless, the discussions were serious, and the various decrees of reunion provide some help in the continuing search for more unity among Christians.

The supersession of the Council of Basel by the Council of Florence, convoked by Pope Eugenius, had larger consequences. The call for more decentralization of church government

The reunion between the Catholic and Orthodox churches was sealed in a document that is known by its opening phrase, *Laetentur caeli*, Latin words that mean "Let the heavens rejoice." The words indicate the joy that the reunion was intended to bring to the members of both churches. Agreement was reached on the four main doctrinal issues that had been in dispute between the two churches for a long time and had been a prime cause of the Papal Schism of 1054. The document was signed on July 6, 1439.

The first issue concerned *Filioque*, a Latin word that means "and from the Son." In the early Middle Ages the Western churches had gradually inserted the word into the Nicene Creed (the fundamental statement of Christian belief) after the phrase "We believe in the Holy Spirit … who proceeds from the Father." The Eastern churches thought this description of the interrelationship of the three aspects of God (the Trinity) misleading or even heretical and considered the insertion of the term into the creed contrary to proper order. The conciliar decree ruled that the word could be justified on theological grounds but that Orthodox Christians were not obliged to include it when they recited the creed.

The second issue concerned whether leavened or unleavened bread should be used when the Eucharist was consecrated at Mass. The compromise reached was that each church should follow its present custom: unleavened bread for Catholics and leavened bread for Orthodox Christians. The third regarded purgatory, the place of temporary punishment that people who were destined for heaven had to endure in order to purge the sins they had committed in this life. Purgatory featured prominently in the doctrine and devotional life of Catholics in the Middle Ages, whereas Orthodox theologians regarded it as almost an invention of the Catholic Church and largely ignored it. The decree recognized purgatory but in a careful way.

The final issue concerned the extent of papal authority. Agreement was reached on this thorny issue by asserting the authority of the pope over all Christians as well as by stating, in a sentence that is open to varying interpretations, that this authority must be seen within the context of church councils—which Orthodox Christians had always seen as central to church government. In addition, the authority of the patriarch of Constantinople within the Orthodox Church was asserted.

▼ *This detail from a fourteenth-century Italian painting portrays purgatory, the place where it was believed baptized Christians who died with sins still to be purged had to go until they were ready to enter heaven.*

was halted or at least slowed for many centuries, right down to the 1950s. The papacy was exalted, and councils that were not under strict papal control came to be viewed with suspicion as a threat to papal authority. In recent years, especially since the Second Vatican Council (1962–1965), interest in councils at various levels has revived among Catholics.

The Council of Florence also had a measure of influence on the Renaissance, though the extent of this influence is debated. The council and the fleeting reunion with the Orthodox Church encouraged eastern Greek-speaking scholars to come to Italy and the West, where some remained. They brought important books and manuscripts from Constantinople to the West, both before and after the capture of the city by the Ottoman Turks in 1453.

The most notable case was John Bessarion (1402–1472), a Greek scholar and bishop in the Orthodox Church. He traveled with the Orthodox delegation to the Council of Florence and continued to accept the reunion after most of the Orthodox Church rejected it. He settled in Italy, was made a cardinal by Pope Eugenius, and became an important patron of Renaissance scholarship as both a writer himself and a supporter of other Greek scholars. Bessarion left his fine library, notable for its large collection of Greek and Latin books and manuscripts, to the city of Venice, which was then a center of the Renaissance.

Finally, the decrees of reunion with the Armenians and Copts had considerable influence upon the later teaching of the Catholic Church. The first decree contained a full treatment of the seven sacraments (baptism, confession, eucharist/mass, confirmation, marriage, orders/priesthood, and last anointing), which were central to the practice and devotional life of Catholicism. Much of this teaching was taken over and repeated by the Council of Trent (1545–1563), which dominated the thought and practice of Catholicism down to the middle of the twentieth century. In this way the decree had a lasting and powerful influence.

The second decree included the statement, "All those who are outside the Catholic Church, not only pagans but also Jews or heretics and schismatics, cannot share in eternal life and will go 'into the everlasting fire prepared for the devil and his angels' [Matthew 28:41] unless they are joined to the Catholic faith before the end of their lives." These forthright, even fierce words proved for a long time to be embarrassing for many Catholics as they tried to take a more positive view of other religions and the salvation of non-Catholics.

◄ *This portrait, painted around 1476 by Justus van Gent, portrays an elderly John Bessarion dressed as a cardinal. In Rome, Bessarion, along with George Gemistus Plethon, his former teacher, attracted a circle of philosophers who were dedicated to the study of Plato.*

FURTHER READING

Gill, Joseph. *The Council of Florence.* Cambridge, 1959.

————. *Personalities of the Council of Florence.* Oxford, 1964.

Tanner, Norman. *The Councils of the Church: A Short History.* New York, 2001.

————. *Decrees of the Ecumenical Councils.* Vol. 1. Washington, DC, 1990.

Norman Tanner

SEE ALSO

• Byzantium • Florence • Humanism and Learning
• Papacy

France

BETWEEN 1300 AND 1650 THE KING-
DOM OF FRANCE GREW TO BECOME
ONE OF THE MOST POWERFUL STATES IN
WESTERN EUROPE.

France's status in 1650 as a great power was partly the result of a three-century-long campaign by French monarchs to establish both a centralized state and a more homogeneous culture within the realm. This process was by no means smooth. War, whether against powerful French subjects or against rival monarchs, provided a driving force for the long-term development of France, but the Black Death in the mid-fourteenth century and the Protestant Reformation in the sixteenth also greatly influenced the course of French history.

France in 1300

By 1300 France had experienced two centuries of demographic and economic growth. This growth underpinned a flowering of French culture and a strengthening of the French monarchy. An increase in trade from around 1100 had fueled rapid urban development, and in the towns the arts and learning thrived. French kings had succeeded in bringing large parts of their kingdom back under their direct rule for the first time in several centuries. Moreover, they also succeeded in forcing many of France's most powerful nobles and churchmen into accepting the monarch as their social and political superior. The key to this development was the monarchy's success in impressing upon its subjects more forcefully than ever before the notion of the divine right of kings—that is, the notion that kings were anointed by God and ruled by God's will.

Despite these developments, in 1300 France lacked a uniform culture and a fully centralized government. The various territories that had come under royal control over the previous centuries maintained most of their own laws and customs. Laws varied from place to place; even within a single village, multiple legal systems might operate at the same time. France also lacked a common language. Those who lived in the northern portion of the kingdom spoke langue d'oïl, the predecessor of modern French, whereas southerners continued to speak langue d'oc, a language much more closely related to

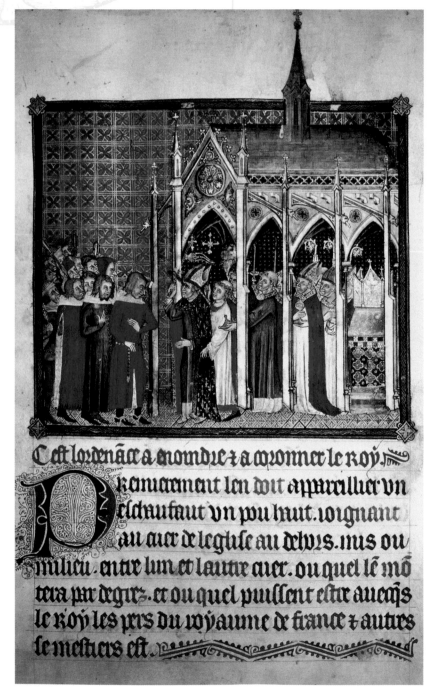

Cest lordenace a enoindre z a coronner le roy.
Premierement len doit appareiller vn eschaufaut vn pou hault. ioignant au euer de leglise au dehors. mis ou milieu. entre lun et lautre euer. ou quel lé mó tera par degrez. et ou quel puissent estre aueqs le roy les pers du royaume de france z autres se mestiers est.

◄ *The close relationship between the French monarchy and the church was evident at the coronation ceremony. In this image from a manuscript of 1365, Charles V is met at the door of Reims Cathedral by the leading churchmen of his realm.*

Latin. (The words *oïl* and *oc* mean "yes" in their respective languages.) In some peripheral regions other languages—Basque, Breton, and Flemish, for example—predominated.

While the power of the monarch had increased in theory by 1300, the reality of royal power always lagged behind. France's territory was large, and communication between one part of the kingdom and another was slow. The king had only a few thousand officials; to govern effectively, he relied heavily on the cooperation of local noblemen, especially in distant regions of the kingdom. The possibility always remained that a powerful lord or an urban or rural community would refuse to accept the dictates of the central government.

The Traumatic Fourteenth Century

Most of the political, social, and economic developments of the previous two centuries were reversed in the fourteenth century. The consequences for both society and government were catastrophic. The Great Famine of 1315 and a series of other poor harvests led to food shortages and malnutrition. Worse was to come: in the summer of 1348, bubonic plague arrived in France. Later known as the Black Death, the fourteenth-century plague epidemic was a disaster of epic proportions. Within ten years between one-quarter and one-third of the population of France had beeen wiped out. After further outbreaks of plague, by 1450 France's population was around half of what it had been in 1300.

The effect of the plague on French society was profound. Nearly one-fifth of France's farmland was abandoned. With so many peasants dead, the dramatic shortage of labor drove up wages. When King John II (reigned 1350–1364), at the behest of noble landowners, tried to limit this wage increase, a peasant rebellion known as the Jacquerie broke out in 1358. While the rebellion was ultimately suppressed by the king and his nobles, serfdom, the medieval form of landholding that tied a peasant to his land, disappeared from almost all of France. With a nobility fearful of further rebellions and competing for a small pool of newly mobile peasant labor, peasants were able to rent land on favorable terms—or in some cases, even purchase land.

The Black Death also increased the opportunities for social advancement. The death of large numbers of nobles, churchmen, and government officials opened up opportunities for commoners to buy land and thus, in some cases, to move up the social ladder. While it is difficult to be certain of the precise figures, historians studying particular regions of France have found that almost one-third of the new noble families that emerged between 1345 and 1660 did so in the sixty years following the first outbreak of the plague. Most of these social climbers came from towns where trading had won them sufficient wealth to buy the lands and titles required.

▲ *The initial outbreak of the Black Death in France killed between one-quarter and one third of the population. Despite their best efforts physicians, such as the one depicted in this fifteenth-century fresco (from the Chapel of Saint-Sébastien in Lanslevillard, in southeastern France), could offer no effective treatment.*

An eyewitness account of the plague outbreak in Paris in 1418:

The death rate in and around Paris this September was higher than it had been in three hundred years, so old men said. No one who was struck by the epidemic escaped, particularly young people and children. So many people died so fast towards the end of the month that they had to dig great pits in the cemeteries of Paris and lay thirty or forty in at once, in rows like sides of bacon ... no one had ever experienced or heard of so dreadful or fierce a pestilence nor one from which so few people once struck by it recovered. More than fifty thousand people died in Paris in less than five weeks. So many priests died that four or six or eight heads of households would be buried with one sung mass; even then it was necessary to bargain with the priests, what price they would do it for.

Quoted in James Collins, *From Tribes to Nation: The Making of France, 500–1799*

The Hundred Years War

When the Black Death arrived, France was already embroiled in a war. In 1328 Charles IV had died without an heir. During the political crisis that followed, two figures emerged with strong claims to the throne: Edward III, king of England and first cousin of Charles, and Philip of Évreux, grandson of an earlier king, Phillip III. Ultimately a council decided that Philip had the stronger claim to the French crown and gave his branch of the royal family, the Valois, the throne. At first, the young Edward accepted this decision. However, increasing tension between the rivals—France's two most powerful figures—broke out into open warfare in 1337. The conflict, known as the Hundred Years War, raged until 1453. At times the war threatened to place the monarch of England on the French throne; at other times it threatened to split France permanently into smaller kingdoms.

The Hundred Years War is best understood as unfolding in three stages. During the first stage, which lasted from 1337 to 1359, Edward III won a series of decisive battles, including those fought at Crécy (1346) and Poitiers (1356). These victories forced Philip's successor, John II, to surrender nearly a third of his kingdom to the English king. The second stage, which lasted from 1363 to 1380, saw a reversal of fortunes when John's successor, Charles V, was able to regain the initiative and drive the English armies from much of the kingdom. The final stage began as a civil war in France between two branches of the ruling Valois family. The king of France, Charles VI, who suffered from bouts of mental illness, lost control of his kingdom. One branch of his family, the Valois dukes of Burgundy, allied themselves with King Henry V of England, while a second, known as the Orléans branch, remained loyal to Charles. At the Battle of

▶ At the Battle of Crécy (1346), the French army suffered a devastating defeat at the hands of the English longbowmen. This illustration of the crucial battle is taken from Jean Froissart's Chronicles, the famed fourteenth-century account of the first seventy years of the Hundred Years War.

NEW WEAPONS IN THE HUNDRED YEARS WAR

Key developments in weapon technologies influenced the course of the Hundred Years War. At the opening of the conflict, the English monarchs were seemingly outmatched, despite their landholdings in France. Compared with France, England was poor and underpopulated. Yet at Poitiers, Crécy, and Agincourt the English dominated their French opponents on the battlefield and scored spectacular victories. The key to English success was the longbow. The English longbowmen effectively countered the weapon that had for so long dominated the medieval battlefield: the armored knight on horseback. Though difficult to master, the longbow fired arrows with greater force and over longer distances than other types of bows could. An expert longbowman could fire ten to twelve arrows a minute, whereas a trained crossbowman could fire only two bolts a minute. The English kings were able to draw on the native populations of England and Wales for expert bowmen. The impact of these troops cannot be overestimated, for their arrows were able to pierce even the chain mail armor of French knights. The sheer number of French nobles who died in battle during the Hundred Years War attests to the power of this new weapon.

The French were never able to respond to the English longbow. They relied on the crossbow, which took much longer to reload and lacked the range of the longbow. However, in the final decades of the Hundred Years War, the French developed the most efficient artillery in Europe, which allowed the French kings finally to overcome their English rivals. Both sides possessed cannon, but the French built an artillery corps of such size that it was able to besiege even the best-fortified sites. During the closing stages of the war, stronghold after stronghold fell to the relentless battery of French cannon.

The kings of France also used their artillery to subdue internal foes in the late fifteenth century. The kings were able to maintain their advantage on the battlefield throughout this period, in part because cannon—and the gunpowder required to fire them—proved so expensive that only the royal treasury could purchase and maintain them in sufficient numbers.

▼ *That the French finally succeeded in defeating their English opponents in the Hundred Years War was thanks mainly to superior French artillery, which could breach the walls of even the most formidable castle. This fifteenth-century manuscript illustration of French forces besieging Ribodane is from a chronicle written by the Burgundian Jean de Wavrin.*

Agincourt in 1415, Henry V won a stunning victory. The ultimate consequence of this triumph was a peace treaty that stipulated that Henry would accede to the throne of France following the death of Charles VI. However, Charles VI's son, Charles VII, won a series of victories over the English armies—thanks in no small measure to Joan of Arc, an inspired and inspirational peasant woman who led a small French force from 1428 to 1430. Although Joan was executed by the English in 1431, by 1453 Charles VII had driven the English from all of their possessions in France except for the northern coastal town of Calais.

The Hundred Years War was of crucial importance in French history. One possible outcome of the series of conflicts could have been the fragmentation of France into several kingdoms, in the manner of the Holy Roman Empire. Instead, Charles's victory ensured that France remained a single political entity. While the conflict was defined primarily as a dynastic struggle between powerful families, it nonetheless provided an important spur to the development of French national identity.

The Recovery of the French Monarchy

By 1453 the Valois royal family had strengthened its position in France. However, after a century of dynastic conflict, during which royal power had collapsed on several occasions, the kings of France were far from completely in control of their kingdom. Indeed, the removal of the English threat had the effect of sparking internal divisions. During the Hundred Years War, French monarchs had regularly granted large territories, known as appanages, to younger sons in order to secure the loyalty of those sons and to ensure that all regions of the kingdom remained firmly in the family's control. Over time, however, these branches of the family began to place their own interests above those of the kingdom and even sought to become princes in their own territories when the main royal line suffered periods of weakness.

At the root of this internal division was the crucial question of whether the king of France had full authority over the entire kingdom or whether his power was tempered by that of the nobility. During the second half of the fifteenth century and the first half of the sixteenth, a series of French kings worked to subdue their most powerful subjects. The kings succeeded in absorbing a number of appanages into the territories ruled directly by the monarchy. This reconsolidation of French territory was a key step in the development of a powerful centralized French state.

Economic and Demographic Recovery

Between 1450 and 1550 the monarchy had succeeded in reviving the political unity of France. During the same period, the population and economic activity of the kingdom also recovered. Although no precise figures exist, it is generally accepted that by the opening decades of the sixteenth century, France's population was growing rapidly and that by 1560 it had reached around 20 million, a level not seen since the dawn of the fourteenth century. France's cities also grew dramatically between 1450 and 1550. Paris, for instance, again reached its pre–Black Death population of 200,000 during this period. The thriving cities were once again centers of both trade and manufacturing.

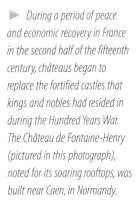

▶ *During a period of peace and economic recovery in France in the second half of the fifteenth century, châteaus began to replace the fortified castles that kings and nobles had resided in during the Hundred Years War. The Château de Fontaine-Henry (pictured in this photograph), noted for its soaring rooftops, was built near Caen, in Normandy.*

In the opening half of the sixteenth century, then, the French economy appeared to be in good shape. Yet there was trouble on the horizon. Agricultural production had been failing to keep pace with the growing population, and thus the price of bread and other goods had risen faster than wages. One historian has estimated that the purchasing power of rural workers around Paris fell by 50 percent between 1450 and 1550. Unemployment and homelessness became problems in both urban and rural areas. However, France's prosperity collapsed only in the second half of the sixteenth century, owing partly to the pressures on the growing population and partly to the outbreak of the wars of religion.

The Renaissance in France

From 1494 France entered a new phase of expansion. French monarchs invaded Italy in wars of conquest, and although the military results of these wars were mixed, their effect on the society and culture of France was profound. While fighting in Italy from the 1490s to the 1550s, French monarchs and the nobles who served in their armies came into direct contact with Italian culture at the height of the Italian Renaissance. When they returned to France, the members of the nobility brought with them many sophisticated Italian habits. Court etiquette became more refined; in order to succeed in the king's service, nobles were expected to display not only military but also intellectual prowess. In addition, kings modeled themselves after the aristocrats of the Italian Renaissance by surrounding their court with displays designed to emphasize

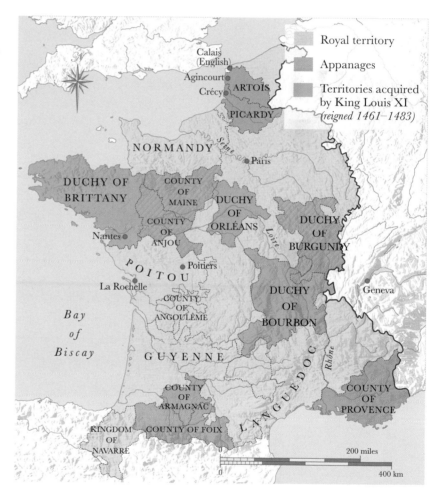

their power and grandeur. As part of this process, French kings became patrons of scholars and artists. For instance, Francis I (reigned 1515–1547), perhaps the most successful French prince of the Renaissance, funded professorships in classical languages, built up a collection of rare books that he allowed scholars to consult in his royal library, and succeeded in securing the services of the Italian artist Leonardo da Vinci at his court.

▲ One key to the monarchy's recovery of power was its ability to regain direct control over key territories within the realm. This map chronicles the gradual disappearance of the independent appanages in the fifteenth and sixteenth centuries.

▲ In 1559 the unexpected death of Henry II, the subject of this portrait by François Clouet (c. 1520–1572), left the French monarchy weak at a moment of rising religious tension.

Czech-, and Hungarian-speaking regions of Europe, whose collective wealth and population exceeded that of France.

The French monarchy neeeded to develop efficient and professional institutions in order to provide resources needed to wage war. These institutions took up permanent residence in Paris, which by the mid-sixteenth century had become the administrative center of France. In the long run, these institutions shifted the focus of power in France to the region around Paris. Indeed, by the opening of the seventeenth century, although French monarchs still visited the palaces of their predecessors in the Loire River valley, they resided primarily around Paris. Nevertheless, despite rapidly growing tax revenues, the Valois monarchs of France were hard pressed to match the resources of their Hapsburg rivals, and the collapse of the monarchy during the early religious wars was partly the inevitable result of the large debts that built up during this dynastic struggle.

The Protestant Reformation in France

In 1300 the Catholic Church in western Europe was led by the pope in Rome. Among the most important national churches that recognized the primacy of Rome was the church in France. Though loyal to the papacy, the French hierarchy was also strongly independent, and in the fifteenth century it cultivated a distinctly Gallic identity and sought to bring its influence to bear on the wider European ecclesiastical scene. Within France the church wielded significant power as one of the largest landowners in the kingdom, as the accepted intercessionary with God and the vehicle through which French Christians might secure their spiritual salvation, and as the chief provider of such social services as hospitals, education, and poor relief.

Despite the damage that Martin Luther (1483–1546) and other Reformers were inflicting on national churches throughout Europe, at the opening of the sixteenth century, the French church was not in crisis. When the ideas of the Protestant Reformation arrived in France, individuals and groups within the church had already been working for decades to reform the financial abuses perpetrated by some members of the

As well as influencing French culture and art, the Italian wars also spurred the growth of royal government in France. During the opening half of the sixteenth century, the Valois monarchs fought a long dynastic war against the rival Hapsburg family. The competition began over the territory of Naples, to which both families laid claim, but their conflict soon spread as the two families fought on multiple fronts across Europe. While France was the largest and wealthiest single kingdom in Europe, the Hapsburgs controlled a series of territories, including Spain and its colonies, the Netherlands, and extensive lands in German-, ecclesiastical hierarchy, to improve the overall quality of the clergy, and to instill greater devotion in the French population. In their critiques of the Catholic Church, these Reformers, who drew much of their inspiration from the Dutch humanist Desiderius Erasmus (c. 1456–1536), identified many of the same problems—and offered many of the same solutions—as Martin Luther had done. However, they differed substantially from Luther in that they viewed unity in the church as crucial and therefore rejected any break with Rome.

Ultimately, however, a Protestant movement that sought to break completely with the Roman Catholic Church did take shape in France. In the 1520s and 1530s a relatively small but growing number of French people adopted Protestant ideas. Holding services in secret, they began to follow different patterns of worship and increasingly took public actions in an effort to convince others to convert to their beliefs. However, it was only between 1540 and 1560, with the emergence of the French Reformer John Calvin as a leading Protestant theologian, that Protestantism took shape in France.

Three aspects of Calvin's thought underpinned his success in France. First, unlike earlier Reformers, Calvin was French and wrote in French. Second, Calvin's followers organized

▲ A contemporary engraving of the States General meeting in Paris on October 27, 1614. Since it comprised representatives of all three estates of the realm, the States General symbolically embodied the whole kingdom.

THE THREE ESTATES

From around 1450, French commentators most commonly described the social structure of their kingdom as being divided into three estates distinguished from one another by the social functions that they fulfilled. The first estate, the clergy, looked after the spiritual well-being of the kingdom. The second estate, the nobility, protected the kingdom from its enemies. The remaining 90 percent of the population made up the third estate, the peasants and townsmen who contributed to society through their labor.

The three-estate system provided the basis for the political organization of the kingdom. When, during a time of crisis, the king of France sought to consult his subjects, he often called the States General (in French, États-Généraux), which brought together representatives from across the realm. The idea of three distinct estates dominated proceedings: representatives of each estate deliberated separately. Each estate had an equal number of representatives, since each was viewed as equally important for the well-being of the realm.

In practice the first two estates received special privileges not accorded to the third. For instance, the first and second estates were exempt from many taxes, as they theoretically made their contribution to society through service rather than labor. While the estate system remained intact from 1300 to 1650, the makeup and influence of the individual estates did not. The most important change was the growth of towns during the period. As a result, the third estate was increasingly dominated by townsmen, a reflection of the growing influence of urban areas on the economic and political composition of France. Furthermore, membership in the second estate was never restricted, and through time many of the most successful urban families entered into the nobility and changed its character.

themselves into consistories, congregations led by a pastor and a council of leading laymen that were able to operate independently if necessary. The local autonomy of the consistories allowed Calvinist congregations to survive and at times even thrive in places where local authorities remained loyal to the Roman Catholic faith and actively opposed Calvinism. Third, Calvin's base in Geneva, which was just across the Swiss border from France, made it easy for Frenchmen to travel to Geneva to train to be pastors of French congregations.

Early Wars of Religion: 1559–1572

By the late 1550s the French Calvinist church, whose members were known as Huguenots, was the only organized Protestant denomination in France. By 1559 Calvinist communities had spread to such an extent that they existed in every province of the realm, although they were strongest in Normandy (in the northeast), Poitou (in the west), and Languedoc (in the south). Most converts to the Reformed faith were highly skilled and literate urban tradesmen. A second group increasingly attracted to the new movement was the nobility, including some of the most powerful families in the realm. At its peak in the early 1560s, the Calvinist church in France counted roughly 10 percent of the population among its members.

Until 1560 the monarchy, by maintaining political peace in France and suppressing Calvin's followers, ensured that the Protestant movement possessed no legal standing in the kingdom. However, following Henry II's premature death on July 10, 1559, and the succession of his young and sickly son Francis II, the kingdom rapidly fell into a period of violent religious and civil war. The initial outbreak of war was sparked by the dominance of Francis II's government by the Guises, one of France's most powerful noble families. The Guises quickly took control of the king's patronage system and placed their supporters in most of the important positions in the realm. Other powerful families aligned themselves in opposition to the Guises, and the divide took on a religious as well as a political character. The Guises became defenders of the Catholic faith, while many of their opponents adopted Protestantism.

Guise dominance of the government lasted only as long as the brief reign of Francis, who died in December 1560. In the place of the Guises, a more moderate government formed around the ten-year-old Charles IX (reigned 1560–1574), the younger brother of Francis,

A sixteenth-century Protestant historian uses evidence from the earliest histories of France to promote the sovereignty of the people over tyrannical or corrupt monarchs:

I think it abundantly clear from these references and from many other similar ones that the kings of Francogallia [ancient France] were constituted by the authoritative decision and desire of the people, that is, of the orders, or, as we are now accustomed to say, of the estates, rather than by any hereditary right. The custom employed by our ancestors in the installation of kings is another powerful argument to the same effect. We may observe from that custom we have remarked a little earlier, which Cornelius Tacitus reported of the Caninefates, the fellow-countrymen of the Franks—namely the placing of the designated king on a shield and his elevation upon the shoulders of those present—this was the custom practiced among our kings. . . . It is to be understood that, in as much as it was the right and power of the estates and the people to constitute and maintain kings, so, if at least all our annals do not lie, the supreme power of deposing kings was also that of the people. The very first man to be made king of Francogallia offers us a remarkable proof of his power. When the people discovered that he was given to shameful acts and libidinous behavior, spending his time in debauchery and fornication, they removed him by public consent and expelled him from Gaul.

François Hotman, *Francogallia*

▼ *The Saint Bartholomew's Day Massacre, the subject of this engraving by Anvers Bouttats, was the bloodiest event of the religious wars. While the massacre failed to break the resistance of the Protestants, as its perpetrators had hoped, its ultimate effect was to place French Protestants on the defensive.*

Masacro Sucedido alos Hugenotes en Paris a 24 de Agosto is72 dia de 'S.Bartolon del mar con mas de 500 Barones y señores Principales.

and his mother, Catherine de Médicis. This government sought but failed to find a compromise between the rival noble factions and the rival faiths. A series of indecisive civil wars in the 1560s ensued as nobles and cities lined up on either side of the religious divide. At the end of each bout of hostility, the monarchy sought to secure a compromise peace that involved some sort of limited toleration of the Protestant minority. These attempts to broker peace failed to last because they proved unacceptable to either party.

A new phase of hostilities began in 1572, when the Catholic party, with at least the tacit support of the king, massacred most of the Huguenots in Paris. The bloodbath, known as the Saint Bartholomew's Day Massacre, spread to over a dozen other cities. The king's implication in the planning of the massacre resulted in a profound break with the Huguenots, who now openly opposed the monarch. In the south of France, where Protestants were most numerous, they fortified the towns against further expected attacks. In doing so, they established what amounted to an independent Protestant confederation, over which the king had little real control. While Catholic forces failed to dislodge the Protestants from this region in the 1570s, after the Saint Bartholomew's Day Massacre the Protestants generally took a more defensive position. They no longer dreamed, as they had in the early 1560s, of converting the whole of France to their faith but rather of defending their church and their congregations from the majority Catholic population.

Au mois de Iuillet de l'an 1593. Ce Prince fit la Ceremonie de son Abjuration dans L'Eglise de St Denis a deux lieües de Paris entre les mains de l'arche= vêque de Bourges et 7. ou 8. Evêques assistans et tous les grands de sa Cour, Gabriel d'Etrée même qui avoit beaucoup Contribué a sa Conversion.

▲ *Despite being next in line to the throne, Henry IV succeeded in gaining the obedience of many of his Catholic subjects only when he officially renounced his Protestant faith in 1593. Henry's abjuration, which took place at Saint-Denis, near Paris, is depicted in this contemporary engraving.*

Later Wars of Religion: 1572–1598

In 1574 the religious struggle entered its final phase when Charles IX died childless and his brother Henry III took the throne. At this point the throne still seemed securely Catholic, but in 1584, when Henry's last living brother died, the king had not yet produced an heir. The next in line to the throne was Henry of Navarre, the leader of the Protestant party. The threat of a Protestant king inspired Catholics, under the leadership of the Guise family, to form the Holy League. The league sought alliances with King Philip II of Spain (a Catholic) and Pope Sixtus V. Open hostilities broke out in 1588, in part owing to Henry III's assassination of leading members of the Guise family, who he feared threatened his authority. The assassinations sparked an open rebellion by the Holy League against Henry III, who was himself killed by a leaguer in 1589.

Following Henry III's death, Henry of Navarre, now Henry IV of France (reigned 1589–1610), faced the difficult task of pacifying the kingdom that he inherited. He could count on support from his Protestant followers, foreign Protestant governments, and those Frenchmen who valued the continuity of the monarchy over other considerations. However, he faced the determined opposition of the Holy League, whose members included Paris and other leading towns. Henry's Catholic opponents argued that,

WHY DID FRANCE REMAIN CATHOLIC?

A number of factors prevented a form of Calvinism from becoming the dominant faith in France. John Calvin's theology had a strong appeal among certain sectors of the population—literate townsmen, intellectuals, and the nobility, for example—but apart from some peasants living on the estates of Protestant nobles, few rural communities were drawn to the new faith. The majority of the nobility, together with the Catholic clergy, royal officials, and other members of France's social elite, remained loyal to the Roman Catholic faith.

Perhaps the most important factor in France's enduring Catholicism was the French monarchy's steadfast adherence to the faith. The monarchy had a compelling reason to remain Catholic: in 1516 Pope Leo X granted French monarchs the right to nominate individuals to most of the important positions within the French church. To turn away from the Catholic faith would have brought to an end this important source of patronage, which the kings used to reward supporters and secure royal influence throughout the kingdom.

In addition, by 1500 the French monarchy had succeeded in establishing the notion that the king ruled by the will of God. The imagery and rituals that underpinned this divine-right conception of monarchy were based on medieval Catholic beliefs. Many of the king's officials were reluctant to tolerate a Protestant minority in the kingdom, for by rejecting the king's religion, the Protestants seemed to be rejecting the king's very right to rule.

as Henry was not a Catholic, he could not take the throne. In 1593 Henry's opponents summoned the States General to name a Catholic king. The key to Henry's success in pacifying France was his renunciation of his Protestant faith in 1593, an act that allowed many wavering Catholics to accept his rule in the hope that he could reestablish peace and order.

By 1598 Henry had subdued the Holy League, which had been unable to agree on a viable alternative king. He also issued the Edict of Nantes (1598), which gave French Protestants limited legal status. This edict proved enduring and ushered in nearly twenty years of peace in the kingdom. The wars of religion were destructive and destabilizing. They also redefined the religious landscape of France. For the first time, more than one faith was legally recognized in the kingdom.

The Rise of Absolutism

Henry IV was the first of a new royal dynasty, the Bourbons. Henry and his son Louis XIII (reigned 1610–1643) rebuilt and then expanded the monarchy's authority in the opening half of the seventeenth century. While Henry inherited the throne in unpromising circumstances, by the time he died in 1610, he had convinced many of the powerful nobles, towns, and other interested groups that respect for his authority was the best way to reestablish peace and prosperity in France. In doing so, he drew on traditional medieval ideas of the king's close relationship to God in order to assert his ability to make decisions for the kingdom that none of his subjects were entitled to question. This powerful idea of kingship, known as absolutism, was more fully developed by Louis XIII and Louis XIV (reigned 1643–1715) and became a key feature of the Bourbon style of government.

Louis XIII also expanded the power of the monarchy by strengthening the government and the army. He crushed the military and political power of the Protestants in France even as he continued to recognize their right to practice their religion. In common with some of his predecessors, Louis engaged in foreign wars that channeled the warlike tendencies of his nobility into projects outside the kingdom. Put together,

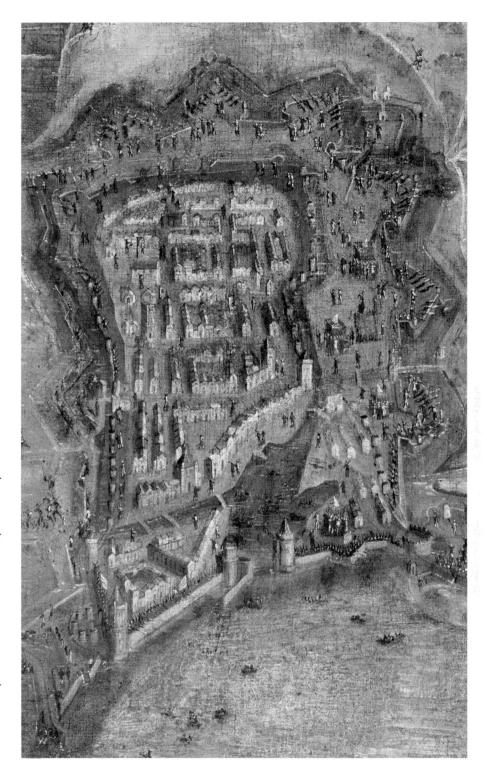

▲ In the 1620s Louis XIII conducted a series of military campaigns against Protestant towns in the kingdom. The 1627 siege of the western seaport of La Rochelle, one of the most powerful Protestant strongholds, is the subject of this seventeenth-century painting. Although Louis's campaigns ultimately destroyed the political power of the Protestants, he allowed them to continue practicing their faith.

these developments solidified the monarchy and drew France together as a nation with a shared identity and, increasingly, a shared set of institutions defined and controlled by the monarchy.

▲ Chenonceaux, a magnificent Renaissance palace on the Cher River in central France, was rebuilt in the sixteenth century by Diane de Poitiers, the mistress of Henry II, and became a favorite of Henry's wife, Catherine de Médicis, after Henry's death.

France in 1650

In 1650 France was a larger and more unified kingdom than it had been in 1300. In 1650 the monarchy, under the child-king Louis XIV, suffered a rebellion known as the Fronde (France's last major rebellion before the French Revolution of 1789). Nevertheless, the long-term future of a single French state was already largely in place. Royal government was far more powerful and professional than it had been. The people viewed themselves as French, and langue d'oïl, the language of northern France (increasingly referred to simply as the French language after 1500), was more and more widespread. A vast majority of the population openly identified themselves as Catholic, an identity forged during the struggles with Calvinists in the sixteenth century. In the second half of the seventeenth century, under the leadership of Louis XIV, France was to become the premier power in Europe—owing in no small part to the formative influences of the previous three and a half centuries. The subjects of Louis XIV, while still somewhat divided along regional lines, considered themselves French more than ever.

FURTHER READING

Baumgartner, Frederic J. *France in the Sixteenth Century.* New York, 1995.

Collins, James B. *From Tribes to Nation: The Making of France 500–1799.* Fort Worth, TX, 2002.

Knecht, R. J. *The Rise and Fall of Renaissance France.* Malden, MA, 2001.

Eric Nelson

Francis I

KING FRANCIS I OF FRANCE
(REIGNED 1515–1547) RULED HIS
NATION AT THE HEIGHT OF THE
NORTHERN RENAISSANCE AND IN
THE OPENING DECADES OF THE
PROTESTANT REFORMATION.

Accession to the Throne

On January 1, 1515, Francis was crowned king of France, but at the time of his birth on September 12, 1494, his accession to the throne had seemed unlikely. He was born into a cadet (younger) branch of the ruling Valois family and became king only when both Charles VIII and Louis XII, his distant cousins, died without male heirs. Francis inherited a monarchy that was growing in strength. Since the conclusion of the Hundred Years War half a century earlier (in 1453), Francis's predecessors had succeeded in reining in the considerable power of the regional lords. Francis's immediate predecessors had also used their strengthened position within France to pursue the Valois family's claims to the territories of Milan (in northern Italy) and Naples (in southern Italy). By the time Francis acceded to the throne, the French monarchy was among the most powerful in Europe, and the Valois dynasty was one of western Europe's most influential families.

From Triumph to Catastrophe (1515–1530)

Francis wasted little time in identifying himself as an active and ambitious monarch. During the final years of his reign, Francis's predecessor, Louis XII, had lost control of almost all the Italian territories claimed by the Valois family. By August 1515, within months of taking the throne, Francis had organized an army and set out for Italy to regain these lands. His invasion of Italy culminated in the Battle of Marignano on September 13, 1515. At Marignano, Francis decisively defeated his opponents in a bloody battle that left him in control of Milan. The following year Francis's opponent, the Holy Roman emperor Maximilian I, failed to retake Milan. Francis could look back on his first two years of rule with no little satisfaction. He had proven his ability in war, reclaimed lands lost by his predecessor, and soundly defeated his chief rival.

However, in the years following the conquest of Milan, the balance of power in Europe began to shift against Francis. During this period Charles of Luxembourg, a member of the rival Hapsburg dynasty, rose through a series of inheritances to rival Francis in power and prestige. By 1515 Charles ruled a string of territories centered on the Netherlands. In 1516 his domain was greatly enlarged when he inherited the significant Spanish territories of Aragon and Castile and the Italian kingdom of Naples.

▶ This scene, a relief on the tomb of Francis I at Saint-Denis, near Paris, depicts the king's decisive victory at the Battle of Marignano (September 13, 1515), where Francis established his reputation as a military leader.

▶ The famous meeting of December 1515 between Francis I and Pope Leo X, depicted in this work by Giovanni Bilivert (1585–1644), led ultimately to the Concordat of Bologna, which granted French monarchs the right to appoint churchmen. Possession of this right made conversion to the Protestant faith less attractive to French monarchs.

A few years later Charles inherited extensive lands in central Europe. In 1519, when he was elected Holy Roman emperor as Charles V, he became Francis's most dangerous rival in Europe. For the remainder of his reign, Francis found himself locked in a struggle with Charles over which dynasty—Valois or Hapsburg—was preeminent in western Europe.

In 1521 open hostilities broke out between Francis and Charles, and by 1522 Francis had lost his conquests in Italy. This setback turned into catastrophe in 1525, when Francis attempted to reverse his fortunes by regaining Milan. The campaign ended in disaster at the Battle of Pavia on February 24, 1525. Francis's army was defeated, and Francis himself was captured. He became the prisoner of Charles and secured his release only in March 1526, when he agreed to the Treaty of Madrid. Among other concessions, the treaty required Francis to cede the duchy of Burgundy, in the eastern part of his kingdom. He was also required to give up his two sons as hostages until he fulfilled his treaty obligations. Upon his return to France, Francis argued

that he had signed the treaty under duress and refused to ratify it. He sought to renegotiate the terms by offering gold rather than territories as a ransom for his sons. At the same time he sought to put pressure on Charles by establishing alliances across Europe and once again invading Italy.

War ensued, but by 1529 neither Francis nor Charles had gained any significant military advantage, and so both were ready to negotiate. From July 1529 peace talks began in earnest between Louise of Savoy, Francis's mother, and Margaret of Austria, Charles's aunt. Under the terms of the resulting Peace of the Ladies, completed on August 3, Charles agreed to return Francis's sons for a ransom of two million gold crowns instead of the duchy of Burgundy. For his part Francis agreed to give up all Valois claims to the duchy of Milan and the kingdom of Naples together with claims to territories on the northeastern border of France. While the terms of the agreement by no means consituted a victory for Francis, he was at least allowed to keep his kingdom intact and recover his sons.

During the sixteenth century the republic of Venice regularly posted ambassadors to the French court. The description of Francis reproduced here was written by one of these ambassadors, Marino Cavalli, in 1547, toward the end of Francis's reign.

The king is now fifty-four years old: his appearance is quite regal, so that even without having his face or his portrait, simply looking at him, one says immediately: "this is the king." His movements are so noble and majestic that no prince can equal him. His character is sturdy, in spite of the excessive fatigues which he has always endured and still endures in so many expeditions and journeys. He eats and drinks a great deal; sleeps even better and, what is more, he thinks only of leading a gay life. He is careful about his dress, which is full of braids and trimmings, rich in precious stones and ornaments. If the king endures bodily fatigues unflinchingly, he finds mental preoccupations more difficult to bear and hands them over almost entirely to the cardinal of Tournon and the admiral. He takes no decision and gives no reply without first listening to their advice: in all things he follows their counsel. But in all the great matters of state, matters of peace or war, his Majesty, who is submissive in everything else, insists on his will being obeyed. In this event there is no one at court, however great their authority, who dares remonstrate with his Majesty. This prince has a sound judgment and wide learning; there is no object, study or art on which he cannot argue pertinently or judge with as much assurance as a specialist. His knowledge is not confined simply to the art of war. He understands not only all that concerns naval warfare but is also very experienced in hunting, painting, literature, languages and the different bodily exercises appropriate to a good knight. Truly, when one sees that in spite of his knowledge and fine speeches, all his martial exploits have failed, one says that all his wisdom is on his lips, not in his mind. But I believe that the adversities of this prince are due to the lack of men able to carry out well his designs.

Quoted in R. J. Knecht, *French Renaissance Monarchy: Francis I and Henry II*

▼ *Francis's strong character is vividly captured in this famous portrait by Jean Clouet (c. 1485–c. 1540).*

Francis and the Protestant Reformation

The opening decades of Francis's reign were dominated by foreign wars, but at home Francis faced another serious challenge: the Protestant Reformation. Throughout his reign Francis maintained his loyalty to the Catholic faith. This loyalty stemmed in part from Francis's own religious beliefs and in part from his success, during the early part of his reign, in securing control over the appointment of Catholic churchmen in France. Under the terms of the Concordat of Bologna, which Francis signed in 1516, Pope Leo X granted Francis and his successors the right to nominate most of the bishops and abbots in France, subject only to approval by the papacy. The agreement allowed Francis to place his preferred candidates in important church positions throughout the land and thus gave him an extremely useful way of making his influence felt in the regions. Francis viewed Protestants as a threat not only to the church but also to his own power and authority.

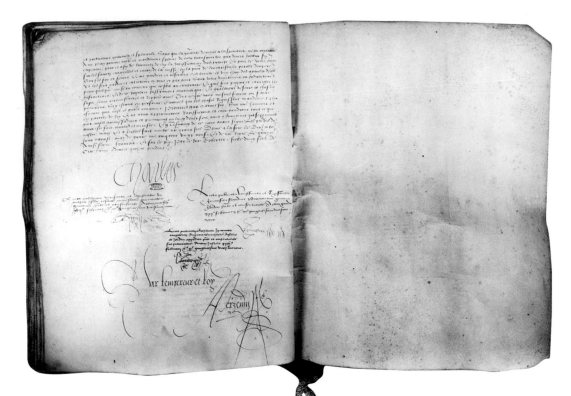

During his reign Francis took stronger and stronger actions to eradicate Protestants from his kingdom. He maintained the view that to tolerate multiple faiths within France would be to threaten the integrity of the state and that any such tolerance would lead only to disorder and civil war. However, Francis was sympathetic, especially early in his reign, to those within his kingdom who sought to reform rather than break with the Catholic Church. Thus, while Francis supported efforts to ban the publication or possession of works by Martin Luther and other Protestants whose stated aim was to overturn the Catholic Church and replace it with a new church, at the same time he often intervened to prevent his royal courts from banning works by French humanists—whose campaigns for a return to the Bible as the primary source of Christian doctrine were not predicated on the abolition of Catholicism.

From the late 1520s Francis persecuted Protestants with greater determination. To a certain extent he was responding to the provocative actions of some Protestants, actions that Francis viewed as challenges to the public peace and to his authority. The key incident that hardened the king's policies occurred in 1528, when a statue of the Virgin and Child that stood at a crossroads in Paris was vandalized. Francis reacted to the vandalism by offering a substantial reward for the capture of those responsible and by paying for a new statue. He also supported increasingly strong actions by his courts to discover and suppress Protestants within the kingdom.

The persecution of Protestants intensified in the later years of Francis's reign, and although the number of Protestants in his kingdom continued to grow, he was able to keep Protestants from practising their faith in public.

Renewed Dynastic Conflict (1530–1547)

The Peace of the Ladies failed to end the rivalry between Francis and Charles. Francis used the years of peace to construct new alliances against Charles while at the same time rebuilding his treasury and army. Despite his strong actions to defend the Catholic Church at home, Francis had no scruples in seeking alliances with Protestant rulers across Europe and even with the Islamic rulers of the Ottoman Empire. In November 1536 Francis once again took direct

ABSOLUTE MONARCH?

The opinions of historians vary as to whether Francis was able to govern absolutely—that is, without consulting his subjects. On the one hand, it is clear that Francis was capable of acting in an authoritarian manner and of tolerating neither opposition nor criticism. On occasion he personally traveled to his royal courts and other assemblies to ensure that they acted on his will. A sense of his authoritarian manner can be gleaned from his assertion to a gathering of representatives in the south of his kingdom that "in times of necessity all privileges cease, and not only privileges but common laws as well, for necessity knows no law." Nevertheless, despite his strong theoretical statements of royal authority, Francis also proved capable of working with local elites to accomplish his goals. This flexibility reflected the fact that he needed the help of nobles, churchmen, and townsmen to raise the resources for his wars. Even at the height of his power, he had only eight thousand royal officials, or one official for every twenty-three square miles (60 km²) of his kingdom. Thus, Francis needed local cooperation in order to raise revenues for war. To secure this cooperation, he was often responsive to local concerns and protective of the special rights and privileges claimed by powerful local groups.

In retrospect, Francis's actions indicate that he believed in the absolute authority of the monarchy but at the same time understood how compromise and cooperation helped him accomplish his goals. Francis sought to increase the monarchy's authority whenever possible but not at the expense of other policy goals. The events of his reign point to the success of this pragmatic approach. He succeeded in raising unprecedented revenues from his kingdom to fund his wars. Yet neither the high nobility nor the clergy rebelled over his growing demands (the single exception was the rebellion of Charles de Bourbon in 1523). Furthermore, Francis's royal courts, towns, and the provincial representative institutions generally cooperated with Francis.

▼ *This unattributed sixteenth-century French equestrian portrait is a reminder that Francis I paid careful attention to the image that he projected.*

action against Charles when he seized the Italian Alpine state of Savoy as part of a wider strategy to regain Milan. In retaliation Charles invaded France, and open war once again broke out between the two powerful rulers.

By 1538 both Francis and Charles had once again exhausted their resources and returned to the peace table. The failure by both sides to secure a clear victory resulted in a profoundly different approach to peacemaking. Francis and Charles made a public reconciliation and sought to remove the tensions over their rival dynastic claims by marrying their sons and daughters to one another and then granting these couples the right to rule over disputed territories.

Although this plan diffused some of the tension between the Valois and Hapsburg dynasties, long-standing enmities proved impossible to suppress, and by 1542 open war broke out again. During the final years of Francis's reign, he fought an increasingly desperate defensive struggle against Charles's onslaught. Peace negotiations began again in the autumn of 1545, but by the time of Francis's death in March 1547, no lasting resolution to the Valois-Hapsburg struggle had taken shape. Francis's son and successor, Henry II, would continue the struggle.

FROM CASTLES TO CHÂTEAUS

Francis spent large sums of money renovating older royal residences and building new ones. One of the most important of his new palaces was his hunting lodge at Chambord, in north-central France. Designed for court life rather than for purposes of defense, Chambord and other such buildings, called châteaus, differed significantly from the castles in which medieval kings had resided. Though he was not the first king to build in this new style, Francis constructed the most ambitious and magnificent châteaus of the period. Chambord testified to the growing power of French monarchs, who no longer needed to worry about defense when constructing their residences. In their unparalleled grandeur and magnificence, the châteaus also embody a new image of the prince that bore the influence of Renaissance Italy, where such concepts of princeliness were first developed. Châteaus on the scale of Chambord, however, surpassed the Italian palaces in both size and grandeur. The building of magnificent princely residences in France continued into the seventeenth century and culminated in Louis XIV's splendid château at Versailles.

Francis as a Renaissance Patron

While Francis devoted much of his time and resources to war, he was also one of the great patrons of the Renaissance. In part owing to his building efforts and his patronage of artists, writers, and scholars, the Renaissance reached its height in France during his reign. In an effort to project an image of royal power and grandeur, Francis rebuilt existing royal residences and built several new palaces whose design incorporated numerous Renaissance ideas and styles. Also a leading patron of Renaissance artists, Francis regularly purchased important works of art. He brought leading Italian Renaissance artists to his court, including Leonardo da Vinci, who was painter and architect to Francis's court from 1516 until 1519, and Benvenuto Cellini, who served Francis in 1536 and then from 1540 to 1545. In the field of scholarship, Francis showed similar enthusiasm as a patron of humanist scholars. During his reign he funded a number of lectureships in Paris for the study of classical Greek and Latin, and he collected rare books in his royal library, which he allowed scholars to consult. Francis also supported literary figures at his court, most notably the poet Clément Marot. Francis's patronage had a profound impact on the flowering of French art, scholarship, and literature that characterized the period from the late sixteenth century through the end of the seventeenth.

▼ *Francis's single greatest building project was the magnificent hunting lodge, known as the Château of Chambord, built between 1519 and 1547 in the Loire region of France.*

FURTHER READING

Baumgartner, Frederic J. *France in the Sixteenth Century.* New York, 1995.

Knecht, R. J. *French Renaissance Monarchy: Francis I and Henry II.* New York, 1996.

———. *Renaissance Warrior and Patron: The Reign of Francis I.* New York, 1994.

Eric Nelson

SEE ALSO

• Charles V • France • Hapsburg Empire
• Holy Roman Empire • Leonardo da Vinci
• Monarchy • Reformation • Renaissance

French Civil Wars

SPARKED BY A SERIES OF MONARCHICAL CRISES AND EXACERBATED BY RELIGIOUS AND POLITICAL FACTIONALISM, THE FRENCH CIVIL WARS (1563–1629) SLOWED FRANCE'S MOVEMENT TOWARD BECOMING A NATION-STATE.

By the sixteenth century France was still far from achieving political centralization, and the king struggled to establish his authority throughout his territory. The fundamental laws of the realm set limits on the royal prerogative. Since these laws distinguished between the person of the king (who was mortal) and the dignity of the crown (which was perpetual), it was deemed acceptable to question the king's authority if that authority was perceived to challenge the laws. The laws insisted above all that the king should be Catholic (as he swore to be in his coronation oath).

▼ This stained glass of around 1562 depicts Huguenots (French Calvinists) attempting to burn Catholic relics. Relics, supposed by many Catholics to have miraculous powers, had been ridiculed by Protestants since the start of the Reformation in Germany.

The king's council and the court were the focal points for the administration and government of the kingdom. The court was itinerant; Paris only gradually became the central seat of government. The move toward political centralization in Paris was helped partly by the enormous jurisdiction of the Paris parliament, which covered two-thirds of the French kingdom. The absence of political unity within the kingdom was underscored by the lack of well-defined borders—indeed, many people living at the eastern frontier were unsure whether they were subject to the French kingdom or to the Holy Roman Empire. Moreover, the French were divided along linguistic and legal lines. The lack of centralized control was also manifest in the outdated and inefficient system of taxation.

The French monarchy was further weakened by the series of dynastic wars fought between the Valois kings and the Hapsburgs, their bitter rivals for supremacy in Europe, between 1494 and 1559. The burdensome costs of these wars (especially of hiring foreign mercenaries) left France in a state of chronic economic instability. When the wars were ended, France's warrior aristocracy, still deeply attached to chivalric ideals, was left without a purpose. Among the economic repercussions of the wars was a sharp contraction in royal pensions. Nobles, inadequately rewarded for their service, became politically disaffected.

The Early Civil Wars: 1563–1572

The wars lasted as long as they did because no side was strong enough to defeat the other conclusively. In 1560 Louis de Bourbon, prince of Condé (1530–1569), became the official protector of the Huguenots (French Calvinists). He subsequently commanded the Huguenot forces in the first three wars. Under his influence the Huguenots sought to overturn the Catholic hegemony in France and establish a Reformed church. During the early skirmishes of the first war (April 1562–March 1563), Condé's initial victories at Orléans, Angers, Tours, Blois, Lyon, and Rouen were soon met and checked by a successful Catholic counteroffensive, which culminated in the Huguenot loss of Tours and Blois.

ORIGINS OF THE FRENCH CIVIL WARS

The primary cause of the French civil wars was the religious conflict between Catholics and Calvinists, which intensified during the 1550s and early 1560s. With the rise of Calvinism and its transformation into a major religious and political movement, the long-standing national myth that France's future security lay in its close association with the Catholic Church was cast into serious doubt. The profound disagreements between Calvinists and Catholics on fundamental points of Christian doctrine and on the rightful structure and role of the church itself made conflict very likely, if not inevitable. Calvinism, a dynamic and highly disciplined political and religious force, posed a considerable threat to the religious unity of the French state. The resilience of French Calvinism was proved by its ability to develop into a mass movement in the face of sustained persecution—around 1,200 churches were established during the 1560s, and at the movement's peak in 1563, there were approximately 1.8 million French Calvinists.

The politicization of Calvinism helped it to become firmly entrenched within French society. At court Calvinism gained some of its most fervent adherents, including Louis, prince of Condé, Gaspard II de Coligny (a close confidant of Charles IX), and Henry of Navarre (the future King Henry IV). Religious disunity added another ingredient to the factional strife among the nobility, strife that had existed before the rise of Calvinism. By winning converts among leading members of the aristocracy, Calvinists became a divisive force in the provinces: according to the system of clientage, the conversion of a powerful noble would leave his clients with little choice but to follow their patron.

The progress toward war was accelerated by the unexpected death of Henry II in 1559 during a jousting accident. As a consequence, France was deprived of an adult male ruler. Henry's successor, Francis II, was easily dominated by the Guises (the family of his wife, Mary Stuart), a situation that accentuated aristocratic rivalries. After the death of Francis II in 1560, the throne was occupied by a minor, Charles IX, who was dominated by his mother, Queen Catherine de Médicis (1519–1589). The lack of an effective monarch—together with Catherine's failure to reconcile the two opposing sides—brought war closer. Catherine's apparent incompetence and naivety notwithstanding, even a strong monarch would have struggled to prevent the civil wars from breaking out, such was the degree of political and religious intransigence manifested by both sides on the eve of the conflict.

▼ *An unattributed portrait of Gaspard II de Coligny, a leading French aristocrat whose conversion to Protestantism during the 1550s was instrumental to subsequent Calvinist success. Following the death of Louis, prince of Condé, in 1569, Coligny took command of the Protestant forces; such was his authority that he became a very close confidant of Charles IX. Indeed, Coligny's close relationship with the king was one of the main reasons why Coligny became the target of an assassination attempt in 1572.*

Similarly, toward the end of the first war, although the Catholic Guise family defeated the Huguenots at the Battle of Dreux (December 1562) and although Condé was eventually captured, the Catholics lost the marshal of Saint-André and the duke of Guise (who were killed) and the key military leader Anne, duke of Montmorency (who was captured). The second war (September 1567–March 1568) was equally inconclusive since the successful Huguenot uprising that led to the seizure of Orléans, Nîmes, and Montpellier was counteracted by the Huguenots' failure to reach Paris and their continued inability to control the monarchy. Each side was unable to inflict a decisive victory on the other during the course of the third war (August 1568–August 1570). The duke of Anjou defeated the Huguenots at Jarnac, in the west-central region of Poitou (March 1569), where Condé was killed, and at Montcontour, in the northwestern region of Brittany (October 1569). Nevertheless, Gaspard de Coligny managed to

reestablish Protestant strength through brilliant maneuvers in the south and southwest (especially in Angoulême, Montauban, and Castres).

The protraction of the civil wars was due also to the interventions of foreign powers. As a result of these interventions, both sides were able to mobilize continual supplies of fresh troops. During the first war Condé negotiated (in September 1562) an English promise of six thousand troops and a loan of 100,000 crowns in return for the northwestern port of Le Havre, while the Catholic Guises gained the active support of Pope Pius IV and King Philip II of Spain. The international dimension of the conflict reemerged during the second war, in which renewed Spanish aid for the Catholics was counterbalanced by the support of John Casimir (the son of Count Frederick III of the German Palatinate) for the Huguenot cause. Spanish intervention increased during the third war, especially when Spain discovered that William of Orange and his brother Louis of Nassau had made an alliance with Condé and Coligny in August 1568

(William of Orange was a Protestant leader who opposed the Spanish Catholics in the Netherlands). The conflicts between Catholics and Protestants in the Netherlands (under Spanish rule) and France thus became increasingly connected. During the course of the third war, the Huguenots received additional support from Wolfgang of Zweibrücken, who led a German army that succeeded in overrunning Burgundy.

The continuation of the wars was due also to the failure of successive peace treaties. The cool reception that both sides of the religious divide gave the Peace of Amboise, which concluded the first war in March 1563, set the pattern for the later treaties. Calvinists, angered by the bias shown toward the nobility (Huguenot nobles were allowed to worship freely), criticized the treaty for not granting sufficient toleration to the broader Huguenot movement (Calvinist commoners were permitted to worship only in one town per judicial district). Catholics, on the other hand, believed that the Huguenots had been granted too many concessions.

▲ *The growth and dynamism of the early Calvinist movement was accompanied by increasing militancy in the late 1550s and early 1560s. Calvinism was considered to be such a threat that French Catholics were willing to resort to violent, even murderous attacks against Calvinists to combat its spread. This contemporary engraving by Franz Hogenberg depicts a massacre of Huguenots by Catholics in a house in Cahors, in southern France, in November 1561.*

▲ *Catherine de Médicis, the subject of this unattributed sixteenth-century portrait, came from the renowned Florentine banking family, the Medicis. Following the death of her husband, Henry II (reigned 1547–1559), Catherine rose to political prominence as regent to her young sons, Francis II and Charles IX. She was faced with the unenviable and apparently insurmountable task of dealing with the religious polarity of the 1560s and 1570s. She has been blamed (by contemporary and modern authors) for the Saint Bartholomew's Day Massacre of 1572.*

Many provincial parliaments initially refused to ratify the peace edict on the grounds that, in failing to defend the country against Protestantism, the king was not honoring his coronation oath. The Peace of Longjumeau (March 1568), which brought the second war to an end, reestablished the provisions of the Peace of Amboise. That the royals attempted to bypass the parliaments by sending the edict to royal governors reflected the monarchy's fear of Catholic opposition. Concessions similar to those outlined in the Peace of Amboise were granted to the Huguenots in the Peace of Saint-Germain (immediately following the third war), although the latter agreement included some additional features. Protestants were now allowed to establish four *places de sûreté* (garrison towns), namely Cognac, La Charité, Montauban, and La Rochelle. They were permitted to worship openly in two towns in each of the twelve *gouvernements* (the largest of the

administrative districts of the kingdom). Unsurprisingly, these concessions encouraged the Huguenots to seek full parity with Catholics and frustrated the Catholics, who now found the Protestants even more difficult to dislodge.

The weakness of the monarchy was a crucial factor in the outbreak and continuation of the religious wars. Catholics and Huguenots made regular attempts to control the monarch and the court. The fear of losing influence at court often provoked an intensification of conflict. The atmosphere of distrust and fear is exemplified by Protestant suspicions concerning the Bayonne meetings (July 1565) between Catherine de Médicis, her daughter, Elizabeth of Spain, and the arch-Catholic duke of Alba. Condé and Coligny were convinced that a Franco-Spanish Catholic plot was afoot to drive out Protestants from the Spanish Netherlands and (ultimately) from France as well. The continuing Guise domination of the French court and the decision of Charles IX to summon six thousand Swiss mercenaries reinforced Protestant suspicions and provoked the Conspiracy of Meaux, a botched attempt on the part of Protestants to capture Catherine and Charles and thus "save" the monarchy from Guise domination. (This event precipitated the outbreak of the second war.) The monarchy also failed to have a commanding military presence: owing to lack of funds, it could not maintain armies in the field for long periods, and owing to the large scale of the conflict, royal troops were too widely scattered.

The Later Civil Wars: 1572–1598

The Saint Bartholomew's Day Massacre was followed by a succession of religious wars that persisted intermittently until the Edict of Nantes in 1598. The fourth war was fought in December 1572, the fifth from December 1575 to May 1576, the sixth from March to December 1577, the seventh from November 1579 to November 1580, the eighth (also known as the War of the Three Henrys) from March 1585 to August 1589, and the ninth from August 1589 to 1598. Like the early conflicts, the later civil wars were characterized by unsatisfactory peace treaties, inconclusive fighting, instances of monarchical weakness, and interventions by foreign powers.

HUGUENOT DECLINE AND RECOVERY

The massacre of Protestants on August 24, 1572, was sparked by a failed assassination attempt on the French admiral and religious leader Gaspard II de Coligny. Although it remains unclear whether Catherine de Médicis was responsible for the attempt, it is extremely likely that the Guises were involved. The fear of Protestant reprisals undoubtedly led the court to sanction a preemptive strike against the Huguenot leadership that culminated in a more or less spontaneous (though not entirely disorganized) massacre.

The Saint Bartholomew's Day Massacre had a devastating impact on Calvinists. Approximately three thousand died in Paris, and as many as seven thousand were killed in the provinces. The huge number of defections accentuated the numerical decline of the Huguenots. The Calvinist population of Rouen, for example, fell from 16,500 in 1565 to between 1,500 and 3,000 in 1572. Many Calvinists went into exile, their confidence in the sincerity of the crown's commitment to reconcile Catholics with Huguenots shattered. Protestants were devastated by the fact that the massacres in Paris had targeted numerous Huguenot nobles, including Coligny. The removal of Protestant leaders inevitably changed the religious and political balance at court. The Protestant decline was greatly exacerbated by Henry of Navarre's subsequent (forced) conversion to Catholicism and confinement within the court.

The Huguenots nonetheless survived as both a political and a religious entity. Indeed, the massacres had important political repercussions that benefited the Huguenots. Members of the moderate Catholic Politique party were shocked by the massacres and came to regard political unity and religious toleration as more important than uniformity of worship. Huguenot opposition took on an overtly political character; the Huguenots waged a war of words against a crown that had morally and politically discredited itself through its capitulation to the extremist Guise policy of extermination. The leading Huguenot political theorists, including Theodore Beza and François Hotman, maintained that resistance to the crown was legitimate when a ruler failed to perform his duties (as long as that resistance was led by the magistracy).

In practice, the Huguenots consolidated their position in southern France by closing their gates to the king's officials and by disregarding the prohibition of Reformed worship. Protestants organized political assemblies during the 1570s, and Huguenots swore an oath of union. Such was the organization of the Protestants in the south that historians have suggested the existence of a Huguenot state-within-a-state. Under the governor of Languedoc, Henry of Montmorency, the Huguenots formed their own army, law courts, and system of taxation, although the large cities, especially Toulouse and Bordeaux, remained outside of Montmorency's control.

◄ Following the Peace of Saint-Germain (1570), it was hoped that the cross-confessional marriage between Henry of Navarre (a leading Calvinist noble) and Marguerite de Valois (Charles IX's sister) in 1572 would secure a lasting reconciliation between Catholics and Protestants. Yet the tensions provoked in Paris by the presence of Protestants and Catholics in close quarters erupted into the Saint Bartholomew's Day Massacre, the subject of this painting by François Dubois (1529–1584).

the duke of Alençon, and Henry of Navarre. The Peace of Monsieur (May 1576), which concluded the fifth war, was forced on the king by Alençon, who had gained the support of Navarre, Condé, and Montmorency. The terms of the treaty included the provision of eight *places de sûretés* and the creation of special tribunals (called *chambres mi-parties*) in the parliaments. This concession allowed for equal numbers of Catholic and Protestant judges in a bid to prevent discrimination (an extremely favorable measure given that it became law only four years after the Saint Bartholomew's Day Massacre).

Inherently weak and irresponsible, Henry III was unable to control Paris, where Catholic extremists saw him as insufficiently robust in his defense of the faith. In response to mounting protests from Catholics, in 1588 Henry assassinated two prominent Catholic agitators, the duke of Guise and the cardinal of Lorraine. This action proved fatal to Henry himself; he was assassinated in 1589. The difficulty experienced by his successor, Henry IV, in regaining the capital (the seat of government) illustrates the extent of the political crisis.

A further important characteristic of the later civil wars was the deteriorating socioeconomic conditions, especially in rural areas. Peasants were under pressure not only from royal taxation but also from the increasing decentralization of the taxation system, a situation that allowed provincial officials to abuse the chaotic context of the civil wars for their own benefit. The passage through the countryside of large numbers of troops, many of whom lived off the land, also devastated the peasants. Rural opposition found expression in the rebellions in Provence (1578), the Rhône valley (1579), and Normandy and in numerous other rebellions in the 1580s and 1590s. The Croquants rebellion, which rose up in the southwest between 1593 and 1595, was by far the most dramatic. The economic instability was aggravated by the general European crisis in the late 1580s and 1590s and by a succession of harvest failures, famines, and plagues. Nevertheless, despite the considerable socioeconomic, religious, and political instability during the later religious wars, Henry IV eventually managed to restore a semblance of order.

▲ *A portrait by François Quesnel (c. 1545–1616) of Henry III, who was unqualified to deal with the intractable religious conflicts of the 1580s and was distrusted by many on both sides of the religious divide. In 1588 Henry ordered the assassination of two leading Catholic agitators; the following year he in turn was assassinated. With his death the Valois line became extinct.*

The later religious wars were also characterized by the further decline of royal authority. Following the death of Charles IX in 1574, Charles's brother, the duke of Anjou, now Henry III, was slow in returning to France from Poland, where he had ruled briefly. An ineffective and weak king, Henry III allowed himself to be influenced by younger male favorites (called *mignons*) and turned a blind eye toward misconduct. Henry did not assert his authority over Montmorency in the south; moreover, he failed to prevent the flight from court of his brother,

THE RISE AND DEMISE OF THE HOLY LEAGUE

Founded in 1576, the Holy League convinced Henry III that he should cancel the majority of concessions granted to Protestants in the Peace of Monsieur (1576) and demanded vigorous wars against the Huguenots. Following the death of the duke of Alençon in 1584, Henry of Navarre, a Protestant, became heir to the throne. In response the league became far more aggressive. Catholic political pamphleteers surpassed their Protestant opponents in their radicalism. The newly founded military confraternities, together with major Catholic nobles and the Spanish (through the Treaty of Joinville, signed in December 1584), expressed their total commitment to the eradication of Protestantism in France. The main focus of the Catholics, the denunciation of Henry of Navarre's claim to the throne, illustrated the importance that they attached to the crown's intimate historical relationship with Catholicism. Leaguers seized Chalon-sur-Saône, Dijon, Mâcon, and Auxonne and by the late 1580s were in control of numerous provinces and cities. In 1588 they took over Paris on the so-called Day of the Barricades (in the process they drove Henry III out of his own capital). Such was the league's commitment to its cause that Henry III, seen as too weak in his defense of Catholicism, was assassinated in 1589. The league became even more determined to prevent the accession of the Protestant Henry of Navarre.

The demise of the Holy League can be attributed to a combination of Henry IV's strengths and the league's weaknesses. Henry IV secured two excellent victories at Arques (September 1589) and Ivry (March 1590), despite the fact that his troops were outnumbered on both occasions. Meanwhile, the league became deeply divided between its aristocratic and urban factions. The split was cemented by the extremism of the Sixteen, the secret council that led the league's activities in Paris. In November 1591 the Sixteen hanged three moderate members of the Paris parliament. In response the duke of Mayenne, leader of the league, was forced to take action. In December he hanged four members of the Sixteen and disbanded the rest. The league was also divided concerning who should succeed Henry IV, especially after the main claimant, the cardinal of Bourbon, died in May 1590. Furthermore, by the early 1590s (after nine civil wars), a significant majority of the French population had become war weary. Henry IV emerged as the only force with sufficient authority to resolve the conflict. The final major obstacle to Henry's accession was removed by his abjuration of Protestantism. Within a year of his conversion to Catholicism, most cities (including Paris, Lyon, and Rouen) proclaimed their allegiance to Henry. The passing of the league was thus assured.

from the duke of Mayenne in October 1595, and in 1596 Mayenne dissolved the Holy League.

Henry III's supporters generally came to Henry IV's side, ostensibly on the grounds that he had (eventually) fought alongside them in the War of the Three Henrys, though they were also undoubtedly enticed by the substantial payments, titles, and offices Henry provided. The restoration of order was facilitated by the people's disillusionment after decades of civil war that had torn society apart (communally, socially, and economically). Nevertheless, Henry insisted on bringing the different noble factions together by declaring war on Spain in January 1595. He had previously fueled anti-Spanish hostility by stressing the league's dependence on foreign troops and money and thereby rallying the population under a banner of French patriotism (despite the fact that he had himself relied on English aid).

The Edict of Nantes and the Conclusion of the Civil Wars

The people's loss of patience with the civil wars was illustrated by their willingness to support the Edict of Nantes (1598), which was similar to preceding peace edicts. Although it was not immediately ratified by all of the provincial parliaments, there was no new outbreak of hostilities, and peace reigned beyond the death of Henry IV in 1610. In May 1598 Henry also concluded the war with Spain by signing the Treaty of Vervins. In the context of the relative peace that followed, Henry worked together with the duke of Sully in strengthening the economy. Following Henry's death, however, peace gradually gave way to war, and Louis XIII raised forces against the Huguenots during the early 1620s. Louis's first minister, Armand-Jean du Plessis, cardinal of Richelieu (1585–1642), sought to weaken the political and military status of the Huguenots, and the western seaport of La Rochelle became a particular target. After La Rochelle's surrender to royal forces in October 1628, the Peace of Alais (1629) stripped the Huguenots of their political and military privileges. While they retained some religious concessions, the Huguenots were no longer allowed to maintain garrisons. From the late 1620s on, Richelieu was forced to defend his religious com-

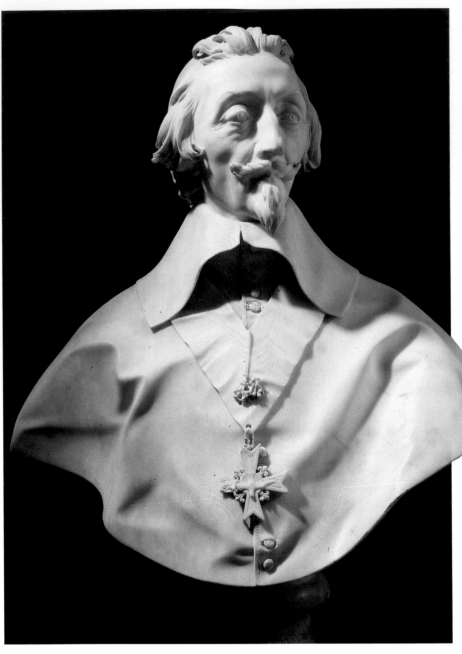

▲ *A marble bust by Gian Lorenzo Bernini (1598–1680) of Cardinal Richelieu, first minister under Louis XIII. Richelieu granted Protestants religious toleration (while undermining their political status) at a time when Catholics were in the ascendancy. In addition, by incorporating the Protestant aristocracy in a foreign military campaign, Richelieu managed to alleviate the religious tensions that had devastated France for decades.*

Henry IV's restoration of order was made possible above all by his conversion to Roman Catholicism in July 1593. Once he had regained control of Paris in March 1594, he was better placed to reestablish monarchical authority. Thanks to considerable financial advancements, the leaguers now sided with the monarchy and guaranteed their loyalty (though some, such as the duke of Mercoeur, excepted themselves from this guarantee). Henry IV received submission

CONFLICTING INTERPRETATIONS OF THE FRENCH CIVIL WARS

The traditional interpretation of the French civil wars has attributed the outbreak of war and the continuing instability of the period to political factors. The historians Lucien Romier and James Westfall Thompson have argued in favor of a political crisis that resulted mainly from the factional rivalry at court. In their view religious factors were less important than political factors; they argue that religion was frequently exploited as a cloak to disguise political motivations. The growth of Calvinism is thus attributed to political disaffection with the Guise ascendancy rather than to genuine religious conviction.

Since the early 1970s, however, social historians have paid closer attention to the socioeconomic and religious motivations of ordinary people, as well as to the interests and motivations of the major protagonists. Henry Heller emphasized the predominance of socioeconomic grievances and thereby downplayed religious causes. While socioeconomic factors cannot be ignored, more recent scholarship has rightly asserted that religion played a major role in the civil wars. The importance of religion can be fully understood only when monarchical, political, and social factors are also taken into consideration. The works of Natalie Davis and Barbara Diefendorf highlight the practical and collective manifestations of religion; religion was a decisive force in early modern society because its significance was understood not merely in terms of beliefs but also in a communal context—that is, in terms of a body of believers. An appreciation of the cultural clash between the Protestant and Catholic communities is fundamental to an understanding of the duration and the intensity of the French civil wars.

▲ A seventeenth-century engraving of three hundred Huguenot families leaving La Rochelle in November 1661 owing to religious persecution. Neither Richelieu nor Cardinal Mazarin (Richelieu's successor) had intended to grant Protestants permanent toleration; the policies of both men were a purely pragmatic means of guaranteeing stability. Even before the 1685 revocation of the Edict of Nantes, French Protestants feared the worst, as religious persecution reemerged from the 1660s on.

promise against the remnants of the Holy League, who were known as the *dévots*. Led by Michel de Marillac, guardian of the seals, and Marie de Médicis, the *dévots* promoted a pro-Hapsburg policy abroad and an anti-Huguenot policy at home. Despite their powerful supporters, the *dévots* were unable to dislodge Richelieu's religious policy. In fact, the Edict of Nantes was revoked only in 1685.

FURTHER READING

Davis, Natalie Zemon. *Society and Culture in Early Modern France.* Stanford, CA, 1975.

Diefendorf, Barbara B. *Beneath the Cross: Catholics and Huguenots in Sixteenth-Century Paris.* New York, 1991.

Garrisson, Janine. *A History of Sixteenth-Century France, 1483–1598: Renaissance, Reformation, and Rebellion.* Translated by Richard Rex. New York, 1995.

Heller, Henry. *Iron and Blood: Civil Wars in Sixteenth-Century France.* Buffalo, NY, 1991.

Holt, Mack P. *The French Wars of Religion, 1562–1629.* New York, 1995.

Max von Habsburg

SEE ALSO

• Calvinism • Catherine de Médicis • France
• Francis I • Henry IV • Monarchy • Paris
• Reformation • Warfare

Galilei, Galileo

THE ITALIAN MATHEMATICIAN AND ASTRONOMER GALILEO GALILEI (1564–1642), A PIONEER IN THE FIELD OF EXPERIMENTAL SCIENCE, MADE IMPORTANT ADVANCES IN THE UNDERSTANDING OF MOTION AND BUILT THE FIRST EFFECTIVE TELESCOPE.

Controversy surrounds almost every aspect of Galileo's life. The historian's task is made more difficult by the fact that the first biography of Galileo, which was written by one of his devoted students, Vincenzo Viviani (1622–1703), contains numerous inaccuracies. Viviani's work is colored by his view of Galileo as a near-mythical martyr to science, a view that influenced many subsequent assessments of Galileo. It is not always easy for a modern scholar to distinguish between the factual and the mythical in accounts of Galileo's life.

Galileo Galilei was born in Pisa, part of the duchy of Tuscany, on February 15, 1564, the eldest of seven children (four of whom survived to adulthood). In his writings he always referred to himself by his first name, and it remains conventional to do so. Galileo's father, Vincenzo, was a composer at the court of the grand duke of Tuscany in Florence. Music always played a part in Galileo's life; he was an accomplished lute player and wove thoughts on musical theory into his mathematical texts.

Vincenzo, who distrusted the church, sent Galileo to a monastery outside Florence for his early education but removed him when Galileo announced that he wished to be a monk. In 1581 Vincenzo enrolled his son as a student of medicine at the University of Pisa in the hope that this course of study would provide Galileo with a lucrative career. It was at Pisa that Galileo first emerged as a gregarious but argumentative young man. He took delight in challenging accepted views, which in his day came largely from the texts of the ancient Greek philosopher Aristotle (384–322 BCE). Aristotle's works still dominated academic study in the sixteenth century; Galileo later claimed that even as a student at Pisa he had spotted the absurdity of Aristotle's theory that balls of different weights would fall at different speeds according to their weight—thus, a ball weighing one hundred pounds would fall one hundred times faster than a ball weighing one pound. There is no firm evidence to support the popular story that Galileo dropped balls from the Leaning Tower of Pisa to prove Aristotle wrong. On the other hand, there is evidence to support the story that Galileo timed the swing of a chandelier in the cathedral of Pisa against his pulse in order to show that a pendulum of a given length would take the same time to complete a swing however long the arc across which it swung.

Medicine did not interest Galileo. Apparently, having heard a lecture on mathematics by the court mathematician, Ostilio Ricci, he fell in love with the subject and became so absorbed in

▼ This 1841 fresco, in Florence's Observatory Academy, depicts Galileo observing a pendulum in Pisa Cathedral. In 1602 a physician used a pendulum to measure a pulse. The first pendulum clocks appeared twenty years after Galileo's death.

The works of Aristotle had been reintroduced to western Europe in the thirteenth century and, through the influence of the Italian philosopher Thomas Aquinas (1225–1274), had become the cornerstone of a Christian theology that allowed for rational enquiry. By Galileo's day, although Aristotelianism pervaded academic study, it no longer seemed innovative. Indeed, much of Aristotle's work had been developed independent of any experimental evidence, and Aristotle's theories were particularly vulnerable to the technological advances of the Renaissance. Galileo brought into question many of Aristotle's theories of motion by showing that they could not be verified by experiment. The observations Galileo made through his telescope were particularly devastating for Aristotelianism since they entirely destroyed Aristotle's idea that the universe consisted of a pure, unblemished substance distinct from the coarse material of which the earth was made.

Galileo's real enemy was not so much Aristotle himself as those who relied on Aristotle's texts irrespective of whether they made sense in the real world. He accepted that Aristotle had ranged so widely that he was bound to have made mistakes. He also pointed out that Aristotle himself believed that experience should be placed above theory and authority. If Aristotle returned to earth now, Galileo argued in a letter he wrote at the end of his life to the Aristotelian philosopher Fortunio Liceti, he would surely take Galileo's side against the Aristotelians.

▲ This aerial view of Pisa, Galileo's birthplace, includes the famous leaning tower. Although Galileo returned to the university there as professor of mathematics in 1589, the stuffy atmosphere did not suit his restless mind, and from the 1590s he challenged many of the conventions of Aristotelian scholarship.

mathematical study that he never completed his medical degree. During the 1580s Galileo came across the works of the ancient Greek mathematician Archimedes (c. 287–212 BCE) and was inspired to write his own works on hydrostatics (a branch of physics that deals with the characteristics of fluids at rest) and materials. Galileo's first original work (which remained unpublished), was a study based on experiments in hydrostatics. This work was followed by a study of the center of gravity of solids. These two studies enabled Galileo, with the help of a patron, to secure a post in 1589 as professor of mathematics at Pisa. He proved something of a rebel by refusing to wear the correct academic dress and openly mocking the more pompous professors.

The Study of Motion

Between 1602 and 1609 Galileo became preoccupied with theories of motion. He sought expla-

in the paths of projectiles (objects launched through the air). According to the accepted view, a projectile would fall straight to the ground when it lost its force. Galileo showed how the path of a falling projectile is a parabola (an arc-shaped curve) and how the rising curve of a projectile and its falling curve are symmetrical. From this principle the maximum trajectory of a cannonball could be calculated. Among Galileo's most important applications of his mathematical knowledge was his law of free fall, a formula that relates the acceleration of a falling object not to the weight of the object (as Aristotle had done) but to the length of time it spends falling.

Whereas Aristotle had argued that it was natural for a body to be at rest, Galileo argued that there was no natural reason (other than air resistance and friction) why a body, once set in motion, should not continue to move at a uniform speed. Motion, Galileo further pointed out, is relative: two bodies moving alongside each other at the same speed may be moving against their background when in relation to each other they appear to be motionless. This principle enabled Galileo to support the theory that the earth might be moving, even though it appears not to be. Although his numerous findings were not yet published, Galileo advertised them to possible patrons as evidence of his achievements.

A Professorship at Padua

In 1591 Galileo's father died, and Galileo became responsible for the financial affairs of his family: two sisters, who needed dowries to marry, and a penniless brother, like his father a musician. Restless at Pisa and in desperate need of more money, Galileo visited Venice and talked his way into a professorship of mathematics at Padua, a city within Venice's mainland territory. At Padua, a far more prestigious university than Pisa, the atmosphere was more congenial for such an original thinker as Galileo. Money always remained a problem, but Galileo used his practical skills to design a geometrical compass, an early form of calculator, which he sold to help make ends meet. (A manual on the use of this device, published in 1606, is Galileo's earliest printed work.) In the same years he formed a stable relationship with Marina Gamba. Although he did not marry her,

nations not only of the different speeds at which various solid objects fall but also of how different materials fall through different substances. What was the relationship between the speed at which an iron ball fell through water and the speed at which it fell through air? Why did a wooden ball fall through air but not through water? (To answer this latter question, he drew on Archimedes' famous experiments with floating objects and showed how a liquid can provide a buoyant force upward.) Faced with the difficulties of measuring the speed of a falling object, he placed balls on inclined planes so that they would move more slowly. By using these planes he could measure the acceleration of a "falling" object more accurately. Next Galileo became interested she bore him his three children (such arrangements were common).

Galileo and Copernicanism

In 1609 Galileo's ideas about motion were still at an early stage of formation and not fully written up, and his salary was still modest. He was not publicly associated with the theory put forward by the Polish astronomer Nicolaus Copernicus in his 1543 work *De revolutionibus orbium coelestium (On the Revolution of Heavenly Spheres)* that the earth and the other planets orbit the sun. Copernicus's theory challenged the long-accepted view, established by the Greek astronomer Ptolemy in the second century CE and supported by the church, that a motionless earth was at the center of the universe. However, a private letter Galileo wrote in 1597 to the great German astronomer Johannes Kepler, whose *Cosmographic Mysteries* (1596) was the first work to take Copernicus's view for granted, reveals that in private Galileo tended toward Copernicanism.

Galileo's observations of the stars gradually distanced him from Aristotle's view that the universe existed as an unchanging and eternal realm circling the earth. The appearance of a supernova in 1604 suggested that the universe did change, but it was the invention of the telescope that allowed Galileo to shatter conventional thinking.

Galileo's discovery that the moon's surface is irregular, described in the following excerpt from a work of 1610, called into question the long-established view of the universe:

There are other spots, smaller in size [than those observed by the naked eye] and occurring with such frequency that they besprinkle the entire lunar surface, but especially the brighter part. They were, in fact, observed by no one before us. By oft-repeated observations of them we have been led to the conclusion that we certainly see the surface of the moon to be not smooth, even, and perfectly spherical, as the great crowd of philosophers have believed about this and other heavenly bodies, but, on the contrary, to be uneven, rough, and crowded with depressions and bulges. And it is like the face of the Earth itself, which is marked here and there with chains of mountains and depths of valleys.

Sidereus nuncius (The Starry Messenger)

◀ *Though blind in later years, Galileo's intellectual vigor remained undiminished, and he was in correspondence with the leading philosophers and scientists of his day until his death. This seventeenth-century painting, of uncertain origin, may show Galileo's devoted pupil Vincenzo Viviani taking a dictation of his master's ideas. Viviani was later to write the first full biography of Galileo.*

The Telescope

The idea of positioning two lenses in a tube in such a way that a viewer looking through the tube sees distant objects magnified is credited to a Dutchman, Hans Lippershey, in 1608. The earliest telescopes magnified objects to only three times their normal size. When Galileo heard of the invention, he quickly realized its potential. Ever the master of practical science, Galileo soon improved the original idea to achieve magnifications of first ten and later twenty times an object's normal size. It was typical of Galileo's expertise that he found the finest glass manufacturer in Florence, perfected the skill of lens grinding, and for the next twenty years personally produced the most advanced telescopes in the world.

What Galileo could see through his telescopes was awe inspiring. The surface of the moon was revealed not to be smooth, as it appeared to be to the naked eye, but mountainous. This discovery destroyed the notion that the planets and stars were perfect orbs with no blemishes. Later Galileo was to see spots on the sun, evidence that this too was no perfect orb. The planet Jupiter could be seen to have four moons. This discovery undermined the traditional view that the earth could not circle the sun because its moon would become "detached." After all, Jupiter, circling either the sun or the earth, retained its moons. Thus, one significant objection to the heliocentric, or sun-centered, view of the universe was undermined. Another important observation was that the planet Venus had phases similar to those of the moon that were consistent with its circling the sun. If all these findings did not amount to incontestable proof for Copernicanism, they certainly cast serious doubt on the Ptolemaic view of the universe.

When Galileo wrote up his observations in *Sidereus nuncius (The Starry Messenger)* in 1610, he caused a sensation throughout Europe. It was not just what he had observed that shocked people; it was the idea that a single scientific invention could challenge an entire worldview—and that the process might be ongoing as technology developed.

The Starry Messenger was also influential in moving on Galileo's career. He desperately needed to escape from university teaching in order to have more time for his research. A post at the court of Cosimo II de' Medici, the grand duke of Tuscany, was an attractive opportunity. After Galileo shrewdly named the four moons of Jupiter the Medicean stars, in May 1610 he was appointed philosopher and mathematician of the Tuscan court for life.

Copernicanism and Christianity

On his first visit to Rome, in 1611, Galileo was welcomed by the Accademia dei Lincei

▼ *Shown here are two of Galileo's own telescopes. Galileo improved the very early telescope so markedly that he can justly be called its inventor. He told the doge of Venice that his telescope would show enemy ships approaching Venice two hours before they could be seen by the naked eye.*

TVBVM OPTICVM VIDES GALILAEII INVENTVM,ET OPVS,QVO SOLIS MACVLAS,
ET EXTIMOS LVNAE MONTES,ET IOVIS SATELLITES,ET NOVAM QVASI
RERVM VNIVERSITATE PRIMVS DISPEXIT A.MDCIX.

("academy of the lynxes"), probably the world's earliest scientific society. The academy was to publish several of his works, including his treatise on sunspots. While in Rome, Galileo was also encouraged to hear that the Jesuits, the formidable Catholic educational order founded in 1540, had carried out their own observations through a telescope and endorsed what he himself had seen. However, he was treading a dangerous path. Despite all the evidence in support of Copernicus's view, the sun-centered system contradicted the traditional literal interpretation of biblical passages that described a stationary earth at the center of things. Conservatives in the Vatican began to move against Copernicanism. In March 1616 *De revolutionibus* was placed on the Index of Forbidden Books.

There was some sympathy for Galileo from an influential cardinal, Robert Bellarmine (1542–1621), but Bellarmine, while ready to consider the evidence for Copernicanism, did not think it compelling enough to overthrow church teaching. Galileo was summoned to Rome and ordered by the pope, Paul V, not to hold or defend the idea that the sun was at the center of the universe or that the earth moved.

The Assayer and The Dialogue

One of Galileo's great achievements was to combine observation through experiment with mathematical interpretation. *The Assayer* (*Il Saggiatore;* 1623) was a manifesto of his views. The fact that it is written in Italian, not Latin as might be expected, suggests that Galileo deliberately wished to distance himself from conventional scholarship. The work makes an important distinction between the measurable mathematical qualities of a substance or object—its weight, size, and the speed at which it moves, for example—and secondary qualities, such as its color or smell.

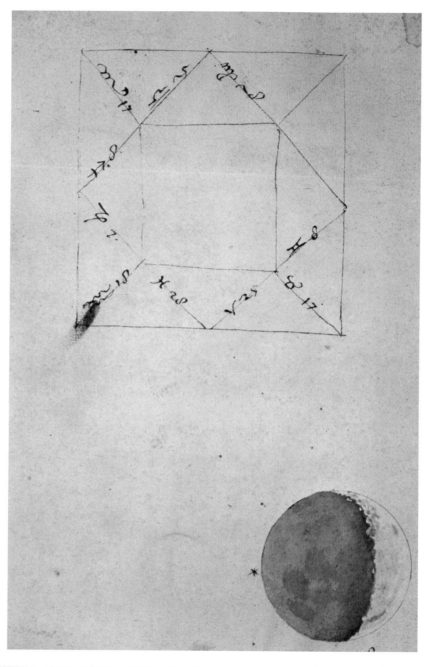

▲ On this page from Sidereus nuncius, *next to an observation of the moon dated January 19, 1610, Galileo sketched an astrological birth chart for Cosimo II de' Medici. Galileo appears to have emphasized the position of the planet Jupiter at the time of Cosimo's birth—the Roman god Jupiter had been associated with the rule of earlier Medici dukes.*

One of Galileo's most famous statements concerns the importance of mathematics in understanding the material world:

Philosophy is written in this grand book—I mean the universe—which stands continuously open to our gaze, but it cannot be understood unless one first learns to comprehend this language and interprets the characters in which it is written. It is written in the language of mathematics, and its characters are triangles, circles, and other geometrical figures, without which it is humanly impossible to understand a single word of it, without these one is wandering about in a dark labyrinth.

The Assayer

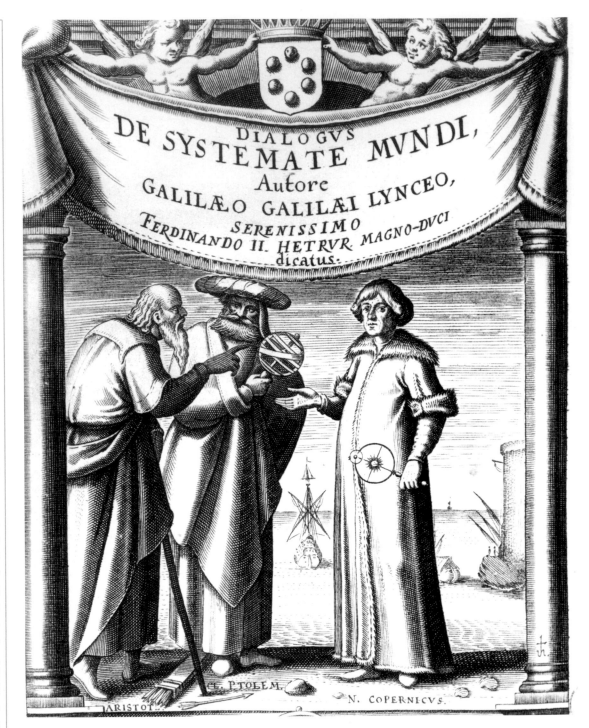

DIALOGVS
DE SYSTEMATE MVNDI,
Autore
GALILÆO GALILÆI LYNCEO,
SERENISSIMO
FERDINANDO II. HETRVR. MAGNO-DVCI
dicatus:

CL. PTOLEM.
ARISTOT.
N. COPERNICVS.

The *Assayer* was so well received that in 1624 Galileo approached Rome to ask for permission to write a comparative study of the two systems, the Ptolemaic and the Copernican. Pope Urban VIII agreed on condition that Galileo keep to the promise of 1616, which in effect ruled that the Copernican view could be stated but not defended. Urban appeared to approve of the first drafts of the *Dialogue concerning the Two Chief World Systems* but abruptly changed his mind when he read the final version. Galileo had pre-

▲ *The frontispiece to this Latin version of the* Dialogue, *published in Leiden (outside papal control) in 1635, shows the three disputants in deep discussion. Galileo credits himself as a member of the Academy of Lynxes and as astronomer to Ferdinand II, grand duke of Tuscany.*

sented the arguments as a dialogue between three figures, the one who supported Ptolemy being called Simplicio ("simpleton"). The final part of the work seemed to suggest that anyone who supported Ptolemy was indeed a simpleton; worse still, Galileo gave Simplicio words to speak similar to those used by the pope himself.

GALILEO VERSUS THE CHURCH

The condemnation of Galileo by the Inquisition is often cited as a classic example of the conflict between science and religion. In fact, Galileo was somewhat unlucky. The church was in the throes of its battle with Protestantism, and in 1546, at the Council of Trent, it had insisted on its absolute authority as the interpreter of the meaning of Scripture. A literal reading of such biblical passages as Joshua 10:12–13, in which the sun and moon stand still at the command of Joshua, suggested that the Bible supported the Ptolemaic view that the sun and moon move around the earth. It was on these grounds that Copernicanism was condemned in 1616 for contradicting "the sense of Holy Scripture, according to the literal meaning of the words and the common interpretation of the church fathers and the doctors of theology." An alternative approach was taken by the great early Christian theologian Augustine of Hippo (354–430). Augustine had argued that when the meaning of a passage in the Bible was unclear, interpretation should be left open until there was strong evidence to support a particular view. In his *Letter to the Grand Duchess Christina* of 1615, Galileo followed Augustine and argued that Copernicanism was just such a case. If Copernicus were proved to be right, the Scriptures must be interpreted in such a way as to support his view. "The task of wise interpreters," he wrote, "is to find true meanings of scriptural passages that will agree with the evidence of sensory experience." It was the clash between these two rival approaches that lay behind the condemnation of Galileo.

Galileo succeeded in uniting physics, mathematics, and astronomy. He broke down the concept, which dated from the time of ancient Greece, that the earth and the heavens were distinct entities, and as a result of his work, it was possible for there to be a comprehensive understanding of the universe as a physical unity. The heavens were no longer the exclusive preserve of God and the church: all were free to speculate on their true nature. Galileo showed that the world was subject to laws that could be understood and tested and that mathematics and experimental evidence reinforced each other. In this respect the great English scientist Isaac Newton (1642–1727) brought Galileo's work to fruition.

▼ *Drawn by Galileo in January 1611, this diagram includes charts of planetary observations for each month plotted on a plan showing the movement of an observed planet.*

Galileo was summoned back to Rome. The Inquisition, the papal body responsible for dealing with those accused of heresy (open contradiction of church doctrine), claimed that in 1616 Galileo had been forbidden to teach Copernicanism. He was forced to recant his views in June 1633 and was punished with imprisonment (mostly in his own home) for the rest of his life. The *Dialogue* was placed on the Index of Forbidden Books.

The Two New Sciences

During his imprisonment and despite increasing ill health, Galileo's intellectual energy was undiminished. In 1638 he completed his last major work, the *Discourses on Two New Sciences*, in which, again through a dialogue, he finally wrote up his thoughts on the science of materials and motion. His work on the former concentrates on the resistance of materials to fracture and the way in which the composition of a material affects this resistance. In his work on the latter, Galileo examines three types of motion: steady, or uniform, motion, the accelerated motion of a falling body, and the violent motion of an object thrown by force.

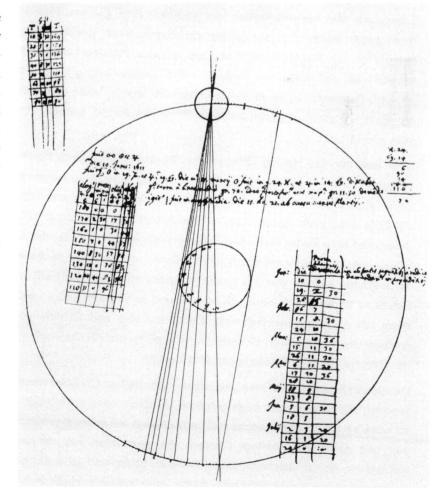

Galileo could not afford to provide dowries for his two daughters by Marina Gamba, and so both became nuns. He was deeply devoted to one of them in particular, Maria Celeste. When she died young in 1634, Galileo wrote, "I feel myself perpetually called by my beloved daughter ... I loathe myself." The father's devotion was reciprocated, as this letter to Galileo from Marie Celeste makes clear:

Most illustrious Lord Father, between the infinite love I bear you, Sire, and my fear that this sudden cold, which ordinarily troubles you so much, may aggravate your current aches and indispositions, I find it impossible to remain without news of you: therefore I beg to hear how you are, Sire, and also when you think you will be setting off on your journey. I have hastened my work on the linens, and they are almost finished. ... My room is terribly cold now, and with my head so infected, I cannot see how I will be able to stand it there, Sire, unless you help me by lending me one of your bed hangings. ... I am most eager to know if you can do me this service. And another thing I ask of you please, is to send me your book, the one that has just been published [i.e., The Assayer] so that I may read it, as I am longing to see what it says. ... Here are some cakes I made a few days ago. ... And to close I send you loving greetings from me and from Suor Arcangela [her sister].

From the convent of San Matteo, the 21st day of November, 1623,

Most affectionate daughter

S[uor]. M[aria]. Celeste

If you have collars to be bleached, Sire, you may send them to us.

Quoted in Dava Sobel, *Galileo's Daughter*

▲ *Galileo had great affection for his daughter Maria Celeste (thought to be the subject of this unattributed portrait), whose life in the convent was marked by hardship.*

been invented, but the work nevertheless represents an early use of scientific method. Uncertain of uncensored publication in Italy, Galileo sent the manuscript to be printed in Leiden, Holland. *Two New Sciences* not only gave a coherent account of Galileo's work but also served as a textbook for students. By the time of its publication, Galileo's health, which had never been good, was failing, and he was almost blind. He died in January 1642.

FURTHER READING

Brecht, Bertolt. *Galileo.* Translated by Charles Laughton. New York, 1991.

Machamer, Peter, ed. *The Cambridge Companion to Galileo.* New York, 1998.

Santillana, Giorgio de. *The Crime of Galileo.* Chicago, 1955.

Sharratt, Michael. *Galileo: Decisive Innovator.* New York, 1996.

Shea, William R., and Mariano Artigas. *Galileo in Rome.* New York, 2003.

Charles Freeman

All Galileo's theories are supported by experimental evidence. For instance, he set up several pendulums swinging together so that he could measure their relative speeds in different situations. Some of the results of his experiments appear to be too good to be true and may have

SEE ALSO

- Aristotle • Copernicus, Nicolaus • Heresy
- Mathematics • Science and Technology
- Trent, Council of

Gentileschi, Artemisia

ARTEMISIA GENTILESCHI (1593–1652), ARGUABLY THE MOST IMPORTANT FEMALE ARTIST OF THE SEVENTEENTH CENTURY, IS BEST KNOWN FOR HER PAINTINGS OF WOMEN, OFTEN IN DRAMATIC SITUATIONS.

Artemisia Gentileschi was born in Rome in 1593. Her father, Orazio Gentileschi, was a friend and follower of the influential and controversial artist Caravaggio (1573–1610). When Artemisia was only eight years old, her mother died. Orazio took Artemisia into his studio and trained her as a painter (the tradition of a woman receiving training from her father was well established). Her early canvases showed exceptional skill. When she was only eighteen, her father wrote that she had no peers, even among masters of painting. Initially her father was her main influence, but she also took inspiration from Caravaggio and Michelangelo, whose work she would have seen in Rome. Unlike most female artists, who were expected to paint only portraits or still lifes, Artemisia concentrated from the outset on what her age considered the highest form of art—historical painting.

In many of her paintings, particularly those executed between 1610 and 1613, Artemisia depicts violent and often disturbing scenes involving women. Some art historians have connected the subjects of her paintings with events from her own life. In 1611, at age seventeen, she was raped by Agostino Tassi, a Florentine painter who had been teaching her about perspective. Tassi promised to marry her, but when he failed to keep this promise, Orazio took Tassi to court. The long trial (in 1612) generated much publicity in Rome. Artemisia was cross-examined under torture and was accused of licentious and provocative behavior. Tassi, who had previously been accused of both rape and incest, was convicted and banished from Rome. Remarkably, the transcripts of the trial have survived.

In November 1612, only one day after Tassi was sentenced to exile, Artemisia married Pierre Antonio Stiattesi, also a painter. The couple left Rome early in 1613 and went to live and work in Florence.

Recognition and Patronage

Artemisia's move to Florence gave her the opportunity to escape the notoriety she had acquired during the trial. She quickly became the protégé of Michelangelo Buonarroti the Younger (Michelangelo's great-nephew), for whom she painted a ceiling. The novelty of a talented woman producing dramatic historical paintings assured Artemisia's success.

Artemisia's most important patron was Grand Duke Cosimo II de' Medici, the head of the ruling family of Florence. Thanks to his influence she became the first woman to gain acceptance and admission to the prestigious Academy of Design in July 1616. The academy trained artists

◄ While Artemisia was visiting Rome in 1625, the French artist Pierre Dumonstier le Neveu made this drawing of her hand. Dumonstier described Artemisia as "the excellent and wise noblewoman of Rome."

1593
Artemisia Gentileschi is born in Rome.

1610
Completes her first major painting, *Susannah and the Elders*.

1613–1620
Moves to Florence, where she adopts her family name of Lomi.

1620–1629
Returns to Rome in debt; travels to Venice and Genoa.

1639
Travels to England to work with her father and brothers.

1641–1652
Returns to Naples and works for the duke of Parma, Ranuccio Farnese II.

1653
Dies.

▶ *The* Penitent Magdalen *(c. 1616) was one of the last works Artemisia painted in Florence. The Magdalene's dramatic rejection of the luxury that surrounds her serves to emphasize both the beauty of her possessions and her virtue in giving them up. The skull lurking in the background is a reminder that life is often fleeting. The artist's signature (Artemisia Lomi) is clearly visible on the chair. While living in Florence, Artemisia preferred her uncle's surname to her maiden or her married name.*

in such disciplines as mathematics, anatomy, and natural philosophy. It is generally thought that Artemisia was not allowed to attend life classes, as it was deemed unsuitable for a woman to study live models.

It was customary for painters to reflect the prevailing Florentine fashion for opulence in their paintings. Also extremely popular was Caravaggism, the adherence to the principles of Caravaggio's style, whose hallmarks include the depiction with theatrical intensity of naturalistic figures who are part of a larger scene or are seen in a burst of activity. Caravaggio's figures are illuminated by strong shafts of light, an effect set off by his dark backgrounds. Artemisia was one of the best-known Caravaggists of her time.

The *Penitent Magdalen* (c. 1616) fuses Caravaggist drama and Florentine opulence. Artemisia uses vibrant colors—gold, maroon, and green—to capture the luxury of Mary

The influence of Caravaggio on Artemisia's style is strongest in such early works as *Susannah and the Elders, Judith Beheading Holofernes, Lucretia,* and *Judith and Her Maidservant,* which are characterized by vivid drama, a naturalized portrayal of the human body, and the technique of chiaroscuro (whereby the painter creates effect through strongly contrasting areas of light and shade). By painting all her figures very close to the picture plane, Artemisia gives the viewer a feeling of intimacy with and participation in the scene depicted. Artemisia had access to female models. Her representations of women are therefore markedly different from those painted by many of her male contemporaries (who had access to male models only). Artemisia's women are hefty, powerful, and active.

The composition of Artemisia's works adds to their dramatic intensity. The figures fill the canvases to overflowing. Susannah, confined to a bare stone step, is forced to writhe away as the lecherous elders invade her space. Judith and her servant Abra, their arms arranged like the spokes of a wheel, work together as one to confine Holofernes. Lucretia's disordered clothing evokes her rape more graphically than if she were naked, and there is nothing in the background to distract the viewer from the dagger she will shortly turn upon herself. Judith and her maidservant are confined to a single dimension and thus have a unity of purpose not seen in other paintings of this subject.

Artemisia's later works, even her reworkings of such familiar subjects as the Judith paintings, have less dramatic intensity—as her figures gradually recede into the canvas, they lose the tendency to shock the viewer. However, the later works demonstrate a more sophisticated technical ability and a more opulent palette.

Magdalene's clothing and surroundings. Mary's sweeping gesture confirms her conversion from faithlessness to belief, and in her facial expression her internal religious experience is manifested externally. (Florentine artists of the late Renaissance were particularly preoccupied with the depiction of facial expressions.) The painting was commissioned by Cosimo de' Medici's wife, Maria Maddalena of Austria, who was known for her piety.

Between 1613 and 1618, Artemisia gave birth to four children, only one of whom, Prudentia, survived. In 1620 Artemisia moved from Florence back to Rome. Her husband, who had proved to be unsuccessful as a painter, had spent much of her dowry and left her owing money to tradespeople and paint suppliers.

Fame

Artemisia's fame was now widespread. Commissions came from Philip IV of Spain and the duke of Alcalá (also in Spain). She attracted the attention of writers, poets, and other artists, who represented her as exceptionally beautiful. When Pierre Dumonstier made a drawing of Artemisia's hand, he commented that the subject was beautiful because it could produce "those miraculous works that delight the eyes of the wisest connoisseurs." Artemisia's reputation as a beautiful woman was not wholly beneficial to her reputation as an artist; her success was connected with her beauty, and she was judged alongside other beautiful women rather than as an artist

▲ *In* Judith Beheading Holofernes *(c. 1620), Judith wears a delicate bracelet on the arm that grips Holofernes by the hair, while the spurting blood forms a ghastly contrast with the delicate fringe of the bed cover.*

among other artists, male and female. However, she received recognition of her artistic talents when she was admitted to the Accademia de' Desiosi ("academy of the desired") in Venice in 1628. When her marriage ended in 1623, she became sole provider for her daughter.

► It is widely believed that this depiction of la Pittura in the Allegory of Painting *(1630s), is a self-portrait. If this assumption is true, Artemisia must have used two angled mirrors to achieve this unusual side view of herself. The figure's fine silk gown expresses Artemisia's belief that artists should be regarded not merely as craftsmen but as professionals on a par with doctors and lawyers.*

During the 1620s artistic tastes in Rome began to move away from Caravaggio's naturalism and toward a more classical approach. In a series of female nudes and portraits, Artemisia depicted a more idealized, much leaner female body than those she had portrayed in earlier works. That the poses adopted by the subjects of *Venus and Cupid* (c. 1625–1627) and *Cleopatra* (1627) are very similar to those found in her father's paintings is proof of his continuing influence on her work. By the late 1620s most of the artists who associated themselves with Caravaggio had left Rome. Artemisia left in 1629 and set up a studio in Naples in the hope of finding a more sympathetic audience.

International Recognition

Artemisia lived in considerable style and luxury during the 1630s. Her paintings were bought by European royalty, and her patrons included kings, princes, and the empress of Austria.

During the height of her success in Naples, Artemisia produced a number of self-portraits and allegories. Some art historians believe that her *Allegory of Painting* (c. 1630–1639) is also a self-portrait. La Pittura, the allegorical figure who symbolizes painting, was traditionally a woman. Paintings of her usually include symbols taken from Cesare Ripa's *Iconologica* (1593), which became the standard handbook of iconography (symbols in art). Such symbols, whose meaning

ARTEMISIA'S WOMEN

Of the fifty-one surviving canvases attributed to Artemisia, forty-nine have female protagonists or give women and men equal pictorial status. Her favorite subject was Judith, of whom she painted seven canvases. Other favorites are Susannah and Bathsheba (whose stories, like that of Judith, form part of Catholic and Orthodox editions of the Old Testament), Mary Magdalene (one of Jesus's followers), Lucretia (a heroine of ancient Rome), and Cleopatra (the first-century-BCE Egyptian queen). The story of each of these women involves some form of struggle against men or against a society dominated by men.

The Old Testament tale of Susannah (in the book of Daniel) tells of a woman who, while bathing, is spied on by two elders of her tribe. When she refuses their advances, the elders threaten to accuse her publicly of adultery. In the early seventeenth century, the story was often painted merely as an excuse to show a naked woman within a religious context. Most paintings of the subject depict Susannah as a passive, even compliant figure. Artemisia's *Susannah* (1610), on the other hand, is clearly suffering after the invasion of her privacy by the conspiratorial elders. Her nakedness is not designed to be alluring; the twists and turns of her body express her physical and mental distress.

The book of Judith, also part of the Catholic and Orthodox Old Testament, tells of a beautiful Jewish widow whose city is under siege. Pretending to flee, she greets the besieging general, Holofernes, and foretells his victory. He invites her into his tent, and when he becomes drunk, she cuts his head off. The Judith portrayed by Artemisia in both versions of *Judith Beheading Holofernes* (1612 and 1620), is a powerful, muscular woman who pins Holofernes down on his bed with her knee. She is completely absorbed in her violent task. Her servant, Abra, appears as an equal, as she does in both versions of *Judith and Her Maidservant* (1612 and c. 1623–1625). In many other representations of the story, the servant is portrayed as a fragile old crone with no emotional connection to Judith.

▼ Artemisia's Susannah and the Elders *(1610), her first major canvas, is an interpretation all the more remarkable given that its creator was only seventeen. The work shows her artistic virtuosity in its fusion of composition and subject matter. The inverted triangle of the well-dressed elders presses down on the naked Susannah, who, seated on bare stone, has no one to turn to for help.*

would have been understood by a contemporary audience, were a way of imparting much information within the restrictions of a painting. In Artemisia's work la Pittura wears a pendant in the shape of a mask, which signifies the imitative function of art; her disheveled hair symbolizes the inspired painter's neglect of her own appearance; and her dress of changing colors alludes to a painter's mastery of light and color. The figure is poised in front of a blank canvas. It is often said that the inspiration behind a painting is more important than the image that results. If the *Allegory of Painting* is a self-portrait, it represents Artemisia's seizure of the opportunity to identify herself, as a female artist, with the art of painting itself.

Financial pressures continued to affect Artemisia's style of painting and choice of subject. She began to repeat certain popular scenes and

The relationship between Artemisia's private life and her work is often debated. Some art historians contend that there is little to suggest that any artists of the Renaissance desired to express their feelings, as distinct from their skills, in their work. However, Cosimo de' Medici stated that every man paints himself. Caravaggio, for example, painted his own likeness into several of his paintings.

Some interpretations of Artemisia Gentileschi's work stress the effects on her art of her rape and torture. While some scholars call for an end to the "disturbing fascination" with her life, others argue that her life and work are inextricably entwined and that her striking originality as an artist stems directly from her personal experiences. Novels, plays, and movies about Artemisia tend to concentrate on dramatic incidents in her life and her alleged beauty rather than on her remarkable achievements as a painter. Although this sensational approach adds little to the understanding of her as an artist, it does point to her continuing appeal.

▲ In Judith and Her Maidservant (1612), the eye of the viewer is drawn to the head in the basket, which contrasts with the bright light shining upon Judith. The tension of the moment is sustained by the realization that Judith is ready to use her sword again if necessary.

cialized in landscape backgrounds, such as Bernardo Cavallino and Domenico Gargiulo.

Orazio Gentileschi had spent ten years in England painting for King Charles I and Queen Henrietta Maria. When Orazio's health began to fail in 1638, he asked Artemisia to help him paint a ceiling in the Queen's House in Greenwich. *The Allegory of Peace and Arts under the English Crown* was finished in 1639, and Orazio died soon after. Charles I bought a number of Artemisia's paintings.

Later Years

Artemisia returned to Naples and stayed there for the rest of her life. Financial troubles continued, and her canvases increasingly repeated subject matter and groups of figures. She trained her daughter, Prudentia, to paint and perhaps helped Prudentia launch her career. The last years of Artemisia's life are poorly documented; she fell ill in the late 1640s and died in 1652 or 1653. The only record of her death is in two epitaphs that unflatteringly refer to her as an adulteress, with no mention of her artistic accomplishments.

subjects (as Orazio had done throughout his career). In one eight-year period she produced three depictions of Bathsheba and a further three of Susannah and the Elders. She sold most of her nudes elsewhere in Europe, as depictions of nakedness were considered inappropriate in Catholic Naples. She produced several paintings during the 1630s in collaboration with other Neapolitan artists, in particular those who spe-

FURTHER READING

Bissell, R. Ward. *Artemisia Gentileschi and the Authority of Art.* University Park, PA, 1999.
Chadwick, Whitney. *Women, Art and Society.* New York, 2002.
Garrard, Mary D. *Artemisia Gentileschi: The Image of the Female Hero in Italian Baroque Art.* Princeton, NJ, 1989.

Jo Hall

SEE ALSO
....
• Caravaggio • Florence • Medicis, The
• Rome • Women

German Towns

At the beginning of the fourteenth century, much of the territory that makes up present-day Germany, Austria, and the Czech Republic fell within the boundaries of the Holy Roman Empire. The empire, an entity controlled primarily (but not exclusively) by the powerful Hapsburg monarchy, was itself a diverse patchwork of regional principalities, large and small towns, and rural villages, most of which became increasingly autonomous between the fourteenth and seventeenth centuries.

▼ *The Peasants' War (1524–1526) created chaos in many key German towns. At its height the conflict involved some 300,000 peasant insurgents. Contemporary estimates put the dead at 100,000.*

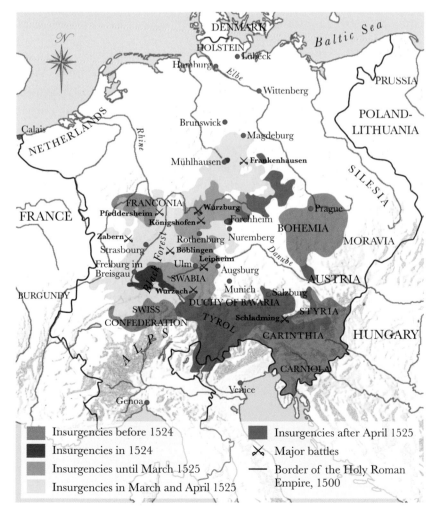

Insurgencies before 1524
Insurgencies in 1524
Insurgencies until March 1525
Insurgencies in March and April 1525
Insurgencies after April 1525
✕ Major battles
— Border of the Holy Roman Empire, 1500

Economics and the Hanseatic League

Europe's most active international trading cities during the High Middle Ages and the Renaissance and Reformation eras that followed were those with easy access to the oceans. In the south such northern Italian maritime cities as Florence, Venice, and Genoa exercised increasing control over Mediterranean trade routes. In the north the towns of the Hanseatic League exercised similar control over Baltic trade routes. The Hanseatic League began in the mid-twelfth century with the alliance of the merchants of two key northern German trading centers, Hamburg and Lübeck. Hamburg had abundant supplies of salt, and Lübeck of herring. Each group of merchants guaranteed the other access to the goods of which it had an abundant supply. Throughout the thirteenth and fourteenth centuries the league spread as towns on key trade routes across northern Europe made agreements with one another on the Hamburg-Lübeck model. The economic success of the Hanse cities won them considerable political status. Yet, notwithstanding those cities' coastal predominance, several independent towns in the Holy Roman Empire's German heartland—most notably Augsburg, Frankfurt, and Nuremberg—also possessed substantial economic power.

While the number of German towns and cities falling within the boundaries of the Holy Roman Empire fluctuated between 1300 and 1650, there were as many as four thousand population centers in the empire during that period. Collectively, these towns and cities were home to 20 percent of the empire's population; two-thirds, however, had no more than two thousand inhabitants, and just a handful housed more than ten thousand. Not surprisingly, those individuals and families who accumulated the greatest wealth lived in the towns that had the most substantial demographic base—and therefore the pool of labor necessary for the production of goods. In addition to Augsburg, Frankfurt, and Nuremberg, the region's most economically powerful towns included Magdeburg, Strasbourg, and Ulm, all three of which were situated in the southern half of Germany.

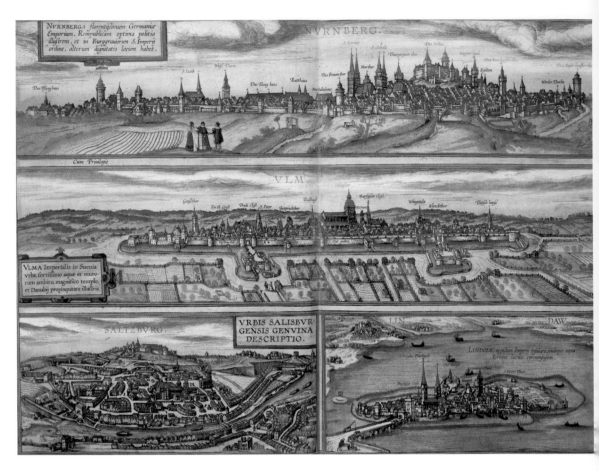

These engravings of the walled towns of Nuremberg (top), Ulm (center), and Salzburg (bottom) are taken from Civitates orbis terrarum (1572), a pioneering atlas of towns throughout the world engraved by Franz Hogenberg and edited by Georg Braun.

People at all levels of society contributed to economic productivity in the towns. Their ranks included members of such established families as the Fugger dynasty of Augsburg, merchants and members of craft guilds, and factory workers, miners, and domestic servants. Collectively, these people extracted raw materials, produced and sold finished goods, and helped to finance the campaigns of figures ranging from local politicians to the Hapsburg Holy Roman emperor Charles V (1500–1558).

The towns of the ethnically German lands of central Europe in particular were administered either in part or in whole by any one or more of three sources of power: the Hapsburg-headed Holy Roman Empire, the nobility (who were in charge of the numerous regions of the empire), and at a local level, influential secular and religious officials and families. Collectively, these power brokers played central economic, political, military, and socioreligious roles in the affairs of towns and, in some cases, the rural villages located along a town's periphery.

As was the case in regions across Europe, towns in the Holy Roman Empire experienced periods of both growth and decline between the fourteenth and seventeenth centuries. Their shifting fortunes led, in many cases, to changes in the types of goods the towns produced and the means they used to generate capital. Until the middle of the sixteenth century, for instance, southern and central German towns were consistently and equally successful in the fields of manufacturing, mining, banking, and long-distance trade. By the end of the century, however, the empire had entered a period of economic stagnation and decline that reached its lowest point during the Thirty Years War (1618–1648).

Augsburg was one of the towns that typified southern Germany's success at the height of an economic boom. The town, which housed one of central Europe's largest textile industries, was the seat of power of the Fugger family. The Fuggers had used their financial influence with the Hapsburgs to secure a virtual monopoly on east-west trade in central Europe.

Local, Regional, and Imperial Politics

Between the fourteenth and seventeenth centuries, the inhabitants of towns in the German

THE FUGGERS OF AUGSBURG

Wealthy families were an influential presence in several German towns of the Holy Roman Empire. Such families frequently used their commercial success to enhance their political influence at local, regional, and international levels. One such family was the Fugger clan of Augsburg (in southern Germany), which amassed one of central Europe's largest fortunes between the fourteenth and sixteenth centuries.

The connection between the Fuggers and Augsburg began in 1367, when a weaver named Hans Fugger (c. 1345–1408) moved to the town. In aiding the development and growth of Augsburg's textile industry, he laid the foundation for the Fuggers' subsequent commercial accomplishments.

Fugger's descendants broadened the family's interests to include the fields of banking, mining, and trade in the decades following his death. Among his descendants was Jacob Fugger II (1459–1525), whose exploits led his contemporaries to refer to him as Jacob the Rich. Most significantly, Jacob cultivated close economic and political ties with the Hapsburg monarchs and Holy Roman emperors Maximilian I and Charles V.

Jacob the Rich profited greatly from Hapsburg-granted concessions to manage the silver mines of the Austrian Tyrol region. He used these profits to strengthen relationships with both Maximilian I and Charles V. Jacob lent Maxmilian I much of the money Maximilian required to pursue a series of military campaigns against the Hapsburgs' many European adversaries. He also donated in excess of one million florins to help secure Charles V's imperial election in 1519; Charles used a substantial proportion of that money to buy the support of the majority of the princes casting votes.

Jacob the Rich and his successors, Raimond (1489–1535) and Anton Fugger (1493–1560), used their imperial connections to maintain de facto control over Augsburg's political affairs in a manner broadly comparable to that employed by the Medicis of Florence. Charles eventually granted members of the family noble status and allowed them to coin their own money in the territory they controlled. In common with the Medicis, the Fuggers were generous patrons of the arts.

In the end, however, the Fuggers' ties to the Hapsburgs proved to be their undoing. Both families reached the height of their power late in the sixteenth century and experienced substantial declines in their respective economic and political fortunes during the conduct and settlement of the Thirty Years War.

▼ *Jacob Fugger II, the subject of this drawing of around 1500 by Hans Holbein the Elder, was referred to by his contemporaries as Jacob the Rich on account of the vast commercial empire he and his family built and presided over from the southeastern German town of Augsburg during the first quarter of the sixteenth century.*

lands of central Europe were typically subjected to three interconnected levels of governmental control. In the context of this three-tiered administrative system, overall power was exercised by the Holy Roman emperor; princes were in charge of geographic regions, and clergymen, religious reformers, and members of wealthy families exercised power at the local level. The role each group played in the direct governance of the population varied from town to town and fluctuated over the decades and centuries according to the economic, military, political, and religious status quo at any given time.

Between 1300 and 1650 the upper tier of the administrative system through which many but by no means all German towns were governed was lodged in the Holy Roman Empire under the auspices of the Hapsburg royal family. Among the most historically significant Hapsburg rulers were Charles V and Ferdinand II (1578–1637), each of whom developed policies that had both direct and indirect implications for German townspeople.

The roles Charles V and Ferdinand II played in governing the territories that fell within the boundaries of the empire were conditioned in part by the Golden Bull of 1356. Enacted by the Holy Roman emperor Charles IV (1316–1378), the Golden Bull decreed that all subsequent emperors were to be selected on the basis of a vote by Germany's princes (known as the electors), who made up the second tier of the system. Consequently, an emperor was usually beholden to the princes who had voted for him and also to those influential town families that had helped to support his election. For example, Charles V and his predecessor Maximilian I (1459–1519) both received substantial sums of money from the Fuggers of Augsburg, whose local and regional political influence rose markedly as a result of their relationship with the Hapsburgs.

Some towns—particularly those listed in the imperial register—were ruled directly by the emperor, and others enjoyed full independence. Most, however, fell somewhere in between. A town with full independence or limited autonomy was usually presided over by a *Bürgermeister* (mayor), who answered to a small electorate drawn from the ranks of established families, merchants, and craft guilds. The *Bürgermeister*, citizens, and noncitizens (a group that included domestic servants, craftsmen's assistants, beggars, and invalids) interacted in the third tier of the system.

Ultimately, because of the interconnectedness of the three tiers, events that affected one part of the system often had an impact on the others, too. The most significant such event, the Thirty Years War, was triggered by Ferdinand II's determination to strengthen Hapsburg control over—and Catholic influence within—the empire. His objectives proved unattainable, and the ultimate result of the subsequent conflict was a substantial increase in the autonomy of the princes and, to a lesser degree, the towns. This greater autonomy was formalized in the Treaty of Westphalia (1648).

Internal and External Security Considerations

One of the primary interests of any political entity, whether a town, principality, nation-state, or empire, is to secure the territory under its control. German towns had to deal with two types of security issues between the fourteenth and seventeenth centuries: on the one hand, they had to maintain internal political and social stability, and on the other, they had to defend their territory against threats posed by external powers. Internally, the gravest threats to stability stemmed from two related sources of popular unrest. One was the dissatisfaction of the lower classes with their standard of living, especially during the numerous food shortages towns across the Holy Roman Empire experienced in the fourteenth and fifteenth centuries. The other was the acrimony between those who embraced the anti-Catholic teachings of the pioneer Reformer Martin Luther (1483–1546) and the Hapsburgs, who were generally supportive of the papacy in Rome.

The chafing of the lower classes broke out in such incidents as the series of civil revolts that erupted in Brunswick in 1374, 1380, 1445, and 1487; on balance, however, these eruptions of civil unrest were transitory in nature and thus led only to brief periods of instability. While considerably less violent in the short term, the acrimony between Protestants and Catholics produced socioreligious changes that proved far more enduring. Sometimes entire towns switched their allegiance from Catholicism to Lutheranism. Such dramatic events threatened the coherence of the Holy Roman Empire from within.

▲ A 1525 drawing of the popular preacher Diepold Peringer, known as the Peasant of Wöhrd, delivering a Lutheran sermon.

THE PEASANTS' WAR (1524–1526)

Conflict between rural and urban dwellers has been a feature of numerous societies throughout history. Its most significant manifestation in the Holy Roman Empire was the Peasants' War.

Unlike traditional conflicts pitting one particular principality or town against another for control over a parcel of territory, the Peasants' War took the form of a wide-ranging series of revolts. The rebellions were an attempt on the part of rural commoners to improve their economic and political power relative to that of the wealthy nobles and families who exercised control over much of the land in central and southern Germany. The revolts, which began in May 1524 with a refusal by the subjects of the Black Forest Abbey of Saint Blasien to pay dues, spread to the larger Swabian towns of Waldshut and Freiburg im Breisgau by the end of the year and to the Franconian towns of Rothenburg and Würzburg to the north by the spring of 1525.

While they had comparable objectives, the peasants who took up arms between the spring of 1524 and the winter of 1526 did not pledge allegiance to any one leader or coordinate their offensives in an effort to permanently seize control of several contiguous principalities or towns. Instead, their revolts served as a precursor of more deep-rooted socioreligious changes to come.

The peasants' revolts were also partly the product of the preaching of Luther and his followers. The numbers of Lutheran sympathizers swelled as a profound distrust of high-level Catholic Church officials spread among members of the lower social classes within and beyond central Europe. They were also the product of centuries of mistreatment by wealthy landowners, princes as well as the scions of established families in the towns.

The Peasants' War did not ultimately result in any immediate, wide-ranging changes in the economic, political, or social status of the rural peasantry. Individually, all of the revolts—large and small—were eventually crushed by the upper classes, whose economic and military resources dwarfed those of the peasants. The movement, however, was indicative of the deeper social and religious transformation that followed over the ensuing century.

External threats to German towns came from three sources: discontent among peasants living in the rural areas surrounding the urban centers; pressure exerted by powerful regional princes on municipal leaders to extract financial or territorial concessions; and larger-scale conflicts pitting the Hapsburgs against other European states, including France, Denmark, and Sweden.

The Peasants' War was one significant although fleeting external threat faced by numerous German towns between 1524 and 1526. Countering the princes' machinations demanded concerted action that extended beyond the local level. In response to repeated attempts by the nobility to add to their possessions at the expense of the towns, several towns formed an alliance known as the Swabian League. The league lasted from 1488 to 1534 before it fell apart owing to religious differences between Catholics and Protestants.

The religious disputes that caused the breakup of the Swabian League also played a central role in triggering the outbreak of the Thirty Years War, a conflict that was as physically devastating for German towns as it was politically devastating for the unity of the Holy Roman Empire. The war unfolded in four phases between 1618 and 1648, with most of the battles contested in the empire's northern, central, and southern German lands.

By the end of the Thirty Years War, which was ultimately settled via the Treaty of Westphalia, the population of the German-speaking segment of the empire had been reduced from a prewar total of 21 million to perhaps as few as 13 million (historical estimates vary). Trade had virtually ceased throughout the empire, and a number of towns (most notably Magdeburg) had been reduced to rubble. In the aftermath of the devastation, Magdeburg and many other towns were left to rebuild their infrastructure and adjust to a future featuring markedly less interaction with and interference from the Hapsburgs.

Intellectual and Religious Thought

The most significant developments in intellectual and religious thought in the German towns of the Holy Roman Empire between 1300 and 1550, those associated with the Protestant Reformation, were the product of three overarching trends: popular dissatisfaction with a Catholic Church whose most prominent officials (especially the pope in Rome and cardinals and bishops based abroad) lived lavishly in comparison with most people; the proliferation of humanist writings that encouraged individuals to think for themselves; and the emergence of individuals, such as Luther, who were willing to challenge the papacy and its supporters among the Hapsburgs and their allies.

Midway through the fourteenth century, much of Europe was devastated by the spread of bubonic and pneumonic plague, diseases referred to collectively as the Black Death. The Black Death had a particularly serious impact on urban areas and markedly reduced the population of the vast majority of towns across the Holy Roman Empire. The uncertainty of life underlay the sale of indulgences, a practice by which corrupt elements within the Catholic hierarchy enriched themselves. (An indulgence was a remission of the punishment due to sin that a pardoned sinner had to undergo on earth and, after death, in purgatory before being admitted to heaven.) Gullible and lazy Christians were led to believe that paying a fee to a local bishop could ease their passage to heaven.

The sale of indulgences, condemned by Reformers as profiteering based on popular fear and superstition, helped create an atmosphere in which a large proportion of the population of German towns proved increasingly receptive to criticism of the church.

▼ *Much of the silver mined in the Tyrol region of Austria during the Renaissance was transported to western European buyers via the towns of southern Germany. Some of that silver was used to mint such coins as this guildiner, or taler, of Sigismund, count of Tyrol (reigned 1439-1496).*

GEOGRAPHY AND TRADE

Geography is a crucial factor affecting the capacity of any political entity to develop productive trade relationships, not only with its close neighbors but also with lands that are farther away. With respect to trade, the geographical position of the many German towns in the Holy Roman Empire was at times advantageous and at others disadvantageous. The commercial success or failure of any given town at any given time was also contingent on the political circumstances of the town, the general security of the region, and the supply of and demand for a particular good.

The central location of the towns both within the empire and within continental Europe was advantageous in two ways. First, the towns served as overland links between the Hanseatic coastal cities to the north and the Italian coastal cities to the south. Second, they served as points of contact along the river and road routes that connected the Hapsburgs' western and eastern possessions. The geographical locations of the towns proved especially useful in transporting the copper and silver mined in the Tyrol region of Austria to markets in central, southern, and western Europe.

However, once goods extracted from English, French, and Spanish colonies in the Western Hemisphere (especially South American silver) began to saturate the European marketplace and the Atlantic trade routes took center stage in the mid-sixteenth and early seventeenth centuries, many German towns sustained substantial economic losses. The insecurity and resultant political instability that enveloped the Holy Roman Empire during the Thirty Years War further reduced both the supply of and the demand for east-west and north-south trade in the lands of the Hapsburgs.

STADT · PILLSEN

Building broadly on the individualistic themes articulated by such humanist philosophers as Giovanni Pico della Mirandola (1463–1494) and Desiderius Erasmus (1466–1536), Luther encouraged Germans to question papal doctrine. In particular, Luther stressed that believers could reach heaven through faith alone and that individuals were perfectly capable of interpreting the Bible for themselves.

Luther, then an Augustinian monk and professor of religion at the University of Wittenberg, posted a treatise—the Ninety-five Theses—on the door of the town's castle church on October 31, 1517. His theses were rapidly reproduced and distributed in German towns across the empire, a process that was fueled by the increasing public disdain for Catholic officials and made practically possible by the growth of the printing industry over the previous half century.

Most printing businesses were headquartered in the towns, where Luther's Protestant movement built its foundation. As Luther's movement grew, it attracted converts from all classes of society, from tradesmen and the scions of wealthy families in the towns to the leaders of principalities across a broad swath of the empire's German heartland. For the princes in particular, Lutheranism served as a means to increase their own power at the expense of the Hapsburgs. In an attempt to avoid losing the political allegiance of the majority of principalities and towns in Germany, Charles V granted the leaders of those entities the right to choose which religion—Catholicism or Protestantism—they would allow their inhabitants to practice. He did so by way of the Peace of Augsburg of 1555. As a result of this treaty, by the end of the sixteenth century, the majority of German towns with populations in excess of a thousand people, including Augsburg, Nuremberg, Strasbourg, and Ulm, had adopted Protestantism.

Ultimately, the marked shift away from allegiance to the Catholic Church proved divisive in the Holy Roman Empire. Many southern towns and principalities (most notably those situated within the duchy of Bavaria) remained loyal to the papacy, while their northern neighbors had a tendency to practice Lutheranism or other strains of Protestantism, such as those established by Ulrich Zwingli (1484–1531) and John Calvin (1509–1564).

In the end, divisions between the Catholic and Protestant principalities and towns of the empire laid the foundations for the outbreak of the Thirty Years War. The final settlement of that bloody conflict, codified in the terms of the Treaty of Westphalia (1648), granted all Germans the freedom to choose which religion they would practice. In the process the treaty locked into place a religious divide that still exists: in present-day Germany most Catholics live in the south, and most Protestants live in the north.

▼ An oil painting by Lucas Cranach the Elder of Philipp Melanchthon, one of Martin Luther's most devoted followers and the author of the Confession of Augsburg (1530).

In April 1530 the Holy Roman emperor Charles V called on the leaders of those towns and regions whose citizens had adopted the Lutheran faith to draft a document explaining their beliefs. In response, Philipp Melanchthon (1497–1560) wrote the Confession of Augsburg, which was presented to Charles V two months later.

Our works cannot reconcile God or merit forgiveness of sins, grace, and justification, but that we obtain this only by faith when we believe that we are received into favor for Christ's sake, who alone has been set forth the Mediator and Propitiation, in order that the Father may be reconciled through him. Whoever, therefore, trusts that by works he merits grace, despises the merit and grace of Christ, and seeks a way to God without Christ, by human strength, although Christ has said of Himself: I am the Way, the Truth, and the Life.... Furthermore, it is taught on our part that it is necessary to do good works, not that we should trust to merit grace by them, but because it is the will of God.... And because through faith the Holy Ghost is received, hearts are renewed and endowed with new affections, so as to be able to bring forth good works.

Confession of Augsburg

FURTHER READING

Hughes, Michael. *Early Modern Germany, 1477–1806.* Philadelphia, 1992.

Ozment, Steven E. *The Reformation in the Cities: The Appeal of Protestantism to Sixteenth-Century Germany and Switzerland.* New Haven, CT, 1975.

Robisheaux, Thomas Willard. *Rural Society and the Search for Order in Early Modern Germany.* New York, 1989.

Scott, Tom. *Society and Economy in Germany, 1300–1600.* New York, 2002.

Strauss, Gerald. *Manifestations of Discontent in Germany on the Eve of the Reformation: A Collection of Documents.* Bloomington, IN, 1971.

Robert J. Pauly Jr.

SEE ALSO
• Augsburg, Peace of • Charles V
• Established Churches • Feudalism
• Guilds and Companies • Hanseatic League
• Hapsburg Empire • Holy Roman Empire
• Lutheranism • Manufacturing • Markets and Fairs
• Nationalism • Peasants' Revolts • Population
• Printing • Reformation • Thirty Years War
• Trade • Universities • Warfare

Giotto

THE FLORENTINE PAINTER, SCULPTOR, AND ARCHITECT GIOTTO DI BONDONE (1266/7 OR 1276–1337) ACHIEVED GREAT FAME DURING HIS LIFETIME AND IS GENERALLY CREDITED WITH MANY OF THE TECHNICAL AND STYLISTIC INNOVATIONS THAT DISTINGUISHED THE ART OF THE ITALIAN RENAISSANCE.

▼ *In this detail from Giotto's Meeting at the Golden Gate, Anne and Joachim, the Virgin Mary's parents, are reunited following Joachim's expulsion from Jerusalem. Giotto masterfully captures the tenderness of the couple's embrace.*

Giotto di Bondone was the son of a farmer from the village of Vespignano, outside Florence. Although little is known about his early life or his artistic training, it has long been presumed that Giotto studied with Cimabue, the greatest Florentine painter of the thirteenth century. Evidence of their association is entirely anecdotal; one legend states that Cimabue, on spying the young Giotto sketching one of his father's sheep on a flat rock, was so taken aback by Giotto's talent that the famous artist begged Giotto's father to allow his young son to study painting with him. The Florentine poet Dante Alighieri (1265–1321) implies a connection, at least in the popular imagination, when he mentions both together in the *Divine Comedy*.

The lack of contemporary documentary evidence of Giotto's life and works is, at least in part, mitigated by the large body of later literature concerning the artist. The most important early source of information is the *Villani Chronicle*, put into verse around 1373 by Antonio Pucci (died 1388). Pucci's claim that Giotto was seventy years old when he died suggests a birthdate sometime in 1266 or 1267. The date of 1276, however, can be found in several sixteenth-century sources. The choice of one birthdate or the other is far more than a trivial biographical detail: it becomes a crucial factor for someone attempting to attribute or date any works tentatively assigned to Giotto.

Cimabue   1588–1637

Cimabue, born Benciveni di Pepo (c. 1240–c. 1302), was the most important Italian painter of the late thirteenth century. Although his style was heavily influenced by Byzantine painting, Cimabue invested his works with a new sense of drama and made innovative experiments in the depiction of three-dimensional space. His figures often appear much more sculptural than those of his contemporaries, many of whom continued in the more linear style adopted from the Greeks. Cimabue's major surviving works include frescoes in the upper church of San Francesco in Assisi (c. 1290), a mosaic of Saint John the Evangelist in the cathedral in Pisa (1301–1302), and the *Santa Trinità Madonna* (c. 1280). There is a long literary tradition that Cimabue taught Giotto. In his *Divine Comedy*, Dante states clearly that Giotto was seen as having surpassed his master.

Major Fresco Cycles

Giotto's painting of the interior of the Arena Chapel in Padua provides the most comprehensive example of his style. It is thought that the fresco cycle was executed sometime between the completion of the chapel in early 1305 and either 1308 or 1309, when a contemporary document mentions one of the final figures that Giotto would have painted there. The overall theme is the redemption of humankind, as demonstrated through the lives of the Virgin Mary and Jesus Christ. Numerous assistants must have helped Giotto complete such a large project so quickly, but the force of Giotto's extraordinary artistic vision is clear. The figures are monumental in scale, with a volume and weight that had been absent from European art since late antiquity. Also new is Giotto's fledgling interest in anatomy; drapery folds no longer merely provide pleasing surface decoration but appear to echo the body parts hidden beneath them. Facial features—small mouths, long noses, and almond-shaped eyes, for example—are easily distinguishable. A highly developed, albeit idiosyncratic, depiction of space and depth is also present in Giotto's Arena Chapel frescos. Lacking the scientific methods of rendering perspective (that is, creating the illusion of three-dimensional space on a flat surface), methods that were perfected by later artists, Giotto uses his eye to create buildings and landscapes that appear to recede into the distance.

Simplicity is perhaps the best word to describe Giotto's painted narrative. Each scene is played out against a stage backdrop, and the artist uses only those props and extraneous figures necessary to ensure that the moment within the story can be properly identified. By focusing on the emotional exchange between the main figures, Giotto heightens the dramatic impact of the scene, which he portrays with a startling degree of psychological insight.

Though his assistants' work is more noticeable in the surviving fresco cycles in the Church of Santa Croce in Florence, Giotto's simple compositions, emphasis on the emotional drama of the scenes, and penetrating psychological insight leave his authorship of these works above speculation. The biographer Giorgio Vasari claims that

Giotto decorated four chapels within Santa Croce, but only the cycles in the private chapels of the Bardi and Peruzzi families survive. There is no contemporary documentary evidence of the cycles' creation, but a date in the 1320s seems most likely on stylistic and iconographical grounds. The Bardi Chapel cycle, the earlier of the two, includes six scenes inspired by the Franciscan movement, while the Peruzzi Chapel is adorned with scenes from the life of Saint John the Baptist and Saint John the Evangelist.

▲ *Cimabue's* Santa Trinità Madonna *(c. 1280) represents an attempt by the artist to depict three-dimensional space, but the decorative linear patterning in the Virgin's gown and the ambiguous positioning in space of the angels surrounding her and the prophets beneath reflect Cimabue's firm grounding in Italo-Byzantine artistic traditions.*

THE ARENA CHAPEL

n February 1300 Enrico Scrovegni, a wealthy Paduan merchant, purchased a large plot of land on which stood the remains of an ancient Roman arena. Enrico wanted to construct a grand villa with the necessary outbuildings—including what would become known as the Arena Chapel. The popular condemnation of Enrico's father, Reginaldo, for growing rich through usury (lending money with interest) weighed heavily upon Enrico, who was condemned by association; the new chapel, dedicated to the Virgin of the Annunciation and of Charity, would not only meet the needs of Enrico and his family but also stand as a permanent monument to the humble penitence of the Scrovegni family before the glory of God.

Work was begun in the spring of 1303, and the chapel was consecrated on March 25, 1305. Giotto, who probably worked there from 1305 until 1309, was commissioned by Enrico to decorate the interior of the chapel, a simple barrel-vaulted space with six windows along the south wall and a small Gothic apse. Giotto and his team executed the painting in *buon' fresco* (painting the pigments onto patches of wet plaster so that the colors bond chemically to the plaster as it dries). They worked from the top of the chapel down both side walls toward the floor.

The overall theme of the frescoes reflects Enrico's concerns with judgment and salvation. The main fresco cycles, which depict the lives of the Virgin Mary and Jesus, conclude with the dramatic Last Judgment scene on the west wall. A variety of iconographical additions, drawn mostly from the *Legenda Aurea* (*Golden Legend*) by Jacobus da Voragine (1230–1298), emphasize the human aspects of the story. On the level of the dado (the lower part of the wall), monochromatic allegorical figures representing the virtues and vices, their stances often echoing actions in the stories above, further relate the narrative to the life of ordinary people.

► *This interior view of the Arena Chapel displays the decorative program executed by Giotto between 1305 and 1309. By examining overlapping patches of plaster and pigment, experts have been able to determine the order in which each fresco sequence was painted.*

In the years after he completed the Arena Chapel frescoes, Giotto's skill at focusing on the emotional interaction between his figures matured. Particularly in the Peruzzi Chapel, the viewer is aware of the subtle subjugation of an entire composition to a central exchange. In *The Raising of Drusiana,* for example, the massing of figures at either side of the fresco (echoed in the organization of the architectural backdrop) leaves a void in the center of the composition that accentuates the emotional drama between Saint John the Evangelist and the woman he has just raised from the dead. Giotto's improved understanding of spatial illusion heightens the viewer's sense of participation in the scene; architectural backdrops are at times cut off abruptly by frames and architectural features within the chapels, and each scene is painted from a slightly different angle in such a way as to afford the viewer, standing at the doorway of the chapel, an optimal vantage point.

The straightforward attribution to Giotto of the fresco cycles in the Arena, Bardi, and Peruzzi chapels stands in sharp contrast to that of the Saint Francis cycle in the upper church of San Francesco in Assisi. Although Giotto is recorded as having worked in Assisi, certain contemporary sources fail to include the frescoes there among Giotto's works. The detailed arguments of the Giotto and non-Giotto camps typically hinge upon discrepancies in the dating of events (including the year of Giotto's birth and the highly disputed dates when artists were working in San Francesco) and several key stylistic differences between the Saint Francis cycle and Giotto's more securely attributed works.

◄ *In this fresco Enrico Scrovegni offers his chapel to the glory of God. Contemporary viewers would have recognized that the figure depicted is Enrico through signs and symbols included by Giotto (such as Enrico's clothing and his position as donor of the chapel, for example) rather than by any physical resemblance of the figure to the man himself.*

THE ASSISI PROBLEM

The Church of San Francesco in Assisi, the mother church of the Franciscan order, comprises an upper and a lower church. The building was completed in 1253 and over the following century underwent extensive decoration. Among the artists of the period who worked there were the Roman Jacopo Torriti (flourished c. 1270–1300), the Sienese Simone Martini (c. 1284–1344) and Pietro Lorenzetti (c. 1280–c. 1348), and the Florentine Cimabue (who was possibly Giotto's teacher). Given the large number of important artists who worked in Assisi, it seems unlikely that Giotto would not have contributed to the decoration in some way. There is no direct documentary evidence to support this argument, however; the earliest writings offer conflicting stories. Later commentaries generally claim that Giotto, because of his skill and fame, must have been at work in Assisi. If Giotto worked in Assisi as a member of Cimabue's workshop, no particular stylistic idiosyncrasies have been detected, and if he worked as a mature master painter and his work was destroyed subsequently, it seems unlikely that no documentary evidence would have survived. Perhaps, then, Giotto is responsible for painting some of the existing decoration for which no definitive attribution survives. The extensive cycle of images of the life of Saint Francis would seem to be the most obvious candidate for such attribution, though certain scholars have suggested that Giotto may also be the master whose work includes the Old Testament story of Isaac.

The Saint Francis cycle, which was executed by several masters but surely overseen by a single person, impresses by its innovative compositions and iconographies; the main artist shares many interests with the Giotto who worked in the Arena Chapel and elsewhere. Those who believe that Giotto was indeed the Master of the Saint Francis Cycle also make the point that the painter of the cycle—if the painter was not Giotto—apparently produced no other works and that it seems unlikely that such a talent would have left no name or other indication of his artistic activities. The main problem with the Giotto theory is chronological. The Saint Francis cycle was certainly completed by 1307 and begun after 1291 (possibly even after 1296). Given this time frame, there is precious little time for Giotto's style to have matured from that evident in Assisi to that displayed in the Arena Chapel (which was probably begun in 1305).

▼ A series of twenty-eight scenes from the life of Saint Francis adorns the walls of the upper church in Assisi; this scene of Saint Francis giving away his cloak, the second in the cycle, was painted by an artist known only as the Saint Francis Master. At least two other artists, whose true names are also unknown, contributed to the Saint Francis cycle.

A master storyteller, the artist responsible for the Saint Francis cycle uses many of the devices favored by Giotto, though arguably in a less confident way. His figures are less monumental than Giotto's, and though he emphasizes emotion and drama, the effect is less powerful than in the Florence and Padua frescoes. The Master of the Saint Francis Cycle (as he is often called) was also interested in depicting space and depth. His work in Assisi is bolder and more experimental than Giotto's rather formulaic work in Padua or in Santa Croce and exhibits a proportional relationship between figures and architecture that is different from that present in Giotto's other works. The attribution of the Saint Francis cycle continues to be hotly debated; it is difficult to imagine how, without the discovery of additional contemporary documentation, the argument will ever be definitively concluded.

Important Works on Panel

The depiction of the Madonna and Child in Florence's Uffizi Gallery is Giotto's best known panel painting. Known as the *Ognissanti Madonna* (because it was once in the Florentine Church of Ognissanti), the panel stands over ten feet (3 m) high and measures nearly eight feet (2.4 m) in width. Known as a *Maestà*, this type of composition—an enthroned Madonna, with the Christ child on her lap, surrounded by adoring angels and saints—was very popular in Italy in the late thirteenth and the fourteenth centuries. Giotto's panel, generally dated to the period immediately following his frescoes in Padua (therefore, completed around 1310) and modeled on thirteenth-century examples, is composed vertically with a small number of onlookers arranged symmetrically. Other early-fourteenth-century depictions of the same subject are often laid out horizontally and filled with much more activity. The best known of these depictions is by the Sienese painter Duccio di Buoninsegna (see page 492).

The figural style of Giotto's *Ognissanti Madonna,* much the same as that employed in the Arena Chapel, emphasizes monumentality, volume, and the suggestion of realistic anatomy. As in Padua, Giotto has taken pains to suggest depth and recession into space, albeit without the

aid of a mathematical method. To indicate spatial depth and recession in the *Ognissanti Madonna,* Giotto relies much less heavily than any of his contemporaries did on the medieval practice of placing a figure or object above another to indicate distance between it and the viewer. Instead, the sense of space within Giotto's composition is firmly established by the obvious projecting and receding lines incorporated within the Virgin's throne. This clarity of composition adds to the overall sense of tranquillity and simplicity always evident in Giotto's work.

▼ *When compared with Cimabue's Santa Trinità Madonna (see page 485), the naturalism and understanding of perspective evident in Giotto's Ognissanti Madonna panel (pictured here) is remarkable given the gap of only thirty years between the two works.*

▶ The Dance of Salome, *from the Peruzzi Chapel in Santa Croce. Compared with Giotto's earlier work in the Arena Chapel, this fresco typifies the artist's mature style. Giotto conveys the interior settings with a confident mastery of spatial illusion.*

The decorative scheme in the Arena Chapel contains two painted panels: a heavily damaged image of God the Father and a crucifix. These works were obviously designed by Giotto as part of the overall decorative scheme for the chapel, but art historians continue to debate the extent of Giotto's personal involvement in their execution. Assistants from Giotto's workshop almost certainly painted the bulk of the two major panels that bear Giotto's signature: *The Stigmatization of Saint Francis* (now in the Louvre, Paris) and the Stefaneschi altarpiece (now in the Vatican Museum). These and various other panels attributed to Giotto are well below the standards of the Arena Chapel panels and the *Ognissanti Madonna*. Some other Giotto panels, such as the *Crucifix* in the Church of Santa Maria Novella, in Florence, may have been painted early in the artist's career, since there are certain stylistic discrepancies with later attributed works. The two signed pieces, however, may well have been executed under Giotto's supervision, since it was not

---

EARLY ITALIAN PANELS: METHODS OF CONSTRUCTION

*S*hifts in liturgical practices in the centuries after 1000 eventually led to the development of the large painted altarpieces once found within all European churches and cathedrals. In Italy in particular, a flourishing panel-painting industry produced great numbers of paintings on wooden panels into the late Middle Ages and beyond. Scientific advances in recent years have led to a much greater understanding of the techniques used to build and paint these panels, but scholars still rely heavily on contemporary documents for information about their construction and execution. In 1437 Cennino Cennini, a Florentine painter trained in the tradition of Giotto, wrote *Il libro dell'arte* (*The Craftsman's Handbook*), the most detailed surviving discussion on this topic. Generations of artists and scholars have studied his technical descriptions, all of which are accompanied by his own anecdotes and helpful hints.

Most Italian panels were constructed from several planks of poplar attached with glue, dowels, and handmade nails to make larger pieces. The panels were then covered with strips of linen and coated with layers of a gypsum plaster known as gesso. Each layer of gesso was finer than the one before until the perfectly smooth surface required for painting and gilding was achieved. After the completion of an underdrawing, all areas to be gilded were covered with *bole*, a greasy red clay, before sheets of gold leaf were applied and burnished (made shiny by rubbing); punched and scratched decoration could then be added. Painting was executed in tempera, made of egg yolk and pigment, and generally applied in a series of layers from darkest to lightest tones. Finally, any remaining gilded decoration (of brocades and draperies) was painted on. There is some evidence that the completed painting often received several coats of varnish to protect the surface.

uncommon during this period for an artist to sign only those pieces from his workshop that were not painted by his own hand; a painting executed by the master himself needed no signature to authenticate it.

Other Works

It is known that Giotto traveled to Rome for the first jubilee year in 1300, when Pope Boniface VIII announced that pilgrims would be granted a special indulgence (a remission of the punishment due to penitent sinners). While there, Giotto executed commissions in the basilicas of Saint Peter and Saint John Lateran, as well as (perhaps numerous) private commissions, notably for Cardinal Stefaneschi. Giotto's stay in Rome would have allowed him to study the early Christian wall paintings still visible in many Roman churches as well as the work of Pietro Cavallini (c. 1250–c. 1330), a Roman painter whose attempts at naturalism (as opposed to the more schematized style inspired by Byzantine painting) certainly influenced Giotto. Most of Giotto's Roman works are lost. The altarpiece commissioned by Cardinal Stefaneschi is probably a workshop product, as may be a fresco fragment from the Lateran Basilica. The *Navicella* (a mosaic depicting Christ walking on water), commissioned by Cardinal Stefaneschi and placed over the entrance to Saint Peter's, was so heavily restored in subsequent centuries that it no longer displays much of Giotto's original work.

Of Giotto's alleged sojourn at the papal court in Avignon around 1305 (mentioned in a contemporary document), there exists no documentary or artistic evidence. Nothing survives of the works that Giotto painted while a resident at the royal court in Naples between 1329 and 1333. In 1334 Giotto was made chief architect of the city of Florence and master of works at the duomo, where he began work on a campanile (bell tower). Giotto died in January 1337.

◀ *Probably only a workshop piece, this panel, which relies heavily on the Saint Francis cycle in Assisi, has been used as evidence of Giotto's authorship of the Assisi frescoes. However, it has also been argued that, since the stigmatization scene in Assisi was widely copied throughout the fourteenth century, the fact that it should appear here with minimal modification may indicate the work of a less innovative artist than Giotto.*

Just as Florentine painting of the trecento (the 1300s) was dominated by Giotto and his followers, the style in Siena was greatly affected by the work of Duccio di Buoninsegna and his successors, Simone Martini and the Lorenzetti brothers, Pietro (1280–1348) and Ambrogio (c. 1290–1348). Duccio's *Maestà* (1308–1311), painted for the main altar in the Cathedral of Siena, set the stage for the development of Sienese painting after 1300.

Sienese painting of this period is more linear than Florentine work, with greater emphasis on the decorative qualities of pattern and line. The sinuous, snaking drapery hems and generally busy compositions of works by Duccio and his followers contrast with the monumental simplicity of Giotto's painting. Duccio's suggestions of depth and volume within his compositions, while more tentative, are every bit as effective as Giotto's, though they always remain subordinate to the overall organization of the flat panel surface.

▶ *Duccio di Buoninsegna (died 1318) utilized an innovative horizontal format for his* Maestà, *a new altarpiece for Siena Cathedral. Although Duccio's compositions are busier than Giotto's, the Sienese painter's understanding of perspective is nonetheless impressive.*

Contribution to Western Art

The debate about Assisi fueled scholarly interest in Giotto's work for hundreds of years and helped establish him as the first great painter of the Italian Renaissance. Giorgio Vasari credits Giotto with having rescued Italian painting from the influence of the Byzantine artists by returning to the ancient practice of modeling forms from nature. Although Giotto's impact on later Italian artists, such as Masaccio and Michelangelo, is undeniable, the works of artists of other early Italian schools, notably Siena, may have had a more profound influence on northern European painting. In a number of important northern works before 1400, the depiction of three-dimensional space and naturalistic facial features owes much to the works of Duccio di Buoninsegna and Simone Martini.

Critical assessments of Giotto often stress what is revolutionary about his work, but in the final analysis, he must be seen as a great artist who called upon his own distinctive talents as well as those of the artists who preceded him. He is as much the heir to the rich traditions of medieval art as he is the founder of the Italian Renaissance.

FURTHER READING

Adams, Laurie, ed. *Giotto in Perspective.* Englewood Cliffs, NJ, 1974.

Derbes, Anne, and Mark Sandona, eds. *The Cambridge Companion to Giotto.* New York, 2003.

Smart, Alastair. *The Assisi Problem and the Art of Giotto: A Study of the Legend of St. Francis in the Upper Church of San Francesco, Assisi.* Oxford, 1971.

Stubblebine, James H., ed. *Giotto: The Arena Chapel Frescoes.* New York, 1969.

Caroline S. Hull

SEE ALSO

• Florence • Painting and Sculpture

Guilds and Companies

GUILDS AND COMPANIES, DIFFERENT TYPES OF TRADING AND CRAFT ASSOCIATIONS, AROSE IN EUROPE IN THE EIGHTH CENTURY AND BY THE FOURTEENTH CENTURY HAD EVOLVED INTO POLITICALLY AND ECONOMICALLY POWERFUL BODIES.

Guilds served important social and economic functions during the Renaissance. They provided groups of merchants, tradesmen, and artisans with protected markets, sources of capital, and economic assistance during difficult times. At least four types of guilds and companies may be distinguished: religious guilds, guilds merchant, craft guilds, and, in the fourteenth century, merchants' and journeymen's companies.

Companies, some of which were chartered by national governments as an effective monopoly in a given region or trade, emerged gradually. In some cases, they were the remnants of guilds, but in general, although the two types of associations existed side by side and sometimes for similar purposes, they were distinct entities.

Religious Guilds

The first guilds, religious guilds, had formed by the late eighth century at the latest. These guilds were an outgrowth of the work of the medieval church, which saw the guild as a way of displacing the pagan banquets and festivals that continued to take place in accordance with long-standing pre-Christian traditions. These earliest guilds were essentially a manifestation of the general desire for society and companionship. The church, recognizing that it was in the nature of people to join together in associations, encouraged the formation of groups that would foster what it regarded as the appropriate religious spirit.

The church was not, however, the sole impetus or driving force behind the formation of guilds. The guilds also owed their origin to the political disorder that was rife in much of Europe during the Middle Ages. At times of political and social instability and uncertainty, people often come together to form groups whose purpose is to provide aid and comfort to its members. In this sense the religious guilds performed an important social function.

The first confirmed mention of guilds is in the Carolingian capitularies (legal decrees drawn up in France under Charlemagne) of 779 and 789. In the ninth century the Synod of Nantes, a provincial meeting of bishops, also referred to guilds. The first known mention of guilds in Norway is from the eleventh century, in Denmark from the twelfth, and in Sweden from the thirteenth. (These dates, of course, do not necessarily denote the first founding of guilds in those countries.)

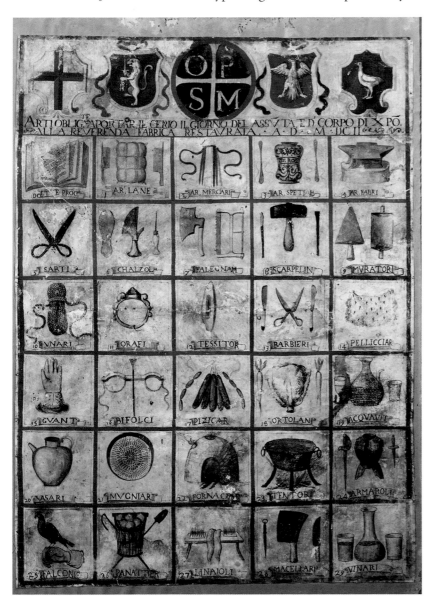

▼ This early-sixteenth-century manuscript page from Umbria, Italy, displays the official insignia of numerous local craft guilds.

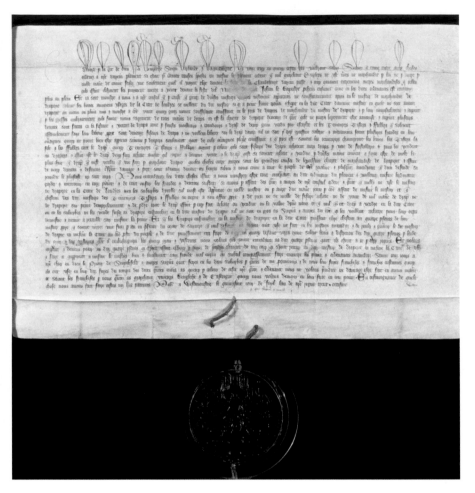

A drapers' guild was founded in London in 1361 and given a royal charter three years later (a draper is a wool and cloth merchant). With this letter of patent, issued in 1438, the guild was incorporated as the Worshipful Company of Drapers. The first corporate body to be granted a coat of arms, the Worshipful Company of Drapers was one of the most powerful companies in London politics; its membership included over one hundred lord mayors.

cial relief would generally receive whatever funds the guild's finances permitted. Benevolences were also provided, albeit to a generally lesser degree, to members who had suffered losses from fire, shipwreck, or thievery. For example, the guild of Saint Catherine, in Aldersgate, London, would assist any member should he "fall into poverty or be injured through age, or through fire or water, thieves or sickness."

In this sense the guild was also a sort of insurance company, of which the members were at once directors and policyholders. By paying the cost of admission into the guild, together with the annual dues, a member was in effect insuring himself against the consequences of any future catastrophic loss. Although the economic self-interest of the guild members in this regard should not be discounted, it is no less true that guilds at this time had much of their original religious character, even as their focus shifted gradually from the religious to the secular.

Guilds frequently took on broader social responsibilities than simply supporting their members in times of trouble and need. They often gave financial assistance even to members of their community who did not belong to the guild. Guilds also lent their often considerable economic clout to the support of local churches, and members took part in masses for the dead and other church activities.

A number of religious guilds also took part in what amounted to local government by providing funding for roads and other civic projects. In a few cases guilds in the fourteenth and fifteenth centuries actually took control of local governments. In general, though, guilds remained independent private organizations that participated in civic affairs only at the margins and restricted the majority of their activities to affairs within their limited sphere of influence.

Further Development of Religious Guilds

Religious guilds flourished in England after the Norman Conquest and were widespread by the thirteenth century. By the fourteenth century they were so integrated into the social and political fabric that an order of Parliament in 1388 referred specifically to the masters and wardens of all guilds. The parliamentary order enjoined every sheriff in England to command the leaders of each guild to provide the king, no later than February 2, 1389, with a full account of the guild's foundation, membership, and intent, as well as with information regarding any documentation pertaining to the guild.

Each member of a religious guild was required to take an oath of admission, make a contribution to the guild as a condition of membership, and contribute annual benevolences, which were used for the well-being of the least fortunate of the guild's members. Guild members received support from the guild under certain circumstances and conditions. An aged, sick, or indigent guild member who petitioned the guild for finan-

The Guilds Merchant

The guild merchant (the term simply means "trading guild") emerged in Norman England after trade increased between England and continental Europe in the wake of the Norman Conquest. It is also possible that the mercantile form of guild was brought over by the Normans and transplanted onto English soil. By whatever

GUILDS AND THE CHURCH

Although the church did not establish religious guilds, the guilds often served religious functions that lay outside either the scope or talents of the church itself. Thus, religious guilds were in effect extensions of the will of the church into society at large. They provided help not only to their members but also to the general community, in keeping with church teaching regarding the need for the faithful to share their material and spiritual blessings with those in need. Although religious guilds were particularly strong in England during the Renaissance, they also played a significant role in the social life of the rest of Europe.

◀ *This stained glass window, in the Cathedral of Saint-Étienne in Bourges, France, includes depictions of the Guild of Weavers—which sponsored the window—and of the parable of the Good Samaritan.*

means the guilds merchant came to be in England, once planted, they took firm root.

A guild merchant was usually established by the royal grant of *gilda mercatoria*. The grant of *gilda mercatoria* was a restrictive covenant that gave its holder substantial control—and sometimes even a monopoly—over the local or regional market for a specific commodity. In addition, the guild merchant frequently empowered its members to charge nonmembers who wished to engage in the craft or activity over which the guild merchant had authority. Thus, the principal function of the *gilda mercatoria* was to allow members a competitive advantage over nonmembers. Town aldermen helped the members of the guild merchant enforce the protection afforded by the grant of *gilda mercatoria*.

The guild merchant, which could be found in most towns and even major cities throughout England, also flourished in Europe. Despite the prevalence of the guild merchant, however, it did not emerge in a number of prominent English towns and cities. The guild merchant was never adopted in London, Norwich and Colchester (both in East Anglia), or the Cinque Ports (a confederation of English Channel ports in southeastern England), where the greater concentration of potential buyers and sellers made it far more difficult to regulate commerce. In major cities the establishment of a guild merchant would probably prove to be of little or no benefit to its members. In general, the guild merchant played a far more influential role in smaller towns than it did in larger ones.

Membership in the guild merchant could even be an economic handicap, since the artificially inflated prices and monopolistic or quasi-monopolistic polices enforced under a grant of *gilda mercatoria* inevitably led to the emergence of a parallel unregulated market in the relevant good or commodity—a black market. While it was a relatively simple matter to shut down such economic competition in a sparsely populated area, where the unauthorized conduct of such trade could be readily detected, in a major city such regulation became all but impossible. The guild merchant therefore remained a predominantly small-town or rural phenomenon.

The Emergence of Craft Guilds

There is no general consensus on the process by which craft guilds emerged and gradually replaced the guilds merchant. This uncertainty is due largely to a lack of information regarding the inclusion or exclusion of craftsmen and artisans from the guild merchant. In at least some cases, it appears that they were admitted on the basis of their being regarded as fellow merchants. They took raw material and produced a product that could be marketed; hence, no sharp division was drawn between artisans and other kinds of merchants until at least the beginning of the thirteenth century.

Even so, craft guilds had existed in England since shortly after the Norman Conquest, and their establishment only slightly postdated that of the guilds merchant. The fact that the guild merchant and the craft guild existed at the same time raises the question of the precise nature of the collaboration or competition between the guild merchant and the craft guild. The original craft guilds that emerged shortly after the emergence of the guilds merchant were relatively few in number, and their number did not increase—nor their distribution spread—for several centuries. It is also probable that the guild merchant and the craft guild shared some members, although it is quite apparent that the guild merchant did not directly give rise to the craft guild. It is possible that where the guild merchant operated alongside the craft guild, the former exercised at least some form of control over the latter, as the guild merchant was often a powerful element in local communities.

The means by which the craft guild gradually supplanted the guild merchant may be most accurately described as a process of undermining. As the more numerous and specialized craft guilds propagated, the influence and territorial extent of the guilds merchant diminished. Individual groups of artisans—silversmiths or weavers, for example—could petition the king for the grant of a royal charter, which would give them the (sometimes exclusive) right to practice their trade or craft in a given area. Each time the king granted such a charter, the power of the guilds merchant was correspondingly reduced, even though the newer craft guilds were officially subordinate to the guilds merchant. This process was more pronounced in towns consisting of boroughs of moderate-to-high population, where

▼ *In this scene from a fifteenth-century French manuscript, a guild master judges the work of a carpenter and stonemason who want to become masters.*

The etymology of the words *guild* and *company* offers a clue to the purpose and intent of each of the two kinds of associations. *Guild* derives from a Teutonic word whose meanings include "penalty" and "payment," the latter having the sense of "expiation," or "atonement." Thus, *guild* carries with it the sense of redemption from guilt (in fact, the word *guilt* may be a cognate form). The etymology further suggests that guilds took it upon themselves to provide a means of atonement for their members; indeed, they were founded as religious or quasi-religious fraternities and often served as an extension of the church into society.

Company derives from two Latin words that mean "together" and "bread." In some of the earliest companies, breaking bread together (the eating of common meals) was widely practiced, as it also was in guilds. Although guilds and companies would ultimately become essentially moneymaking operations, both were at heart social organizations that took on more strictly economic characteristics with the passing of time.

the necessity for more specialized craft workers spurred the faster growth of the craft guilds. In more rural areas the prevalence of agriculture as the dominant economic activity left the guilds merchant in a much stronger position relative to the upstart craft guilds.

From Craft Guilds to Companies

By the first half of the fourteenth century, craft guilds had gained ascendancy in much of Europe. Under King Edward III (reigned 1327–1377), the influence of craft guilds in England increased with ever-greater rapidity as the country experienced the beginnings of early industrialization and Edward encouraged the growth of specialized trades that would facilitate further economic development.

By the beginning of the fifteenth century, master craftsmen began to shift the focus of their efforts from producing or overseeing the production of their wares to more strictly mercantile pursuits. Concurrently, the term *guild* had fallen into relative disuse and was being replaced by *mistery* or *company*. The word *guild* (usually spelled *gild*) was still commonly used in northern Europe but had become very rare elsewhere by the sixteenth century.

As the number of guilds decreased, companies increasingly assumed what had historically been the guild's roles and prerogatives. These companies were generally referred to either as merchants' companies or journeymen's companies. The merchants' companies did not generally make the goods they sold, nor did they usually even fulfill the trade master's historical role of instructing and supervising apprentices and jour-

neymen. On the whole, members of merchants' companies were just that—merchants. As such, the merchants' companies were clearly to be distinguished from the old guilds merchant, which boasted both merchants and artisans among their membership.

▼ In this 1532 portrait by Hans Holbein the Younger of a merchant named Georg Gisze, the assortment of objects that surround the merchant are a clear indication that he wanted to be depicted as a typical Renaissance humanist.

Merchants' companies sold the products of others, an activity that brought them into conflict with journeymen's companies. Journeymen's companies were originally established in the fourteenth century by artisans and tradesmen as a defensive bulwark against merchants' companies. The two sorts of companies frequently operated at cross purposes, since the merchants wanted to obtain the products of the artisans and tradesmen at the lowest possible price (with the object of getting a more profitable resale), while the artisans and tradesmen of the journeymen's companies naturally wanted to maximize the profit from the sale of their wares.

Although this struggle between merchants and journeymen was in evidence throughout continental Europe and in England, it was most pronounced in northern Europe. Indeed, this battle for economic dominion was a major influence on mercantile life in Germany during the fifteenth century.

Joint-Stock Companies

The joint-stock company was another form of corporate organization, distinct from the various guilds and the merchants' and journeymen's companies that emerged from the guilds. Although the joint-stock company shares some of the characteristics of the guild, it does not owe its origin to this earlier system of joint cooperation; the guild predates the establishment of the first joint-stock companies by at least several hundred years.

A joint-stock company was an association of individuals who each contributed a capital sum to the company. Each member thus held transferable shares in a joint stock of capital, and each took a commensurate share in the profits of the joint enterprise. Joint-stock companies generally invested in more speculative projects, particularly trading ventures in remote lands, where the commercial and political risk was high.

Joint-stock companies were established by royal prerogative, as were some guilds, but they had very different aims. Whereas a guild was established in order to further the goals of its members, a joint-stock company was typically chartered by the monarch in order to advance the nation's mercantile interests abroad. In this respect the joint-stock company differed from what was called a regulated company, which resembled a trade guild and held a royally decreed

▼ *The Grote Markt was the commercial center of Brussels (and thus one of the most important trading markets in Europe) from the early fifteenth century on. Every year, during the Ommeganck (literally, "walk around"), the guilds of Brussels processed through the Grote Markt. This painting by Denys van Alsloot captures the Ommeganck of 1615, during which the guilds paraded in honor of Archduchess Isabella, who was made queen of the crossbowmen's guild.*

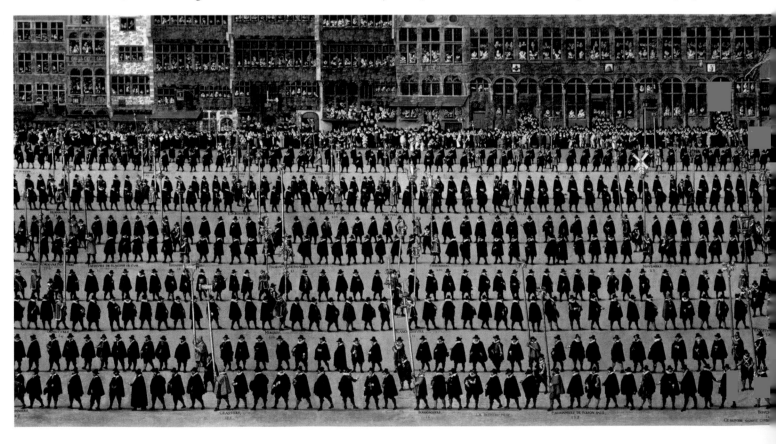

AMALGAMATION OF THE CRAFT GUILDS

One curious characteristic of the craft guilds was their tendency to amalgamate, that is, come together into a larger unit. The frequent combining of several smaller guilds into one larger guild was clearly evident in fifteenth-century England and became even more evident in the sixteenth and seventeenth centuries. Nor was continental Europe immune to this tendency, where such amalgamation was common as early as the fourteenth century, particularly in the Netherlands.

Amalgamation took different forms. In some cases, several smaller guilds (usually involving related crafts) came together into one larger guild. This union provided less individual control, naturally, but far greater collective clout. It also happened that all of the guilds in a given town or region would combine into one far larger and more powerful guild. In such cases it was not unheard of for guilds to exercise considerable political power and even to take over the administration of the town or region in which they were located. The guild was by its nature a fraternal organization whose formation was motivated in large part by a desire to protect its members' narrow interests from society as a whole. That amalgamation would take place seems logical, since amalgamated guilds could provide both greater protection for their members and more extensive control over local and regional markets.

monopoly on trade between the mother country and another country or region. Although regulated companies operated by the leave of the monarch, they were essentially private enterprises.

Even though private individuals ran a joint-stock company, it was essentially an extension of royal authority. The period from the fourteenth century through the seventeenth offers up

numerous examples of joint-stock companies tightly controlled by the monarchy. King Richard II of England granted a royal charter to the Merchant Adventurers of England in 1390; Queen Elizabeth chartered the famous and long-lived East India Company in 1600; and William and Mary chartered the Bank of England in 1694. Although not technically part of the king's or queen's government, such companies operated at the pleasure of the crown and were chartered under mandates designed to further the interest of the monarchy.

The carrying out of this intention was, however, often easier to demand in principle than to realize in practice. Generally speaking, joint-stock companies tended to go their own way, notwithstanding any limitations imposed by their charter, principally owing to defects in the very nature of the joint-stock company. To begin with, the individuals who contracted debts in the company's name could not be held to account, no matter how poor their judgment had been. Even outright fraud perpetrated in the company's name usually went unpunished, if not undetected. In addition, once a charter was granted, there was great difficulty in compelling a joint-stock company to adhere to it. In many cases a joint-stock company acted directly contrary to the public interest and the interest of the same crown that had provided its charter—in other words, it did the very opposite of its intended function.

shares, rather than an incorporated association like the joint-stock company. Despite a certain improvement in structure, the common-law companies were still subject to abuses by unscrupulous individuals who used them to advance fraudulent schemes.

In the end guilds and companies suffered from the same fundamental flaw: as voluntary associations of like-minded individuals, they had the capacity to act contrary to the interests of their surrounding community, which they were supposed to serve. The fundamental differences between guilds and companies are a function of their respective time periods more than of any other single criterion. Guilds came first, and companies, by and large, came later. The fraternal and religious guilds of the early Renaissance gave way to the large and often abusive companies of the late Renaissance, which—under royal charter—often acted contrary to the interests of the crown and people they were chartered to serve.

Chartered Companies in General

The types of companies discussed represent only a few of the many kinds of chartered companies. Chartered companies are so called simply by virtue of having been granted a charter by a governmental authority, usually a king or queen. In addition to England, France and Holland were also active in the granting of charters to companies. Chartered companies were granted monopolies, usually in areas either already colonized or in the process of being colonized by the power granting the charter. As such, chartered companies—while not actually part of the government granting the charter—were intended to be instruments of its power. As European colonial powers competed for dominance in India, Africa, and the New World, each found it convenient to grant exclusive mercantile rights to a single company that would—in theory at least—be amenable to control and limitation by the granting power. As already noted, this aim was seldom realized in practice.

The granting of charters to private companies even extended into the Baltic region. Henry IV of England chartered the Eastland Company in 1404 for the express purpose of engaging in exclusive trade in the Baltic Sea. This company's

▲ *A miniature of a notary (an official who certifies documents to give them legal force), from a fourteenth-century Italian manuscript called the* Book of the Guild of Notaries.

Establishment of Common-Law Companies

In response to the more obvious abuses of the joint-stock company, the common-law company was established. Common-law companies proliferated in the late seventeenth century. Although in many ways they represented an improvement over the joint-stock company, they were subject to different forms of abuses. The common-law company, which is the direct ancestor of the present-day publicly traded company, differed from the joint-stock company principally in its being a large partnership that issued transferable

▲ On May 2, 1670, King Charles II of England granted this royal charter to the Hudson's Bay Company, which was charged with finding a northwest passage (a route across or around North America linking the Atlantic Ocean to the Pacific), occupying the lands adjacent to Hudson's Bay, and carrying on any trade with those lands that might prove profitable. The company came to play a prominent role in the economic and political fortunes of Canada.

charter was confirmed 175 years later, in 1579, by Queen Elizabeth I. In some cases chartered companies also played a significant role in the establishment of diplomatic relations. For example, the activities of the Russia Company (an English body) led to Great Britain's first meaningful contact with Russia as well as its first direct trade with the Levant (the lands on the eastern shore of the Mediterranean) and with Persia.

The influence of the famous East India Company in the Asian holdings of the British Empire is well known, but of no less significance was the Hudson's Bay Company, which engaged in trade in what would later become Canada and the United States. Although chartered companies were never more than quasi-governmental—and were in nearly every case at least technically independent entities—they played very significant roles in opening up the world that presented itself during the Renaissance and the Reformation.

FURTHER READING

Epstein, Steven A. *Wage Labor and Guilds in Medieval Europe.* Chapel Hill, NC, 1991.

Johnson, Paul. *The Renaissance: A Short History.* New York, 2000.

Daniel Horace Fernald

SEE ALSO

• Agriculture • Elizabeth I • England • London
• Manufacturing • Trade

Hanseatic League

FOUNDED IN THE MID-TWELFTH
CENTURY, THE HANSEATIC LEAGUE WAS
AN ALLIANCE OF GERMAN TOWNS AND
OVERSEAS MERCHANT COMMUNITIES
THAT HAD CONTROL OF THE TRADE
MARKETS OF NORTHERN EUROPE
UNTIL AROUND THE MIDDLE OF THE
FIFTEENTH CENTURY.

Medieval Europe did not consist of large central-ized kingdoms or empires. Rather, land and power were divided among local feudal lords. Most trade markets were likewise localized throughout the early Middle Ages. From the twelfth century on, the more important local markets began to expand to encompass larger regional areas. By the fifteenth and sixteenth centuries, merchant alliances of one form or another had spread throughout the continent, and the reach of these alliances was beginning to extend beyond regional confines.

Sailing in the Middle Ages was a precarious business. Although rather crude navigational books gave information about sea depths and landmarks, sailors had few navigational tools at their disposal. Most sailing was done by "coast-ing" within sight of the shores. Piracy was also a serious problem. Owing to these various dangers in the shipping of cargoes, some German mer-chants began to form partnerships known as Hansas. Each merchant spread his risk by divid-ing his cargo among several ships. If one ship was pirated, no single merchant's entire investment would be lost. Soon these Hansas became more beneficial to their members, and the practice of forming alliances spread. A merchant's base of operation was his factory, which consisted of a retail outlet on the bottom level, a storehouse on the second level, and offices and private resi-dences on the top level. In some foreign towns merchant associations set up *kontors* (permanent trading posts) with the permission of, or some-times even at the request of, the local ruler.

Origins of the League

As the Hansas proliferated in the late thirteenth and early fourteenth centuries, mutual trading rights and pledges of security were extended beyond the merchant associations themselves to include entire towns. The Hanseatic League, formed around the middle of the twelfth century, united the Hansas (associations and trading towns) under a single body of legislation that protected all its member merchants and their goods.

The number of towns involved in the league in some capacity varies depending on the sources; estimates range from seventy to two hundred Hansas. The chief town of the league was Lübeck, located on the northern German coast-line of the Danish Sound (an inlet of the Baltic Sea). As the Germans pushed eastward and settled towns in the Slavic lands of the Baltic, merchant associations began to develop into leagues of merchants. The lack of a strong cen-tralized government during this time made it more beneficial for merchants to join forces in order to protect their interests and to create greater opportunities for economic success.

▼ *This seal, which dates from the early thirteenth century, bears the emblem of the Hansa of Water Merchants, one of the many groups that formed a protective merchant alliance.*

LÜBECK

Lübeck is located in northern Germany slightly inland from the Baltic Sea. Adolf II of Schauenburg established the city in 1143. With the Danish Sound to the north and two winding rivers on either side, the new city had a peninsular location that was easy to defend. In order to entice more inhabitants, Adolf sent messengers to surrounding areas, such as Flanders, Holland, and Westphalia, with invitations to all those interested in acquiring some land. The plan was a success: settlers flooded into the city.

The town of Bardowiek, ruled by Henry the Lion, duke of Saxony, suffered from the outflow of merchants seeking to take advantage of the economic opportunities Lübeck offered. Henry issued an embargo on the trading of all items other than foodstuffs with Lübeck. In 1157 Lübeck was destroyed by fire, and merchants were not prepared to rebuild it unless Henry was willing to lift the embargo. In response to this demand, Henry built a rival town that he named, for himself, Lewenstat ("lion's town"). The town's location was not ideal because only small boats could reach it. Henry finally approached Count Adolf and forced Adolf's vassal to give up his rights to Lübeck. A new city of Lübeck was definitively founded in 1159 and soon prospered owing to the trade privileges bestowed upon it.

Merchants quickly returned to the new Lübeck to rebuild its churches and other buildings. Henry sent messengers to Denmark, Sweden, Norway, and Russia to inform them that the new town was now open for business. Traders from all around the Baltic Sea were welcomed to use Lübeck as a port of call. Its central location on the northern German coast of the Baltic Sea made it a natural crossroads for trade routes. Over time, it would become as important a trading hub in northern Europe as Constantinople was for southern Europe and southwestern Asia.

As activity in Lübeck increased, thanks to the efforts of Henry the Lion, the population grew considerably in a short period of time. Subsequently, other towns began to develop on the northern shores of the Holy Roman Empire. Among them were Reval (the present-day Estonian capital of Tallinn), Riga (the present-day capital of Latvia), Danzig (present-day Gdańsk, in Poland), Stralsund and Bremen (in northwestern Germany), Bergen (in Norway), and a great many others.

▼ An engraving by the Swiss artist Kaspar Merian (1627–1686) of Lübeck, considered to have been the capital of the Hanseatic League.

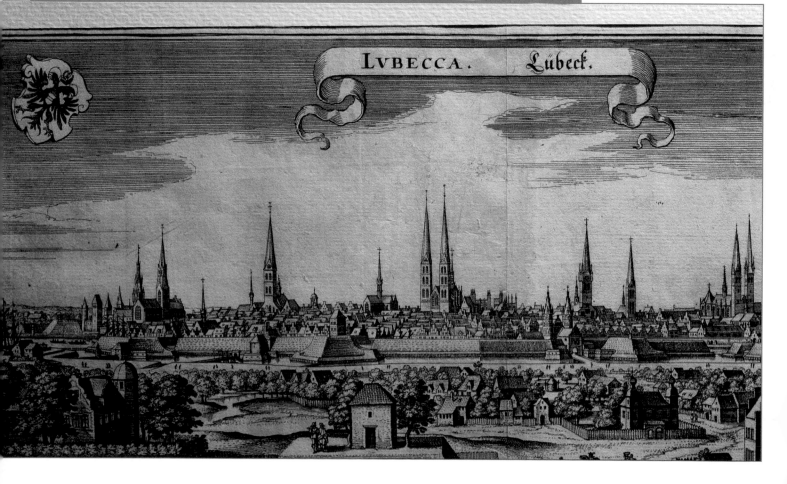

LVBECCA. Lübeck.

▶ *This image of Hamburg, its harbor bustling with Baltic cogs, comes from the city charter of 1497. Hamburg's strategic importance derived from its control over the salt routes that led from Lüneburg.*

The alliance forged by the cities of Lübeck and Hamburg in the mid-twelfth century marks the beginning of the Hanseatic League. Lübeck is at the eastern end of the southern base of Jutland (the Danish peninsula), while Hamburg is at the western end. Fish was a primary food in the diet of European Christians during this time. The Catholic Church called for fasts before many holy days and forbade the consumption of meat on Fridays. Most Catholics substituted fish. The location of Lübeck afforded the town easy access to substantial herring stocks. If they could tap into those stocks and begin trading them elsewhere, there were potentially great profits for entrepreneurs willing to take the risk. Refrigeration, however, did not exist at the time, and raw fish generally perished quickly.

A common preservative for fish and other raw meats was salt. Hamburg, located on the other side of the Jutland peninsula, had easy access to the salt produced at Kiel. The salting and drying of meat and fish extended their shelf life and made it more feasible to transport them. Therefore, it was only a matter of time before merchants from Hamburg and Lübeck formed a trade alliance so that each could benefit economically from the abundant resources of the other. This original alliance became a model after which other northern German and Scandinavian cities formed their own alliances. By the mid-thirteenth century the league included Bremen and other key towns in the west; in the east the league had expanded to include Livonia (present-day Latvia and Estonia).

Expansion and Decline of the League

Most Hansa towns were founded as independent cities or gained their independence through the political power of the league. An independent town's allegiance lay with the Holy Roman emperor rather than with a local noble. The Hansa towns were strategically located along the major trade routes. The league would develop great political power because of its economic success. The ships used in the trade market were well equipped militarily to protect the merchants from pirates and from overzealous rival nobles. Such factors put the league in a position to wield some measure of influence over imperial policy-making decisions. Its power, envied by many merchants and nobles, created social tensions that sometimes sparked off rivalries among league members.

Although each city had its own merchant association, the alliance formed a diet (parliament) for the purpose of governing intercity trade and regulating common policies. Yet this centralized governing body rarely convened, and when it did, so few towns sent representatives that it was difficult to make appropriate decisions for the entire league. Furthermore, the diet was bedeviled by divisive regional politics.

▶ *At the center of this image from the renowned* Evangeliar *(gospel book) of Henry the Lion, Henry may be seen kneeling next to his wife, Matilda. Behind Henry stand his father, Henry the Proud; his mother, Gertrude; and her parents, Lothar III and Richenza. Behind Matilda are her father, King Henry II of England; his mother, Queen Matilda; and an unknown person.*

Henry the Lion 1129–1195

Henry X "the Proud" of Bavaria was killed in 1139 while fighting to regain his duchies. His son, Henry the Lion, continued the war and restored the duchy of Saxony, in northern Germany, in 1142. Henry was the leader of the house of Welf, which was at odds with the Hohenstaufen family. Frederick I Barbarossa, a cousin of Henry and a Hohenstaufen, became Holy Roman emperor in 1155 and restored the southern province of Bavaria to Henry just one year later. Henry then made efforts to expand his authority beyond the Elbe River, which marked the eastern border of Saxony. He gradually took over much of the pagan territory bounded by the Elbe in the west, the Oder River in the east, and the Baltic Sea in the north. He encouraged settlement in the lands he conquered and converted many pagans to Christianity, an act that he knew would win him support from the papacy.

In 1168 Henry married Matilda, the daughter of Henry II of England. His conquests brought him animosity from other German nobles, but he maintained the support of the emperor. In 1176 Frederick, engaged in a war in Italy, requested Henry's assistance. Henry bargained that he would do so only if the imperial city of Goslar were given to him as payment. Frederick refused Henry's request and was subsequently defeated in Italy and forced to surrender to the pope. Part of the peace agreement demanded that the former Saxon church lands acquired by Henry be restored to the church. Henry resisted; the Saxon nobles allied with the church. Frederick, who was called in to judge Henry's case, confiscated the lands in 1180. The duchies of Bavaria and Saxony were partitioned, Henry's armies were defeated, and Henry retained only the province of Brunswick and the city of Lüneburg.

While Frederick was leading the Third Crusade, Henry organized an effort to reoccupy Saxony. Conflict between the Welfs and Hohenstaufens continued after Henry's death in 1195. His younger son became Holy Roman Emperor Otto IV in 1209.

► In this photograph, the wax seals of various European cities are attached to the Document of Confederation of the Hanseatic League.

THE BALTIC COG

Capable of carrying a cargo of 150 tons and a crew of around eighteen, the cog, a vessel that had much in common with the Viking knarrs, was the primary ship used by Hansa merchants until at least the fourteenth century. In 1962, during dredging of the Weser River, a cog dating from 1380 was recovered and preserved. In 1987 construction of a replica began in Kiel; the replica ship was launched in October 1989.

Consequently, regional assemblies began to form, and they met frequently. Because the league was geographically divided into three primary regions, the regional assemblies came to be known as thirds. In the west the Rhenish third controlled the trade of the Rhine River valley of northwestern Germany. The Wendish third included the Baltic maritime trade based in Lübeck. In the east the Prussian third was based on the trade of the lands of the Teutonic Order.

By the turn of the fifteenth century, the Hanseatic League was failing to deal with threats to its continued success. To the south of the Hanseatic route, an east-west trade route had developed that included such towns as Frankfurt, Nuremberg, Leipzig, and Poznań. Rather than drive out the competition, as it had done to previous trade rivals, the league sat by as the new route cut into its profits.

To the north the league was facing a challenge from Erik of Pomerania (c. 1381–1459), king of Denmark, Norway, and Sweden. Erik was claiming the duchy of Schleswig. When Hamburg and Lübeck challenged his claim, Erik opened Norwegian trade markets to Dutch and English merchants. Although the league seemed victorious after Sweden deserted Erik's side, pressure from Erik's successor, Christopher III, eventually compelled the Wendish towns to allow free trade in the Baltic. Thus, the league found itself in open competition with the Nordic Union of Scandinavian merchants and the Dutch Baltic traders. The Hanseatic League's last diet, held at Lübeck in 1669, was attended by representatives of just nine towns.

FURTHER READING

Dollinger, Philippe. *The German Hansa.* Translated by D. S. Ault and S. H. Steinberg. Stanford, CA, 1970.

Lavery, Jason. *Germany's Northern Challenge: The Holy Roman Empire and the Scandinavian Struggle for the Baltic, 1563–1576.* Boston, 2002.

Brian A. Carriere

SEE ALSO
• German Towns • Holy Roman Empire • Trade

Hapsburg Empire

THE HAPSBURGS DOMINATED THE POLITICAL LIFE OF MUCH OF EUROPE FROM THE FOURTEENTH CENTURY THROUGH THE EIGHTEENTH. THEIR EMPIRE WAS LARGELY THOUGH NOT ENTIRELY COEXTENSIVE WITH THE HOLY ROMAN EMPIRE.

The Hapsburg family name derives from the castle of Habsburg, which was originally known as Habichtsburg ("hawk's castle"). Habichtsburg was built in 1028 by the bishop of Strasbourg and one Count Radboto, the bishop's brother-in-law. The most likely candidate for the actual founder of what would come to be called the Hapsburg line is Guntram the Rich, who died around 950. Guntram was the father of Lanzelin, who was the father of Radboto. Radboto's son, Werner, is the first person known with certainty to have borne the title count of Hapsburg.

By the mid-sixteenth century, when the start of the Reformation was already thirty-five years in the past, the Hapsburgs had extended their influence far beyond the limits of their ancestral regions at the confluence of the Aar and Rhine rivers and were arguably the dominant political force on the continent. Members of the Hapsburg family held numerous titles—including duke, archduke, king, and emperor—in Austria, Hungary, Spain, Bohemia, and various other areas of western and central Europe. Despite shifting alliances with the Vatican, the Hapsburgs, staunch Roman Catholics, proved to be formidable allies of the church in their response to the challenge presented by the Protestant Reformers.

Rapid Expansion, Division, and Reunification

Considering their relatively humble origins several hundred years earlier, by the fourteenth century the Hapsburgs (or Habsburgs—both spellings are widely used) had assumed considerable political power and territorial dominion. One key to their early success was a family policy of investing political power and governmental authority communally in all adult males rather than in any single individual. In this way the Hapsburgs avoided having their domain break down into tiny sovereign duchies and principalities and retained their centralized—though shared—power base. This arrangement is sometimes referred to as condominium, a system under which numerous individuals retain authority over a territory. Although this system quite naturally frustrated the individual ambitions of many within the Hapsburg clan, it served the family well by fostering comity and encouraging cooperation, rather than competition, among the male family members in whom undivided, communal political authority was vested.

The first major blow was struck to this system of condominium in 1364, when Rudolf IV, king of Bohemia, entered into an agreement with his younger brothers to divide their common domain into what amounted to essentially autonomous principalities. Albert III, awarded the duchy of Austria, assumed the title of archduke. Leopold III became master of Styria, the Tyrol, and Carinthia. Control over their holdings was to be passed on to their heirs.

▼ *A thirteenth-century Austrian painting on a wooden panel of Rudolf I (1218–1291), who inaugurated the Hapsburg dynasty when he was made king of Germany and Holy Roman emperor in 1273.*

CONDOMINIUM

Derived from the Latin prefix *con,* which means "with" or "together," and the word *dominium,* which means "lordship," the term *condominium* refers to a system of shared rule or joint political leadership in which two or more individuals possess an undivided interest in the governance of an area or region. Elements of the system of condominium persist in modern political life. In the United States, for example, two politicians elected as senators from a given state each represent the entire state. (Members of the House of Representatives, on the other hand, represent a specific district within a state.) A senator shares his or her political authority with another senator, who also represents the entire state.

Although the modern American system is obviously a form of power sharing different from that practiced by the Hapsburgs, it has much the same function and effect. If each state were divided in two, with each half represented by one senator, each senator might be tempted to vie against the other for political advantage, and the governance of the state would be fractious and divisive. Instead, the state is represented in its entirety by two separate individuals whose advantage is best served if they work cooperatively in the interest of their constituents. Much the same effect was achieved by the Hapsburgs' system of condominium, which encouraged those who shared power to work together to achieve common aims.

The adoption of the system of condominium was a crucial element of the Hapsburgs' early and enduring success. Historically, one of the greatest challenges facing family dynasties has been their tendency to come apart owing to internal tensions caused by the ambitions of self-seeking family members. Because the system of condominium encouraged a united front, the Hapsburgs achieved dramatic territorial expansion and economic prosperity in a remarkably short period. The Hapsburgs' eventual abandonment of condominium was one of several major factors that ultimately brought about the fragmenting of their lands and the weakening of their power.

The effective partition of the Hapsburg holdings would ultimately lead to a decline in the influence of the Austrian line of the family. Albert III had one son, Albert IV, who died in 1414. Albert IV had one son, also Albert. Albert V had two daughters, Anna and Elizabeth, and one son, Ladislaus Postumus. The death of Albert V in 1439 made Ladislaus the ward of Albert's cousin Emperor Frederick III. Frederick also served as regent for another cousin—Sigismund, the only child of his uncle Frederick IV. Sigismund held the family lands in Styria and Tyrol, while

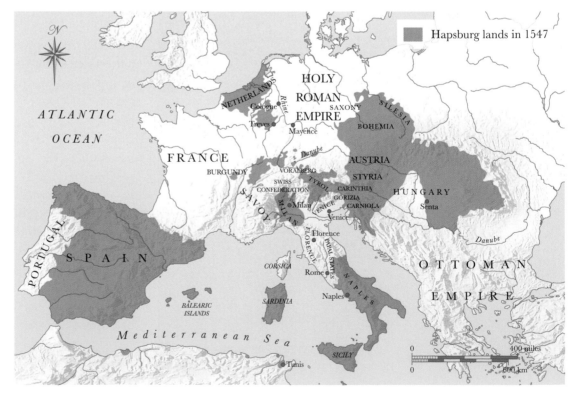

► *The Hapsburg possessions in Europe in 1547. In that year Charles V secured a victory over the Protestant League of Torgua at the Battle of Mühlberg and arrived at a truce with the Ottoman Empire, whose armies continually threatened Hungary. The map does not include the extensive Spanish possessions in the New World.*

Ladislaus was heir to the Hapsburg's Austrian lands. When Ladislaus died childless in 1457, the holdings of the Austrian line were taken over by the Styrian line in the person of Sigismund, who died in 1496. With the extinction of the Austrian and Styrian lines, the family's interests were once again united in the person of Frederick III's son, Maximillian I.

Accumulation of Titles and Power

In the period from the turn of the thirteenth century to the end of the fifteenth, the Hapsburgs gained a remarkable ascendancy over central Europe, their historical power base, and also—via cleverly arranged marriages—western Europe. Rudolf I, who died in 1291, had been king of Germany, a title that was assumed by his son, Albert I, who died in 1308. The electors responsible for the succession to the German throne chose someone outside of the family line to succeed Albert I, but the Hapsburgs regained power in 1314, when Frederick I was named to the post—which he held until 1322. From 1322 until the election of Albert II in 1438, the Hapsburgs suffered a long exile from supreme political power in Germany.

From 1438 until the family's final fall from power nearly 500 years later, the titles of Holy Roman emperor and king of Germany belonged to the Hapsburgs (there was only one brief interruption to Hapsburg domination, from 1742 to 1745). By skillful diplomacy the Hapsburgs expanded their power base west and south from Austria and Styria into the Tyrol, Vorarlberg, Carinthia, Gorizia, and Carniola. They were less successful in their attempts to retain their holdings in Switzerland and lost control of the Bohemian and Hungarian thrones when Ladislaus Postumus died without having married. The loss of these lands represented a significant reversal of fortune for the wily and resilient Hapsburgs.

The Hapsburgs rebounded under Maximilian I (1459–1519). With the newly reunified holdings of the Hapsburg family all under his control, Maximilian moved to extend the Hapsburgs' influence, wealth, and power. He renewed his strength in Austria, the historical seat of family power, and expanded westward via a shrewd mar-

riage in 1477 to Mary of Burgundy, the daughter and heiress of Charles the Bold, duke of Burgundy. This marriage dramatically increased Maximilian's holdings with a swath of land that would serve as a protective buffer on the western flank of his family's traditional holdings in Austria and central Europe. Mary died in 1482, and in 1494 Maximilian married the duke of Milan's daughter, Bianca Sforza (this marriage did not, however, lead to the hoped-for extension of Hapsburg power into Italy). A shrewd diplomat but amateur military tactician, Maximilian's ill-conceived and poorly executed military campaigns nevertheless cost him far less than he gained via his astute marriage to Mary of Burgundy.

▲ When Maximilian I married Mary of Burgundy, the subject of this fifteeenth-century portrait by Niclas Reiser, he added to Hapsburg possessions the considerable territories of the duchy of Burgundy.

Further Expansion East and West

Maximilian had one son, Philip I, who died in 1506, thirteen years before Maximilian's own death in 1519. Philip I, who apparently inherited his father's talent for skillful political maneuvers and adroitly orchestrated marriages, expanded the Hapsburg holdings into Iberia by marrying Joan the Mad, the daughter of Ferdinand and Isabella, the king and queen of Spain. Philip I had two sons, Charles and Ferdinand.

When Philip died, his son Charles assumed his father's titles and lands in the Netherlands and Spain. When the emperor Maximilian died in 1519, Charles arranged, in part by paying hefty bribes to key electors, to be made Holy Roman emperor as well. Charles V was the last Holy Roman emperor to be crowned by a pope. In an effort to quell discontent stemming from the perception of his overarching dominion of Hapsburg lands, in 1522 Charles ceded the Austrian portion of the empire to his brother, Ferdinand, via the Treaty of Brussels. Also in 1522, Ferdinand married Anne, the daughter of Ulászló II (1456–1516), king of Hungary and Bohemia. Among the four children Anne bore Ferdinand was the future emperor Maximilian II.

In 1526 King Louis II, Ferdinand's brother-in-law, died without leaving any heirs. Ferdinand attempted to profit from this event by claiming the thrones of Hungary and Bohemia. He justified these claims by citing his marriage to Anne and declared additionally that he was entitled to

▶ *A striking feature of this 1519 Hapsburg family portrait by Bernhard Strigel is the famous Hapsburg jaw, a facial characteristic accentuated by generations of inbreeding.*

the two titles by treaty. Although his claims were initially rejected, Ferdinand did manage to have himself elected king of Bohemia later that same year. He fared only slightly worse in Hungary, where his dominion was split between himself and János Zápolya, whom a counterparty elected king at the same time Ferdinand was elected to the post by the majority.

This final expansion represented the political apogee of the Hapsburg clan. With a combination of military success, skillful diplomacy, and shrewdly conceived marriages, the Hapsburgs had created an empire that extended from the Danube River to the Atlantic Ocean. The Holy Roman Empire of Charles V was buoyed by internal commerce, overseas trade, and the riches brought back from the New World by the Spanish conquistadores. Charles ruled Spain and its many colonies, the Netherlands, much of central Europe, and portions of northern Italy. Ferdinand controlled part of Hungary, the Tyrol, much of Austria, and Bohemia.

By now Charles and Ferdinand were not only extremely powerful but also extremely wealthy, and the extent of their combined dominion in fact grossly understated the true nature of their economic power. The Hapsburgs were a force to be reckoned with, and despite numerous conflicts and even setbacks during their day, Charles and Ferdinand kept the Hapsburgs very much at the forefront of European power.

Charles's Abdication and the Gradual Partition of the Empire

Owing to a combination of military and political setbacks, Charles V gradually removed himself from active involvement in various aspects of

political life and various areas of the Hapsburg empire. This process culminated in 1556, when Charles formally abdicated as Holy Roman emperor and turned that post over to his brother, Ferdinand, who became Emperor Ferdinand I.

Charles's abdication and reassignment of his holdings had the effect of partitioning the Hapsburg lands quite clearly into Spanish and Austrian spheres. While Ferdinand became emperor, Charles's son, Philip, became King Philip II of Spain. Charles also granted Philip the Netherlands, the islands of Sardinia and Sicily, and the Italian city-states of Milan and Naples. Unlike his father, Philip was a true Spaniard, and as effective as his rule was in his native land, he had great difficulty governing his northern provinces, notably the Netherlands, which broke away in 1609 and was formally lost in 1648 by the Treaty of Westphalia.

▲ *This illustration, from a manuscript of the* Memoires *of the Burgundian courtier Philip de Commynes (1447–1511), shows the marriage of Mary of Burgundy to Maximilian I, an extremely auspicious event for the Hapsburg family. Burgundian territory, sandwiched as it was between France and the Holy Roman Empire, was of supreme strategic importance in European politics.*

The Hapsburgs retained a large amount of political and economic power into the early twentieth century, when the end of World War I saw the final partition of Hapsburg lands. Just over a century earlier, the Hapsburgs had been dealt a significant though not entirely decisive blow when, in 1806, a triumphant Napoléon Bonaparte dissolved the Holy Roman Empire, an act that further fragmented the already divided Hapsburgs and dramatically reduced their base of power.

The Hapsburgs and Catholicism

The Hapsburgs were a staunchly Catholic family whose religion figured heavily in the politics of their expansion and in their defense of their power. As the Hapsburg family grew in power and prestige, the vision of a restored Roman Empire seemed ever more attainable. The Hapsburg empire, however, would be free from the remnants of paganism that had stained the purity of the first Christian Roman Empire, which originated with the conversion of Constantine the Great in the early fourth century. The Hapsburg Holy Roman Empire would be a greater fulfillment of the desire for a universal Catholic empire than even Constantine could have envisioned.

Catholicism was central to the Hapsburgs, and while they were not always scrupulous in their adherence to church doctrine in their public or personal lives (Charles V, for example, had two children out of wedlock), there is no doubt that faith played a pivotal role in the rise of the Hapsburgs.

The Hapsburgs were particularly distressed at the Muslim occupation of some of the eastern portion of the Hapsburg domain, although their distress was not quite matched by military zeal—the Hapsburgs generally left such fighting to local principalities. Charles V was a noteworthy exception for his active defense of the Catholic lands of the Holy Roman Empire against the Turks. He also took up the crusade against Süleyman I "the Magnificent" and defeated the Ottomans at Tunis.

The defense of Hapsburg holdings against encroaching Muslims was not definitively won until 1697, when Prince Eugene of Savoy, at the

▲ *Part of a page from a fifteenth-century Greek manuscript. The impaled fox represents the Ottoman sultan Bayezid I (reigned 1389–1402); the three swords bear the flags of the papacy, the Venetian republic, and the Hapsburg empire, which together formed a holy alliance against the Ottomans.*

The rest of the seventeenth century was no kinder to the Spanish Hapsburgs. France successfully nibbled away at Hapsburg holdings on the French border and in France's sphere of influence and thus further reduced their power and prestige. With the Treaty of Nijmegen (1678), Spain formally conceded even more of its northern European territories. When King Charles II of Spain died without heirs in 1700, the line of Hapsburg kings of Spain ended.

The Austrian line of Hapsburgs got through the seventeenth century in far better shape; having fully grasped the long-term dangers to its integrity and power posed by partition, the Austrian Hapsburgs adopted a policy of strict primogeniture. Although this strategy represented a clear break with the already neglected notion of rule by condominium, it was quite effective in keeping the family from breaking up into small (and only nominally loyal) fiefdoms and principalities.

How did the originally Germanic Hapsburgs come to rule the renewed Roman Empire? First, it is worth noting that the Holy Roman Empire was initially a largely political device whereby the bishop of Rome (that is, the pope) attempted to extend his political power and impose some order on European Christendom in the last two centuries of the first millennium. The Hapsburgs did not come into the title until five hundred years later, in the fifteenth century. Once ensconced on the throne, however, the Hapsburgs proved to be remarkably skillful at retaining it. Hapsburg support of the Catholic Church during the Reformation and Counter-Reformation was a significant element in the family's ability to retain power, despite differences with the electors responsible for choosing successors to the emperor's seat and despite tensions with several popes over territorial and political disputes.

◀ Despite his initial opposition to the accession of Charles V to the imperial crown, in 1530 Pope Clement VII crowned Charles at a lavish ceremony in Bologna, in northern Italy. In this painting, by Cornelius Schut, of the coronation, the three cardinals who also participate in the placing of the crown on the emperor's head are the archbishops of Cologne, Treves, and Mayence. Charles V was the last emperor crowned by a pope.

behest of the Holy Roman emperor Leopold I, defeated the Turks at Senta, in present-day Serbia—a victory that would help to define the boundary of Europe and the Middle East for centuries to come.

The Hapsburgs' concerns were not, of course, entirely otherworldly. They were very much embedded in the political and social climate of their day, a time in which even popes went to war to defend their territory and prerogatives. While the Hapsburgs cannot accurately be described as altruistic in their motivations or actions, neither can there be any serious doubt over the sincerity of their desire to oppose the growth of Protestantism in the West or to defend Catholic lands against the threat of Muslim encroachment in the East.

Charles V and Martin Luther

Although many prominent members of the Hapsburg family were noteworthy for their dedication to the Roman Catholic Church and their opposition to the Reformation, the Holy Roman emperor Charles V stands out as a particularly strong defender of the Catholic faith.

Charles's dedication may come as something of a surprise given the fact that when he was elected Holy Roman emperor in 1520, at the age of only nineteen, his ascension to the imperial throne was initially opposed quite strongly by the Vatican. The reason for the Vatican's opposition was Charles's hereditary claim, as king of Aragon, to the papal fief of Naples. Even so, Pope Leo X did not persist in his opposition and reconciled himself to the coronation of the young emperor.

▲ *This silk flag, which bears the Hapsburgs' coat of arms (a double-headed eagle) dates from around 1700.*

There is little question that Charles V was a loyal Catholic, despite occasional differences with the papacy in Rome (and a few personal indiscretions). The disputes between Charles and the papacy were typically concerned with territorial and secular issues rather than religious ones. In religious matters Charles seemed to take to heart one of the principal original purposes of adding "Holy" to the Roman Empire that had been revived with the support of the Catholic Church several hundred years previously. Charles was vigorous in his opposition to the Protestant princes of Germany and to the man who was arguably their most influential religious leader, the Reformer Martin Luther (1483–1546).

Indeed, in 1521 Charles V undertook to oppose Luther with unexpected vehemence and ardor at the Diet of Worms, a meeting of the assembly of the Holy Roman Empire held in southwestern Germany. Charles's opposition was motivated in large part by his natural concern to put down the territorial ambitions of a number of Protestant princes both within and on the border of Hapsburg lands. Charles was continually skirmishing and bargaining with these princes in order to maintain some level of order in and around his northern possessions. As the Holy Roman emperor, much of the authority that Charles wielded stemmed from the recognition of his being invested with the divinely derived authority of his office. Thus, any challenge to the authority of the church or the pope also represented a direct challenge to Charles's rule in these disputed territories.

Reformation and Counter-Reformation

For the Hapsburgs the Reformation and Counter-Reformation presented challenges and opportunities. The need to defend Catholic domains against the growing threat of Protestantism severely limited the pope's ability to circumscribe the great family's territorial and political ambitions. This situation effectively gave the Hapsburgs a free hand in areas where the papacy perceived Protestant heresy to be a threat to the authority of the Catholic Church and, of course, church lands. The Holy See could not afford to alienate such a powerful ally by intruding too obviously into the Hapsburgs' conduct and policy within these rebellious domains.

Indeed, after the abdication of Charles V, the Holy Roman emperors Ferdinand II and Ferdinand III used their active support for the Counter-Reformation as a justification for expanding the power of the office of Holy Roman emperor. The loss of the Thirty Years War in 1648 (a war that was fought largely but not exclusively between Catholics and Protestants in Germany) put an effective end to any dreams of universal Hapsburg dominion and underscored the severely divided nature of the Holy Roman Empire, which, in the eyes of many, was neither holy nor Roman—least of all was it even an empire.

Even so, the Hapsburgs remained Catholic stalwarts through the Counter-Reformation and served as self-styled guardians of Europe against the encroachments of the twin threats of Protestant doctrines and militarily aggressive (as well as highly capable) Turkish Muslims. The Hapsburgs cultivated an image of chivalric knights standing athwart the onrushing tide of barbarism, an image that achieved a form of reality with the creation of the Order of the Golden Fleece in the fifteenth century.

The Hapsburgs shared in the ultimate failure of the goal of the Counter-Reformation: to bring the departed Protestants back to the church of

◀ *This miniature, from Guillaume Fillastre's 1473* Book of the Golden Fleece, *depicts a chapter (ceremonial meeting) of the order. Duke Philip the Good of Burgundy set up the Order of the Golden Fleece in 1430 as a means of rewarding his most loyal nobles with social honorability and political power.*

ing to keep the forces of Islam out of the heart of the continent.

There can be little question concerning the pervasive social, political, economic, and religious importance of the Hapsburgs during the early modern and modern periods. For good or ill, this great family influenced the courts of all the nations of Europe, as well as some courts of nearby western Asia. Without the Hapsburgs' steadfast (albeit self-interested) support of the Roman Catholic Church during the upheaval produced by the Reformation and Counter-Reformation, there is no question that the fate of Europe, and indeed of the world, would have been markedly different.

FURTHER READING

Kann, Robert A. *A History of the Habsburg Empire, 1526–1918.* Berkeley, CA, 1974.

Milton, Joyce, and Caroline Davidson. *The House of Hapsburg: The Spanish Hapsburgs; the Hapsburgs in Central Europe.* New York, 1980.

Daniel Horace Fernald

SEE ALSO

Rome. This vexing failure came about in spite of sincere and earnest effort on the part of the Counter-Reformers. The Hapsburgs' success in defending the territory of central Europe is less ambiguous, whatever judgment may be formed of the end result. Despite their sometimes lackluster performance in opposing the Ottoman Turks on the eastern borders of the empire, the Hapsburgs' presence at Europe's center provided both direct and indirect support for those fight-

Henry IV

THE FIRST BOURBON KING OF FRANCE, HENRY IV (1553–1610) BROUGHT PEACE TO HIS KINGDOM IN 1598 AFTER NEARLY FORTY YEARS OF RELIGIOUS WARFARE.

Born Henry of Navarre in 1553, Henry IV acceded to the throne of France in 1589 following the death of the last Valois king, Henry III. In the decades before his accession, the future Henry IV ruled two small territories, Béarn and Navarre, located in the southwestern part of modern-day France. Henry was also a leader of the French Protestants, but his conversion to Catholicism in 1593 allowed him to secure his position as king of France and ultimately to broker a lasting religious peace in France after nearly four decades of violent religious conflict.

▼ *This engraving by Theodore de Bry depicts Henry in 1589, the year in which he became king of France.*

Early Loyalties: Protestant or Catholic?

Henry IV lived through the French wars of religion, a time when the nobility of France was divided into Protestant and Catholic factions. In common with many of his contemporaries, a combination of political factors and personal inclinations prompted Henry to change his religious faith several times during his life. At the time of his birth in the 1550s, the Protestant movement in France was rapidly gaining strength. Indeed, Henry's mother, Jeanne d'Albert, was an early convert to Protestantism. His father, Antoine de Bourbon, shifted between the Catholic and Protestant faiths, in part owing to political considerations.

Faced with the alternating influences of his mother and his father, Henry switched between Protestantism and Catholicism several times in his formative years. During his youth his mother raised him as a Protestant, but while living with his father at the royal court in 1562, he was convinced to embrace the Catholic faith. Upon leaving the court in 1567, he returned to the Protestantism of his mother. However, he was forcibly reconverted to Catholicism at the royal court in 1572, in the aftermath of the Saint Bartholomew's Day Massacre (in which several thousand Protestants were killed). In 1576 he escaped from the royal court and once again renounced Catholicism for the Protestantism of his earliest days.

Leader of the French Protestants

Following his flight from the royal court in 1576, Henry became an increasingly important political figure in France. He stood third in line to the French throne, and his royal blood made him one of the most important figures in the Protestant party. However, it was more than social status that placed Henry at the forefront of the Protestant movement. He also proved to be an adept politician and a talented military leader. He led Protestant troops in the 1570s and 1580s in successful defense of Protestant regions of the south. By 1584, the year in which the political and dynastic crisis that would eventually propel him to the throne of France broke out, Henry

CHRONOLOGY

1553
Henry is born.

1562
Converts to the Catholic faith.

1567
Returns to the Protestant faith.

1572
Marries Marguerite de Valois; is forced to reconvert to Catholicism while at the royal court.

1576
Flees the royal court and returns to his Protestantism.

1576–1589
Becomes the leader of the Protestants in France.

1589
Succeeds to the throne of France.

1593
Renounces Protestantism again.

1595
Pope Clement VIII lifts the excommunication on Henry IV; Henry is thus able to rejoin the Catholic Church.

1598
Henry proclaims the Edict of Nantes, which provides the basis for peace between Protestants and Catholics in his kingdom.

1610
Henry is assassinated.

was a seasoned political and military commander. This experience served him well during his reign.

Political Crisis

The death of Henry III's younger brother, the duke of Alençon, created a political crisis. It was widely known that Henry III was unlikely to father a son. Therefore, according to the prevailing laws of succession, Henry of Navarre, the leader of the Protestant faction in France, was next in line to the throne. In the early 1580s around 90 percent of the kingdom remained loyal to the Catholic faith, and after two decades of bloody religious conflict, many Catholics viewed the accession of a Protestant to the throne as a disaster. A group of powerful Catholic nobles and townsmen organized the Holy League, which was dedicated to ensuring that the next French king was a Catholic.

Relations between Henry III and the Holy League deteriorated when the king refused to take forceful action against the Protestant Henry of Navarre. Relations broke down completely in the summer of 1588, when Henry III ordered two leading figures in the league, Henry I of Lorraine, the duke of Guise, and Henry's brother, Cardinal Louis II of Lorraine, murdered. The Holy League responded by openly rebelling, and most of the major cities of the realm, including Paris, closed their gates to their monarch. In the summer of 1589 a fanatical follower of the league assassinated Henry III.

Although Henry of Navarre was now in a position to claim the throne, significant obstacles

◄ This series of engravings by Franz Hogenberg depicts the assassination of King Henry III in 1589 and the execution of his killer, Jacques Clément. Before he died, Henry III acknowledged Henry of Navarre as his legitimate successor (this event is depicted in the picture at bottom left).

stood in his way. Given that the pope had excommunicated him as a heretic, it was unlikely that Catholic subjects would accept his rule. Moreover, the Holy League was determined to stop him from taking the throne. Indeed, the members of the league called a council to choose a new king.

Accession to the Throne

Henry may initially have hoped to secure the throne without abandoning his Protestant faith. He enjoyed the support of his Protestant followers, foreign Protestant governments, and some moderate Catholics who placed the stability of the monarchy above religious concerns. These groups argued that Henry, being the closest male relative of the former king, had the right to take the throne. However, the powerful Holy League interpreted the situation differently. They argued that all previous kings of France had been Catholic and that Henry's excommunication from the Catholic Church made him ineligible to ascend the throne. Leaguers declared that the nation, through a representative council, should choose a new king.

In the early 1590s Henry won a series of military victories that helped him to sustain his claim to the throne. Nevertheless, he lacked the military might to force the league to submit to his will. In the end, however, he was able to draw on his political skills to secure the throne despite strong opposition. Crucial to his success was his ability to split the Holy League and to draw certain towns and important nobles to his side. In this project he was aided by the fact that his opponents could not agree on a viable alternative candidate for the throne. After the death of Henry's elderly uncle, Charles, cardinal of Bourbon, no other French candidate with a good claim to the throne survived, and many Frenchmen, even within the Holy League, opposed any foreign candidate. In this atmosphere Henry attracted important nobles and towns to his side through financial incentives, important titles, and special privileges. These concessions proved attractive to many rebellious groups, especially when faced with the bitter arguments within the league over who should be the next king.

Renunciation of Protestantism

Henry's strategy of luring leaguers to his side through patronage succeeded only after his renunciation of Protestantism in 1593. His decision to leave the Protestant faith in the hope that

► This engraving, from Giuliano Giralda's 1610 Life of Henry IV of France, depicts the dramatic ceremony in the Church of Saint-Denis during which Henry renounced the Protestant faith. This act was the foundation on which Henry ultimately convinced many of his Catholic subjects to accept his rule.

STYLE OF GOVERNMENT

fter thirty years of religious war, Henry sought to rebuild royal authority in France and to broker peace between the religious factions. By redefining medieval ideas of royal authority, Henry strengthened his ability to make decisions for his kingdom that none of his subjects could question. Key to his effort to redefine royal authority was his assertion that, as king of France, he had a special understanding, granted to him by God, of issues of royal government. According to this assertion, no subject could comprehend an issue as fully as the king could, and therefore no subject was in a position to question his decision. In reality, Henry was careful to consult and listen to powerful figures in his kingdom, but this assertion of divine understanding protected his decisions from direct opposition and ultimately became the basis for the absolutist system of government associated with his son, Louis XIII, and grandson, Louis XIV, in the seventeenth century.

Cum privilegio Regis. P. Firens excudit.

◀ Scrofula, a disease similar to tuberculosis, was once known as the king's evil owing to an old tradition that it could be cured by the mere touch of a king. The tradition of touching people who had the king's evil began in France under Philip I (reigned 1059–1108). This engraving by Pierre Firens (died c. 1636), which depicts Henry IV touching soldiers to cure their scrofula, was a piece of propaganda designed to trumpet Henry's true fitness to rule as king of France.

the pope would allow him to rejoin the Catholic Church was a risky one. This course of action alienated many of his Protestant supporters, and because of his shifts in religious allegiance before 1576, it remained uncertain whether his Catholic subjects would believe that he was sincere in this conversion. This concern was particularly problematic; it may explain why he did not immediately renounce Protestantism upon the death of Henry III in 1589. Instead, several years elapsed before he sought to convert. During this interval he made it known that he was receiving instruction in the Catholic faith. Only after carefully laying the groundwork did he finally

seek to embrace Catholicism in 1593. While many doubted his sincerity, his conversion did allow the more moderate leaguers to compromise with the king without forsaking their commitment to their faith.

This moment proved to be decisive in Henry's bid to take the throne. In March 1594 Henry retook Paris, and in September 1595 Pope Clement VIII officially accepted him into the Catholic Church by granting a papal absolution. These events turned the tide in Henry's favor, and by 1598 all the major nobles and towns of the kingdom had made their peace with their new monarch.

Brokering Peace between Protestants and Catholics

By 1598 Henry had succeeded in pacifying his kingdom. However, if he was to secure his rule, he still had to broker a lasting peace between the Protestant and Catholic factions. For most of four decades the wars of religion (1562–1598) had destabilized the French kingdom and weakened the monarchy. Henry sought to use his position as former leader of the Protestants and current Catholic king of France to broker a religious compromise. In 1598 he issued the Edict of Nantes, which granted Protestants the right to practice their religion in designated localities and also, through a series of secret stipulations, guaranteed their security by granting them certain towns as Protestant strongholds with garrisons paid for by the king. While this ruling met with opposition from both Protestants and Catholics, Henry was ultimately able to secure compliance from both parties, and the edict became the basis for lasting religious peace.

Henry secured this edict in part through political skill. He was able to convince his former Protestant allies that he would protect them and their freedom to practice their faith. At the same time he steadily increased the confidence among his Catholic subjects that he would secure the ultimate triumph of Catholicism in France, in part by personally promoting initiatives to revive the Catholic Church. This adept balancing act was crucial to the reestablishment of peace in France—at least outwardly—after nearly forty years of conflict.

The Revival of France

In the final decade of his reign, Henry sought to repair the damage wrought by the religious wars. He inherited a bankrupt treasury but through careful management was able to place royal finances back on a solid foundation. By 1610 the kingdom had largely recovered, and Henry once again sought to expand French influence in Europe. In fact, he was planning for the first time since the 1550s to take France to war with Spain, its traditional enemy, when in May he was assassinated by a deranged man named Ravaillac, who did not believe in the sincerity of Henry's conversion to Catholicism.

FURTHER READING

Buisseret, David. *Henry IV.* Boston, 1984.

Greengrass, Mark. *France in the Age of Henri IV: The Struggle for Stability.* New York, 1995.

Knecht, R. J. *The French Wars of Religion, 1559–1598.* New York, 1996.

Eric Nelson

SEE ALSO

• Calvinism • Catherine de Médicis • France
• French Civil Wars • Paris

▼ *A detail of a contemporary engraving showing the attempted assassination of Henry IV by Jean Chastel in December 1594 (the engraver has labeled him Pier du Castel). Through the window on the left may be seen the subsequent execution of Chastel, who was torn apart by horses.*

Henry VIII

THE VIVID AND EVENTFUL REIGN OF
KING HENRY VIII OF ENGLAND,
WHICH LASTED FROM 1509 TO 1547, IS
MOST NOTABLE FOR HENRY'S REJEC-
TION OF THE AUTHORITY OF THE POPE
AND HIS ASSUMPTION OF THE SUPREME
LEADERSHIP OF THE ENGLISH CHURCH.

Born in 1491, Henry VIII was the second surviving son of King Henry VII, founder of the Tudor
dynasty, and his wife, Elizabeth of York.
Following the death of his elder brother, Arthur,
Henry became heir to the throne, and in 1503 he
was created prince of Wales. In 1509 Henry VII
died, and Prince Henry became King Henry
VIII. He married his brother's widow, the
Spanish princess Catherine of Aragon, in the

▼ *This portrait of a young
Henry VIII was made around
1525 by Lucas Horenbout.*

same year as his accession, and the two were
crowned together on June 24. Contemporaries
praised Henry's youthful beauty, his fair skin, his
great height, and his physical prowess at hunting,
jousting, and sport.

The young king's priorities did not lie in the
day-to-day administration of the kingdom.
Instead, his preferred pastimes were hunting and
participating in tournaments, the mock battles
and jousts that honed the military abilities of the
knightly elite. Henry saw himself primarily as a
warrior, and his immediate aim was to make his
reputation in Europe by waging war against
France, England's traditional enemy. Henry
declared war on France in 1512, and for the next
two years England was embroiled in a highly
costly conflict that had very little point or lasting
significance.

Owing to Henry's military priorities and his
preoccupation with leisurely pursuits, he relied
upon his ministers and servants to maintain the
smooth and peaceful governance of the kingdom.
In 1513 Thomas Wolsey, a lowborn cleric, rose to
prominence through his administrative abilities
and boundless capacity for hard work. Wolsey
became the king's principal minister; his
promotion to office within the administration and the church was dazzlingly swift,
and in 1518 the papacy bestowed on
him the ultimate honor by making him
legatus a latere—the pope's official representative in England.

Wolsey, who remained Henry's
chief minister until 1529, maintained
his powers by making himself indis-
pensable to the king. He grew exceptionally wealthy and became a great
builder and patron of the arts. Wolsey's
power and the state of magnificence in
which he lived provoked hostility from the
old nobility, who also resented his low birth.
He was accused of ruling as an *alter rex*—an
alternative monarch. Yet the reality was that
Wolsey's great powers had been granted by the
king: the ultimate power lay with Henry, and if
Wolsey were to lose the king's favor, the foundations of his greatness would be ruined.

THE FIELD OF THE CLOTH OF GOLD

Although Henry wanted above all to achieve military glory fighting the French, continued and successful war with France was not a possibility. His chancellor Cardinal Wolsey endeavored to convince Henry that peace could be as magnificent and glorious as war. In 1518 Wolsey orchestrated the Treaty of London, a truce signed by King Francis I of France and the Holy Roman emperor, Charles V, under the mediation of Henry and Wolsey himself. The latter two gained much reflected glory from the treaty.

Such truces rarely lasted long, and in 1520 Henry was looking to form an aggressive alliance with one monarch against the other. He and Francis I met in northern France in a visit that was ostensibly designed to demonstrate their friendship but in reality displayed their extreme rivalry. The meeting lasted three weeks and consisted of a series of entertainments—including feasts, jousts, and masques—intended to demonstrate the wealth, physical ability, and cultural sophistication of each king and his court. The event became known as the Field of the Cloth of Gold because the tents erected to house the courts were made of cloth woven with strands of gold. The cost of the Field of the Cloth of Gold was enormous (among the more opulent features were fountains that flowed with wine), and the significance short-lived, as Henry had already decided to ally with Charles V in an invasion of France that failed miserably. In reality, by the early sixteenth century England was an inferior power that lacked the economic and military resources of France and Spain.

The King's "Great Matter"

Henry finally provided Wolsey with a problem that the cardinal was unable to solve. Henry and his wife, Catherine, had one child, a daughter named Mary, but Henry desperately wanted a male heir to succeed him. The only previous

▲ *This copy of an unattributed sixteenth-century painting conflates in a reimagined landscape numerous events that took place during the Field of the Cloth of Gold (June 7–24, 1520). Henry VIII leads an English procession from the town of Guînes to the castle. In front of him are Thomas Wriothesley, the garter king of arms, and Thomas Grey, marquess of Dorset, carrying the sword of state. Cardinal Wolsey rides beside the king, and on the far left behind him is Charles Brandon, duke of Suffolk.*

occasion on which a female had inherited the English crown had occurred in the twelfth century, and the country had been plunged into civil war as a result. Convinced that Catherine, now in her forties, would be unable to conceive again, Henry sought a way to rid himself of his wife so that he could marry again.

In 1501 Catherine had married Henry's brother, Arthur, who had died less than six months later. To be allowed to marry his dead brother's wife, Henry had sought a dispensation from the pope. He now began to worry that his marriage was sinful in the eyes of God and that the pope's decision had been wrong. His concerns seemed to be borne out by a passage from the Old Testament, Leviticus 20:21, according to which a man who has sexual relations with his dead brother's wife will remain childless. In 1527 Henry began to take the first official steps to annul his union with Catherine.

Henry had also found a replacement. In 1526 he became infatuated with Anne Boleyn, whose refusal to be his mistress made him determined to make her his wife. Henry turned to Wolsey to secure from the pope an annulment of Henry's marriage to Catherine, but there were many significant obstacles. Catherine herself refused to retire into a nunnery; she declared that she had never consummated her marriage with Arthur (that is, she had never had sexual relations with him). Furthermore, she discovered a biblical text that contradicted the Leviticus passage: Deuteronomy 25:5 obliges a man to marry his widowed sister-in-law if his brother dies without an heir.

Despite Wolsey's best efforts, all attempts to procure the annulment were thwarted when Charles V, the powerful Holy Roman emperor and Catherine's nephew, consolidated his domination of Italy by sacking Rome in 1527. Pope Clement VII was temporarily taken prisoner and was effectively unable to act against Charles's wishes. Charles was absolutely unwilling to see his aunt disgraced.

Anne Boleyn and her allies at court grew increasingly hostile to Wolsey, whose failure to procure the annulment made him more and more vulnerable. After the collapse of the hearing of Henry's case, Wolsey was charged with an

▲ The subject of this portrait, which was painted around 1503 by Michiel Sittow, is generally believed to be Catherine of Aragon. Henry was then heir apparent to the English throne.

offense under the fourteenth-century statute of praemunire, that is, the offense of preferring foreign (usually papal) jurisdiction above the jurisdiction of the crown. Wolsey pleaded guilty and resigned from political office. He died a year later while on his way to London to answer charges of treason.

Anne Boleyn | c. 1507–1536

Anne Boleyn had been educated at the French court; her impact in England derived from her continental sophistication—her dancing, musicality, witty conversation, and fashionable dress. Anne's refusal to become Henry's mistress undoubtedly fueled his obsessive desire for her, while her strong-minded, argumentative personality fascinated and frustrated him.

Anne showed a great interest in religious reform. She was a keen reader of scripture and a significant patron of early Reformers. One of them was Thomas Cranmer, the future archbishop of Canterbury; he and several other key figures in England's Protestant Reformation under Edward VI owed the advancement of their careers to Anne's patronage.

Anne did not provide Henry with the male heir that he wanted. Soon after their daughter, Princess Elizabeth, was born in 1534, Jane Seymour, lady-in-waiting to both Catherine of Aragon and Anne, appeared to be threatening Anne's place in Henry's affections. Anne's fall from power in 1536 resulted largely from Thomas Cromwell's hostility. Cromwell, who apparently became convinced that Anne was his political enemy, presented Henry with fabricated evidence of her adultery with several of his courtiers and with Anne's own brother. Horrified, Henry became bent on revenge. Anne was guilty of flirtation at the most, and of those men condemned with her, all declared their innocence except one, who confessed his guilt under severe psychological pressure (and possibly torture) on the part of Cromwell. The king's last kindness to Anne was to hire a French swordsman to carry out her execution. He married Jane Seymour the following day.

This unattributed English portrait of Anne Boleyn dates from around 1534, the year in which Anne gave birth to Elizabeth.

The Break with Rome

Henry began to try other methods of pressuring the pope into granting his divorce. He commissioned scholars and clerics to research the theoretical justifications for the annulment. The result was a document, the *Collectanea satis copiosa*, in which it was claimed that the pope exercised no spiritual jurisdiction over the king of England and that the king need recognize no superior authority in his dominions. These ideas were compounded by Henry's introduction to Reformist ideas about the ecclesiastical power of princes. Anne Boleyn had brought to Henry's attention the writings of William Tyndale, whose *Obedience of the Christian Man* (1528) claimed that the papacy had usurped the rightful temporal power of secular rulers over the church. Henry saw himself as the loyal servant of the papacy. Yet he guarded his sovereign power ever more jealously and became increasingly convinced that he alone possessed the authority to solve his marital problem.

In 1531 Thomas Cromwell, a convinced Reformer and a skilled and ruthless politician, rose to prominence at court. Prompted by Cromwell, Henry demanded that the clergy recognize his supreme spiritual and temporal headship of the English church. Cromwell exploited hostility in Parliament toward ecclesiastical law to launch an attack on the jurisdiction of the clergy. Cowed into submission, the clergy eventually surrendered their jurisdictional independence and reluctantly acknowledged Henry's total authority over the church.

Meanwhile, Anne was pregnant by the end of 1532. She and Henry were married in secret by Anne's protégé, the Reformer Thomas Cranmer, who had been made archbishop of Canterbury. Cranmer also declared the marriage with Catherine void and Princess Mary an illegitimate child. Henry's assumption of the headship of the church was formalized in Parliament in a series of acts. Among them was the 1534 Act of Supremacy, which officially declared that Henry was "the only Supreme Head on earth of the Church of England."

To ensure compliancy, all members of the clergy and the nobility were forced to swear the Oath of Supremacy, an official acceptance of Henry's headship and of his marriage to Anne Boleyn. The number of those that refused was not great, but they included men of international reputation. Thomas More, the great English humanist; Bishop John Fisher, the leading English theologian; and a handful of monks from the more prestigious religious orders were executed for their refusal.

The Henrician Reformation

Henry's break with Rome was at first nothing more than a legal repudiation of papal jurisdiction. However, a tiny minority of English men and women had been strongly influenced by religious change on the continent, and of these Anne Boleyn, Thomas Cranmer, and above all Thomas Cromwell used their power and influence in the 1530s to try to move the church in England in the direction of moderate reform. This task was a dangerous undertaking, not least because Henry's conventional and conservative piety was bolstered by a strong interest in theological debate and a profound wariness of doctrinal change.

In 1536 Henry and his bishops worked on the Ten Articles, a statement of religious faith that bore the influence of Lutheranism while remaining far from a definitive statement of Reformed beliefs. The doctrine of purgatory and the efficacy of praying for the souls of dead sinners in order to shorten their time in purgatory were questioned, and the veneration of icons and saints was condemned. The Lutheran doctrine of justification by faith alone was endorsed in a watered-down version; it was undermined by an insistence on the continued need for good works.

THE PILGRIMAGE OF GRACE

The most significant opposition to Henry's policies, the Pilgrimage of Grace of 1536, was a popular rising of around 30,000 protestors in the north of England. Discontent over the dissolution of the smaller monasteries had been most pronounced in the north. Cromwell's injunctions of 1536 furthered fears of a general attack on the traditional church that were compounded by other grievances, such as a fear of excessive taxation. The rebels marched under banners that represented their commitment to traditional religion and proclaimed their aims to be "for the preservation of Christ's church of this realm of England ... for the reformation of that which is amiss within this realm and for the punishment of heretics and subverters of the laws." The rebel leader Robert Aske, a lawyer, organized petitions of the rebels' grievances to be submitted to the king. Aske also managed negotiations with the court in London. The king, whose forces were woefully inadequate to put down such a large and well-organized rising, was forced to allow the duke of Norfolk, leader of the royal troops, to negotiate with the rebels and promise concessions. Trusting Henry's words, Aske disbanded the rebel armies and accepted the king's invitation to court at Christmas in 1536. Henry had no intention of making good any of his promises, and a new outbreak of violence gave him the chance to declare his promises void and to crush the rising. Aske was arrested with the other leaders, and Norfolk oversaw the "dreadful execution" of over two hundred people. Their dismembered bodies were displayed as a warning to Henry's subjects of the evils and dangers of rebellion.

► A photograph of the ruins of the Benedictine Abbey of Saint Mary in Glastonbury, in southwestern England. Among the country's oldest and richest monasteries, Glastonbury Abbey was one of hundreds throughout the country that were sacked during the dissolution of the monasteries (1536–1540). Most of the abbey's limestone was eventually quarried and used for other buildings.

Between 1536 and 1538 Cromwell issued injunctions to all English parishes demanding the removal of some images from churches and reducing the number of saints' days and holy days. Cromwell and Henry sanctioned the destruction of shrines and relics, which were central to popular religious practice. These moves in a Reformed direction were accompanied by an immensely significant event, the translation of the Bible into English in 1537. The other major religious change of the 1530s was the forcible suppression of monasticism in England. Henry shut the smaller monasteries in 1536 through a parliamentary act that used the claim of monastic corruption to launch a Reform-influenced attack on the principle of monasticism. The larger houses surrendered or were destroyed, and in April 1540 the last monastery was closed.

In 1536 the Pilgrimage of Grace, a popular rising, demonstrated the deep attachment to the traditional church in northern England. Henry himself grew increasingly concerned about radical heresy, and the next statements of faith, the Six Articles of 1539, together with the *King's Book* (1543), a revision of the 1537 *Bishops' Book*, have been seen by historians as a triumph for conservatives and traditionalists. Among other specifically non-Lutheran tenets, the new statements expounded the king's repudiation of the Reformed doctrine of justification by faith alone. The stance on the efficacy of prayer for the souls of the dead was rather more ambiguous. Henry saw himself as forging a middle path between traditional and radical religion. Although the English church in 1547 was far from being a Protestant church, many of the old religious certainties and traditional features of religious life (shrines, relics, and monasteries, for example) had been dismantled.

Politics and Marriage

After Henry's marriage to Anne's successor, Jane Seymour, Anne and Henry's daughter, Princess Elizabeth, was declared illegitimate—as her half sister Mary had been. Jane provided the much longed for heir, the future Edward VI, but died soon after his birth. Henry soon cast around for another wife, and Cromwell, believing in the need for alliance with other Protestant powers, urged Henry toward a marriage with Anne, sister to the duke of Cleves, a minor German ruler. Although he was delighted with Anne's portrait, Henry was horrified by the reality of his German wife's manner and appearance, and after a few months of marriage, he was able to put Anne aside by procuring a speedy annulment on the grounds of nonconsummation.

Thomas Cromwell, the engineer of Anne Boleyn's execution in 1536, was executed in 1540, when a group of religious conservatives led by Thomas Howard, duke of Norfolk, conspired to accuse him of radical heresy. The same year, Henry married Catherine Howard, Thomas Howard's eighteen-year-old niece. Accused of immoral conduct before and during her marriage to Henry, Catherine, like Anne Boleyn, was executed for adulterous treason; unlike Anne, she was probably guilty—at least of intent. Henry's final bride was Catherine Parr, an attractive widow whose intelligence and understanding of the king's personality allowed her to manage Henry and to outlive him. Catherine

promoted reform discreetly, particularly by sponsoring the publication of religious works in the vernacular. At the end of Henry's reign, both she and Thomas Cranmer survived attempts by their conservative enemies to destroy them with accusations of heresy. Catherine did so by making a gratuitous public display of submission to the king's superior judgment.

Final Years: War and the Succession

In the 1540s Henry returned to the overriding obsession of his youth, namely the glorious pursuit of war. In 1544 he invaded France in the hope of marching on Paris. His only gain was Boulogne, a town on France's northern coast that was extremely expensive to hold. He was forced to make peace with France; as part of the agreement, Boulogne would remain in English hands for eight years. Meanwhile Henry also declared war on Scotland in 1542 and inflicted on the Scots a crushing defeat at Solway Moss. The Scottish king, James V, died soon after and left his baby daughter, Mary, as heir to the Scottish throne.

▼ In 1537 the German painter Hans Holbein the Younger became the court painter to Henry VIII. Among the numerous glorious portraits he painted of members of and visitors to the court is this 1540 picture, one of the most enduring images of the king. Holbein acted not only as a portraitist but also as a fashion designer: he designed Henry's state robes and left drawings for everything from buttons and buckles to weapons, horse outfittings, and bookbindings for the royal household. Indeed, Holbein did not so much document as create the visual aspect of Henry's court.

▲ *Commissioned by Elizabeth I in the 1590s and attributed to Lucas de Heere, this work is called* An Allegory of the Tudor Succession. *To Henry's right are Mary Tudor and her husband, King Philip of Spain; behind them is Mars, the Roman god of war. To Henry's left are Edward VI and the most prominent figure, Elizabeth, who ushers in an allegorical figure representing peace.*

Henry sought to turn the minority of the Scottish monarch to England's favor. If Mary were to marry Henry's son, Edward, the dynastic union of England and Scotland would be achieved. The proposed marriage was formalized in the Treaty of Greenwich (1543). The Scots, however, broke the treaty and the engagement. In response Henry sent Edward Seymour, earl of Hertford (and brother of Jane Seymour), to ravage the Scottish border and lowland countries, a campaign known by the Scots as the "rough wooing." This aggressive act merely hardened the Scots' resolve to oppose the English.

In 1546, his health deteriorating, Henry made a will in which he designated his son as his next heir and his daughters, Mary and Elizabeth, as heirs after Edward. He also nominated a council of statesmen and administrators to govern in Edward's name after Henry's death. His effort to ensure that Reformers were in the majority probably indicate that in his very last years Henry's concern was to protect the supremacy and the particular nature of his church against the possible reversals of conservatives in the next reign. Henry expected Edward Seymour, Prince Edward's uncle, a tacit evangelical, to lead the council, although he tried to ensure that power reside with the body of the council rather than one man or one faction.

Henry died on January 28, 1547, and was buried next to Jane Seymour. Henry's carefully laid plans for the regency of his son were cast aside after his death. Seymour took command of the council and elevated himself to the position and title of lord protector and duke of Somerset. Seymour, Thomas Cranmer, and a group of powerful Reformers were able to introduce thoroughgoing religious change; the short reign of Henry VIII's son, Edward VI, was the era of the true Protestant Reformation in England.

FURTHER READING

Haigh, Christopher. *English Reformations: Religion, Politics, and Society under the Tudors.* New York, 1993.

MacCulloch, Diarmaid, ed. *The Reign of Henry VIII: Politics, Policy and Piety.* New York, 1995.

Rex, Richard. *Henry VIII and the English Reformation.* New York, 1993.

Scarisbrick, J. J. *Henry VIII.* Berkeley, CA, 1997.

Starkey, David. *The Reign of Henry VIII: Personalities and Politics.* London, 1985.

Alexandra Gajda

SEE ALSO

• Church of England • Elizabeth I • England
• Francis I • More, Thomas • Scotland

Heresy

LIKE OTHER RELIGIOUS MATTERS, THE TEACHING OF HERESY AND THE PRESENCE OF HERETICS WERE PERSISTENT CONCERNS IN EUROPEAN SOCIETY FOR THEIR POLITICAL AND SOCIAL CONSEQUENCES AS WELL AS THEIR STRICTLY RELIGIOUS ONES.

Heresy in Western Europe

The English theologian Robert Grosseteste (1175–1253) defined *heresy* as "an opinion chosen by human perception, contrary to the Holy Scripture, publicly avowed, and obstinately defended." For the church to find someone guilty of heresy according to this definition of the word, it had to prove the supposed heretic had committed a number of acts. First, a member of the church had to assert a doctrine that was deemed unorthodox; that is, it contradicted the church's teaching. However, the mere assertion of an unorthodox opinion did not amount to heresy. A heretic was a person who, even after having the heretical nature of his or her beliefs explained, continued obstinately to hold them.

Implicit in Grosseteste's definition are several important presumptions that helped shape the understanding of heresy in western Europe. He presumed, first, that there was a single orthodox body of official beliefs (specifically, those of the Roman Catholic Church) and, second, that all Christians had to assent to these beliefs and any deviation from them was a crime. A third presumption was that the church should punish anyone who deviated from orthodoxy and indeed should be determined to do so.

Thus, a heretic was a very clearly defined figure. By definition, a follower of another religion was not a heretic, nor was a member of the church who, upon receiving instruction in orthodoxy, renounced his or her errors. Moreover, until the church defined a set of beliefs and became determined to enforce them, heretics were unlikely to be identified or prosecuted.

In western Europe the prosecution of heretics began in earnest only after 1000. Two forces within the church drove the new concern about heresy and heretics. First, a series of reforms—known as the Gregorian reforms after their initiator, Pope Gregory VII (c. 1020–1085)—swept through the church. With these reforms Gregory and his followers sought to establish uniformity of belief throughout the church. In the process of defining standards and enforcing reforms, the church discovered believers who upheld unorthodox beliefs and practices. Second, this reform initiative drew the support of many believers. Some worked within the church toward orthodox goals, but some in the reform movement chose to pursue goals that the church defined as unorthodox.

◀ *This fresco, in the Church of San Francesco in Assisi, Italy, depicts the story of a man who, imprisoned for heresy by the bishop of Tivoli, repented and called on the aid of Saint Francis. When the man's shackles fell off and the prison doors burst open, the bishop, recognizing the evidence of divine intervention, knelt and gave praise to God.*

Dealing with Heretics

By the 1100s the church had recognized that a number of unorthodox groups existed within its ranks and that it needed to take new measures to combat these groups. Churchmen set up a number of mechanisms for defining orthodoxy in greater detail and for dealing with those who refused to accept the church's teachings. In the process of defining orthodox theology, the church established the principle that Christianity was based on a collection of truths that were divinely revealed and that any opposition to these revealed truths either implied ignorance of the church's teachings or amounted to an attempt to undermine the church's authority.

In terms of the punishments meted out to those who opposed orthodox teachings, a number of key developments took shape during the period. First, it was established that both church and state in western Europe had an interest in prosecuting heretics. At the base of this attitude was the assertion that, since heresy was the equivalent of the crime of treason against God, heretics were a threat not only to themselves but also to the whole community. This notion of heresy as treason demanded that heretics be punished severely. Underlying this rationale was the issue of obedience. By willfully rejecting the authority of the church, heretics were denying the authority of their superiors.

A second development was the formation within the church of institutions designed to detect and combat heresy. The church sought in part to reeducate the people in areas in which heresy was rife by dispatching preachers to teach orthodox doctrines. They also developed a special set of courts, known collectively as the Inquisition, whose task was actively to discover and prosecute heretics. In its efforts to do so, the Inquisition operated in conjunction with the governing authorities of western Europe.

The jurisdiction of church courts extended only to the punishment of those who admitted their faults. An eleventh-century church law decreed that unrepentant heretics could be burned. Since churchmen were not allowed to take life, these unrepentant heretics were turned over to secular officials for punishment. The close collaboration between church and state was revealed in the public punishment of groups of heretics in a ceremony known as the auto-da-fé. Secular rulers were active participants in the rooting out and punishment of heresy and heretics. Viewing heresy as a threat to society, they frequently used military force to disperse or convert heretical communities. This pattern of action, which continued to operate throughout the Renaissance and the Reformation, took shape in the 1200s as the Catholic Church sought to combat two important heresies, those of the Waldensians and the Cathars.

▼ *This detail, from a painting by Pedro Berruguete (1450–1504) entitled* Auto-da-fé presided over by Saint Dominic de Guzmán, *shows a heretic being brought to judgment by a Dominican monk.*

Two heretical movements combated by the church in the twelfth century shaped the prosecution of heresy during the Renaissance and the Reformation. The first movement, whose members were known as Cathars or Albigensians, represented a fusion of a protest movement against the wealth of the church and a heretical belief that the universe contained two gods, one good and one evil. This belief, which challenged the basic teachings of the church, spread in the twelfth, thirteenth, and fourteenth centuries and became especially strong in parts of southern France and the Italian Alps.

The church struggled to eradicate this heresy. After a papal legate he sent to Provence was murdered, Pope Innocent III ordered the preaching of a crusade against the Cathars in 1208. Eventually, the participation of King Louis IX in 1229 led to a decisive military triumph. At the same time the pope dispatched preachers to the region and set up the first inquisition to seek out the remaining Cathars and punish them.

The second heresy, known as the Waldensian heresy, originated with Peter Waldo, a former businessman from the southern French town of Lyon. Around 1173 Waldo gave all of his possessions to the poor and began to live a life of poverty in imitation of Jesus's apostles. At the same time he began to preach publicly what he believed was the essence of Jesus's teachings. He sought the church's blessing for his activities, but his bishop ordered him to cease, as he and his followers were untrained laymen who were not qualified to teach orthodox Christian ideas. When Waldo and his followers continued to preach in defiance of the ban, they were condemned as heretics. Despite prosecutions of Waldensians, the movement attracted followings in France, Germany, parts of eastern Europe, and Italy. While the Cathars had been suppressed by the time of the Reformation in the sixteenth century, the Waldensians continued to practice in secret, especially in mountain valleys of the southern Alps. The Waldensians ultimately assimilated into the Calvinist faith, with which they shared a number of beliefs.

The Inquisition

The most effective response to the newly defined threat of heresy in western Europe was the Inquisition, a church court established in the 1230s. The Inquisition remained a key feature of the church's response to heretics, and after the Protestant Reformation, the courts continued to operate in Roman Catholic territories, where they attempted to limit the spread of Protestantism. Although the church had set down laws against heresy as early as the fourth century, the inquisitors took advantage of two developments to create a more effective system to combat heresy. First, a rich body of theological literature had developed after 1000; it discussed and defined heresy very precisely. Second, there had been a revival in the study of the law practiced in the later Roman Empire. Christianity was the empire's official religion from the reign of Theodosius (379–395), and later Roman law set down a wide range of penalties for the crime of heresy.

▶ *This scene from a fifteenth-century French chronicle depicts the expulsion in 1209 of Cathar heretics from the town of Carcassonne by the forces of the French king, Philip Augustus.*

These two developments were further advanced by the creation during this period of a new legal procedure known as the *inquisito*. In the past, church courts had relied on accusations from the community to initiate cases. The new process allowed the inquisitors of their own accord to conduct investigations and bring prosecutions. Thus, the church for the first time actively sought out and punished heretics. Over the course of time, a series of popes strengthened the inquisitorial system. Various popes asked the Dominicans and Franciscans, two orders of friars (monks who combined monastic life with work at large in the community), to operate inquisitorial courts in conjunction with local bishops.

Since they were skilled theologians, the friars were well suited to the task.

Early in the Inquisition's history, certain procedures became part of its judicial method. In common with most secular courts of the time, the Inquisition regularly concealed the names of witnesses from suspects and held trials in secret. It sometimes used torture to secure a confession when the court lacked sufficient evidence to convict a person accused of heresy. These policies have contributed to the Inquisition's bad reputation. However, by the fifteenth century, inquisitors had become extremely wary of confessions gained through torture, and its use became less common.

After the successful suppression of the heretical Cathars in southern France in the 1220s, inquisitors became a permanent presence in many Catholic courts of Europe throughout the Renaissance and later. Perhaps the most important inquisitorial body during this period was the Spanish Inquisition, which played a key role in thwarting Protestant influence in Spain during the sixteenth century and in ensuring that those families of Jewish heritage who had been forced to convert to Christianity by Ferdinand and Isabella in the late fifteenth century did not return to the Jewish faith.

The Witch Hunts

As the inquisitors uncovered heretics among the general population of western Europe, they also became concerned about the widespread practice of magic. During and after the Renaissance nearly everyone in Europe, including trained theologians, believed in the existence of magic. All across Europe, people called on supernatural forces to protect their crops, cure disease, or recover lost items. However, at the same time most agreed that magic could also be used for evil purposes. Since the conversion of western Europe to Christianity, the church had sought to require believers to turn exclusively to the church for supernatural protection and help. Church authorities promoted the cult of the saints, whose intercession, it was believed, could be of service to the Christian in day-to-day life. The church also offered sacramentals—holy water, for example—to help protect Christians

▼ *This illumination comes from a fourteenth-century manuscript of the Decretals of Gregory IX, who was pope from 1227 to 1241. Gregory, presiding over a sitting of the Holy Inquisition (which he helped to found), is shown receiving from a kneeling inquisitor a list of people accused of heresy.*

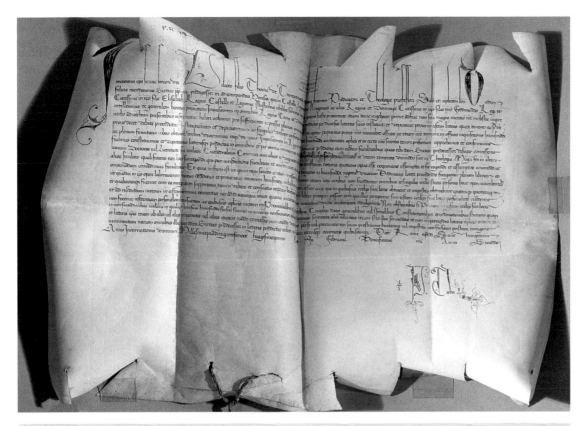

◀ In the papal bull pictured here, Pope Innocent VIII in 1487 appointed Tomás de Torquemada inquisitor general of Spain and gave him authority to prosecute heretics.

Tomás de Torquemada ▌ 1420–1498

The Dominican monk Tomás de Torquemada was a driving force behind the creation of the Spanish Inquisition. As confessor to King Ferdinand and Queen Isabella, he encouraged the Spanish monarchs to seek out and punish both practicing Jews and the so-called crypto-Jews—those Jews who had been forcibly converted to Christianity but still continued to practice Judaism secretly. Torquemada was influential in convincing the Spanish monarchy to petition the pope for an inquisition into crypto-Judaism, but he made his greatest impact in 1483, when he was appointed inquisitor general. As leader of the united Inquisition, which had been formed to root out crypto-Jews and other heretics in the Spanish kingdom, Torquemada created an efficient, organized court structure that proved far more successful (and far less cavalier) than other courts in finding and prosecuting heretics.

Under Torquemada's direction, the Spanish Inquisition tried large numbers of people. Perhaps two thousand were executed, roughly 2 percent of those convicted. His leadership did not meet with the full approval of Pope Alexander VI, who appointed four more inquisitors general. Torquemada, however, maintained the support of Ferdinand and Isabella, who in 1492, as much for political as for religious reasons, issued an order expelling all Jews and Muslims from their kingdom. This order made the work of the Inquisition more pressing, and even after his retirement in 1494, Torquemada wielded a great deal of influence within the institution that he had organized.

After his death in 1498, Torquemada's successors reduced the number of arrests and prosecutions; however, the centralized structure of the Spanish Inquisition remained in place for its duration. Scholars credit the Spanish Inquisition with helping to ensure that the Protestant faith would fail to take root in Spain; the court itself survived into the nineteenth century.

against misfortune. As part of its efforts to shepherd its flock, the church sought to define supernatural forces as either divine (issuing from God and being mediated through the church) or demonic (issuing from the devil). During the Middle Ages the church sporadically punished local healers and sorcerers for practicing demonic magic. However, until the twelfth century the devil was not generally thought of as a potent force. Therefore, the church rarely sought the execution of sorcerers; sorcery was viewed as harmful to the soul of the individual user of magic rather than a danger to the community as a whole.

IOAN PREN
& his Bid

IACKE

GILL

▲ By the sixteenth century authorities had come to view witches as dangerous figures who plotted with the devil against their own community. In many regions witches received death sentences for their perceived crimes and were either burned or hanged. This image, from an English pamphlet of 1589, depicts the public hanging in Chelmsford, Essex, of three witches: Joan Prentice, Joan Cony, and Joan Upney.

After 1100 a number of factors led to a reassessment of the devil's power—and with it the power of evil sorcerers. The church's new interest in prosecuting heretics prompted the Inquisition to take note of the widespread practice of demonic magic in the West. At first, there was some debate over whether the Inquisition had jurisdiction over sorcerers. However, church lawyers, especially those associated with the Inquisition, increasingly viewed the activities of witches as tantamount to heresy, the crime that the Inquisition had the most obvious claim to investigate and punish. Key to this perception was the definition of the power used by witches as diabolical (coming from the devil). This assumption led to a second, that the devil, being evil, would not share his powers without receiving something in return.

Many theorists identified the making of a pact as the devil's chief strategy. This pact required a witch to promise to worship the devil and forsake God in return for being granted magical powers. To theologians this pact made witches traitors to God. From this inference came the related idea that witches, like heretics, constituted an organized group opposed to orthodox Christianity. Churchmen progressively emphasized something known as a sabbat, a gathering at which the devil's followers engaged in rituals that parodied Christian worship, paid homage to the devil, and performed such repulsive acts as feasting on human flesh and boiling babies to make broth.

This evolving conception of witches made them among the most feared and fearsome enemies of the church. Moreover, the belief that witches met at sabbats in part to plan evil deeds led churchmen and state authorities alike to seek out groups of witches. Under torture those accused of witchcraft made confessions in which they also named other participants in the sabbat. These confessions provided the basis for widespread prosecutions of hundreds of witches discovered within small areas over a short period of time. While estimates of the scale of the witch hunts vary, most scholars believe that between roughly 1300 and 1700 more than 100,000 witches were prosecuted in Europe and perhaps 60,000 of those convicted were executed. While over three-quarters of those prosecuted were women, witchcraft was not exclusively a female crime. Roughly one-quarter of all the witches prosecuted in Europe were male, and in some regions, especially Scandinavia, a majority of them were male.

Very few witches were convicted in Inquisition courts after 1400, in part because

This letter of 1320, written by an Italian cardinal to the inquisitors of Carcassonne and Toulouse, demonstrates how the church defined the imagined activities of witches as a crime of heresy:

Our most holy father and lord, by divine providence, Pope John XXII, fervently desired that the witches, the infectors of God's flock, flee from the midst of the House of God. He ordains and commits to you that, by his authority against them who make sacrifice to demons and adore them, or do homage unto them by giving them as a sign a written pact or other token; or who make certain binding pacts with them, or who make or have made for them certain images or other things which bind them to demons, or by invoking the demons plan to perpetrate whatever sorceries they wish; or who, abusing the sacrament of baptism, themselves baptize or cause to be baptized an image of wax or some other material; and who themselves make these things or have them made in order to invoke the demons, or if knowingly they have baptism, orders, or confirmation repeated; then, concerning sorcerers and witches, who abuse the sacrament of the eucharist or the consecrated host and other sacraments of the Church by using them or things like them in their witchcraft and sorcery, you can investigate and otherwise proceed against them by whatever means available, which are canonically assigned to you concerning the proceeding against heretics. Indeed, our same lord amplifies and extends the power given to Inquisitors by law as much as the office of the inquisition against heretics, and, by this certain knowledge, likewise the privileges in all and singular cases mentioned above.

Quoted in Alan Charles Kors and Edward Peters, eds., *Witchcraft in Europe 400–1700: A Documentary History*

▶ *Central to the authorities' concerns about witches was the belief that they attended sabbats, gatherings where they worshiped the devil, hatched plots to cause harm, and created dangerous magical potions. This woodcut depicting just such a sabbat was made by Hans Baldung (1484–1545).*

Inquisition judges became increasingly well educated in law and viewed any supposed evidence that witches were able to perform magic with a great deal of skepticism. Nevertheless, the prosecution of witches continued during the Reformation. Both Martin Luther (1483–1546) and John Calvin (1509–1564), the two leading theologians of the Reformation, accepted without question the existence of witches and, in common with their Catholic counterparts, advocated the punishment of witches (Calvin was particularly zealous in this regard). Examples of intense witch hunting can be found in both Protestant and Catholic territories in the sixteenth and seventeenth centuries. Zealous witch hunting was not, however, ubiquitous. Some areas had professional, legally trained judges and influential courts of appeal that operated outside the communities where the witchcraft accusations took place. In those areas the courts tended to maintain rigid standards for the admissibility of evidence. Therefore, it was less likely that a defendant would be prosecuted for crimes that involved supernatural components.

▶ *The Oxford University professor John Wycliffe, depicted in this contemporary engraving, was a theologian whose ideas inspired a heretical movement in England known as Lollardy.*

Lollardy and Hussitism

Two new and related heresies emerged in the Christian West during the fourteenth and fifteenth centuries. The first, Lollardy, sprang from the teachings of John Wycliffe (c. 1330–1384), a professor at the University of Oxford. Wycliffe first rose to prominence in the 1370s, when he put forward the idea that the political power of the church should be eliminated in England and that the church should return to the example of Jesus's apostles by, among other things, embracing poverty. Wycliffe's ideas were particularly popular among those in England who saw the church as corrupt and the pope as an ally of England's enemy, France.

Wycliffe also advanced a series of more controversial ideas that were ultimately condemned as heretical. One key idea was that God had preordained before birth who would be saved and who damned. This idea ran counter to the church's teaching that faith, good works, and the sacraments could help a believer achieve salvation. Wycliffe also denied the doctrine of transubstantiation (the miraculous transformation, at the Eucharist, of the substance of bread and wine

into the body and blood of Christ). By doing so, he not only denied an essential church doctrine but also downplayed the role of the sacraments in the saving of souls. Finally, he argued that the Bible should be interpreted literally and should be translated into English so that ordinary people could more easily read it. By envisaging a more direct relationship between the Christian believer and God, Wycliffe removed the church from its role as sole intercessionary.

Wycliffe's followers translated the Bible into English and established small groups that kept his teachings alive in secret through the fifteenth century. They survived despite the increasing suspicion of the ecclesiastical and political authorities. The archbishop of Canterbury condemned Wycliffe's works as heretical in 1411, and in 1428 Wycliffe's body was dug up and reburied outside a Christian cemetery—an act that symbolized the church's rejection of his teachings. The similarity between Wycliffe's ideas and those of the first Reformers has led some scholars to label Wycliffe a proto-Reformer.

Wycliffe's ideas also had an immediate impact in the central European territory of Bohemia, where a group of critics were already preaching against ecclesiastical wealth. Through Jan Hus, a charismatic preacher at the University of Prague, Wycliffe's ideas found a following in Bohemia. Hus was called to explain his ideas before the Council of Constance, a general church council held in 1415, but, despite a promise from the Holy Roman emperor of safe conduct, Hus was tried and convicted by the council and burned as a heretic. Hus's death sparked an uprising in Bohemia by his Czech-speaking followers, who succeeded in holding off the emperor's armies. The radical wing of the uprising advocated a number of heretical ideas, including the rejection of the special status of churchmen and the use of Czech rather than Latin in church services. In 1430, at the Council of Basel, a more moderate wing of the group that by now had become known as Hussites agreed to lay aside some of the group's more radical ideas in exchange for peace with the church authorities. The movement survived into the sixteenth century; after being accused of being a Hussite, Martin Luther read Hus's works and recognized how similar their ideas were.

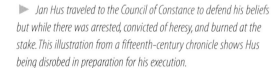 Jan Hus traveled to the Council of Constance to defend his beliefs but while there was arrested, convicted of heresy, and burned at the stake. This illustration from a fifteenth-century chronicle shows Hus being disrobed in preparation for his execution.

In a foundational work of Renaissance humanism, Giovanni Pico della Mirandola (1463–1494), one of the most outspoken advocates of the Renaissance view of human potential, defined an optimistic vision of humankind. Three of the nine hundred controversial theses that make up this 1486 work were condemned by the church as heretical.

God the Father, the supreme Architect, had already built this cosmic home we behold.... But, when the work was finished, the Craftsman kept wishing that there were someone to ponder the plan of so great a work, to love its beauty, and to wonder at its vastness. Therefore, when everything was done (as Moses and Timaeus bear witness), He finally took thought concerning the creation of man. But there was not among His archetypes that from which He could fashion a new offspring.... [God chose to give man characteristics of both heavenly and earthly creatures.] O supreme generosity of God the Father, O highest and most marvelous felicity of man! To him it is granted to have whatever he chooses and to be whatever he wills. Beasts as soon as they are born (so says Lucilius) bring with them from their mother's womb all they will ever possess. Spiritual beings, either from the beginning or soon thereafter, become what they are to be for ever and ever. On man when he came into life the Father conferred the seeds of all kinds, and the germs of every way of life. Whatever seeds each man cultivates will grow to maturity and bear in him their own fruit. If they be vegetative, he will be like a plant. If sensitive, he will become brutish. If rational, he will grow into a heavenly being. If intellectual, he will be an angel and the son of God. And if, happy in the lot of no created thing, he withdraws to the center of his own unity, his spirit, made one with God, in the solitary darkness of God, who is set above all things shall surpass them all.

Oration on the Dignity of Man

Heresy and the Renaissance

The emergence of humanism and the rebirth of classical learning during the Renaissance challenged medieval theology in a number of ways. In Italy the chief challenge came from the revival of classical Greek philosophy, particularly the works of Plato (c. 428–c. 348 BCE) and his later Roman follower Plotinus (205–270 CE). In Florence the work of two scholarly students of Plato caused considerable controversy. The first, Marsilio Ficino (1433–1499), envisaged the human being at the center of a great chain of being. According to Ficino a man had the ability by his own free will to rise up the chain toward heaven or to fall down toward the earth. This view was potentially heretical, since it ignored the role of Christ's resurrection in human salvation. The second scholar, Giovanni Pico della Mirandola, a disciple of Ficino, argued even more forcefully for the power of free will and also sought to demonstrate the basic harmony among the doctrines of all religions, including ancient pagan religions and Islam. Pico's ideas were investigated on several occasions because, in seeking the essence of all religions, he implicitly removed Christianity from its preeminent position among faiths.

With the spread of Renaissance ideas to northern Europe, another challenge to medieval orthodoxy emerged as scholars began to reexamine the oldest surviving copies of the Bible. Their goal was to apply what they had learned from their studies of ancient Greek and Latin texts to creating a "purer" translation of the Bible that was linguistically as close as possible to the oldest biblical texts. A group of evangelical humanists led by the Dutchman Desiderius Erasmus (c. 1466–1536) applied new techniques in the study of language to the Bible. Erasmus rejected the method of enquiry of the medieval Schoolmen, who arrived at theological truths through refined logical argumentation. The new interpretations of the Bible by Erasmus and his followers tended to emphasize the view that the essence of Christianity lies in moral formation rather than ritual action.

The church was relatively tolerant of these new ideas as long as they remained the subject of debate among scholars. However, toleration of these new approaches to scholarship ended

▶ *In a mid-seventeenth-century oil known as* The Church as Ship *(attributed to Jacob Gerritsz Loef), the artist allegorically depicts the Catholic Church's victory over Hus, Calvin, Luther, and other heretics. In Loef's own Netherlands, however, whatever victory there was for Rome was limited to the realm of the allegorical.*

abruptly in the opening half of the sixteenth century, when, at the outbreak of the Reformation, Catholic and Protestant authorities alike tightened their control of scholarly debate.

The Reformation

The permanent split of western Europe into Protestant and Catholic churches heightened the concern of both churchmen and secular authorities about heresy. While they differed over the nature and content of orthodox Christian belief, major Protestant and Catholic theologians all agreed on the validity of the definition of heresy that had been developed in the Middle Ages. Catholic churchmen defined all the Protestant groups, including Lutherans, Calvinists, Zwinglians, and Anabaptists, as heretics. Adherents of all of these sects were at different times punished by Catholic authorities.

Protestants rejected Roman Catholic accusations of heresy. Key Protestant thinkers, however, never explicitly labeled Roman Catholics as heretics, although more than one Reformer condemned un-Reformed Catholic belief and practice as idolatry. Lutherans, Calvinists, and Zwinglians did actively prosecute and punish as heretics other Protestants, however, especially Anabaptists. Zwingli supported a 1526 law that punished Anabaptists in Zurich with drowning for their practice of adult baptism, and in 1553 Calvinist authorities in Geneva burned the free-thinker Michael Servetus as a heretic.

During the Middle Ages heresy was essentially defined as the obstinate upholding by a member of the Christian church of beliefs that ran counter to official church teachings. However, the eagerness to prosecute heretics that was shared by Roman Catholic and Protestant authorities after the Reformation was also driven by a second widely held belief—that heresy was disruptive to the structural integrity of society and that a heretic was thus guilty of committing a crime against the state as well as one against the church. One basis for this belief was the theory of the divine right of kings—the view, advocated by monarchs across Europe, that a king held his position by the will of God. By its very nature a group within a state that worshiped a different god or worshiped the Christian God in a differ-

ent way was often open to accusations of not recognizing the government's right to rule. Thus, when peace was established between Protestant and Catholic rulers in the Holy Roman Empire in 1555, the treaty specifically decreed that the religion of the ruler of each territory would also be the faith of his subjects.

HERESY AND THE SCIENTIFIC REVOLUTION

By the beginning of the seventeenth century, some Catholic theologians had come to view certain new scientific ideas as heretical. In particular, the theory that the earth orbited the sun—first advanced by the Polish astronomer Nicolaus Copernicus (1473–1543)—challenged the widely accepted belief that the earth stood motionless at the center of the universe. Copernican cosmology became a matter of greater interest to the church after 1609, when the Italian scientist Galileo Galilei (1564–1642) used his telescope, a new invention, to observe the heavens. His published observations about the shape and workings of the solar system seemed to contradict church teachings. The church was concerned that the theories and findings of Copernicus and Galileo might be used to undermine the orthodox position on the creation of the universe. It followed that if the new claims were true, then the church's creation theology, which was based on the book of Genesis, was erroneous.

While Copernicus died before his theories had attracted great attention, Galileo publicized his findings widely. Called before the Inquisition in Rome, Galileo was charged with holding and defending heretical positions, and though never imprisoned, he spent his last eight years under house arrest.

▲ This unattributed painting fancifully depicts the trial of Galileo Galilei by the Roman Inquisition in 1633. The inquisitors placed Galileo under nominal house arrest for life.

The inability of rulers to eradicate rival faiths from their territories ultimately forced them to experiment with the idea of religious toleration. The Treaty of Westphalia, the signing of which at Münster in 1648 forms the subject of this engraving, brought an end to the Thirty Years War, a bitter and bloody conflict that largely (but not exclusively) pitted Protestants against Catholics.

Tolerance of multiple faiths within a community remained unthinkable. One revealing example of how this concern for the social fabric was shared by Protestant and Catholic authorities alike involved the besieging of the German city of Münster by a combined Lutheran and Catholic army in 1534 and 1535. Within the town was a group of radical Anabaptists who had seized power and were implementing an increasingly radical agenda based on their belief that Christ would soon return to earth. The Anabaptist leaders outlawed private property and legalized polygamy (the practice of having more than one wife). The threat to social norms posed by the Anabaptists of Münster was so compelling that Lutheran and Catholic authorities worked together to destroy it.

Heresy after the Reformation
Following the Reformation, in Protestant and Catholic territories alike, the precise nature of the rituals believers participated in and the beliefs they held defined them as either true members of the church or heretics in the eyes of the church authorities. Thus, one long-term outcome of the Reformation was the campaign by various Christian authorities to exert unprecedented influence over the practices and beliefs of individuals within their communities. Both Protestant and Catholic churches made clear statements of what they considered orthodox doctrines to be and also improved the training of the clergy so that they would be better able to teach those orthodox doctrines to the faithful.

Clear statements of dogma, such as the Augsburg Confession for Lutherans and the decrees of the Council of Trent for Catholics, not only drew well-defined theological lines between Protestantism and Catholicism but also made prosecution for heresy easier. The concerted and often coordinated efforts of state and church authorities to instill orthodox beliefs in all the faithful within their jurisdiction led to a pattern of local uniformity of religious belief. This long-term campaign has come to be known as confessionalization.

Toleration and Heresy
In the seventeenth century some European powers were forced to acknowledge that two well-established faiths coexisted within their territory. Faced with this reality, a number of states

reluctantly experimented with religious pluralism—that is, they decreed that everyone in a region need not adhere to the same religion. Henry IV, the king of France from 1589 to 1610, was the first monarch to create a successful and lasting agreement that recognized the legal practice of Catholicism and Protestantism in the realm. In the Holy Roman Empire rulers attempted a similar experiment with religious pluralism through the Treaty of Westphalia (1648), the agreement that officially brought an end to the Thirty Years War.

These experiments with religious pluralism were forced upon rulers; the French experiment was ultimately rejected by King Louis XIV in 1685. Nonetheless, the experiments mark an important stage in the history of religion in western Europe, since they separated the theological problem of heresy—which understandably continued to preoccupy churchmen who sought to guide and regulate the beliefs of their followers—from a state's impulse or requirement to prosecute dissenters. This separation would, in the eighteenth and nineteenth centuries, lead to the development of the modern Western concept of religious freedom.

FURTHER READING

Evans, Gillian Rosemary. *A Brief History of Heresy.* Malden, MA, 2002.

Lambert, Malcolm. *Medieval Heresy: Popular Movements from the Gregorian Reform to the Reformation.* Malden, MA, 2002.

Levack, Brian P. *The Witch-Hunt in Early Modern Europe.* New York, 1995.

Eric Nelson

▲ On March 25, 1560, hundreds of Protestants were killed at Amboise, in central France. This depiction of the massacre—carried out in retaliation for a failed conspiracy against the Catholic house of Guise—was engraved by Franz Hogenberg and later colored.

SEE ALSO

• Augsburg, Peace of • Bibles • Bohemia • Copernicus, Nicolaus • Erasmus, Desiderius • Established Churches
• Ferdinand and Isabella • France • French Civil Wars • Galilei, Galileo • Henry IV • Holy Roman Empire
• Humanism and Learning • Lutheranism • Magic • Pico della Mirandola, Giovanni • Platonism • Preaching
• Reformation • Spain • Thirty Years War • Trent, Council of

Hobbes, Thomas

ONE OF THE MOST SIGNIFICANT
PHILOSOPHERS OF THE SEVENTEENTH
CENTURY, THOMAS HOBBES (1588–
1679) IS CREDITED WITH BRINGING TO
THE FORE MANY IMPORTANT FEATURES
OF MODERN LIBERAL POLITICS,
INCLUDING INDIVIDUALISM, THE SOCIAL
CONTRACT, AND GOVERNMENT BY
CONSENT.

▲ *An unattributed mid-seventeenth-century portrait of Thomas Hobbes. He believed a strong monarchy was the best defense against social chaos.*

Thomas Hobbes was born in Malmesbury, in the English county of Derbyshire, in 1588. His father, a priest, abandoned the family when Thomas was very young. As a result, the younger Hobbes was raised principally by his wealthy uncle, Francis. Hobbes. He studied philosophy and logic at Oxford University and, after earning a bachelor's degree in 1608, became a tutor for a family of prominent aristocrats, the Cavendishes, and later for another family, the Clintons. Hobbes tutored the youths in both households in philosophy, politics, and mathematics.

Early Scholarship and Ideas

In 1610 Hobbes embarked on a trip to the European continent. While there, he developed a deep interest in contemporary scholarship and decided that, instead of remaining a mere tutor, he wanted to contribute to contemporary debates on politics and the nature of humanity. Hobbes left Europe convinced that, in spite of the great advancements being made in the sciences, many intellectuals too often lazily relied on past scholarship instead of striving for the advancement of learning.

Hobbes met with Francis Bacon (1561–1626) several times and became friends with the great English intellectual. During this period Hobbes also became increasingly opposed to democracy. He gradually came to believe that only a monarchy could provide the stability needed for a society to advance. He was especially mistrustful of revolutions and rebellions and the disorder and chaos they tended to create. In 1628 Hobbes published a translation of the works of the ancient Greek historian Thucydides. He hoped his book would warn people of the inherent danger in democracy—that it could descend into mob rule.

Hobbes made further journeys to Europe from 1629 to 1631 and then from 1634 to 1637. These journeys changed the course of his life by convincing him that scholarship on politics and history should be based on the scientific method. Hobbes became fascinated by the physical sciences, including geometry and mathematics. While in Europe he took a variety of classes in chemistry, geometry, and general science in order to stay abreast of current developments in the sciences. He wanted to apply to the study of people and politics the scientific methods being used to gain insight into natural history and astronomy. On his second and third trips to Europe, he began developing ideas on how to apply science to the study of politics.

Hobbes rejected the predominant view that humans were spiritual beings and instead insisted that people, like other animals, receive all knowledge from their senses (and not from divine inspiration). Since all knowledge came from the senses, Hobbes reasoned that all human intelligence was based on people's perceptions of the material world. Hobbes contended that people categorize all external stimuli as either pleasurable (in the case of food, wealth, and warmth, for example) or painful (in the case of hunger, poverty, and cold). People seek pleasure and try to avoid pain. For Hobbes, the only significant difference between humans and animals is that people possess rationality: people will accept some pain if they believe that they will later be rewarded with greater pleasure.

Hobbes argued that, since power enables people to gain more pleasure and avoid pain, people naturally seek greater power. As a result of this competition for power, humans are combative and warlike. This characteristic tends to create a climate of anarchy and lawlessness in human society. Hobbes argued that, in their natural state, people are full of violence and greed and that one person will readily inflict harm on another in order to gain power. According to Hobbes only a strong government can keep people safe from this violence. In knowledge of this fact, reasoning people are willing to secure their safety by agreeing to surrender some freedom and accept the rules and laws of a society (a form of pain since it involves the loss of freedom). Hobbes's materialism rejected both the idealism of the ancient philosophers and Christian notions of human spirituality. Hobbes's ideas anticipate the development of behavioralism as a way of explaining human actions, and many scholars consider the English philosopher the founder of modern behavioral studies.

Hobbes also became a staunch materialist; he rejected the philosophy of such idealists as Plato and Aristotle and came to believe that the key to understanding human behavior was to study the physical world rather than speculate on the metaphysical. During his trips to Europe, Hobbes interacted with some of the most renowned thinkers and scholars of his day, notably the Italian astronomer Galileo Galilei (1564–1642).

CHRONOLOGY

1588
Thomas Hobbes is born in Malmesbury, England.

1603–1608
Studies at Oxford University.

1636
Meets Galileo and becomes fascinated by geometry; begins to apply scientific methodology to the study of human nature.

1640
Goes into exile in France as the English civil wars commence.

1646
Begins tutoring the future English king Charles II in Paris.

1651
Publishes his greatest work, *Leviathan;* begins a twelve-year dispute with Bishop Bramhall on free will.

1668
Completes the historical work *Behemoth,* but Charles II forbids its publication.

1679
Dies on December 4.

1682
Behemoth is published.

◄ *Hobbes believed that the 1649 execution of Charles I, depicted on this contemporary broadsheet, ushered in a period of anarchy and chaos in England.*

▶ *The monk and renowned intellectual Marin Mersenne, the subject of this engraving by Balthazar Moncornet (c. 1600–1668), taught philosophy and mathematics in Paris and was at the center of a group of famous scholars. Mersenne was best known for his work on prime numbers and number theory.*

The English Civil Wars

Hobbes's materialism was first expressed in *The Elements of Law, Natural and Politic*. Although he finished the book in 1637, he was unable to publish it until 1640. In the book he argued for the importance of an absolute monarchy in order to fend off the anarchy that would otherwise result from the competition among people for political power. At the time England was in the midst of a confrontation between King Charles I and Parliament over the power of the monarchy. A committed supporter of the king, Hobbes believed that his life was in danger. He went into exile in Paris in 1640.

In Paris, Hobbes joined a circle of prestigious intellectuals led by Marin Mersenne (1588–1648), who was a mentor to the great philosopher René Descartes (1596–1650), among others. Hobbes engaged in a lively and long-running debate with Descartes over human nature. He also worked with a number of scholars involved in scientific explorations in the fields of chemistry and mathematics.

Although he supported the monarchy, Hobbes displeased many Royalists by objecting to the important role the church played in contemporary government. In 1642 he wrote *De cive (On Citizenship)*, in which he argued that universal standards of morality were wrong and that a government should not try to enforce a single set of ethics for all of its citizens. The work became the first in a trilogy on political philosophy. The attack on the Catholic Church made Hobbes unpopular with many in Paris. Nonetheless, his intellectual prowess was well respected by all. After the publication of *De cive*, Hobbes turned to nonpolitical subjects. He studied optics and wrote about vision and images in *A Minute of First Draught of the Optiques* (1646).

Hobbes returned to England in 1651 and tried to make peace with Oliver Cromwell's antimonarchist government. He lived in London until 1675, when he moved back north to Derbyshire, the area of his birth, and devoted himself to scholarly research and writing.

THE DARK WORLD OF *LEVIATHAN*

In his masterpiece *Leviathan*, Hobbes portrays life as brutal and full of pain. He begins by comparing the human form and the way people interact with one another with the structure of a state and the interaction between one state and another. Hobbes argues that, just as the head controls the rest of the body, a government must have absolute control over a country. Just as countries go to war to gain more territory or wealth, people fight one another for power and prestige. The fierce competition among states matches the natural state of anarchy into which human society collapses in the absence of sufficient regulation. Interactions at both levels are carried out in the grip of constant fear, mistrust, and violence.

This natural anarchy creates a kind of rough equality among people. While some are stronger than others, even the strong cannot maintain order by themselves. For instance, Hobbes writes that any person is capable of killing any other person. Even the strongest man must sleep. A group of the weak could attack and kill even the strongest man while he slumbers.

Hobbes contends that people want to live in a peaceful and secure society that will uphold their right to protect their position and property in the face of thievish rivals and usurpers. Consequently, people organize themselves into communities. Even within these communities, however, there are some who cannot be trusted. Therefore, people establish structures to protect themselves. These structures are the governments that provide law and order by using—or threatening to use—force against those who would violate the rules of society. At the core of Hobbes's argument is the notion that it is rational for people to accept the rule of government so that they can seek to improve their lives without fear of attack by others. This argument was radical for its time because it asserted that people accepted moral and ethical values out of self-interest and fear of punishment, not for spiritual or religious reasons.

Writing about the social contract, Hobbes argued that governments are formed when people agree to surrender some of their freedom to the state in exchange for protection from violence, theft, and other attacks. Hobbes believed that a government had to have absolute authority because people will try to break their side of the contract and violate social rules if they perceive that the reward for doing so outweighs the punishment. For Hobbes the perfect government controlled all aspects of society, including the allocation of property and wealth. The ideal government even controlled employment by deciding who did what job and regulated the press and individual speech through censorship. Only through such strict governmental control could people be protected from themselves.

Leviathan

Hobbes's return to England also marked the publication of his greatest work, *Leviathan* (1651). The work was the result of Hobbes's experience of the English civil wars and his observations of the anarchy and disorder that the conflicts caused. Hobbes believed that the civil wars had seriously eroded the fabric of English society and that the violence and upheaval of the conflicts lent substantial credence to his theory that monarchy was the best form of government. The book explained the major points of Hobbes's political philosophy and introduced the concept of the social contract. Many of Hobbes's concepts were rejected, but the idea of the social contract, later developed by the English political philosopher John Locke (1632–1704) and the American statesman Thomas Jefferson (1743–1826), became the basis for theories of constitutional government.

◄ The formal title of Hobbes's masterpiece is Leviathan; or, The Matter, Forme, and Power of a Common-Wealth Ecclesiasticall and Civil, 1651. *The design of the title page of the first edition, pictured here, was intended to convey a sense of the book's view of government.*

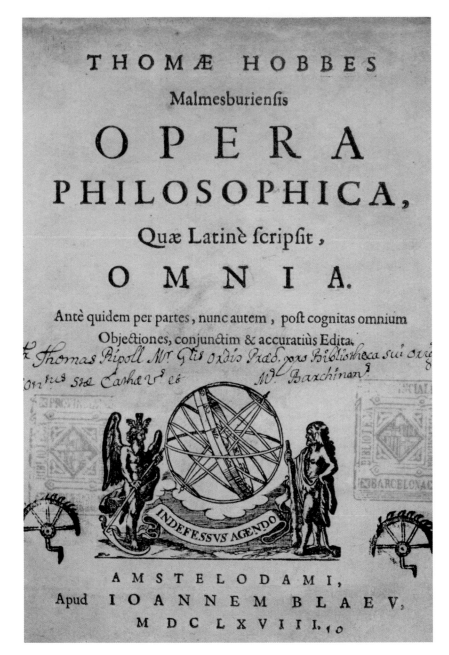

THOMÆ HOBBES
Malmesburienſis
OPERA
PHILOSOPHICA,
Quæ Latinè ſcripſit,
OMNIA.

Antè quidem per partes, nunc autem, poſt cognitas omnium
Objectiones, conjunctim & accuratiùs Edita.

[handwritten annotations]

INDEFESSVS AGENDO

AMSTELODAMI,
Apud IOANNEM BLAEV,
MDCLXVIII.

▲ *While England banned many of Hobbes's works, he was widely published in other countries. In 1668 most of Hobbes's major works, including* On Citizenship *and* Leviathan, *were collected, edited, and published in Amsterdam. Above is the title page of the collection.*

theological grounds. Over the next twelve years, Hobbes and Bramhall wrote a series of responses to each other's criticisms and arguments. Bramhall responded to Hobbes's *Of Liberty and Necessity* (1654) with *A Defense of True Liberty and Antecedent and Extrinsical Necessity* (1655), to which Hobbes in turn responded with *The Questions concerning Liberty, Necessity and Chance* (1656).

New Challenges

In 1655 Hobbes published *De corpore (On the Body),* and in 1657 he completed his political trilogy with the publication of *De homine (On Man).* Together with *De cive,* these works constituted Hobbes's effort to integrate scientific methodology and political theory. Although this initiative was bold and foreshadowed later developments in political science, many of Hobbes's conclusions proved flawed. For instance, in *De corpore* many of Hobbes's assumptions about mathematics contradicted the established principles of geometry. Hobbes defended his mathematical arguments even when most scholars rejected his ideas. His unwillingness to accept the criticism of others on this matter undermined his standing within the community of scholars and intellectuals.

In addition to his mathematical work, Hobbes continued to engage in a variety of scholarly activities. In 1668 he completed a massive history of the English civil wars entitled *Behemoth; or, The Long Parliament.* Although the work was supportive of the monarchy and highly critical of the rebellion, Charles II forbade its publication. Hobbes also completed a translation of both the *Iliad* and the *Odyssey* in 1675 (by which time he was eighty-six years old). Toward the end of his life, Hobbes became an increasingly active supporter of education. For example, he arranged to have the king fund a local school in Derbyshire.

Although he remained very active, Hobbes's later years were difficult. He was publicly unpopular, and many scholars ridiculed his ideas, especially on mathematics. In light of his contributions to philosophy and mathematics, he was disappointed that the Royal Society did not elect him a fellow. In addition, he became

The English government banned *Leviathan* for its radical ideals and antireligious overtones. Most anti-Royalists rejected Hobbes's work because it endorsed the principle of monarchy. When the great fire of London broke out in 1666, some blamed Hobbes's work for incurring God's wrathful vengeance. King Charles II even forbade Hobbes from publishing any more original books after the fire.

The publication of *Leviathan* began a long-running intellectual dispute between Hobbes and John Bramhall, the Anglican bishop of Derry and later archbishop of Armagh (in northern Ireland), on the subject of free will. Bramhall's objections to Hobbes's philosophy were based mainly on

John Aubrey (1626–1695), a member of the Royal Society, wrote about prominent English intellectuals in a series of manuscripts that were later collected into a book called *Brief Lives.* This 1679 letter from James Wheldon, included in *Brief Lives,* describes Hobbes's friendship with prominent thinkers of the day:

Lucius Cary, Lord Falkland was his great friend and admirer and so was Sir William Petty; both which I have here enrolled amongst those friends I have heard him speak of, but Dr. Blackburne left them both out (to my admiration). I asked him why he had done so. He answered, because they were both ignote [unknown] to foreigners. His acquaintance with Sir William Petty began at Paris, 1648 or 1649, at which time Mr. Hobbes studied Vesalius' Anatomy, and Sir William with him. He then assisted Mr. Hobbes in drawing his schemes for his book of optics, for he had a very fine hand in those days for drawing, which drafts Mr. Hobbes did much commend. His Excellency in this kind conciliated them the sooner to the familiarity of our common friend Mr. S. Cowper.

When he was at Florence he contracted a friendship with the famous Galileo Galilei, whom he extremely venerated and magnified; and not only as he was a prodigious wit, but for his sweetness of nature and manners. They pretty well resembled one another, as to their countenances, as by their pictures doth appear; were both cheerful and melancholic-sanguine; and had both a consimility of fate, to be hated and persecuted by the ecclesiastics.

Descartes and he were acquainted and mutually respected one another. He would say that had he kept himself to geometry he had been the best geometer in the world but that his head did not lie for philosophy.

James Wheldon

◀ *This portrait of Hobbes by Isaac Fuller (1606–1672) depicts the philosopher in later life. The intellectual passion of his younger years unquenched, Hobbes continued to publish even as his health prevented him from physically writing.*

afflicted with a form of palsy, a disease marked by uncontrollable tremors that prevented him from writing, and so he had to dictate his final works to a secretary. He died on December 4, 1679. Three years after his death, Charles II's government finally issued the required license to allow the posthumous publication of *Behemoth.*

FURTHER READING

Sorrell, Tom. *Hobbes.* New York, 1986.

Spragens, Thomas A. *The Politics of Motion: The World of Thomas Hobbes.* Lexington, KY, 1973.

Warrender, Howard. *The Political Philosophy of Hobbes: His Theory of Obligation.* New York, 2000.

Watkins, John W. N. *Hobbes's System of Ideas.* Brookfield, VT, 1989.

Tom Lansford

SEE ALSO

• Bacon, Francis • Descartes, René
• English Civil Wars • Galilei, Galileo • Monarchy
• Philosophy • Science and Technology

Holy Roman Empire

ALTHOUGH A LOOK AT A MAP OF THE HOLY ROMAN EMPIRE FROM THE LATE MIDDLE AGES THROUGH THE EARLY MODERN PERIOD SUGGESTS THAT THE EMPIRE WAS FOR CENTURIES A FORCE TO BE RECKONED WITH, ITS INTERNAL DIVISIONS ENSURED THAT IN PRACTICE NO EMPEROR EVER WIELDED AUTHORITY PROPORTIONAL TO THE SIZE OF HIS DOMAIN.

▼ *Featured in this 1532 panel, by Lucas Cranach the Elder, are three electors of Saxony: (from left to right) Frederick the Wise (1482–1556), John the Steadfast (1468–1532), and John Frederick the Magnanimous (1503–1554). The Saxon princes were vital to the political landscape of the late medieval and early modern periods, and electoral Saxony was integral to the protection of the Lutheran cause, particularly during the rule of Frederick the Wise.*

The Holy Roman Empire encompassed most of central Europe from the Baltic and North seas and the Danish kingdom in the north to the Swiss Confederation and the Venetian Republic in the south. The empire's western frontier bordered France, while to the east the imperial lands faced the Polish, Bohemian, and Hungarian kingdoms and the increasingly threatening Turks. Given the immense geographical range of the empire, it is hardly surprising that its inhabitants spoke a variety of languages and dialects, although various forms of German predominated. Throughout the early modern period, Latin continued to be the favored language of academics, although German began gaining increased prominence in the late fifteenth century, thanks largely to the emergence and rapid spread of the printing press.

A majority of the people living within the boundaries of the empire were Roman Catholics, at least until the early sixteenth century. The spiritual leadership of the papacy was accepted by most, with a single major exception—the Jews (who, it is estimated, made up no more than 1 percent of the empire's population). The Holy Roman Empire represented a unified western Christendom that was broken up by the onset and expansion of the Protestant Reformation. By 1555 Lutheranism had gained legal and official recognition within the empire.

From its inception, the Holy Roman Empire tended to be dominated by a single elected emperor, a position reserved exclusively for men. From 1273 emperors were formally chosen by a powerful group of seven princes called electors: the archbishops of Mainz, Trier, and Cologne, the king of Bohemia, the count palatine of the Rhine, the duke of electoral Saxony, and the margrave of Brandenburg all served as electors. Once elected, it was the emperor's responsibility to defend the empire from any foreign enemies and to maintain peace internally. To that end emperors presided over the imperial diet (in German, the Reichstag), where laws were discussed and edicts promulgated. The sheer size of the empire made it very difficult for an emperor or any centralized authority to control—a situation that the German princes were content to live with.

The sentiments expressed in these comments by a sixteenth-century French writer typify the self-confidence felt by many in the Holy Roman Empire:

Now just as the Tartars, Turks, Mamelukes, and Persians have by their valor drawn to the East the glory of arms, so we here in the West have in the last two hundred years recovered the excellence of good letters and brought back the study of the disciplines after they had long remained as if extinguished. The sustained industry of many learned men has led to such success that today this our age can be compared to the most learned times that ever were.... The invention [of printing] has greatly aided the advancement of all disciplines....The invention is attributed to the Germans and began in Mainz; it was then employed in Venice and subsequently spread over all Latin Christendom, brought to its perfection by Nicholas Jenson, Aldus, the Giunti, Froben, Badius, Robert Estienne, and others.

Louis Le Roy, *On the Vicissitudes and Variety of Things in the Universe*

Imperial Institutions and Royal Dynasties

During the late medieval period, the Holy Roman Empire was dominated by three main dynasties: the Luxemburgs, the Wittelsbachs, and the Hapsburgs. Throughout the early modern period, a powerful family base was the decisive prerequisite for strong rule. The Luxemburgs and Hapsburgs had the distinct advantage of having access to eastern central Europe; the Hapsburgs acquired the Austrian lands, while the Luxemburgs gained control of the Bohemian lands.

The golden age of the Luxemburg dynasty came with the reign of Charles IV, which lasted from 1347 to 1378. Charles IV helped to reform imperial institutions and laws. He refined the German constitution and in 1356 established the Golden Bull, which focused on the rights and status of the German princes and especially the electors, whom Charles IV wanted to limit in number to seven. These constitutional changes were reflected in the final evolution of the empire's title. Its official designation, Holy Roman Empire of the German Nation, indicated that the emperor's powers were limited to German lands. Above all, Charles sought not only to make the administration of the empire more efficient but also to exclude his dynastic rivals (the Hapsburgs and the Wittelsbachs) from the electoral body.

The principal reason for the success of the Luxemburgs, the Bohemian lands, became their nemesis. After Emperor Sigismund (reigned 1410–1437) abrogated the safe-conduct he had extended to the Bohemians Jan Hus (1369–1415) and Jerome of Prague (1370–1416) and agreed to their execution for holding heretical

beliefs, a devastating civil war broke out in Bohemia in the late 1410s. The so-called Hussite wars prevented Bohemia, as well as the Luxemburgs, from becoming the major force within the empire. The demise of the Luxemburgs paralleled the growing influence of the Hapsburgs. The threat posed by the Wittelsbachs was eventually negated during the course of the Landshut War (1503–1505), in which an internecine Wittelsbach quarrel culminated in the family's downfall.

▲ *Charles IV (pictured here praying) was the most prominent representative of the Luxemburg dynasty. It was common for members of aristocratic and imperial dynasties to commission works of religious art, such as this anonymous altarpiece, to reinforce the close link between religion and politics.*

THE REFORMS OF MAXIMILIAN I

Before becoming emperor in 1493, Maximilian Hapsburg was already an important political force in the Holy Roman Empire. In February 1468 he was elected king of the Romans, and in 1477 his marriage to Mary of Burgundy brought him significant new lands. The wealth of Burgundy, one of the leading states in western Europe, far exceeded any riches that the Hapsburgs had been able to muster until that point.

Maximilian acceded to the throne in 1493. His power was reinforced by the continued existence of the Swabian League, an association of imperial cities motivated principally by their shared mistrust of the westward expansion of the Wittelsbachs. The early years of Maximilian's reign were dominated by attempts at imperial reform and by his determination to counter the invasion of Italy by King Charles VIII of France (reigned 1483–1498). Maximilian's demands for money for this project provoked debate about the empire's constitution. In order to finance the Italian campaign, the diet authorized the first general direct head and property tax, known as the Common Penny.

The elector of Mainz, Berthold of Henneberg, sponsored the most important projects of imperial reform in 1495. Berthold's reforms resulted in the establishment of the governing council (Reichsregiment) at the Diet of Augsburg in 1500. The council was initially to consist of the seven imperial electors and thirteen others appointed by the German princes. Yet the emergence of this institution presented an increasing threat to imperial power, and Maximilian undermined the council's authority by announcing that he would not accept any of its decisions in his own territories. The emperor was helped in his attempts to limit the power of the council by the fact that the growth of royal government outweighed the divergent multiplicity of princely interests.

The system of imperial circles (Reichskreise) was also established as a result of imperial reforms in the early 1500s. The circles were regional alliances established for the purpose of maintaining peace and security. By 1512 there were ten circles: Austrian, Burgundian, Electoral Rhenish, Franconian, Bavarian, Swabian, Upper Rhenish, Lower Rhenish-Westphalian, Upper Saxon, and Lower Saxon. Bohemia, Moravia, and Silesia were not represented by this system, though they did remain part of the empire. The circles became useful agencies for collecting taxes, for recruiting troops, and for nominating judges to the imperial court.

Although Maximilian was responsible for significant measures of imperial reform, his most significant contribution lay in tightening the link between the Hapsburg dynasty and the imperial throne. He sponsored Conradus Celtis (1459–1508), whose writings linked the house of Hapsburg to the rulers of ancient Rome, and he financed the propagandist work of such noted artists as Albrecht Dürer (1471–1528) and Bernhard Strigel (1460–1528).

▶ Maximilian I was extremely successful in promoting the Hapsburg dynasty's fortunes and reputation. A strong advocate of humanism, he provided patronage for many of the period's leading scholars (including Conradus Celtis) and artists (among them, Albrecht Dürer and Bernhard Strigel, who painted this image).

Eurus
Ionis
Colen ʒ

Sophiam me Greci vocant Latini Sapienciam
Egipcn & Chaldei me muenere Grecis cripsere
Latini tium fulere Germani ampliauere :—

Zephir?
Aer.
Sanguine?

PHILO   SOPHIA

QVI MALEDICT PRINCPI SVO MORTE MORIATVR · EX · XXI

Quicquid habet Coelum quid Terra quid Aer & aequor
Quicquid in humanis rebus & esse potest
Et deus in toto quicquid facit igneus orbe
Philosophia meo pectore cuncta gero :—

36   37

Although the Hapsburgs came to dominate the imperial title, the office continued to be elective. The thirteenth-century insistence on seven electors persisted throughout the early modern period. Because the emperor received his crown through election rather than inheritance, rival candidates resorted to bribery to win the post. It was common for a would-be emperor to make concessions—that is, to agree to make certain political decisions in the event that he was elected. These electoral agreements became part of imperial law and tradition. The power of the electoral vote forced emperors to operate within narrow political constraints. Furthermore, the emperor ruled only with the consent of the imperial diet—in the words of the historian William Maltby, "a representative assembly whose sheer size and diversity of interests made agreement almost impossible." In the 1490s Maximilian I had gained the approval of an imperial court to resolve disputes between states, but the fact that the majority of judges were to be named by the diet and not the emperor is illustrative of the limits of imperial authority.

Northern Renaissance

The Holy Roman Empire became one of the leading centers of the Renaissance in northern Europe. The northern Renaissance, in common with the Renaissance in Italy, was dominated by a revival of scholarly interest in the art, architecture, literature, philosophy, and society of classical Greece and Rome. One important religious dimension of the Renaissance was Christian humanism, a movement that sought to apply the new understanding of classical languages to biblical scholarship in order to return Christianity to its essence and its origins. In addition to retranslating and reinterpreting the Bible, Christian humanists extended their interests to broader

▲ *These woodcuts by Albrecht Dürer (1471–1528), the foremost German artist of the Renaissance, accompany Conradus Celtis's 1502 work* Quattuor libri amorum (Four Books of Love). *On the left is a depiction of Maximilian I. On the right, the enthroned figure of Philosophy is surrounded by four medallions that symbolize the cultural achievements of Egypt, Greece, Rome, and Germany. The engraving expresses Celtis's view that the Germany of his time was the heir to those great ancient civilizations.*

conceptions of reform with a view to ridding the church of clerical abuses within the ecclesiastical hierarchy as well as eradicating monastic corruption.

The Dutch humanist Desiderius Erasmus (c. 1466–1536), the leading figure of the northern Renaissance within the Holy Roman Empire, was a prolific author and a renowned biblical scholar as well as an outspoken critic of what he perceived to be church abuses. During the early years of the Reformation, there were significant points of agreement between Erasmus and the leading Reformer, the German Martin Luther (1483–1546), especially in their emphasis on the Bible as the primary source of knowledge of God and their outspokenness against institutional corruption in the church. Yet Erasmus was essentially a reformer of the church from within, not a radical. Reluctant to disrupt the unity of the church, he ultimately broke with Luther in a public theological dispute over the issue of free will.

A further characteristic of the northern Renaissance is reflected in the works of the humanist Ulrich von Hutten (1488–1523), whose writings, in common with those of his predecessor Conradus Celtis (1459–1508), have a patriotic German tone. In a period well before German unification, Hutten gave powerful voice to those aspiring to "Germanness." Though a difficult concept to penetrate, Hutten's Germanness is characterized by the anti-Roman slant of his writings, particularly his nationalistic resentment of a foreign pope whose authority was transmitted through members of the higher echelons of the church. Opposition to the ecclesiastical hierarchy was accentuated when the higher clergy's political authority and influence exceeded its spiritual role. In short, the northern Renaissance within the empire was a varied movement with both secular and religious agendas and was principally promoted and advocated by the intellectual elites.

Reformation in the Holy Roman Empire

The intricacies of Luther's theological agenda were simplified and transmitted to the masses in printed and illustrated pamphlets and by Lutheran preachers. The Lutheran message was accepted in a considerable number of regions and localities, especially in the cities, and Luther also received princely patronage.

Cities were particularly receptive to the Reformation message. Since a larger proportion of the urban population was literate (between 10 and 30 percent, in comparison with an average

▶ Given the intricacies of Luther's mature theological program, it was essential for him and his followers to simplify his message for popular consumption. This woodcut of around 1520, which contrasts Roman Catholic and Lutheran doctrines, is typical of the highly effective ways in which Lutherans presented their teachings.

across the empire of 5 percent), Lutherans in the cities were able to take particular advantage of the printing press. The Reformers gained support in schools—and in some cases universities—and were highly skilled at making their own views heard and shaping public opinion. Well-educated German humanists offered a stern resistance to Rome and encouraged a qualified opposition to clerical abuses, particularly the sale of indulgences. (An indulgence was a means of commuting the punishment due to a penitent sinner, during life or in purgatory, by paying a sum of money to the church.) Luther's followers were able to harness the anticlerical feeling that was already well established in the cities.

Reform also flourished in cities located along trade routes, where the Lutheran message was transmitted via the merchant classes. Although different social classes were drawn to the Reformation message, the bulk of support came from the artisanal classes. Particularly receptive to Lutheranism were imperial cities, the towns with no immediate overlord other than the emperor

▲ This portrait of Martin Luther was painted by Lucas Cranach the Elder (1472–1552), who was court painter to Frederick the Wise of Saxony from 1505 to 1550. Celebrated as the originator of Protestant painting, Cranach painted numerous portraits of his friend Luther, as well as pictures of other Reformers and Reform-related subjects.

IMPERIAL POWER AND THE EARLY REFORMATION

With the death of Maximilian in 1519, his grandson Charles (who was already king of Spain) was elected as Charles V. Charles's election had hinged largely on the vote of Frederick the Wise of Saxony, the most powerful of the seven electors. This circumstance explains why Charles was not more determined in his actions against Luther—Luther resided in electoral Saxony, Frederick's territory. For Luther, Frederick's protection was vital; it ensured that Luther was not suppressed in the aftermath of the controversy provoked by the issuing of the Ninety-five Theses in 1517. Luther's theses laid the foundations for a more radical theological program; the Augsburg (1518) and Leipzig (1519) disputations that followed sought to control and silence Luther and led to an increasing separation between Luther and his opponents.

Following Luther's official excommunication from the church in 1520, Frederick's protection of Luther prevented Charles from immediately dispatching the Reformer to Rome. The same protection guaranteed Luther a genuine and effective safe-conduct to the Diet of Worms in 1521 (the Bohemian reformer Jan Hus had not enjoyed the same good fortune). Immediately following the Diet of Worms, Luther was placed under an imperial ban. For his own safety Luther was kidnapped on Frederick's orders and taken to Wartburg Castle. Although Charles V was increasingly convinced that Luther had fundamentally betrayed the church, he opted not to intervene.

Charles was relatively powerless against Luther because he did not have full political control of the Holy Roman Empire. Without a proper standing army, he was utterly dependent on the princes for their financial and military support, not only for the administration of the empire but also (what was more important) for its protection against foreign invaders, notably the Turks. Charles's inability to enforce the Edict of Worms was a result of his lack of political control as well as of his personal absence from Germany during the 1520s. At the Diet of Nuremberg (1524), for example, the princes declared that they were willing to enforce the Edict of Worms but only to the extent that it did not provoke rebellion, disobedience, and murder. In this way, the representatives of the diet succeeded in pacifying the emperor by accepting his demands while reserving the right to ignore them.

The opening page of the Gospel of Saint Matthew from Luther's 1530 Bible. Luther's translation of the Bible was central to the identity of the Lutheran movement. The text itself represented the authority upon which Lutheranism was based. The first edition of Luther's complete translation of the Old and New Testaments was published in 1534.

just as keenly as urban communities did. Yet Reformers also encountered considerable obstacles as they tried to spread their message in the countryside, particularly the high levels of illiteracy and the shortage of Protestant clergy and preachers. Furthermore, Catholic rituals were deeply entrenched within rural communities—the sacraments had social and cultural dimensions in addition to their liturgical significance. In the countryside theological questions mattered little. These circumstances explain in large part why the Protestant Reformation was such a divisive force within rural regions. Nevertheless, profound dissatisfaction among the peasantry with the religious status quo, together with a number of socioeconomic grievances, erupted in the peasant rebellions that destabilized the Holy Roman Empire in the mid-1520s.

The suppression of the peasant rebellions by a coalition of princes was backed by Luther, who repudiated the violence of the insurrection and sought to distance himself as far as possible from the uprising. The princes' success served to increase their political self-awareness and self-confidence. They became less willing to compromise as the religious crisis intensified in the subsequent decades of the Reformation. Throughout the 1520s they became more active in preventing the enforcement of the Edict of Worms, which called for the arrest of Luther and the outlawing of his writings. Princely support for Reform took on a military dimension—in addition to a political and diplomatic one—with the creation of the League of Torgau in 1526. By 1529 the evangelical movement was sufficiently entrenched to risk a calculated act of defiance—the Protestation, a document signed by six princes and fourteen imperial cities that openly challenged the emperor's authority. These developments prepared the way for the establishment of the Schmalkaldic League, a formal military alliance of Protestant princes. This league of princes eventually secured the survival of Protestantism against the troops of Emperor Charles V, who sought to put down Luther's movement by force in the late 1540s and early 1550s and almost achieved this goal with victory over the Schmalkaldic League at the Battle of Mühlberg in 1547.

that were concentrated primarily in the southwestern corner of Germany. Pressure groups within town councils could play a major role in promoting the Reformation, as was the case in Nuremberg. Trade guilds could also leave a lasting imprint on the course of religious reform—in Basel, more than twelve guilds placed pressure on the town council to adopt Lutheranism.

The spread of Reform in the countryside ensured that Lutheranism became a mass movement. Local village leaders saw the Reformation as an opportunity to establish greater control over their parish church. They especially embraced the anticlerical tone of Luther's message, since rural communities felt the absence of the kind of pastoral care they wanted

DYNASTIC RIVALRY AND THE TURKISH THREAT

Even after he inherited a massive empire upon his election in 1519, Charles V continued to increase his possessions. Charles's accumulation of vast lands inevitably threatened his neighbors, a factor that would lead him into decades of military conflict. Charles was particularly suited to warfare; he saw himself as the archetypal Renaissance monarch, a warrior king for whom status and honor were paramount. Moreover, his advisers, most notably Chancellor Gattinara (1465–1530), promoted the concept of universal monarchy, according to which Charles was expected to seek peace and stability within the empire in order to gather and unite Catholic forces everywhere in a campaign to defeat the Protestant and Turkish threats.

The warmongering style of Charles V's rule was encouraged by the long-standing rivalry between the Hapsburgs and the Valois, then the ruling family of France. These tensions were further exacerbated by the fact that the French king, Francis I, had been a contender for the imperial throne. The dynastic conflict was intensified when Charles and Francis vied to gain ascendancy over the Italian peninsula, both no doubt attracted by the wealth and power of the Italian city-states. Despite Francis I's recapture of Milan (which had been lost by his predecessor, Louis XII) in the early 1520s, he could not prevent Charles V from winning a decisive victory at the Battle of Pavia (in which Francis himself was captured) in 1525. Francis was forced to abandon all claims in Italy and the Netherlands in exchange for his freedom. On his return to France, the French king renounced his promises; these recurrent territorial disputes continued between Charles V and the Valois dynasty for decades. Although Charles gained some control over the Italian peninsula, this war was fought at considerable expense.

The Hapsburgs were also threatened by the Turks, who, during the early sixteenth century, continued to expand under the sultans Selim I (reigned 1512–1520), who added Egypt, Syria, and southwestern Anatolia, and Süleyman I "the Magnificent" (reigned 1520–1566), who added Bohemia and Hungary. Charles V was naturally opposed to the Turks on religious grounds, and his opposition was reinforced by the Turkish invasion of Hungary, which brought the Turks within striking distance of the empire. The reality of the Turkish threat was highlighted in 1529, when Süleyman besieged Vienna with 100,000 troops. Although they gradually withdrew, the Turks secured central Hungary in the truce of 1547 and established Transylvania as a nominally independent state under Turkish rule; in exchange they acknowledged Ferdinand's control of western Hungary (for which privilege Ferdinand paid an annual tribute).

◀ The Truce of Nice between Francis I and Charles V, negotiated by Pope Paul III in 1538, forms the subject of this fresco. Charles's reign was plagued by a succession of Hapsburg-Valois wars, particularly in the Italian lands. In practice, truces amounted to little more than brief respites from fighting during which each side reorganized and realigned its troops.

▲ *Charles V came to believe that Lutheranism could be eradicated only by force. The brief victory that he secured at the Battle of Mühlberg in 1547 (the subject of this painting by Titian) was short lived, as the Protestant forces reorganized themselves and secured French support.*

Religious Polarity: Coexistence and Conflict, 1555–1648

In 1555 Charles V and the German princes negotiated the Peace of Augsburg, which established a permanent legal basis for the existence of Lutheranism in the Holy Roman Empire. Although opposition to the Peace of Augsburg existed, it hardly amounted to a serious threat to the emperor, at least initially. In contrast with France and the Dutch provinces, where religious conflict sparked violent civil wars, the Holy Roman Empire enjoyed a period of relative peace from 1555 to 1618. Ferdinand I, who succeeded his brother, Charles, as emperor in 1556, pursued two seemingly contradictory religious policies. On the one hand, he tried to reconcile Lutheranism with Catholicism and was willing to urge Catholics to accept clerical marriage and communion for the laity under both forms (bread and wine); on the other hand, he encouraged the Jesuits to set the Counter-Reformation

in motion in his domains. In political terms, central to Ferdinand's dynastic aims was the city of Vienna, a vantage point from which he could monitor the empire's eastern frontier.

Before his death Ferdinand divided the Hapsburg territories among his three sons, Maximilian, Charles, and Ferdinand, and tried to ensure the succession of the eldest, Maximilian. However, the headship of the house of Hapsburg went not to Maximilian (who reigned as emperor from 1564 to 1576), but to Ferdinand's nephew, Philip II of Spain.

Maximilian II became even more tolerant of Protestantism than his father had been—chiefly, perhaps, because toleration was the only means of avoiding the destruction of the empire. Maximilian's tolerant attitude was also reflected in the horror with which he reacted to the brutal suppression of the Dutch Calvinists by the duke of Alba in the 1560s and 1570s and to the Saint Bartholomew's Day Massacre of Huguenots (Calvinists) in France in 1572. Both sides of the religious divide mourned Maximilian's death, principally because he had succeeded in maintaining peace. His legacy was continued, albeit in a different way, by his son Rudolf.

Through imperial propaganda campaigns, Maximilian II called for internal unity under Hapsburg leadership in the face of external (especially Turkish) threats. At this stage there was no substantial opposition to imperial authority, partly because there was no recognized leader among the princes; now that Lutheranism had been granted official recognition everywhere, electoral Saxony no longer played the authoritative role it had played in the past. Despite the relative security of imperial power, the empire became deeply unstable following the accession of Rudolf II (reigned 1576–1611). Rudolf's lack of real interest in or grasp of politics allowed the empire to proceed toward confessionalization (the process by which Protestant and Catholic authorities alike delineated their orthodoxy in specific theological terms and by which each strove for uniform adherence to all aspects of that orthodoxy among their believers). Thus, religious polarity, the foundations for which had been laid in 1555, now took on a political dimension.

Ferdinand I   1503–1564

Ferdinand rose to prominence when he became ruler of the Austrian hereditary lands under the treaties concluded at Cologne, Worms, and Brussels in the early 1520s. In 1522 he married Anne, sister of King Louis II of Hungary, and following Louis's death in 1526, Ferdinand was elected king of Bohemia and Hungary (though with Turkish domination of eastern Europe, he never had full control of those territories). In 1531 Ferdinand was elected king of the Romans, and on the abdication of his brother, Charles V, in 1556, he was appointed Holy Roman emperor. From the outset Ferdinand differed from Charles in that he was more compromising and had little affection for the Spanish branch of the Hapsburgs.

Although a devout Catholic, Ferdinand was reluctant to resort to force in his dealings with Protestantism. The fact that he was more pragmatic than Charles V can be attributed to the proximity of Ferdinand's hereditary lands to both the heartland of the Reformation and the Turks. Within Bohemia and Hungary, Ferdinand had little choice but to accept the growth of Protestantism, especially in Bohemia, which had already been deeply influenced by Hussitism (the reform movement led by Jan Hus). After 1526 religious life in the Bohemian lands was characterized by a diversity of religious practice. By 1550 the Hungarians had largely abandoned the Catholic Church. Even in Austria and in the hereditary lands, the Reformation made progress, though the Peace of Augsburg (1555) gave Ferdinand a considerable advantage. Following the principle embodied in the Latin phrase *cuius regio eius religio,* the religion of the people was that of their ruling prince, and so Ferdinand regained some control of the hereditary lands. Still, only Carinthia remained overwhelmingly Catholic, while Styria and Upper Austria became largely Lutheran.

Ferdinand's central concern, one that largely explains his pragmatism in religious matters, was the protection of the eastern part of the Holy Roman Empire in the face of Turkish aggression. In 1529, at the end of the first decade of the Lutheran Reformation, the Turks were besieging Vienna. From that moment on, if not before, eradicating the Turkish threat became Ferdinand's primary objective. As the historian Jean Bérenger has written, for the next two centuries, "the geo-strategic role of the capital changed radically: previously the crossroads of the Austrian monarchy's communications and commerce, Vienna was now a frontier post." The Austro-Turkish conflict, which came to a conclusion in 1568 with the Peace of Adrianopolis, thus remained a massive political, economic, and psychological burden on Ferdinand, as it did on his successor, Maximilian II (reigned 1564–1576).

◄ *Though a devout Catholic, Ferdinand I—at age twenty-one the subject of this painting by Hans Maler—was pragmatic in religious affairs. Rather than be allowed to devote himself to the total suppression of Lutheranism, Ferdinand was forced to compromise with the Protestant princes in order to protect his territorial interests, the hereditary Hapsburg lands in Austria.*

THONAV FLVS.

INSEL
S. ANDRE.

Pest. G. Die Ober Vorstatt.
Ofen. H. Das Zolhaus.
Hauptstatt I. Warme Bäder.
Vorstatt K. S. Gerhardis perg.
er Judenstat L. Die Schiffprucken.
Vorstatt M. Der Christen Leger.

E CONTERFACTVR DER STADT OFEN VND PEST WIE ES VON DEN CHRISTEN BELEGERT WORD:

▲ *A 1602 illustration of Buda and Pest—the chief Hungarian cities, then under Ottoman control—besieged by the forces of the Holy Roman Empire. In 1526 the death of Louis II, of the Hungarian Jagiellon dynasty, at the Battle of Mohács opened the door to Hapsburg supremacy in eastern Europe. Although the Hapsburgs were regularly elected to the Bohemian and Hungarian thrones, in practice the Turks dominated the region and would continue to do so until their failure to capture Vienna in 1683.*

There were also tensions between different Protestant groups, especially the Lutherans and Calvinists. The latter, who had been excluded from the provisions of the Peace of Augsburg, gradually gained greater confidence and won political support. By the 1580s there was a Catholic willingness to concede that Protestants predominated in northern Germany, but religious coexistence in such areas as Cologne and Strasbourg was a far more controversial issue. Owing to religious differences, Rudolf found it difficult to gain the support of the princes for his war against the Turks; this lack of support partly explains why the war ended in a stalemate. In fact, the Palatinate, which had by now converted to Calvinism under John Casimir (reigned 1576–1592), had organized active opposition to the taxes levied for the Turkish campaign. Furthermore, Maximilian I, duke of Bavaria (reigned 1597–1651), sought to establish a major Catholic stronghold in southern Germany and even had imperial pretensions.

The formation of religious leagues in the first two decades of the seventeenth century essentially laid the foundations for the Thirty Years War (1618–1648). Internally, the empire was further undermined by economic stagnation, a situation that provoked a series of peasant rebellions between the 1580s and 1620s. Externally, foreign powers (notably France and Spain)

Rudolf II   1551–1612

Rudolf II was the only Hapsburg to make Prague the capital of the Holy Roman Empire, an act that transformed the city into a major cultural center. Rudolf, well-educated and a competent linguist, took an interest in imperial government only until 1600. During this period he ruled with relative competence and referred regularly to the advice of Bohemian Catholic nobles. Yet after 1600 Rudolf refused to discuss policy with any degree of thoroughness. To make matters worse, he delegated authority to Wenzel Eusebius von Lobkowitz, the president of the privy council, who appointed a succession of intransigent Catholics to the council. All in all, the imperial diet met only five times during Rudolf's reign.

Rudolf was also faced with the reemergence of the Turkish threat. Following relative peace on the eastern frontier from 1568 to 1593, the so-called Fifteen Years War (1593–1608) broke out between the Ottoman and Holy Roman empires. Although imperial troops outnumbered the Turkish army, neither side made advances during the conflict, which was fought mainly in Hungary. Imperial authority was further undermined by a rebellion, led by the Hungarian István Bocskay in the early 1600s, that was motivated principally by the fact that Turkish occupiers seemed to be more willing than the Hapsburgs to respect the privileges and religious liberties of the Hungarian estates.

The Hapsburg anxiety to eradicate Protestantism was epitomized by Archduke Matthias, Rudolf II's brother, who hoped that reconquest of Protestant lands would prepare the way for a thorough Counter-Reformation. Despite these intentions, Matthias was sufficiently pragmatic to accede to the Hungarians' religious demands; under the treaties of Vienna and Zsitva-Torok, signed by both sides, the Lutheran and Calvinist confessions gained official recognition.

In spite of Rudolf's apparent political ineptitude, he became known for his patronage of the arts and sciences. In addition to collecting art, Rudolf invited a significant number of talented artists and intellectuals to his court, most famously the Italian painter Giuseppe Arcimboldo (1537–1593) and the Flemish painter Bartholomeus Spranger (1546–1611). The court became an influential locus for scientific research and discovery; among its most illustrious guests were the astronomer Tycho Brahe (1546–1601), a Danish exile, and his successor Johannes Kepler (1571–1630), the German astronomer and mathematician.

Rudolf's political incompetence nevertheless convinced his brother, Matthias, that Rudolf was no longer capable of ruling the empire. Matthias summoned the imperial diet at Pressburg and, without consulting the emperor, had himself elected king of Hungary. As his powers were increasingly questioned, Rudolf withdrew from public life and enclosed himself in his Prague castle. The clear disunity within the imperial family strengthened the Bohemian and Hungarian estates, a crucial development given that Rudolf had changed the geographical focus of the empire by placing Prague at its center.

◀ Rudolf II, the subject of this portrait by Hans von Aachen, strikes many as the most intriguing of all the Hapsburg rulers. Having moved the court from Vienna to Prague, Rudolf attracted to it some of the most talented artists and scientists of his age.

The theories espoused by the great Italian painter Leonardo da Vinci (1452–1519), who traveled to northern Europe, certainly resonated with artists working within the Holy Roman Empire:

If you scorn painting, which is the sole imitator of all the manifest works of nature, you will certainly be scorning a subtle invention, which with philosophical and subtle speculation considers all manner of forms: sea, land, trees, animals, grasses, flowers, all of which are enveloped in light and shade. Truly this is science, the legitimate daughter of nature, because painting is born of that nature; but to be more correct, we should say the granddaughter of nature, because all visible things have been brought forth by nature and it is among these that painting is born. Therefore we may justly speak of it as the granddaughter of nature and as the kin of God.

Leonardo da Vinci, *Notebooks*

▼ *The full title of this work by Peter Paul Rubens is* The Meeting of Ferdinand II and His Son the Cardinal Infante Ferdinand before the Battle of Nordlingen in 1634. *Rubens, one of the most prolific artists of the seventeenth century, played an important role in the promotion of the Catholic cause. Ferdinand's commitment to Catholicism is illustrative of the complex interweaving of political and religious divisions that lay behind the Thirty Years War.*

became involved in imperial affairs owing to the the Jülich-Cleves succession crisis (a contested succession in the duchy of Jülich-Cleves between Protestant and Catholic claimants). Rudolf's weakness and that of his successors Matthias (reigned 1612–1619) and Ferdinand II (reigned 1619–1637) had allowed the German princes to develop their own power bases, which would provide them with sufficient strength to wage a devastating war. The Thirty Years War plunged the empire into considerable socioeconomic and political instability and halted the movement toward German unification for centuries.

FURTHER READING

Bérenger, Jean. *A History of the Habsburg Empire.* Translated by C. A. Simpson. New York, 1994.

Dixon, C. Scott. *The Reformation in Germany.* Malden, MA, 2002.

Greengrass, Mark. *The Longman Companion to the European Reformation, c. 1500–1618.* New York, 1998.

Hughes, Michael. *Early Modern Germany, 1477–1806.* Philadelphia, 1992.

MacCulloch, Diarmaid. *Reformation: Europe's House Divided, 1490–1700.* New York, 2003.

Maltby, William S. *The Reign of Charles V.* New York, 2002.

Pettegree, Andrew, ed. *The Reformation World.* New York, 2002.

Wheatcroft, Andrew. *The Habsburgs: Embodying Empire.* New York, 1995.

Max von Habsburg

Households

DURING THE RENAISSANCE THE HOUSEHOLD WAS A FUNDAMENTAL SOCIAL AND POLITICAL UNIT FOR ALL CITIZENS, FROM THE WEALTHY NOBLE TO THE HUMBLE PEASANT.

The household was socially and politically significant in a variety of ways during the Renaissance and Reformation. For the peasant or servant, the size of the household was primarily an economic consideration, while for wealthy families the size, reputation, and honor of the household was a key determiner of social status. During the Renaissance the household was a center for many aspects of life, religious as well as secular, ceremonial as well as quotidian. Although there were distinct differences between the household of the common citizen and that of the wealthy noble, fundamental aspects of basic household structure and function were common to households of all sizes and degrees of prosperity.

Varieties of Households

The number of inhabitants within a Renaissance household varied enormously and depended principally on the wealth of the household. The

▼ This group portrait by Isaac Luttichuys (1616–1673) is said to show the well-to-do Kuysten family.

peasant sustenance farmer would commonly live with a small nuclear family. Wealthier peasant households would sometimes have a servant or two. If the means were available, a male heir might remain in his family home after marriage in order to inherit the property rights. In some households this chain extended down several generations. Furthermore, with a little more wealth, multiple sons could remain in a household after marriage to share in the fruit of the household's labors. For the very wealthy, including lords and nobles, the number of inhabitants in a single household could be extremely large. The family home might hold a large immediate family together with an abundance of servants, kinsmen, orphaned relatives, and other people connected to the family.

In general, three main types of households can be identified. Most common during the Renaissance was the nuclear family, a household that contained a husband and wife, their offspring, and at most a few servants.

The second form of household was the stem-family household. The stem family was similar to the nuclear family but allowed for heirs of inheritance to remain in the household after marriage. Thus, if a family had two sons, the first would be allowed to remain in his home after marriage to await his inheritance. If the heir-in-waiting had a son who reached marrying age before his father had inherited the household, he too was allowed to remain in the house with his wife and children. The stem-family household was strictly heir based, however, and the opportunity to remain in the house was not open to family members other than heirs.

The largest type of household would contain an extended family together with any number of kinsmen and nonrelatives. Parents, children, grandchildren, aunts, uncles, and cousins would at times reside together, along with a multitude of servants, possibly lodgers renting rooms, and distant relatives who had fallen on hard times. While poorer families occasionally lived in extended-family homes, in general a large household was a mark of wealth and power. Poorer families could simply not afford the expense of

▲ Antoine Le Nain
(c. 1588–1648) and his brothers
Louis (1593–1648) and
Matthieu (1607–1677) are
known for producing collectively
such realistic depictions of French
peasant life as this image of a
poor rural family.

housing an extended family under one roof. For the nobility and the social elite, however, there were many advantages to be found in a large household. A good family name and reputation, essential to powerful members of society during the Renaissance, could be provided by a large, well-run household.

Life in the Household

In spite of industrial advances, the life of most Renaissance households revolved around agricultural pursuits. A more modest household, headed by a peasant farmer, might manage only a small tract of land and provide its landlord with payment in the form of a percentage of the crop yield. Husband, wife, child, and servants were expected to help with the farming.

The lords and masters of manors, those who received a proportion of the produce of the land that was worked by their tenant farmers, kept high-ranking servants called household officers. These officers presided over judicial matters in the lands and managed the manors. Larger manors entailed more power and responsibility and a larger household. Power was delegated hierarchically among the various members of a manorial household.

The manufacturing of goods during the Renaissance was likewise centered on the household. For the tradesman a front room made an adequate shop, and apprentices often became members of his household. Work and sales were completed within the home. Thus, for the manufacturer as for the farmer, daily household life centered around work.

Members of a Renaissance household had various responsibilities, in addition to their regular work. It was generally the wife's job to manage the home by making sure that meals were prepared and linens were washed. In a small home the wife would do this job herself, and in a larger home she would manage servants who carried out the domestic tasks. Child care also fell under the umbrella of the wife's responsibilities. In general, children were taught skills in the home that would later benefit the business of the household. The youngest servants and any apprentices were included among the children of the household and educated accordingly.

Religious training was also part of normal household life for Catholic and, after the Reformation, Protestant households alike. For smaller households religious training was often part of the general education. That is, servants and family members would see to the religious education of minors in the household. It was not uncommon for larger manors to maintain a personal chapel and chaplain who would see to the family's spiritual needs, as well as to the general religious training of the household's younger members. A chapel was also a key means by which a noble family could project an image of wealth, stability, and respectability.

The great households of the period, those that managed large tracts of land and encompassed subordinate households, were invested with limited judicial powers. The resolution of legal matters within the confines of a particular manor were very often left to the discretion of the lord of the managing household or his designee. Thus, many large households had a household manager who was given specific judicial responsibilities.

Political power was invested in the great households of lords and nobles; it was common for the very wealthy to entertain important guests. Since wealth was a source of social and political influence, wealthy households made little effort to conceal their prosperity, of which a large household was one of the more obvious indicators.

▲ The Villa Rotonda, in Vicenza, in northeastern Italy, was designed by Andrea Palladio, who started building it in 1550. Construction was completed by Vincenzo Scamozzi.

Keeping more servants than a household needed was often considered good household policy (finances permitting), as doing so served to reinforce the image of wealth and stability many families sought to project. Servants tended to the needs both of the house itself and of any guests and took care of the land management. Nobles decorated the interior of their home with an eye toward impressing their frequent visitors. Often interior decoration was themed around the ancestry of the house's master (noble lineage was an extremely important indication of the family's power and prestige). The smaller household, on the other hand, was in general little more than a taxable unit that possessed negligible political power.

The Large, Wealthy Household

Many factors contributed to the large size of the wealthy household. Chief among them was the simple matter of wealth. A large household was clearly more expensive to maintain than a smaller one was. The ability to maintain a large household also conferred prestige, as doing so required sound managerial skills, financial acumen, and a great deal of money. Much of the authority held by a noble derived from a distinguished family line. A large, old family signified wealth that had been maintained across the generations. The easiest way to keep a family strong was to keep it large and unified.

Families displayed their wealth in any way possible. Lavish decoration, exquisite estates, expensive parties, the finest of fashions, and other outward extravagances were the norm for larger, wealthier households. Noble families were powerful, and alliances made them stronger. Thus, it was always important for a family to make a good impression upon those as rich as or richer than itself. Often marriages were designed to merge particular families for political or economic gain. A noble family was able to arrange the marriage of its young daughters with an eye to forging or renewing alliances with other influential and wealthy families. It was understood in the noble household that everyone benefited if the household benefited. For this reason, almost every decision was made to better the household and to strengthen its position.

Women in households were expected to maintain high standards of personal conduct and public morality. To behave otherwise was to besmirch the family's good name and, by extension, to weaken the entire household. In particular, a woman was expected to remain sexually chaste until marriage and to honor the sanctity of the marriage bed thereafter. Men, however, were not always held to the same standard of behavior.

According to the hierarchy of authority in the household, in general matters a woman was subservient to the master of the house, whether that

▶ *This unattributed oil painting of around 1580 depicts a ball held in honor of foreign visitors in the house of a wealthy Venetian family.*

master was her husband, her father, her brother, or another leading male figure. Whereas the major decisions of the household were left to the men, women were charged with the myriad of tasks involved in general inner household management from day to day.

The Household and Power

For a young man in Renaissance Europe, social opportunities were often associated with the family name. Powerful figures paid heed to the bloodlines of those with whom they associated. It was, accordingly, a tremendous advantage to come from a wealthy or noble family of good reputation. Conversely, a serious crime committed by a member of a noble familiy could prove fatal to that family's reputation. The threat of tarnishing the family name provided a strong incentive for proper conduct. In the case of a truly heinous or egregious crime, a family could lose certain legal privileges its status had gained it and be barred from winning them back for several generations.

It has been argued that family name was more important than personal qualities in Renaissance society. Family reputation was paramount and not only for those of noble heritage. In many cases rich mercantile families coveted a good reputation even more than noble families did, since newly rich families lacked the prestigious lineage that their aristocratic counterparts could boast.

Power was passed down within the great households from heir to heir. This system of inheritance was commonplace and was considered quite proper. As individuals acquired power, wealth, and privilege, it was expected that

they would use these considerable advantages for the benefit of the members of their household. Anybody who received a job in the court of a monarch, for example, exploited this position to provide family members with jobs involved in the running of the country and, if at all possible, with the accompanying privilege of inheritability. This practice was common and at times even encouraged.

▲ This 1443 fresco by Domenico di Bartolo depicts a marriage ceremony, an event of supreme importance in Renaissance society. While a good marriage could dramatically improve a family's fortunes, a bad one could ruin a household.

In a book published in 1526, the Dutch humanist scholar Desiderius Erasmus examined marriage from many viewpoints. The following excerpts comment somewhat humorously upon the role of a woman within the household:

A girl whose parents have taught her to manage a household has acquired a skill which is by no means to be disdained. She will never find any shortage of jobs to do in the home.

The female sex can sometimes give advice worthy of a man.

Many have found it profitable to follow their servants' advice … and so you should be all the more eager to accept your wife's.

Desiderius Erasmus, *The Institution of Marriage*

soluto matrimonio quemad modum eos vetatur

causa semper et ubiq; p cipua est. nam et publice

▲ This thirteenth-century French manuscript illustration depicts the official dissolution of a marriage by a bishop—an event that could have resulted only from one of the narrowly defined forms of marital breakdown.

Since noble families vied for power during the Renaissance, it was not uncommon for disputes, often serious ones, to arise between households. Long-standing feuds were by no means uncommon. A disagreement or dispute that began over a trivial matter between even two relatively insignificant members of their respective households could easily escalate into a full-blown feud in which all members of each household would be expected to participate zealously for the preservation of family honor as well as for the pursuit of some social advantage.

Law Pertaining to the Household

When a man and a woman, both from well-to-do families, married during the Renaissance period, the notion of two becoming one in marriage was more than just a biblical formula. Upon marriage the political and economic advantages pertaining to the bride's family affiliation generally devolved to her new husband. In addition, political and familial authority within

the household was almost completely the domain of the male. Divorce in the modern sense—legal dissolution of a marriage—was not allowed under Catholic law. There were some cases, however, in which a couple could be granted "divorce from table and bed."

In the case of divorce from table and bed, remarriage was not permitted. Divorce from table and bed was granted for six officially recognized reasons: consanguinity (that is, the spouses were too closely related), religious disbelief, entering holy orders, physical abuse, sexual impotence, and offenses of a sexual nature (including adultery).

It was also possible, however, to contest a divorce. One could do so on three grounds: equal guilt (that is, if the husband and wife were both guilty of the same indiscretion), condonation (whereby the resumption of sexual relations implied forgiveness on the part of one partner for the indiscretion of the other), and connivance (that is, if one partner had knowingly been the agent of the other's indiscretion). Ecclesiastical courts could grant an annulment, to all intents and purposes a complete dissolution of the marriage that left the divorced parties free to remarry. Annulments stated that, for a reason deemed acceptable by the courts, the original marriage was null and void. Allocations for divorce were more abundant in Protestant countries. It was commonplace, for instance, for adultery to be understood as grounds for a full divorce in Protestant regions.

The Reformers took varying views on divorce. The German Martin Luther (1483–1546), one of the figureheads of Reform, came to accept four grounds for divorce by the church: unfaithfulness, refusal of marital duties, sexual impotence, and desertion. Luther's compatriot and colleague Philipp Melanchthon (1497–1560) reduced the number of acceptable grounds to two—desertion and unfaithfulness. Most of the more radical Reformers agreed that divorce was acceptable on the grounds of adultery but were less certain about other grounds. The Frenchman John Calvin (1509–1564), another major figurehead of Reform, and his colleague Théodore de Bèze were more hesitant to allow divorce but came to the conclusion that

THE BARDI FAMILY

During the early part of the Renaissance period, the Florentine Bardi family of merchant bankers began establishing banks throughout the Italian city-states, as well as in other parts of Europe (notably in England, France, and Flanders). By the fourteenth century the Bardis had amassed such great wealth that they were considered the richest family in Florence. They increased their wealth greatly by lending money to rulers across Europe and by bargaining for monopolies in the trading of commodities (English wool, for instance).

When King Edward III of England, who had taken on a large loan from the Bardi family, defaulted on his obligations in 1345, the Bardis' bank failed. This disaster dealt the family's prospects a major—though not fatal—blow. In spite of this very significant reversal of family fortunes, the Bardis remained a major force within Florence and beyond for centuries to come.

Much later, toward the end of the sixteenth century, Giovanni Bardi (1534–1612) invited a group of musically talented friends (known as the Camerata) into his palazzo. During this and subsequent gatherings the Camerata experimented with musical instruments and developed methods of using instruments in combination with solo voices for theatrical ends. Out of these experiments developed *dramma per musica*, a form of art that, under the name opera, became a popular and important musical and dramatic medium.

it was acceptable on the grounds of unfaithfulness and separation due to religious differences. Other Reformers espoused more liberal views on divorce, including among the acceptable reasons for divorce such grounds as insanity, one partner being a threat to the life of the other, and eventually (though quite controversially) mutual consent. In response to this more relaxed attitude, in 1563 the Catholic Church wrote into its canon law that under no circumstances—not even on grounds of infidelity—could Christian marriage be ended by divorce.

▼ *This image of a castle feast accompanied by music and dancing is from the Bible of Borso d'Este, a lavish illuminated manuscript created between 1455 and 1461 by some of the leading Italian artists of the day.*

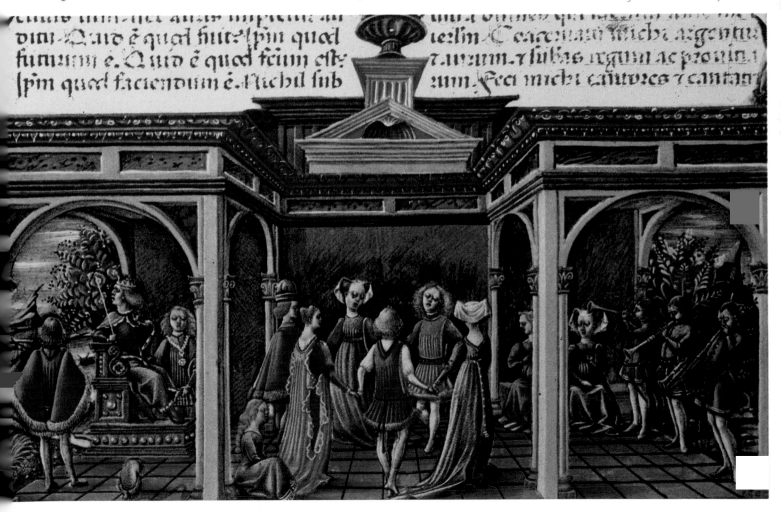

During the later part of the Renaissance, some interesting regional variations on divorce law emerged. Scotland, for example, permitted divorce on the grounds of desertion from 1573. For cases where adultery was invoked as grounds for divorce, remarriage was permitted; the adulterer was not, however, allowed to marry the person with whom he or she had committed the adulterous act that led to the divorce. In Denmark divorce was permitted if one of the spouses had committed incest, contracted leprosy, or fled justice. In the Netherlands divorce was permitted if one of the married partners was imprisoned for life.

Tax Laws Pertaining to the Household

Tax laws were related directly to the household. Instead of taxing individual citizens, it was standard practice to tax only the head of the household. The master of the house would work out the financial position of individual household members, but tax responsibility rested squarely on his shoulders.

Inheritance laws were of supreme importance to the larger households of the Renaissance. Inherited wealth constituted a huge portion of the money and land held by rich families. The Roman Catholic Church allowed for legal kinship to extend back four generations—in other words, third cousins were legally recognized as kin. Some secular laws allowed for consideration of kinship to extend even farther back, but usually it was determined more practically. Those members of the family who were known and seen occasionally were considered kinsmen. The more wealthy or powerful the household, the farther back kinship might be deemed to stretch. A distant extension of kinship was especially important for nobles, who kept careful records of their ancestry in order to demonstrate

► *The* Très riches heures du duc de Berry, *one of the finest examples of manuscript illumination, was created in the fifteenth century by the Limburg brothers. Ostensibly a prayer book and calendar, the manuscript is decorated with numerous images of the magnificent residences of Jean de France, the duke of Berry— including this image of a banquet, which adorns the page for the month of January.*

LUTHER ON EARTHLY DELIGHTS

Martin Luther wrote poignantly about the temptations of the flesh. Traditionally, priests, nuns, and monks were sworn to celibacy, an oath that Luther himself had taken as a young monk. Speaking of his own trials, he recalled sleeping on stones and torturing himself in order to fight his carnal desires, only to find those desires intensified.

Luther sympathized with young men caught up in lustful thoughts and pointed out that such thoughts resulted from natural forces. He commented that young love intoxicates and is not easily manageable. For this reason, he argued, one should not be too quick to judge harshly those who are not celibate. Even in the bond of marriage, Luther pointed out, it is difficult to remain chaste. Luther broke with Catholic teaching of the time to oppose the condemnation of sexual relations between man and wife when the goal of procreation was not the sole impetus.

Luther made his feelings on this subject clear in his correspondence with Philip of Hesse. Philip was married but unsatisfied with his wife. He desired another companion but would not keep a mistress. Luther delivered a list of Old Testament citations that seemed to justify bigamy, and so Philip took a second wife. Luther did, however, advise Philip to remain quiet about his second marriage. Luther's fellow Protestants were particularly outraged, as they considered Philip's act to be a crime and an abomination, directly contrary to the teachings of Scripture.

their descent from some great hero or lord. At times family genealogies were even falsified to provide a more favorable heritage.

The Household Model

Because the household was the fundamental unit of Renaissance society, its structure was replicated throughout various institutions. Good household management was a sign of nobility and strength. Thus, a monarchical court was expected to be run in a similar way to a well-managed household. In much the same way, schools, which originated in a schoolmaster's home, adopted a householdlike structure. As schools became larger and moved out of homes, they continued to follow the basic management model of a household. Monastic institutions were also managed and organized by the same standard.

Delegation of function within a hierarchy was a feudal concept that became part of daily life for the Renaissance citizen. This model of management worked well for Renaissance institutions because, among the larger families, it was well known and everyone was accustomed to it. Every noble child had been raised in a noble home and had accordingly been educated in proper household management. Each citizen was aware of what was expected within a household and how authority was distributed among the members of a household.

FURTHER READING

Barzun, Jacques. *From Dawn to Decadence: 500 Years of Western Cultural Life.* New York, 2000.

Campbell, Gordon. *The Oxford Dictionary of the Renaissance.* New York, 2003.

Rummel, Erika, ed. *Erasmus on Women.* Toronto, 1996.

Daniel Horace Fernald
Zachary C. Parmley

▲ *A 1640 portrait of a comfortable family living in Hamburg by a German artist known only as the Hamburg Master.*

SEE ALSO

• Agriculture • Banking • Education
• Erasmus, Desiderius • Feudalism • Manufacturing
• Music • Nobility and Rank • Women

Index

Illustration Credits

Éditions Usborne

Mon grand livre illustré
Les dinosaures

Laura Cowan

Illustrations : **Gianluca Foli**
Maquette : **Zoe Wray**
Expert-conseil : Darren Naish, université de Southampton

Pour l'édition française :
Traduction : Nathalie Chaput
Rédaction : Renée Chaspoul et Nick Stellmacher

Liens internet

Pour en savoir plus sur les dinosaures, va sur **www.usborne.com/quicklinks/fr** et
entre le titre de ce livre. N'oublie pas de lire « La sécurité sur Internet » sur le site
Quicklinks d'Usborne. Nous recommandons d'encadrer les enfants lorsqu'ils utilisent Internet.

Sommaire

*Chaque scène présente des dinosaures
qui vivaient à la même époque.*

Bonjour, les dinosaures !

Il y a des millions et des millions d'années, bien avant le premier homme, des formes de vie telles que tu n'en as jamais vues apparaissaient sur la Terre. Parmi elles, il y avait de « terribles lézards », ou dinosaures. Essaie d'imaginer ce qu'il se passait dans ces temps lointains.

Au commencement, sur la Terre, il n'y avait rien, ni plantes ni animaux, uniquement des roches.

POP !

À partir de ce néant, l'évolution de la vie s'est déroulée, lentement, sur des millions et des millions d'années.

PLOUF !

TIKTAALIK

SPLASH !

MÉDUSE

Les premiers dinosaures sont apparus il y a environ 200 millions d'années.

Salut, le dinosaure !

DIMÉTRODON

Le nom d'un animal qui n'est pas un dinosaure est inscrit dans un cartouche blanc.

COELOPHYSIS

Il y avait des plantes, comme les fougères, mais pas de fleurs.

Le nom d'un animal qui est un dinosaure est inscrit dans un cartouche noir.

Les premiers dinosaures n'étaient souvent pas plus gros qu'un chien ou qu'une vache. Plus tard, des dinosaures de tailles et d'aspects divers feront leur apparition.

AAAAR !

Certains dinosaures avaient des plumes, d'autres des poils ou bien des écailles.

Quelques-uns avaient une grosse tête, une grande queue, des dents tranchantes et des griffes acérées.

Ils pouvaient être tout petits ou plus gros que n'importe quel animal ayant jamais existé sur Terre.

STAURIKOSAURE

Voici le monde des dinosaures.

RIOJASAURE

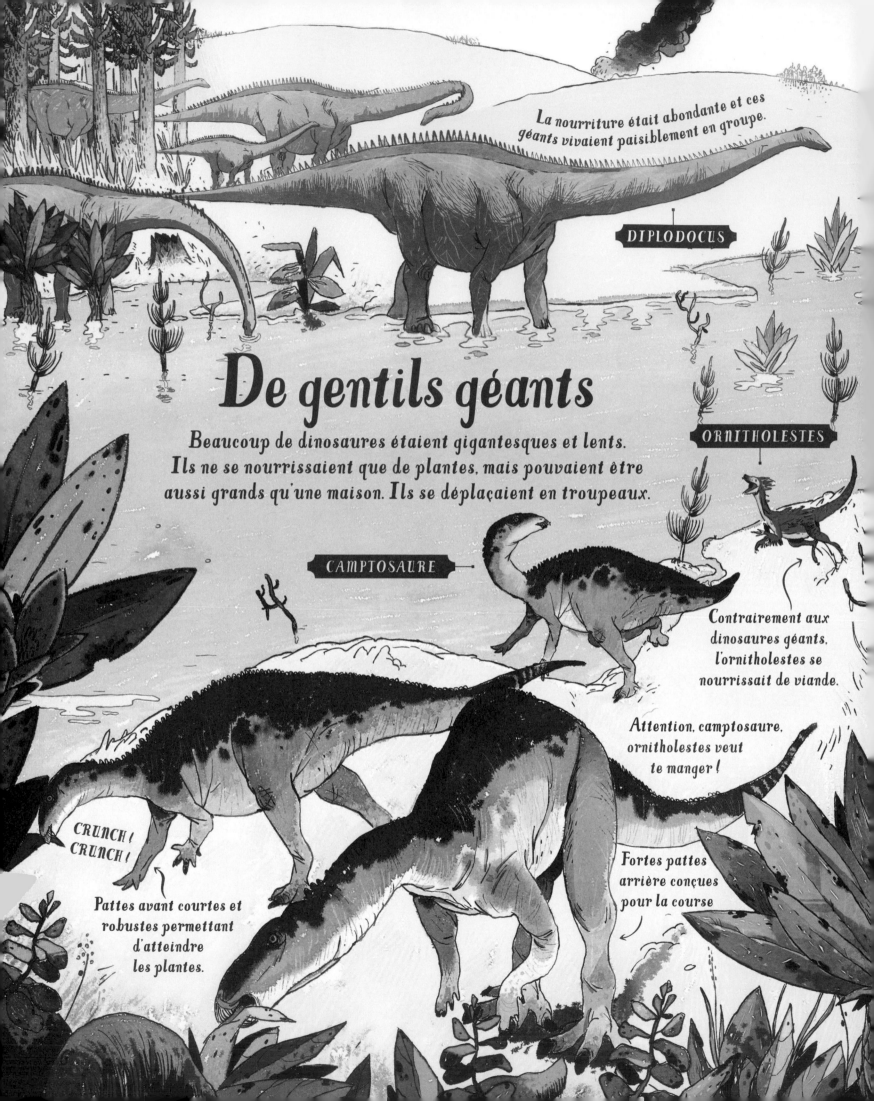

La nourriture était abondante et ces géants vivaient paisiblement en groupe.

DIPLODOCUS

ORNITHOLESTES

De gentils géants

Beaucoup de dinosaures étaient gigantesques et lents. Ils ne se nourrissaient que de plantes, mais pouvaient être aussi grands qu'une maison. Ils se déplaçaient en troupeaux.

CAMPTOSAURE

Contrairement aux dinosaures géants, l'ornitholestes se nourrissait de viande.

Attention, camptosaure, ornitholestes veut te manger !

CRUNCH !
CRUNCH !

Pattes avant courtes et robustes permettant d'atteindre les plantes.

Fortes pattes arrière conçues pour la course

Les prédateurs

Les dinosaures n'étaient pas tous des herbivores qui vivaient en troupeau.
Des dinosaures plus terribles encore mangeaient d'autres dinosaures.

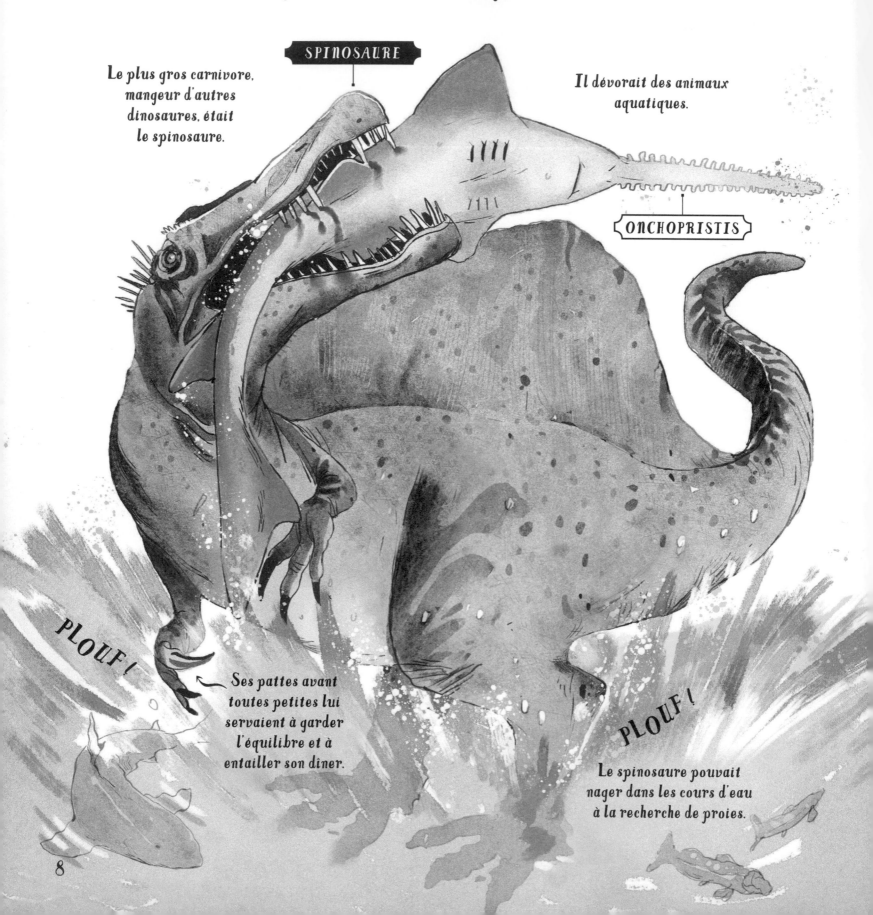

SPINOSAURE

Le plus gros carnivore, mangeur d'autres dinosaures, était le spinosaure.

Il dévorait des animaux aquatiques.

ONCHOPRISTIS

PLOUF !

Ses pattes avant toutes petites lui servaient à garder l'équilibre et à entailler son dîner.

PLOUF !

Le spinosaure pouvait nager dans les cours d'eau à la recherche de proies.

Le tyrannosaure était bien le roi des dinosaures. Si d'autres étaient plus gros, lui, était le plus féroce et le plus craint.

TYRANNOSAURE

EDMONTOSAURE

RAAAH!

Pourquoi ? Parce qu'il mangeait de tout, et parfois même ses congénères.

Ce petit dinosaure ressemblait à un poulet terrifiant.

GRrrrrrrr !

ANZU

Euh ! Oh ! Anzu va-t-il être avalé tout cru ?

MICRORAPTOR

Les plus petits

Beaucoup de dinosaures n'étaient pas plus gros que des pigeons et n'avaient pas l'air très effrayants. Certains étaient couverts de plumes brillantes.

Le microraptor utilisait sa queue en vol pour changer de direction.

FIIIIT !

Ses ailes étaient conçues pour planer et flotter au gré du vent.

Parfois, les ailes du microraptor paraissaient noires.

À d'autres moments, elles avaient des reflets violets, bleus et verts.

ZOUM !

Est-ce un papillon ?

Non, mais cela lui ressemble.

Le kalligramma était un insecte qui vivait il y a plus de 100 millions d'années.

CLAP ! CLAP !

KALLIGRAMMA

D'un battement d'ailes, le kalligramma pouvait monter, descendre ou voleter.

ARGENTINOSAURE

Des combats de géants !

L'argentinosaure était l'un des plus grands dinosaures ayant jamais existé. Le giganotosaurr paraissait minuscule à ses côtés, alors qu'il était énorme et... affamé de viande de dinosaure !

GIGANOTOSAURE

GNARF !
GNARF !

Dents inadaptées pour mordre les autres dinosaures mais capables de brouter la végétation.

LE COMBAT !

Toutes dents et griffes acérées prêtes à entailler la chair, le giganotosaure attaquait à plusieurs.

Du museau au bout de la queue, l'argentinosaure était aussi long que trois bus alignés.

L'argentinosaure se défendait en se servant de son énorme queue et de ses robustes pattes.

CLAAAC !

GRRRRRR !

GNARF ! GNARF !

LE COMBAT !

Une bande de giganotosaures pouvait-elle venir à bout du plus gros dinosaure de tous les temps ? À voir....

PSSSSST ! Si ces dinosaures ne te paraissent pas vraiment gros, reporte-toi pages 30-31 pour te faire une idée de leur taille.

Le camouflage

Certains dinosaures excellaient dans l'art du camouflage — ils se cachaient de leurs prédateurs comme de leurs proies.

Ces petits dinosaures, appelés sinornithosaures, étaient tigrés. Leurs rayures, qui jouaient avec la lumière filtrant dans le sous-bois, leur permettaient de se fondre dans le feuillage.

SINORNITHOSAURE

RRRRR !

Le sinornithosaure ne dormait ni la nuit ni le jour. Quand il était fatigué, il somnolait brièvement.

Ces insectes feront un délicieux en-cas !

Combien de sinornithosaures vois-tu ?

BOUH !

Le sinornithosaure rôdait entre les arbres et dès qu'un insecte se montrait... il s'en délectait !

La parade

Certains dinosaures se fondaient dans leur environnement, mais d'autres, au contraire, paradaient pour effrayer leurs ennemis ou pour faire la cour.

Semblable à un gros oiseau, le zhenyuanlong ne pouvait pas voler.

ZHENYUANLONG

Le zhenyuanlong exhibait ses plumes colorées pour avertir les autres mâles.

Quittez mon territoire.

En plus d'être belles, les plumes tenaient chaud.

Mais il cherchait aussi à attirer les femelles.

Venez admirer mes plumes.

Ce mâle déployait les plumes de sa queue en éventail pour parader devant une femelle.

L'épidexiptéryx se servait aussi des plumes de sa queue pour se tenir en équilibre sur les branches.

EPIDEXIPTERIX

Vous êtes si beau !

L'épidexiptéryx était un dinosaure de la taille d'un écureuil. Il restait sans doute dans les arbres pour éviter de rencontrer les impressionnants dinosaures qui chassaient au sol.

Les nouveau-nés

Raconte-moi la naissance d'un dinosaure. En fait, tout commence dans un œuf relativement petit...

MAIASAURE

Une femelle maiasaure pondait entre 30 et 40 œufs à la fois. Chaque œuf avait la taille d'une grosse orange.

La femelle maiasaure tapissait son nid de feuilles et de plantes pour tenir ses œufs au chaud.

Un petit dinosaure se développait dans chaque œuf.

Quand vais-je sortir de ma coquille ?

Crrrrrrrrrrac !
Tap-tap !

Des mois plus tard, les coquilles se fendillaient...

Même chez les dinosaures, la vie d'un nouveau-né était fragile ; il était petit et le monde bien vaste. Mais les maiasaures vivaient en troupeau et s'entraidaient.

La femelle s'occupait de ses petits. Elle les nourrissait de plantes déchiquetées et les protégeait.

PIIP !

PIIP !

PIIP !

PIIP !

PIIP !

... et les nouveau-nés éclosaient.

TAP-TAP !

PIIP !

PIIP !

19

Dinosaures du désert

Certains dinosaures vivaient dans le désert. Comme de nos jours, il y a 80 millions d'années, le désert était un lieu aride, sauf pour les dinosaures.

Dans un désert, la nourriture est rare. Il n'y a pas autant de végétation qu'ailleurs et beaucoup plus de poussière. Pendant la journée, le soleil brûle.

Certains dinosaures sommeillaient dans la journée, car la chaleur intense les empêchait de bouger.

PROTOCÉRATOPS

RRRRR

D'autres ne se souciaient pas de la chaleur, car ils se déplaçaient avec une extrême lenteur.

PIRACOSAURE

Le protocératops se reposait le jour pour mieux se nourrir de végétaux la nuit.

CRRRRUNCH !

POUM !

POUM !

POUM !

20

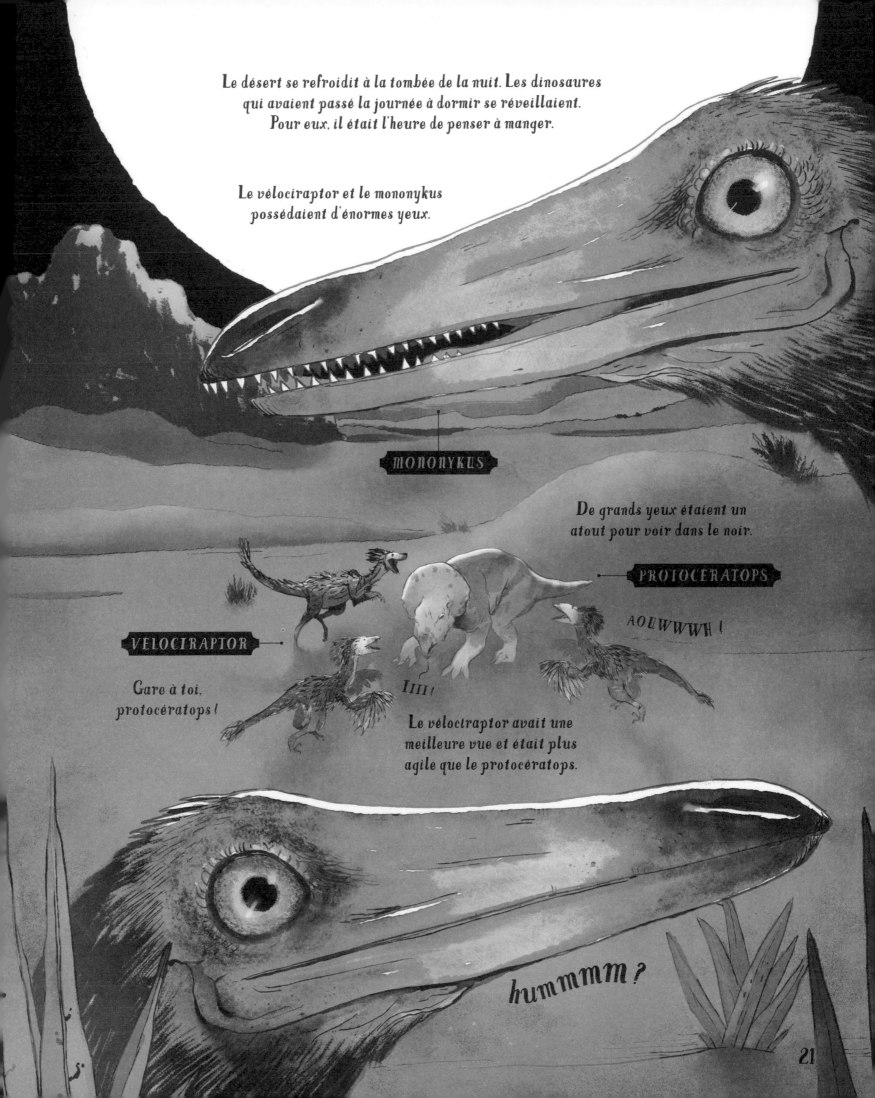

Le désert se refroidit à la tombée de la nuit. Les dinosaures qui avaient passé la journée à dormir se réveillaient. Pour eux, il était l'heure de penser à manger.

Le vélociraptor et le mononykus possédaient d'énormes yeux.

MONONYKUS

De grands yeux étaient un atout pour voir dans le noir.

PROTOCÉRATOPS

VÉLOCIRAPTOR

AOUWWWH !

Gare à toi, protocératops !

IIII !

Le vélociraptor avait une meilleure vue et était plus agile que le protocératops.

hummmm ?

21

Le vol des ptérosaures

Aucun dinosaure ne volait, mais le ciel était parcouru par toutes sortes de reptiles volants étonnants : les ptérosaures.

PRÊT !

BONDIR !

DÉCOLLER !

TROPEOGNATHUS

Le corps des ptérosaures était recouvert d'un épais duvet de pycnofibres (des sortes de poils).

L'eau regorgeait de poissons – un mets de choix pour les ptérosaures.

TAPEJARA

TUPUXUARA

Les os des ptérosaures étant creux, légers et remplis d'air, les reptiles flottaient dans le ciel.

Le tupuxuara était doté d'une crête osseuse. Mais à quoi servait-elle ?

À le rafraîchir en laissant s'échapper la chaleur ?

À naviguer dans le ciel ?

À parader ?

Personne ne le sait… encore.

THALASSODROMEUS

Miam, miam, délicieux, ce petit dinosaure !

Attention, ptérosaures ! Les crocodiles sont à l'affût !

SNAP !
SNAP !

PTERANODON

STYXOSAURE

SQUALICORAX

AMMONITE

Impressionnant le requin ?
Pas pour le styxosaure, qui
n'en fait qu'une bouchée !

Dans les mers

Les dinosaures ne peuplaient pas non plus
les océans, mais les formes de vie marine
étaient aussi grosses et effrayantes
que les terrestres.

BACULITE

TYLOSAURE

PTYCHODUS

Mâchoire puissante pour broyer les coquillages.

ARCHÉLON

La plus grande tortue ayant jamais existé ?

Oui, grande comme une voiture !

DOLICHORHYNCHOPS

Iiiii !

CRAC !

CŒLACANTHE

Le cœlacanthe est un poisson qui vit toujours dans le fond des mers, comme il y a des millions d'années.

Le tylosaure se délectait d'animaux proches du styxosaure, comme le dolichorhynchops.

Adieu, les dinosaures !

Les dinosaures ont vécu sur la Terre pendant plus de 150 millions d'années avant de disparaître. Que leur est-il arrivé ?

BANG

PIOUUUH !

BOUM !

De nombreux volcans se seraient-ils réveillés en même temps pour cracher des cendres et de la lave sur toute la planète ?

RÓAAAAAAAAAAAAAAAAAAAAAAAAAAR !

AAAAAAAAAAH !

La planète se serait réchauffée ?   Ou refroidie ?

BRRRRRRR !

KOF !
KOF !
KOF !

Plusieurs causes pourraient être responsables de leur disparition. Un jour, une météorite de la taille d'une ville serait tombée de l'espace.

De la poussière aurait été projetée dans le ciel.

L'impact aurait déclenché un cataclysme.

BOUUUUM !

BAAANG

Le froid et les ténèbres auraient envahi la Terre, entraînant la disparition des plantes.

Tous les ptérosaures, ainsi que de nombreux autres animaux terrestres et marins, seraient morts.

Les dinosaures aussi auraient disparu, enfin. Mais pas tous, pas complètement....

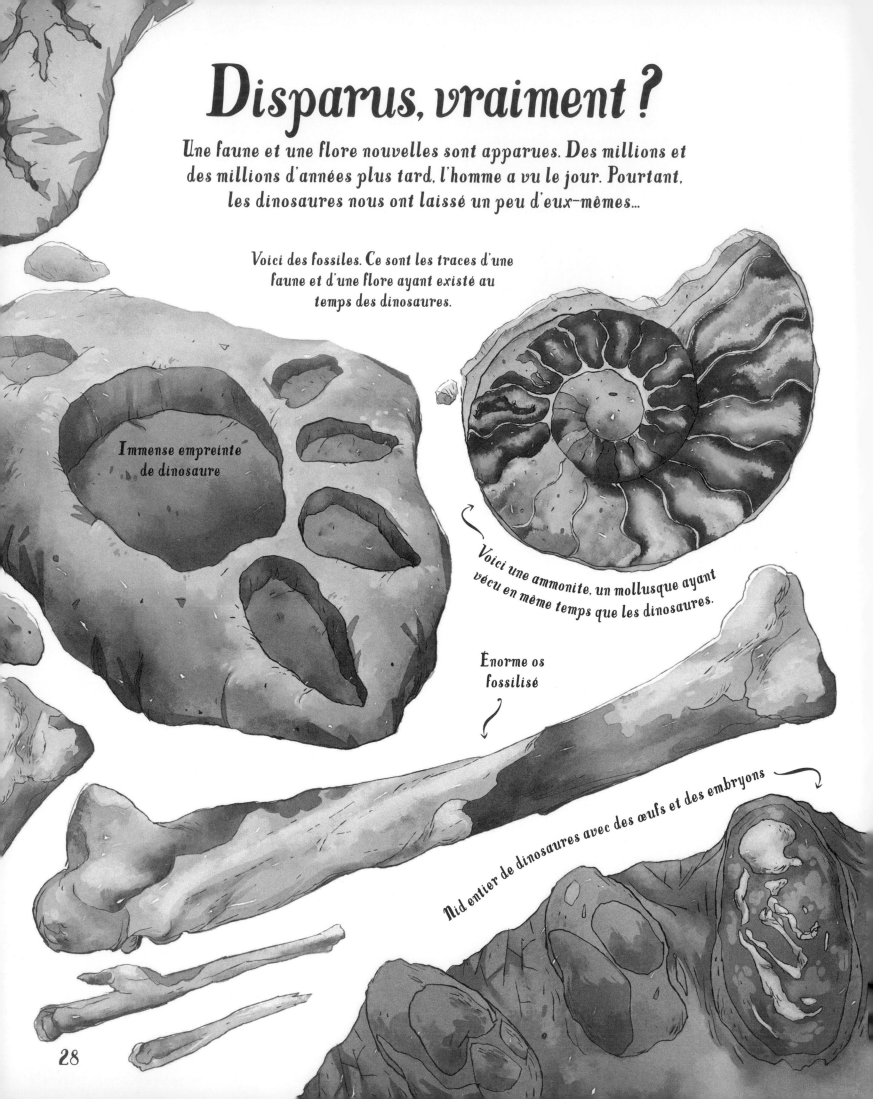

Disparus, vraiment ?

Une faune et une flore nouvelles sont apparues. Des millions et des millions d'années plus tard, l'homme a vu le jour. Pourtant, les dinosaures nous ont laissé un peu d'eux-mêmes...

Voici des fossiles. Ce sont les traces d'une faune et d'une flore ayant existé au temps des dinosaures.

Immense empreinte de dinosaure

Voici une ammonite, un mollusque ayant vécu en même temps que les dinosaures.

Énorme os fossilisé

Nid entier de dinosaures avec des œufs et des embryons

On ne cesse de découvrir de nouveaux fossiles. Ils nous en disent un peu plus sur l'aspect et la vie des dinosaures.

Cette queue recouverte de plumes a été figée dans de l'ambre, une résine fossile issue des conifères, qui durcit avec le temps. Jusqu'à très récemment, personne ne savait que les dinosaures pouvaient avoir des plumes.

En se fossilisant, cette dent s'est changée en une pierre irisée, l'opale.

Fossile d'un squelette de vélociraptor

On dirait un caillou, mais c'est une empreinte du cerveau d'un dinosaure fossilisé.

Sais-tu que les oiseaux descendent des dinosaures ? Il y a des millions et des millions de générations de cela, certains dinosaures furent les ancêtres des oiseaux.

Voilà pourquoi les dinosaures n'ont pas tous complètement disparu...

Qui es-tu ? Tu me ressembles un peu...

Bonjour !

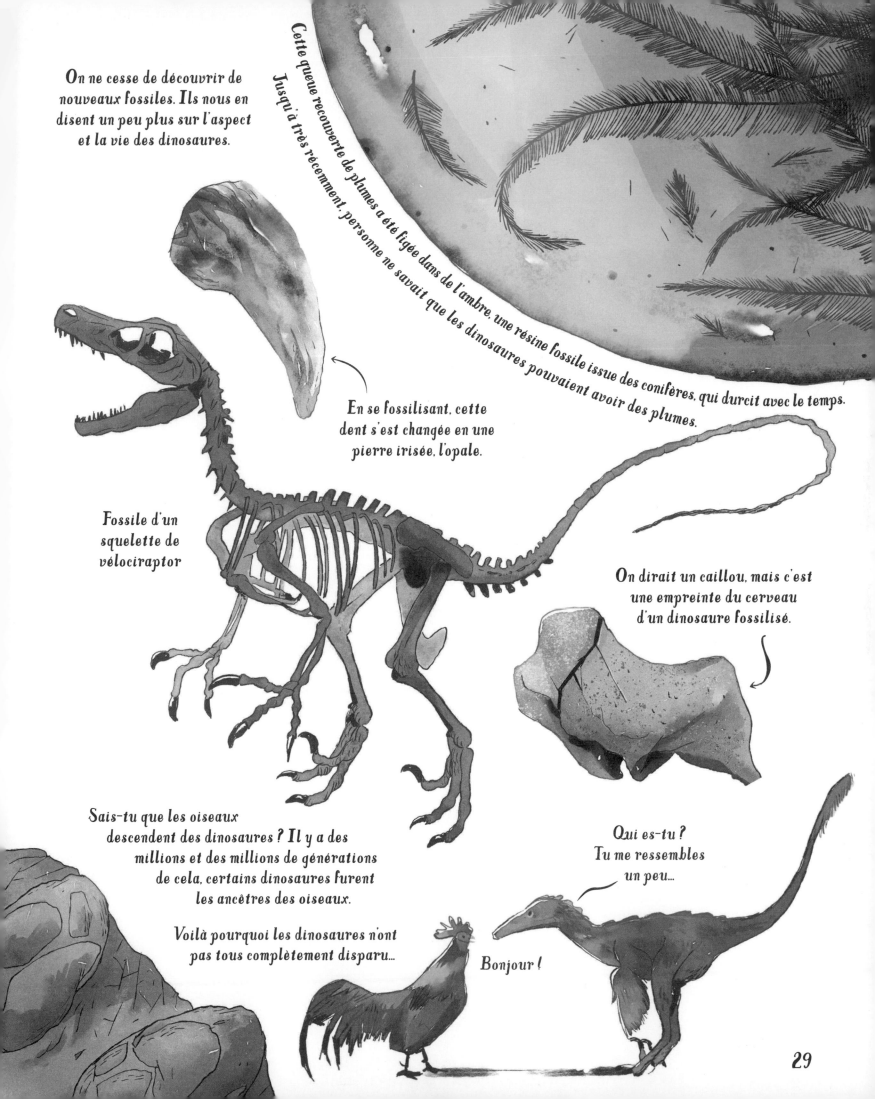

29

TYRANNOSAURE

Grrrrr !

Zoum !

TUPUXUARA

Miam !

ARGENTINOSAURE

STÉGOSAURE

À comparer...

Les dinosaures de ce livre n'ont pas tous la même taille. Compare-les pour savoir si le microraptor était vraiment petit par rapport à l'énorme argentinosaure ?

RIOJASAURE

MICRORAPTOR

HOMME

ANZU

BRONTOSAURE

Grrrrr !

COELOPHYSIS

SINORNITHOSAURE

ZHENYUANLONG

PROTOCÉRATOPS

Pip ! Pip !

GIGANOTOSAURE

ÉPIDEXIPTÉRYX

Sniff ! sniff !

MAIASAURE

30

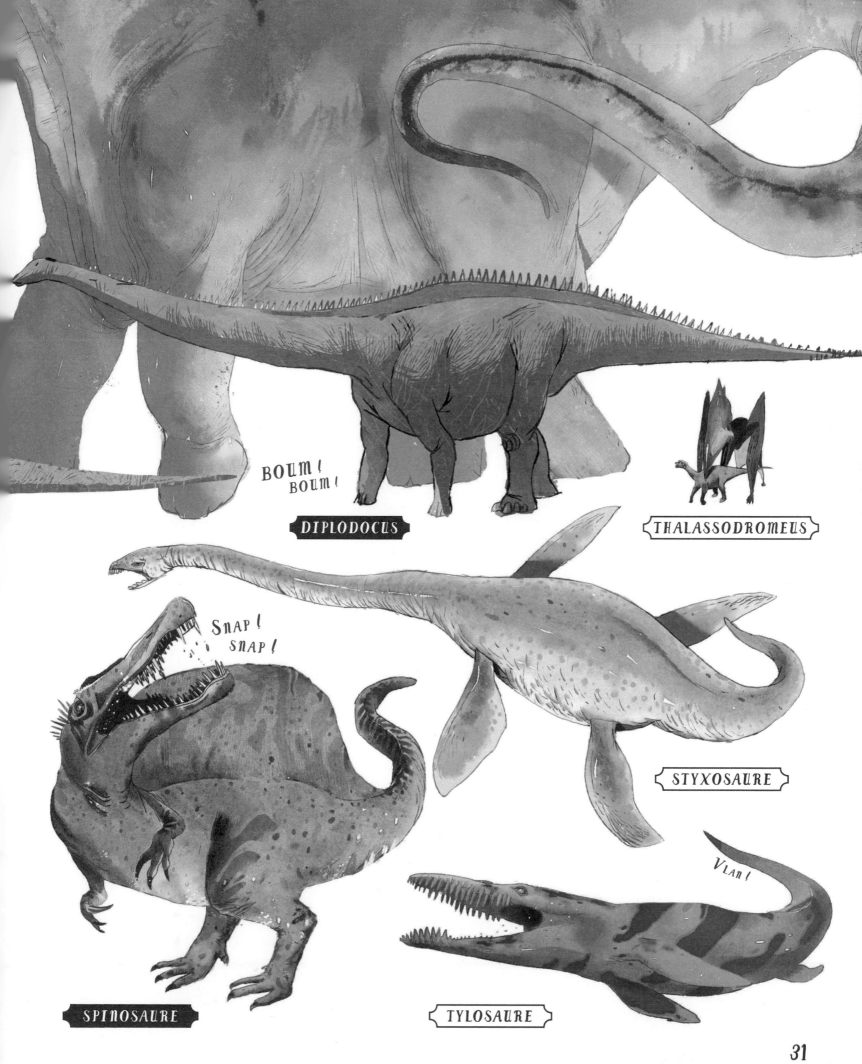

BOUM! BOUM!

DIPLODOCUS

THALASSODROMEUS

SNAP! SNAP!

STYXOSAURE

SPINOSAURE

Vlan!

TYLOSAURE

31

Index

Directrice de la collection : Ruth Brocklehurst
Illustrations numériques et retouches : John Russell

© 2017 Usborne Publishing Ltd. Usborne House, 83-85 Saffron Hill, Londres EC1N 8RT, Grande-Bretagne.
© 2017 Usborne Publishing Ltd. pour le texte français.